American Negro Slavery

AMERICAN NEGRO SLAVERY

A MODERN READER
THIRD EDITION

EDITED BY
ALLEN WEINSTEIN
FRANK OTTO GATELL
DAVID SARASOHN

NEW YORK
OXFORD UNIVERSITY PRESS
1979

Library of Congress Cataloging in Publication Data

Weinstein, Allen, comp.
  American Negro slavery.

  Bibliography: p.
  1. Slavery in the United States—History—
Addresses, essays, lectures.   I. Gattell, Frank Otto,
joint comp.   II. Sarasohn, David, joint comp.
III. Title.
E441.W42   1979   326'.0973   78-59690
ISBN 0-19-502470-2

To the memory of David Potter

Preface

The good reception afforded the first two editions of *American Negro Slavery: A Modern Reader* is one of two principal reasons for the appearance of a third and substantially revised version. In 1973, the editors noted that systematic work had barely begun on the specific problem, isolated by Orlando Patterson among many others, of producing major works which interpreted the nature of the social and cultural response of blacks to their enslavement. Happily, that gap no longer exists. The last half-dozen years have seen the publication of several major works on slavery, studies dealing not only with the slaves' worlds, but with the socioeconomics of the institution as well as the intellectual problem of slavery. In view of the ground-breaking and provocative material which appeared during the late 1950s and throughout the 1960s, the proliferation of significant new material on slavery is no surprise. But the volume and high quality of much of what has lately appeared in print must gratify those who believe that historians can and do respond to calls for meaningful work on significant topics—though all would agree that the "new crop," far from closing out the subject, will doubtless stimulate more debate and produce yet another wave of studies. This third edition of *American Negro Slavery* incorporates major examples of new research; well over half the selections are new ones. And, as was the case with earlier editions, we have tried to provide balanced, one-volume coverage of North American slavery's history and a usable introduction to its literature.

Table of Contents

I: SLAVERY AND THE AMERICAN IDEA

• When the Revolutionary generation made its appearance, slavery was still a national institution. By the time the last major Revolutionary figures had passed from the political stage, early in the nineteenth century, slavery had become sectionalized—restricted to the Southern and Border states. By 1800 most Northern states were well along the road to abolition without any accompanying social upheaval. Even in the South, where many leaders in the American struggle for independence proposed eventual emancipation, men such as Jefferson denounced slavery and searched for methods of eliminating it gradually. Yet Southern critics of the institution could not stem the rising tide of support for maintaining Negro slavery within their region. Nor did they succeed in devising an abolition plan that they felt comfortable advocating publicly, much less enacting into law. William W. Freehling examines the mixture of failure and achievement in the Founding Fathers' response to the problem and points out the quandary they confronted when trying to cope with the question of Negro bondage.

The Founding Fathers and Slavery

WILLIAM W. FREEHLING

Only a few years ago, in a historical age now grown as arcadian as Thomas Jefferson himself, no man needed to defend the Founding Fathers on slavery. However serious were their sins and however greedy seemed their pursuits, the men who made the American Revolution

From "The Founding Fathers and Slavery" by William W. Freehling, *The American Historical Review* 77 (February 1972): 81-93. Copyright © 1972 by William W. Freehling. Reprinted by permission of the author.

were deemed to have placed black slavery at bay. Patriots such as George Washington, historians used to point out, freed their slaves. If Jefferson emancipated few of his, the condemnation of Jeffersonian ideology and the curse of a declining economy were fast driving Virginia's slavery to smash. Only the fabulous profits made possible by Whitney's invention of the cotton gin and the reactionary abstractions perpetuated by Calhoun's repudiation of Jefferson breathed life into the system and waylaid the Fathers' thrust toward peaceful abolition.

This happy tale, once so important and so widely believed, now lies withered by a decade of attack. Scholars such as Robert McColley, Staughton Lynd, William Cohen, and Winthrop Jordan have assaulted every aspect of the old interpretation.[1] Some revisionists write to correct excesses in the former view. Others are driven by a New Leftist contempt for reformers who repudiate radicalism and a modern-day repugnance for liberals contaminated by racism. Whatever their separate reasons and however qualified their individual positions, these scholars, taken together, have hammered out a new image of the Founding Fathers. The image is not attractive. In an era of racial turmoil, the racist taints portrayed by Jordan seem even more grotesque than the grasping materialism described by Beard.

The Declaration of Independence, it is now argued, was a white man's document that its author rarely applied to his or to any slaves. The Constitution created aristocratic privilege while consolidating black bondage. Virginia shrank from abolition, for slave prices were too high and race fears too great. Jefferson himself suspected blacks were innately inferior. He bought and sold slaves. He advertised for fugitives. He ordered lashes well laid on. He lived in the grand manner, burying prayers for freedom under an avalanche of debt. In all these evasions and missed opportunities Jefferson spoke for his age. For whatever the virtues of the Founding Fathers, concludes the new view, they hardly put slavery on the road to ultimate extinction. It seems fitting, then, that when Southerners turned their backs on the Declaration and swung toward reaction in the wake of the Missouri crisis, the sage of Monticello himself helped point the way.

Many admirers of Jefferson, aware of a brighter side, scorn this judgment and yearn for a reassessment. The following essay, while in sympathy with their position, is not written for their reasons. More is at stake than Thomas Jefferson; indeed Jefferson's agonized positions on slavery are chiefly important as the supreme embodiment of a generation's travail. Moreover, the historian's task is not to judge but to explain; and the trouble with the new condemnatory view is not so much that it is a one-sided judgment of the Founding Fathers as that it distorts the process by which American slavery was abolished. The new charge that the Founding Fathers did next to nothing about bondage is as misleading as the older notion that they almost did everything. The abolitionist process proceeded slowly but inexorably from 1776 to 1860: slowly in part because of what Jefferson and his contemporaries did not do, inexorably in part because of what they did. The impact of the Founding Fathers on slavery, like the extent to which the American Revolution was revolutionary, must be seen in the long run, not in terms of what changed in the late eighteenth century but in terms of how the Revolutionary experience changed the whole of American antebellum history. Any such view must place Thomas Jefferson and his contemporaries, for all their ironies and missed opportunities, back into the creeping American antislavery process.

If men were evaluated in terms of dreams rather than deeds, everyone would concede the antislavery credentials of the Founding Fathers. No American Revolutionary could square the principles of the Declaration with the perpetuation of human bondage. Only a few men of 1776 considered the evil of slavery permanently necessary. None dared proclaim the evil a good. Most looked forward to the day when the curse could be forever erased from the land. "The love of justice and the love of country," Jefferson wrote Edward Coles in 1814, "plead equally the cause of these people, and it is a moral reproach to us that they should have pleaded it so long in vain."[2]

If the Founding Fathers unquestionably dreamed of universal American freedom, their ideological posture was weighed down equally unquestionably with conceptions of priorities, profits, and prejudices that would long make the dream utopian. The master passion of the age was not with extending liberty to blacks but with erecting republics for whites. Creative energies poured into designing a political City on the Hill; and the blueprints for utopia came to be the federal Constitution and American union. When the slavery issue threatened the Philadelphia Constitutional Convention, the Deep South's ultimatums were quickly met. When the Missouri crisis threatened the Union, Jefferson and fellow spirits beat a retreat. This pattern of valuing the Union more than abolition—of marrying the meaning of America to the continuation of a particular government—would persist, producing endless compromises and finally inspiring Lincoln's war.

The realization of the Founding Fathers' antislavery dream was blocked also by the concern for property rights articulated in their Declaration. Jefferson's document at once denounced slave chains as immoral and sanctioned slave property as legitimate. It made the slave's right to freedom no more "natural" than the master's right to property. Liberty for blacks became irrevocably tied to compensation for whites; and if some proposed paying masters for slaves, no one conceived of compensating South Carolina planters for the fabulous swamp estates emancipation would wreck.

The financial cost of abolition, heavy enough by itself, was made too staggering to bear by the Founding Fathers' racism, an ideological hindrance to antislavery no less important than their sense of priorities and their commitment to property. Here again Jefferson typified the age. As Winthrop Jordan has shown, Jefferson suspected that blacks had greater sexual appetites and lower intellectual faculties than did whites. This racism was never as hidebound as its twentieth-century varieties. Jefferson kept an open mind on the subject and always described innate differences as but his suspicion. Still it is significant, as Merrill Peterson points out, that Jefferson suspected blacks were inferior rather than suspecting blacks were equal.[3] These suspicions, together with Jefferson's painfully accurate prophecy that free blacks and free whites could not live harmoniously in America for centuries, made him and others tie American emancipation to African colonization. The alternative appeared to be race riot and sexual chaos. The consequence, heaping the cost of colonization on the cost of abolition, made the hurdles to emancipation seem unsurmountable.

Jefferson and the men of the Revolution, however, continually dreamed of leaping ahead when the time was ripe. In 1814, while lamenting his own failure, Jefferson urged others to take up the crusade. "I had always hoped," he wrote Edward Coles, "that the younger generation receiving their early impressions after the flame of liberty had been kindled in every breast . . . would have sympathized with oppression wherever found, and proved their love of liberty beyond their own share of it." As late as 1824, five years after his retreat in the Missouri crisis, Jefferson suggested a federally financed postnati abolition scheme that would have ended slavery faster than the plan proposed by his grandson, Thomas Jefferson Randolph, in the famed Virginia slavery debate of 1832.[4]

The ideological stance of Jefferson and other Founding Fathers on slavery, then, was profoundly ambivalent. On the one hand they were restrained by their overriding interest in creating the Union, by their concern for property rights, and by their visions of race war and miscegenation. On the other hand they embraced a revolutionary ideology that made emancipation inescapable. The question is, How was this theoretical ambivalence resolved in practical action?

The answer, not surprisingly, is also ambivalent. Whenever dangers to Union, property, or racial order seemed to them acute, the Founding Fathers did little. In the short run, especially in those Deep Southern states where the going was stickiest, they did almost nothing. But whenever abolition dangers seemed to them manageable, Jefferson and his contemporaries moved effectively, circumscribing and crippling the institution and thereby gutting its long-range capacity to endure.

The revisionist view of the Founding Fathers is at its best in emphasizing slavery's short-run strength in Jefferson's South. In Virginia both secure slave prices and frenzied race fears made emancipation a distant goal. Jefferson as legislator did no more than draft abolitionist resolutions, and his revisions of the Virginia slave code did little to ease the lot of slaves and something to intensify the plight of free blacks. Jefferson's proposed clause, requiring a white woman who had a black child to leave the state within a year or be placed "out of the protection of the laws," speaks volumes on why abolition came hard in Virginia. South of Virginia, where percentages of slaves and profits from staple crops ran higher, abolition was more remote. Planters who worked huge gangs of slaves in pestilential Georgia and South Carolina's lowlands never proposed peacefully accepting the end of their world.

The federal Constitution of 1787 also reflected slavery's short-run strength. Garrison's instinct to consign that document to the flames was exactly right, for the Constitution perpetually protected an institution the Fathers liked to call temporary. Safeguards included the three-fifths clause, destined to help make the minority South political masters of the nation for years, and the fugitive slave clause, destined to help return to thralldom men who had risked everything for freedom. Moreover, to lure Georgia and South Carolina into the Union, the Fathers agreed to allow any state to reopen the African slave trade for twenty years. When South Carolina seized the option from 1803 to 1807 the forty thousand imported blacks and their hundreds of thousands of slave descendants paid an awesome price for the creation of the white man's republic.

After the Constitution was ratified, slavery again showed its strength by expanding over the West. "The years of slavery's supposed decline,"

Robert McColley points out, "were in fact the years of its greatest expansion."[5] In the age of Jefferson black bondage spread across Kentucky and engulfed Alabama and Mississippi. Furthermore, Jefferson as president acquired slave Louisiana, and Jefferson as elder statesman gave his blessings to the resulting diffusion of the system. If in the 1780s Jefferson had believed, as he did in 1819, that diffusing slavery made it more humane, the antislavery clause in the Northwest Ordinance might have been scotched and this essay could not have been written.

Slavery showed its strength not only in Jefferson's Virginia legislature, Philadelphia's Constitutional Convention, and Louisiana's black deltas but also at Monticello itself. By freeing their slaves George Washington and John Randolph lived up to Revolutionary ideals. These men, however, were exceptions. Thomas Jefferson, who freed nine while blithely piling up debts that precluded freeing the rest, was the rule. The plantation life style, with its elegant manner and extravagant tastes, lessened the chance of reducing debts and allowing quick manumission on a massive scale. That life style, in Virginia and throughout the South, was as integral a part of slavery as was South Carolina's hunger for Africans and the Southwest's commitment to cotton.

The master of Monticello, finally, revealed the towering practical strength of slavery in the notorious case of Sally Hemings, his mulatto house servant. Those who enjoy guessing whether Jefferson sired Sally's many offspring can safely be left to their own speculations. The evidence is wildly circumstantial and the issue of dubious importance. Of greater significance is the way Jefferson and his contemporaries handled the ugly controversy. Alexander Hamilton could cheerfully confess to ellicit relations with a white woman and continue with his career. Jefferson's supporters had to ward off all talk of the embarrassing Sally, for interracial sex would ruin anyone's reputation. Nor could Jefferson handle the problem resolutely in the privacy of his own mansion. Firm action would, as Dumas Malone points out, "have looked like a confession that something was wrong on the mountain."[6] Better to look the other way as Sally's light-skinned children multiplied. Better to keep blacks enchained for a time than risk a nation polluted by allegedly lascivious Sallys. Better, in short, to live uneasily in a corrupted City on the Hill than blurt out the full horror of America's nightmare.[7]

The old view, then, that slavery was dying in Jefferson's South cannot withstand the revisionist onslaught. The system was strong and, in places, growing stronger; and the combination of economic interest, concern for the Union, life style, and race prejudice made emancipationists rare in Virginia and almost nonexistent in South Carolina. Jefferson, no immediate emancipationist, refused as president to endorse an antislavery poem that had been sent to him for his approval. He could not, he said, "interpose with decisive effect" to produce emancipation. To interpose at all was to toss away other reforms.[8] Here as always Jefferson reveals himself as the pragmatic statesman, practicing government as the art of the possible. An idealist might fault him for refusing to commit political suicide by practicing utopian politics. But all the evidence of Robert McColley shows that as a practical politician Jefferson accurately gauged impassable obstacles. The point is crucial: long before Garrison, when Jefferson ruled, peaceful abolition was not possible.

What could be done—what Jefferson and his contemporaries did—was to attack slavery where it was weakest, thereby driving the institution south and vitiating its capacity to survive. In a variety of ways the Founding Fathers took positive steps that demonstrated their antislavery instincts and that, taken together, drastically reduced the slavocracy's potential area, population, and capacity to endure.

The first key reform took place in the North. When the American Revolution began slavery was a national institution, thriving both north and south of the Mason-Dixon line. Slaves comprised 14 per cent of the New York population, with other figures ranging from 8 per cent in New Jersey to 6 per cent in Rhode Island and 3 per cent in Connecticut and Pennsylvania. In these states, unlike Virginia, percentages of slaves were low enough to permit an unconclusive variety of reform.

Still, prior to 1776, abolitionists such as John Woolman found the North barren soil for antislavery ideas. As John Jay recalled, "the great majority" of Northerners accepted slavery as a matter of course, and "very few among them even doubted the propriety and rectitude of it."[9] The movement of 1776 changed all this. The humanitarian zeal of the Revolutionary era, together with nonslaveholder hatred of slave competition and universal acknowledgment that the economy did not need slavery, doomed Northern slavery to extinction. In some states the doom was long delayed as Northern slaveholders fought to keep their bondsmen. Slavery was not altogether ended in New York until 1827 and in New Jersey until well into the 1840s. By 1830, however, less than one per cent of the 125,000 Northern blacks were slaves. Bondage had been made a *peculiar* institution, retained alone in the Southern states.[10]

No less important than abolition in old Northern states was the long and bitter fight to keep bondage from expanding. In 1784 Jefferson drafted a congressional ordinance declaring slavery illegal in all Western territories after 1800. The proposed law, keeping bondage out of Alabama and Mississippi no less than Illinois and Indiana, lost by a single vote, that of a New Jerseyite ill in his dwelling. Seldom has a lone legislator lost so good a chance to turn around the history of a nation. "The fate of millions unborn," Jefferson later cried, was "hanging on the tongue of one man, and heaven was silent in that awful moment."[11]

Three years later, in the famed Northwest Ordinance of 1787, Congress decreed slavery illegal immediately in the upper Western territories. The new law left bondage free to invade the Southwest. But without the Northwest Ordinance slavery might have crept into Illinois and Indiana as well, for even with it bondage found much support in the Midwest.

In the years before 1809 Indiana settlers, led by William Henry Harrison and the so-called Virginia aristocrats, petitioned Congress again and again to allow Midwestern slavery. Indiana's pro-Harrison and anti-Harrison parties were both proslavery; they disagreed only on the tactical question of how to force Congress to budge. When Congress refused to repeal the ordinance, the Indiana legislature in 1805 passed a black indentured servitude act, in effect legalizing slavery. Indiana census takers, more honest than the legislature, counted 237 slaves in the territory in 1810 and 190 in 1820.

In 1809, when the part of Indiana that was most in favor of slavery split off as the new territory of Illinois, the battleground but not the issue shifted. The climax to the territorial phase of the Midwestern quest for slavery came in the Illinois Constitutional Convention of 1818, when proslavery forces, after winning a bitterly contested election to the convention, settled for a renewal of the territorial indentured servitude law because they feared that an explicit slavery law might jeopardize statehood.

With statehood secured the battle over slavery in Illinois continued in the 1820s. The hero of the antislavery forces was Edward Coles, an enlightened Virginian deeply influenced by Madison and Jefferson. Coles, who came to Illinois to free his slaves and stayed to protect the

Northwest Ordinance, narrowly defeated his proslavery rival for governor in 1822. In 1824 he helped secure, by the close vote of 6,640–4,973, final victory in a referendum on a proslavery constitutional convention. With Coles's triumph, slavery had again been restricted to the South.[12]

The crusade for slavery in Illinois and Indiana, lasting over a quarter of a century and so often coming so close to victory, forms a dramatic example of the institution's expansive potential in the age of the Founding Fathers. The proslavery drive was turned back in part because of race phobias and economic desires that obsessed nonslaveholding Midwestern farmers. But in an area where victory came so hard no one can deny the importance of the Northwest Ordinance and Edward Coles's crusade in keeping slavery away.

A third antislavery victory of the Founding Fathers, more important than Northern abolition and the Northwest Ordinance, was the abolition of the African slave trade. This accomplishment, too often dismissed as a nonaccomplishment, shows more clearly than anything else the impact on antislavery of the Revolutionary generation. Furthermore, nowhere else does one see so clearly that Thomas Jefferson helped cripple the Southern slave establishment.

The drive to abolish the African slave trade began with the drafting of the Declaration of Independence. Jefferson, with the concurrence of Virginia and the upper South, sought to condemn King George for foisting Africans on his colonies. South Carolina and Georgia, less sure they had enough slaves, demanded the clause be killed. Jefferson acquiesced. Thus was prefigured, at the first moment of national history, the split between upper and lower South that less than a century later would contribute mightily to the disruption of the republic.

At the Constitutional Convention, as we have seen, lower South delegates again postponed a national decision on slave importations. This time a compromise was secured, allowing but not requiring Congress to abolish the trade after twenty years. A year before the deadline Jefferson, now presiding at the White House, urged Congress to seize its opportunity. "I congratulate you, fellow citizens," he wrote in his annual message of December 2, 1806, "on the approach of the period when you may interpose your authority constitutionally" to stop Americans "from all further participation in those violations of human rights which have been so long continued on the unoffending inhabitants of Africa, and which the morality, the reputation, and the best interests of our country have long been eager to proscribe."

Although the law could not take effect until January 1, 1808, noted Jefferson, the reform, if passed in 1807, could make certain that no extra African was dragged legally across the seas.[13] In 1807 Congress enacted Jefferson's proposal.

The new law, although one of the most important acts an American Congress ever passed, did not altogether end African importations. Americans illegally imported approximately one thousand blacks annually until 1860. This is, however, a tiny fraction of the number that could have been imported if the trade had been legal and considered legitimate. Brazil imported over a million and a half slaves from 1807 to 1860, and the Deep South's potential to absorb bondsmen was greater. South Carolina alone imported ten thousand blacks a year in the early nineteenth century, before the law of 1808 went into effect. Louisiana creole planters sought unsuccessfully to make Jefferson's administration grant them the same privilege.[14] The desire of Virginia slaveholders to keep slave prices high no doubt helped feed the abolition of the trade, just as the desire of Illinois nonslaveholders to keep out blacks helped give Edward Coles his triumph. In both cases, however, the Revolutionary generation's conception of slavery as a moral disaster was of undeniable significance.

The law that closed the trade and saved millions of Africans from servitude on new Southwestern plantations also aided slaves already on those plantations. The great Southwestern boom came after the close of the African trade. Slaves could not be "used up," no matter how fantastic yearly profits were, for the restricted supply kept slave prices high. By mid-nineteenth century, moreover, almost all blacks were assimilated to the Southern way, making possible a paternal relationship between master and slave that could ease exploitation. One does not have to romanticize slave life or exaggerate planter paternalism to recognize that bondage would have been crueler if millions of Africans had been available in Mississippi and Louisiana to escalate profits.

The contrast with nineteenth-century South America, where the trade remained open, makes the point with precision. Wherever Latin Americans imported so-called raw Africans by the boatload to open up virgin territories, work conditions reached a level of exploitation unparalleled in the New World. Easy access to fresh recruits led to using up laborers; and the fact that slaves were unassimilated foreigners precluded the development of the kind of ameliorating relationship that was possible between master and bondsman in North America.[15]

The law profoundly affected North American whites as well as

blacks. Most notably, it shut off the South's importation of labor during the period when immigrants were pouring into the North and the
two societies were locked in mortal combat. If the trade had remained
open, the operation of the three-fifths clause would have given the
South greater congressional representation, and a massive supply of
Africans might well have helped Southerners to compete more successfully in the race to Kansas and the campaign to industrialize. As it
was, with the trade closed, fresh immigration fed the Northern colossus
by the hour while Southerners fell ever more desperately behind.

Perhaps the most important long-run impact of closing the trade
was to help push bondage deeper into the South, thereby continuing
the work the Fathers had begun with Northern abolition and the
Northwest Ordinance. Now that African markets were closed the new
Southwest had to procure its slaves from Northern slave states. By
1860 the resulting slave drain had significantly reduced percentages of
slaves and commitments to slavery throughout the border area stretching from Delaware through Maryland and Kentucky into Missouri.
Whereas in 1790 almost 20 per cent of American slaves lived in this
most northern tier of border slave states, the figure was down to 10
per cent and falling by 1860. On the other hand, in 1790 the area that
became the seven Deep South states had 20 per cent of American
slaves and by 1860 the figure was up to 54 per cent and rising. During
the cotton boom the shift was especially dramatic. From 1830 to
1860 the percentage of slaves in Delaware declined from 4 to 1 per
cent; in Maryland from 23 to 13 per cent; in Kentucky from 24 to 19
per cent; in Missouri from 18 to 10 per cent; and in the counties to become West Virginia from 10 to 5 per cent.[16]

By both reducing the economic reliance on slavery and the psychic
fear of blacks this great migration had political consequences. Antislavery politicians, echoing Hinton R. Helper's appeals to white racism,
garnered thousands of votes and several elections, especially in Missouri, during the 1850s.[17] It was only a beginning, but it was similar
to the early stages of the demise of slavery in New York.

While the end of the slave trade indirectly drained slaves from the
border South another Revolutionary legacy, the tradition of individual
manumissions, further weakened the institution in the Northern slave
states. Although Jefferson did not live up to his dictum that antislavery
planters should free their slaves, many upper South masters followed
precept rather than example in the antebellum years. The Virginia law
of 1806, forcing freed slaves to leave the state in a year, did not halt

the process as absolutely as some have supposed. Virginia laws passed in 1819 and 1837 allowed county courts to grant exceptions. The ensuing trickle of manumissions was a festering sore to the Virginia slave establishment.[18]

Meanwhile, in two border states, manumission sabotaged the institution more insistently. Delaware, which had 9,000 slaves and 4,000 free blacks in 1790, had 1,800 slaves and 20,000 free blacks in 1860. Maryland, with 103,000 slaves and 8,000 free blacks in 1790, had 87,000 slaves and 84,000 free blacks in 1860. These two so-called slave states came close to being free Negro states on the eve of Lincoln's election. Indeed, the Maryland manumission rate compares favorably with those of Brazil and Cuba, countries that supposedly had a monopoly on Western Hemispheric voluntary emancipation.[19]

The manumission tradition was slowly but relentlessly changing the character of states such as Maryland in large part because of a final Jeffersonian legacy: the belief that slavery was an evil that must some day be ended. Particularly in the upper South, this argument remained alive. It informed the works of so-called proslavery propagandists such as Albert T. Bledsoe; it inspired Missouri antislavery activists such as Congressman Frank Blair and the mayor of St. Louis, John M. Wimer; and it gnawed at the consciences of thousands of slaveholders as they made up their wills.[20] Jefferson's condemnation of slavery had thrown the South forever on the defensive, and all the efforts of the George Fitzhughs could never produce a unanimously proslavery society.

In summary, then, the Revolutionary generation found slavery a national institution, with the slave trade open and Northern abolitionists almost unheard. When Jefferson and his contemporaries left the national stage they willed to posterity a crippled, restricted, peculiar institution. Attacking slavery successfully where it was weakest they swept it out of the North and kept it away from the Northwest. They left the antebellum South unable to secure more slaves when immigrants rushed to the North. Most important of all, their law closing the slave trade and their tradition concerning individual manumissions constituted a doubly sharp weapon superbly calculated to continue pushing slavery south. By 1860 Delaware, Maryland, Missouri, and the area to become West Virginia all had a lower percentage of slaves than New York possessed at the time of the Revolution, and Kentucky's percentage was not much higher. The goal of abolition had become almost as practicable in these border states as it had been in the North in 1776. As the Civil War began, slavery remained secure in only eleven of the fifteen slave states. Meanwhile black migration toward the tropics showed every capacity to continue eroding the institution in Virginia and driving slavery down to the Gulf.

If the Founding Fathers had done none of this—if slavery had continued in the North and expanded into the Northwest; if millions of Africans had been imported to strengthen slavery in the Deep South, to consolidate it in New York and Illinois, to spread it to Kansas, and to keep it in the border South; if no free black population had developed in Delaware and Maryland; if no apology for slavery had left Southerners on shaky moral grounds; if, in short, Jefferson and his contemporaries had lifted nary a finger—everything would have been different. Because all of this was done, slavery was more and more confined in the Deep South as the nineteenth century progressed.

No one spied these trends better than the men who made the Southern revolution of 1860–61. Secessionist newspaper editorials in the 1850s can almost be summed up as one long diatribe against Jeffersonian ideology and the policy to which it led. Committed lower South slaveholders knew the world was closing in on them at the very time the more Northern slave states could not be relied on. Seeing the need not only to fight off Republicans from without but also to halt erosion from within, radical Southerners applauded the movement to re-enslave free blacks in Maryland; many of them proposed reopening the slave trade so that the Gulf states' hunger for slavery could be fed by imported Africans instead of black Virginians; and they strove to gain Kansas in large part to keep Missouri.

When this and much else failed and Lincoln triumphed, lower South disunionists believed they had reached the moment of truth. They could remain in the Union and allow the noose to tighten inexorably around their necks. They would then watch slavery slowly ooze out of the border South and permit their own domain to shrink to a handful of Gulf and lower Atlantic states. Or they could strike for independence while the upper South retained some loyalty to bondage, thereby creating a confrontation and forcing wavering slave states to make their choice. This view of the options helped to inspire the lower South's secession, in part a final convulsive effort to halt the insidious process the Founding Fathers helped begin.[21]

When war came the lower South's confrontation strategy was half successful. Four of the eight upper South states seceded in the wake of Sumter. But four others remained loyal to the North. In the most Northern slave states, Delaware, Maryland, Kentucky, Missouri, and also in the area to become West Virginia, the slave drain and manumission processes had progressed too far. When the crunch came, loyalty to the Union outweighed loyalty to slavery. Abraham Lincoln is said to have remarked that while he hoped to have God on his side, he had to have Kentucky. The remark, however apocryphal, clothes an important truth. In such a long and bitter war border slave states were crucial. If they, too, had seceded, the Confederacy might have survived. The long-run impact of the Founding Fathers' reforms, then, not only helped lead lower South slavocrats to risk everything in war but also helped doom their desperate gamble to failure.

Any judgment of the Founding Fathers' record on slavery must rest on whether the long or the short run is emphasized. In their own day the Fathers left intact a strong Southern slave tradition. The American Revolution, however, did not end in 1790. Over several generations, antislavery reforms inspired by the Revolution helped lead to Southern division, desperation, and defeat in war. That was not the most desirable way to abolish slavery, but that was the way abolition came. And given the Deep South's aversion to committing suicide, both in Jefferson's day and in Lincoln's, perhaps abolition could not have come any other way.

This conclusion would have brought tears to the eyes of Thomas Jefferson. Jefferson wrote St. George Tucker in 1797 that "if something is not done, and soon done" about slavery, "we shall be the murderers of our own children."[22] In 1820 he saw with a prophet's eye how that murder would take place. The Missouri crisis, coming upon him like "a Firebell in the Night," almost caused him to shrink from even his own antislavery actions. The "momentous question," he knew, was the "knell of the Union," if not in his own time inevitably soon enough. "I regret that I am now to die in the belief," he wrote John Holmes,

> that the useless sacrifice of themselves by the generation of 1776, to acquire self-government and happiness in their country, is to be thrown away by the unwise and unworthy passions of their sons, and that my only consolation is to be, that I live not to weep over it.[23]

No sadder note survives in American literature than this scream of failure from one of the most successful of the Founding Fathers. The irony is that the ambiguous antislavery posture of Jefferson and his contemporaries helped place the nation, unintentionally but perhaps irrevocably, in lockstep toward the blowup. In the late eighteenth century a statesman had two ways to lessen the chance of a civil war over slavery. He could ease the racial, sexual, and materialistic fears that made the lower South consider emancipation anathema. Or he could scotch the antislavery idealism the slavocracy found disquieting. Jefferson, mirroring his generation and generations yet unborn, could do neither. Both his antislavery beliefs and his fear of the consequences of those beliefs went too deep. He was caught up too completely in America's most anguishing dilemma. The famed wolf he complained of holding by the ears was his own revolutionary tradition no less than blacks chained in violation of that tradition.

Like reluctant revolutionaries before and since, Jefferson sought to have it both ways. He succeeded, as such men will, in starting something destined to get out of hand. He helped protect slavery where it was explosive and helped demolish it where it was manageable. Meanwhile, he helped give informal sanction to the lower South's worst racial fears at the same time that he helped intensify those fears by unintentionally driving more blacks toward the tropics. Over a seventy-five year period the Founding Fathers' reforms helped add claustrophobia to a lower South psyche inflamed enough in 1787. When that happened the day of the soldier was at hand.

If in 1820 Jefferson pulled back shuddering from the horror he saw ahead, his imperfect accomplishments had taken on a life of their own. And less than a half century later, though hundreds of thousands lay slain by bullets and slaves were but half freed, mournful bells in the night would herald the realization of his most radical dream.

NOTES

Earlier versions of this article were read before the Johns Hopkins History Seminar and at the annual meeting of the American Historical Association, Dec. 30, 1970. Benjamin Quarles, James Banner, Jr., Cecelia Kenyon, and especially David Donald offered cogent criticisms on those occasions. Others made helpful suggestions after reading written drafts: Alison Freehling, the late Adrienne Koch, R. Nicholas Olsberg, C. Vann Woodward, Eric Foner, Arthur Zilversmit, William Cohen, Bernard Bailyn, Robert McColley, John Shy, Bradford Perkins, and especially Kenneth M. Stampp. My thanks to them all.

1. Robert McColley, *Slavery and Jeffersonian Virginia* (Urbana, 1964); Staughton Lynd, *Class Conflict, Slavery and the United States Constitution* (Indianapolis, 1968); William Cohen, "Thomas Jefferson and the Problem of Slavery," *Journal of American History*, 56 (1969): 503-26; Winthrop D. Jor-

dan, *White Over Black: American Attitudes Towards the Negro*, 1550–1812 (Williamsburg, 1968). For the fullest summation of the position, see Donald L. Robinson, *Slavery in the Structure of American Politics* (New York, 1971).

2. Thomas Jefferson to Edward Coles, Aug. 25, 1814, in Paul Leicester Ford, ed., *The Works of Thomas Jefferson* (New York, 1904–05), 11: 416.

3. Jordan, *White Over Black*, 429-81; Merrill D. Peterson, *Thomas Jefferson and the New Nation: A Biography* (New York, 1970), 263.

4. Jefferson to Coles, Aug. 25, 1814, Jefferson to Jared Sparks, Feb. 4, 1824, in Ford, *Works of Jefferson*, 11: 416, 12: 335-36.

5. McColley, *Slavery in Jeffersonian Virginia*, 3.

6. Dumas Malone, *Jefferson the President: First Term, 1801–1805* (Boston, 1970), 498.

7. See the stimulating comments on the matter in Jordan, *White Over Black*, 468, and Eric McKitrick, "The View from Jefferson's Camp," *New York Review of Books*, Dec. 17, 1970, p. 37.

8. Jefferson to George Logan, May 11, 1805, in Ford, *Works of Jefferson*, 10: 141-42.

9. Jay to Granville Sharp [1788], in Henry P. Jackson, ed., *The Correspondence and Public Papers of John Jay* (New York, 1890–93), 3: 342.

10. Arthur Zilversmit, *The First Emancipation: The Abolition of Slavery in the North* (Chicago, 1967).

11. Quoted in Peterson, *Jefferson*, 283.

12. The Indiana-Illinois story can best be followed in Jacob P. Dunn, Jr., *Indiana: A Redemption from Slavery* (Boston, 1888); Theodore Calvin Pease, *The Story of Illinois* (Chicago, 1949), 72-78; and, Adrienne Koch, *Madison's "Advice to My Country"* (Princeton, 1966), 144-51.

13. James D. Richardson, ed., *A Compilation of the Messages and Papers of the Presidents* (Washington, 1910), 1: 396.

14. Philip D. Curtin, *The Atlantic Slave Trade: A Census* (Madison, 1969).

15. See the judicious remarks in C. Vann Woodward, *American Counterpoint: Slavery and Racism in the North-South Dialogue* (Boston, 1971), 97-106.

16. U.S. Census Bureau, *The Statistics of the Population of the United States: Ninth Census—Volume I* (Washington, 1872), 3-8.

17. Helper is too often treated as a lone voice crying in the wilderness when in fact he was the man who summed up in book form an argument heard constantly in the upper South. See, for example, the files of the St. Louis *Democrat*, Baltimore *Patriot*, and Wheeling *Intelligencer* during the 1850s.

18. See, for example, John C. Rutherfoord, *Speech of John C. Rutherfoord of Goochland, in the House of Delegates of Virginia, on the Removal from the Commonwealth of the Free Colored Population* (Richmond, 1853).

19. James M. Wright, *The Free Negro in Maryland, 1634–1860* (New York, 1921).

20. The Wimer-Blair position is best laid out in the St. Louis *Democrat*. See also Albert T. Bledsoe, *An Essay on Liberty and Slavery* (Philadelphia, 1856), and the ambiguities omnipresent in such upper South newspapers as the Baltimore *American* and Louisville *Courier* throughout the fifties.

21. I hope to demonstrate at length the positions outlined in the last two paragraphs in my forthcoming *History of the South, 1850–61*, to be published by Harper and Row. The best sources on fire-eater positions in the 1850s are the Charleston *Mercury*, New Orleans *Delta*, and *DeBow's Review*. The clearest statements of the connection between lower South secession and upper South wavering are in John Townsend, *The South Alone Should Govern the South* (Charleston, 1860), and Henry L. Benning, *Speech . . . November 6, 1860* (Milledgeville, Ga., 1860). For a preliminary estimate of how the same thinking affected the Virginia Secession Convention, see William W. Freehling, "The Editorial Revolution, Virginia, and the Coming of the Civil War: A Review Essay," *Civil War History*, 16 (1970): 64-72.

22. Jefferson to St. George Tucker, Aug. 28, 1797, in Ford, *Works of Jefferson*, 8: 335.

23. Jefferson to John Holmes, Apr. 22, 1820, in *ibid.*, 12: 158-60.

• The slave trade was the least defended—and the least defensible—part of the business of slavery. It had no friends, but many practitioners. When American politicians argued about slavery, the slave trade (as part of the right of masters to obtain and dispose of their slave property) hovered over the debaters. In the previous selection, William W. Freehling discussed the trade in his overview of the Revolutionary generation's ethos regarding slavery. Here, David Brion Davis analyzes the nuances of the slave trade debate at the Constitutional Convention in 1787 and the controversial compromise which allowed the international slave trade to continue unhampered by federal action for twenty years. Davis demonstrates how both the slave-state and the free-state delegates at Philadelphia strove for a formula that would be feasible as well as fuzzy. Notice the conflicting and self-serving interpretations of the clause's meaning. This amalgam may not have been the enlightened precision that constitution-makers are supposed to display in concocting governments, but, in view of the realities of sectional interests and the already recognized North-South antagonism, union among the states dictated this sort of arrangement.

The Constitution and the Slave Trade

DAVID BRION DAVIS

When the first Continental Congress agreed in 1774 to prohibit the importation of slaves, along with more innocent commodities, high moral principle gave added thrust to economic retaliation. But questions of morality and sincerity have tended to obscure the fundamental demand on which most of the colonists could agree: the right of localities to control slave importation as part of their larger right to self-determination. This demand did not necessarily mean hostility toward the slave trade. In 1750, for example, the colonists of Georgia, having demonstrated that laws could not keep settlers from acquiring slaves, succeeded in reversing the original free-soil policy of the Trustees and the British government. Because of Georgia's late start as a plantation economy, in 1760 there were only 3,500 blacks in a population of 9,600. The demand soared during the following decade and remained strong in 1774, when Georgians vehemently opposed the Continental Association's boycott. As late as 1793, when alarmed by the St. Domingue revolution, Georgia chose to exclude only slaves from the West Indies and Florida, contagious areas that might pass on the insurrectionary fever. Otherwise, legal imports continued for five more years, supplemented by a growing migration of South Carolinians accompanied by their slaves.[1]

South Carolina complied more willingly with the nonimportation agreements, in part to reduce debts and allow local merchants, as one manifesto put it, "to settle their accounts, and be ready with the return of liberty to renew trade." Certainly the South Carolinians had no desire to see nonimportation become permanent national policy, nor did they wish to become dependent on Virginia's surplus supply of labor, which of course included Virginia's most unruly and dangerous blacks. Yet self-determination allowed for the legal suspension of

From *The Problem of Slavery in the Age of Revolution* by David Brion Davis (Ithaca, N.Y.: Cornell University Press, 1975), pp. 119-31. Copyright © 1975 by Cornell University Press. Reprinted by permission of Cornell University Press.

slave imports as a means of conserving specie, restoring economic stability, and preventing optimistic debtors from purchasing Negroes instead of paying their creditors. South Carolina's law of 1787 suspend-
ing the slave trade for three years was, in fact, part of an act requiring
the rapid recovery of debts.[2]

Patrick S. Brady has shown that the division between debtors and
creditors was actually less important than the division between "low-
country" and "up-country" in determining South Carolina's slave-
trade policy. The planters of the rice coast, who were well-stocked
with slaves and who stood to gain by rising slave prices, not only favored continuing the suspension of imports from Africa but objected
particularly to the domestic slave trade from Virginia and North Carolina. Well before the boom in short-staple cotton, triggered in 1793 by
Eli Whitney's gin, the up-country regions surrounding Camden and
Columbia had begun a burst of enormous population growth and were
clamoring for more slaves than the low-country areas could supply. By
1787, to complicate matters further, the sea-island districts of Beaufort
and Colleton had begun cultivating long-staple, luxury cotton; because
of their isolation from the domestic slave trade, these planters looked
to Africa for their labor.[3]

By 1792 the news from St. Domingue reinforced the position of the
dominant rice planters and helped to prolong the ban on slave importation. It was not until 1803 that the demands of King Cotton, am-
plified by the opening of Louisiana, finally took precedence over fear
of insurrection. Even then, the legislature voted to exclude any black
who had ever been in the West Indies and, with apparently uninten-
tional irony, required that slaves brought in from other states have
"good character; and have not been concerned in any insurrection or
rebellion."[4] To be a slave in South Carolina, one had to meet the
highest moral standards. Nevertheless, to the dismay and anger of her
sister states to the north, South Carolina legally imported, from 1803
to 1808, nearly 40,000 Africans—presumably all of "good character."

In Virginia the market for African-born slaves had long been confined to new or small planters, traders, speculators, or miscellaneous
people who simply wanted a servant. Yet as Darold D. Wax has
pointed out, "throughout the colonial period, whenever economic
conditions permitted, Virginia planters willingly purchased freshly
imported Negro slaves." Until the late 1760s, Virginia had been allowed considerable leeway in taxing imported Africans. In 1772, however, the House of Burgesses self-righteously requested the crown to

accept a heavy duty on such "a Trade of great Inhumanity." When the crown disallowed the act, the Virginians could piously claim they had never really wanted Negro slaves but had been forced to accept them by the perfidious English. Patriotic edicts did not necessarily mean effective enforcement. For example, in September, 1773, an American slaving captain wrote his Rhode Island employers from Fredericksburg, reporting that since no one had shown up at an emergency meeting of the Association, which was supposed to prevent importations, he had disposed of all but two of his slaves, receiving especially fine prices for the children.[5]

Nevertheless, Virginia took the lead in making a disavowal of the slave trade a part of Revolutionary ideology. Even though the commonwealth was happy to supply slaves to her neighbors, her public policy opposed any further growth of Negro population, whether slave or free.

To put the non-importation agreements in proper perspective, we should note that the best recent estimates indicate that the period from 1780 to 1810 represented the peak of the slave trade to North America. Moreover, in 1820 the slave population of the United States was approximately three times greater than it had been at the outset of the Revolution.[6] On the other hand, the increase might have been still larger if the Revolution had not disrupted previous patterns of trade, if ten of the rebellious states had not followed Virginia's ideological lead, and if planters in Mississippi Territory and Louisiana had later won their appeals for direct slave imports from Africa.

With this background in mind, the decisions of the Constitutional Convention become more meaningful. It was a Virginian, George Mason, who reminded the delegates that western settlers were already crying out for slaves, and that it would be futile for Virginia to cut off further importations of Africans if they could be shipped to the West by way of South Carolina and Georgia. The central question was whether the expansion of slavery should be sanctioned or impeded, or in Mason's words, whether the general government would have power "to prevent the increase of slavery."[7]

On July 23, Charles Cotesworth Pinckney, a South Carolinian educated at Oxford and the Middle Temple, announced that he would vote against the Constitution if it lacked some security against the future emancipation of southern slaves. Three days later the Committee of Detail, chaired by another South Carolinian, John Rutledge, began working on a draft of the Constitution. Although many South-

erners were ardent nationalists who wished to create a strong and vigorous central government, they also feared that the Congressional
power "to regulate commerce among the several states" could be used
as a weapon against slavery and as a device for exploiting the plantation economy. The Committee of Detail failed to adopt the explicit
guarantee demanded by Pinckney, but agreed to restrict the commerce
clause by adding two sections protecting the economic and social interests of the Deep South. One was the requirement of a two-thirds
majority in both legislative houses for the passage of import duties and
laws regulating foreign trade. The other stipulated that "no tax or
duty shall be laid by the Legislature on articles exported from any
State; nor on the migration or importation of such persons as the several States shall think proper to admit; nor shall such migration or importation be prohibited."[8]

Some northern delegates took alarm at the Deep South's bid for
economic freedom. On August 8, two days after the submission of the
draft, Rufus King lost patience with orderly procedure. He provoca-
tively linked the issue of representation to the continuation of the
slave trade and to the prohibition of taxes on exports. He could never
agree, he said, to let slaves be imported without limitation, for aug-
menting the South's representation would bind the government to
defend the region against insurrection, yet leave the government powerless to tax slave produce. Roger Sherman, of Connecticut, tried to
separate the slave trade from the issue of representation, which he
thought already settled. But Gouverneur Morris then expanded on
King's sectional attack, delivering a sweeping indictment of the South's
"nefarious institution" which had turned Virginia and Maryland into
"barren wastes" of misery and poverty, and which now induced the
Georgian and Carolinian to go to Africa, where, "in defiance of the
most sacred laws of humanity," he "tears away his fellow creatures
from their dearest connections & dam(n)s them to the most cruel
bondage," only to be rewarded by "more votes in a Govt. instituted
for the protection of the rights of mankind."[9]

Suggestions that the northern public found slavery morally repug-
nant gave a cutting edge to demands for economic concessions. But
Morris's rhetoric also exploited the contradictions underlying American liberty and union, contradictions which the Convention had tried
to forget. On August 21 and 22, when the delegates directly faced the
slave-trade issue, there was danger of impasse and failure. Charles
Pinckney informed the assembly that ancient Greece and Rome furnished illustrious precedents for South Carolina, and that in all ages

one-half of mankind had been slaves. Although he added that the southern states, if left alone, would probably stop importations, his cousin Charles Cotesworth candidly explained that this meant "only stop them occasionally as she now does." The Deep South stood firm in threatening to reject the Constitution if the Committee's clause were rejected. Charles Cotesworth Pinckney accused the Virginians of favoring an end to the slave trade so they could monopolize the domestic supply of Negroes. In any event, as John Rutledge pointed out, the Convention had no business dealing with religion or morality; the only question was whether mutual interests would allow the southern states to be parties to the Union.[10]

Angry southern threats shifted the contest back from the high ground of abstract principle to the easier terrain of immediate interests and mutual concessions. Roger Sherman gave voice to the mood of accommodation when he said it would be better to allow the southern states to go on importing slaves than to have them leave the Union. Gouverneur Morris, having paid tribute to the sacred laws of humanity, suggested that a bargain might be struck if a special committee considered the slave trade along with taxes on imports and exports.[11]

On August 24 this committee of eleven submitted its recommendations, which embodied one of the crucial compromises of the Convention. As explained by Charles Cotesworth Pinckney, it had been in South Carolina's interest to ally with Virginia and the former majority of states desiring restrictions on navigation acts; however, in view of the northeastern states' "liberal" attitude on the slave trade, he was willing to recognize the commercial losses the Northeast had suffered as a result of the Revolution, and withdrew his support for the requirement of a two-thirds legislative majority for import duties and other commercial regulations.[12]

The "liberal" attitude Pinckney had in mind was the agreement by northeastern delegates that there should be no prohibition on the importation of slaves prior to the year 1800. On the Convention floor Pinckney moved that the date be advanced to 1808, which won New England's support, though Madison predicted that twenty years would bring as much evil as an indefinite period of slave trading. Before the Convention finished its work, it placed the prohibition on interference with the slave trade beyond the power of Constitutional amendment. Only the equal suffrage of states in the Senate shared this high sanctuary of immunity. And as part of the package of northern concessions, Article IV, on full faith and credit, included the provision that no fugitive slave could be freed by the laws of any state into which he escaped, and that all fugitives were to be delivered to their rightful owners.[13]

During subsequent decades there would be endless and involved debate on whether the Constitution implicitly challenged or gave positive sanction to the South's peculiar institution. Many of the framers, including Madison, had scruples against openly acknowledging that human beings could be property. The use of the euphemism "persons" could not disguise the support given to slavery by the three-fifths compromise and the clause respecting fugitives. The slave-trade provision was another matter, since in 1808 a restraint on Congress could suddenly become a delegated power; in Charles Pinckney's words, it was a "*negative pregnant*, restraining for twenty years, and giving the power after."[14]

There is some evidence that "migration" referred to what today would be called "immigration," a word whose modern implications Jeremy Belknap helped to popularize in the 1790s.[15] It is likely that northern members of the Committee of Detail were willing to accept a continuance of the slave trade so long as no national restrictions could be imposed on immigration from Europe. Such immigration would presumably keep the North from falling behind the South in population and political power. Oliver Ellsworth, who represented Connecticut on the Committee, reassured northern delegates that an increase in white population would provide a pool of cheap labor that would eventually render slaves useless. In a different context, Charles Pinckney feared that the absence of uniform rules on naturalization and citizenship would allow new states to encourage unrestricted immigration. If the words "migration" and "persons" were simply a concession to northern interests as well as sentiment, the Committee may have intended the clause to refer solely to the movement of Negroes and whites from other countries to the United States.[16]

On the other hand, the original purpose of the clause was to prevent the federal government from ever interfering with state regulations regarding the migration or importation of persons. And as we have seen, both Virginia and South Carolina placed restrictions on the migration of slaves from other states, even when accompanied by their masters. In 1792, South Carolina suspended the domestic slave trade along with foreign importations.[17] Given the restrictive purpose of the clause, the word "migration" must have been all-inclusive.

After the Convention had agreed on the twenty-year limitation, Gouverneur Morris offered two reasons for changing the wording of what was to become Article I, Section 9: inclusion of "persons" and "migration" might lead to national restrictions on immigration after 1808; and also the Convention should show that it had tolerated the slave trade only in compliance to the wishes of three states. Accordingly, Morris proposed the substitute phrase—if acceptable to the states concerned—"importation of slaves into N. Carolina, S. Carolina & Georgia." George Mason said he had no objection to using the word "slaves," but thought that naming the three states might give offense. John Dickinson, still desiring to except states that had already permanently outlawed the slave trade, suggested the less specific wording: "the importation of Slaves into such of the States as shall permit the same shall not be prohibited by the Legislature of the U———S——— until the year 1808." The Convention decided not to sanction slavery so openly, and thus kept the original phrase "such persons." But by retaining the word "migration" and inserting the qualifier "now existing" after "several States," the delegates opened the way for violently conflicting interpretations.[18]

In the Congressional debates over the Alien Law of 1798, Federalists ultimately conceded that until 1808 the migration clause gave states exclusive control over admitting (though not deporting) aliens. But Jonathan Dayton, who had been a Convention delegate from New Jersey, contended that "such persons" applied only to slaves, and that "the sole reason assigned" for not using "slaves" was "that it would be better not to stain the Constitutional code with such a term." Abraham Baldwin, a former Georgia delegate who challenged Dayton in the House of Representatives, correctly remembered that some of the Convention members had observed "that this expression would extend to other persons besides slaves, which was not denied, but this did not produce any alteration of it." Baldwin also recalled, however, that the original phrase had "used the word 'slaves' *instead of* 'migration,' or 'importation,' of persons" (*my italics*). He thus implied that "migration" could have referred to slaves as well as immigrants, and to a mode of arrival distinguishable from "importation." Even Madison, who in 1819 hotly denied that the framers had intended to include interstate movement, did not deny that the word "migration" included slaves: the term, he wrote, allowed "those who were scrupulous of acknowledging expressly a property in human beings, to view *imported* persons as a species of emigrants, whilst others might apply the term to foreign malefactors sent or coming into the country."[19]

Yet both Morris and Dickinson had opposed the expansion of slavery and had omitted "migration" from their substitute motions. And as Madison later pointed out, if southern delegates had supposed that the word included internal movement between the states or into the territories, they would surely have avoided using it. In 1820, when the clause served as one of the justifications for barring slavery from Missouri, Charles Pinckney argued that it had been adopted as a potential check on immigration to the North, in order to balance the South's losses from closing the slave trade. He also asserted that the Convention had made a solemn compact: in exchange for the South's concessions on the slave trade, the North had agreed that Congress would have no power ever to touch the question of slavery.[20]

But this solemn compact never became explicit law. The southern delegates apparently failed to recognize the subtle implications of adding a time limitation to the original wording of the Committee of Detail. They succeeded in removing export duties from the temporary prohibition of Article I, Section 9, but the other phrases, chosen to put maximum restrictions on the commerce clause, now carried the opposite implications. The power of regulating commerce, subject to broad or narrow interpretation, now specifically included the power of prohibiting the migration or importation of persons. Even the effect of Article V, removing the provision from the reach of Constitutional amendment, was necessarily limited to a twenty-year term.

The very vagueness of the wording could be used to widen the potentially antislavery powers granted by the Fifth Amendment and by the clauses concerning interstate commerce, the general welfare, and the need for republican state governments. The Constitution could thus be interpreted as granting Congress the power to manumit contraband slaves, to prohibit the coastal and interstate slave trade, to bar slavery from the territories, to enlist slaves in the armed forces, or to purchase Negroes and emancipate them. Moreover, the phrase "several States now existing" suggested that Congress did not have to wait twenty years to apply its powers to new states or territories. Even Madison conceded that Article I, Section 9, had given Congress immediate power to stop the importation of foreign slaves into new states.[21]

The "true" meaning of the Constitution's provisions on slavery cannot be known, precisely because they were the products of an uneasy bargain and were deliberately shrouded in ambiguity. Agreement on concrete economic issues, or in blunter terms, a deal, could not resolve an unnegotiable conflict over the future of American slavery.

Delegates who returned to the New England and Pennsylvania ratifying conventions could encourage the assumption that the power to be granted Congress in 1808 would become the basis for eradicating slavery from the country. James Wilson, in a famous speech to the Pennsylvania convention, is supposed to have said there could never be another slave state. Yet Virginians, who had strongly favored an immediate end to the slave trade, were confident that the Constitution posed no threat to slavery itself. And in the South Carolina legislature, where there was some fear that the Constitution might be used as a tool for northern interference with slave property, delegates swore that they would never have agreed to confederate without winning agreement on the right to import slaves. They reassured skeptics that the Deep South would even be able to defend the slave trade after 1808, when its power and support in Congress would presumably be invincible.[22]

Northern and southern delegates could tell the people in their respective sections that slavery had been given a mortal wound or the most secure protection; but ultimately both sections had agreed to defer the question to the future. Unlike Parliament's resolutions of 1792, which called for a definite ending of the slave trade at a specified date, the Constitution was open-ended, stating simply that Congress could not prohibit the trade for twenty years. Both opponents and defenders of slavery had faith that time was on their side. And both sides, if disposed to place the Union above inflammatory sectional interests, had strongly implied that the continuance of the Union would depend on the fulfillment of their expectations.

NOTES

1. Darold D. Wax, "Georgia and the Negro before the American Revolution," *Georgia Historical Quarterly*, LI (March, 1967), 63-75.
2. Patrick S. Brady, "The Slave Trade and Sectionalism in South Carolina, 1787–1808," *Journal of Southern History*, XXXVIII (Nov., 1972), 601-20. Peter H. Wood has shown that even by 1720 blacks constituted more than one-half the population of South Carolina; in 1741 the colony enacted a temporary prohibitive duty on slave imports ("More like a Negro Country: Demographic Patterns in Colonial South Carolina, 1700–1740," paper given at 1972 M.S.S.B. Conference on Systems of Slavery, University of Rochester).
3. Brady, "Slave Trade and Sectionalism," pp. 601-20.
4. *Ibid.*, p. 612.
5. Darold D. Wax, "Negro Import Duties in Colonial Virginia: A Study of British Commercial Policy and Local Public Policy," *The Virginia Magazine*, LXXIX (Jan., 1971), 29-44; Robert McColley, *Slavery and Jeffersonian Vir-

ginia (Urbana, Ill., 1964), pp. 163-67, and *passim;* "Slavery Miscellaneous," Box 1, D21, D35, New-York Historical Society.

6. Robert William Fogel and Stanley L. Engerman, *Time on the Cross: The Economics of American Negro Slavery* (2 vols., Boston, 1974), I, 24, 86-89; II, 30-33; Stella H. Sutherland, *Population Distribution in Colonial America* (New York, 1936), p. 271; Bureau of the Census, *Negro Population, 1790–1915* (Washington, 1928), p. 53. Because of the natural increase in the slave population, new imports from Africa had a lessening impact both on the price and total population of slaves. But if Fogel and Engerman are right in their demographic estimates, the period of state prohibition coincided with the period of greatest slave imports.

7. Max Farrand, ed., *The Records of the Federal Convention of 1787* (4 vols., New Haven, 1937), II, 370. For a detailed analysis of the subject, see Donald L. Robinson, *Slavery in the Structure of American Politics, 1765–1820* (New York, 1971), pp. 207-47.

8. Farrand, ed., *Records,* II, 95, 183.

9. *Ibid.,* II, 220-23, Morris added, with questionable sincerity, that he would sooner submit to a tax sufficient to emancipate all the slaves than saddle posterity with such a Constitution.

10. *Ibid.,* II, 371, 373-74.

11. *Ibid.,* II, 374.

12. *Ibid.,* II, 400, 449-50.

13. *Ibid.,* II, 415; Jonathan Elliot, ed., *The Debates in the Several State Conventions, on the Adoption of the Federal Constitution* (Philadelphia, 1876), I, 372-73.

14. Farrand, ed., *Records,* III, 443.

15. See "immigration," *Oxford English Dictionary.* At the Convention, Mason "was for opening a wide door for emigrants; but did not chuse to let foreigners and adventurers make laws for us & govern us" (Farrand, ed., *Records,* II, 216). Yet Rutledge could refer to "an emigrant from N. England to S.C. or Georgia" (*ibid.,* p. 217). No consistent distinction was then drawn between an "immigrant" and "emigrant," nor between an "emigrant" from abroad and one from another state.

16. Farrand, ed., *Records,* II, 371; III, 120. Charles Pinckney was clearly wrong when he later argued that the word "migration" had been chosen because "it was supposed, that, without some express grant to them of power on the subject, Congress would not be authorized ever to touch the question of migration hither, or emigration to this country, however pressing or urgent the necessity of such a measure might be" (*ibid.,* III, 443). In the draft of the Committee of Detail, Congress could *never* have prohibited "the migration or importation of such persons as the several States shall think proper to admit." On the other hand, Pinckney may have been right in suggesting there was an understanding that the power to limit the importation of slaves should be linked with the power to limit white immigration.

17. McColley, *Slavery and Jeffersonian Virginia,* pp. 165-66; Brady, "Slave Trade and Sectionalism," p. 608.

18. Farrand, ed., *Records,* II, 415-16. Whatever the meaning of "migration," its application to the territories was not affected by the twenty-year restriction on Congressional power, which pertained only to "the several States

now existing." Although James Wilson and others thought that the authorized
ten-dollar duty could apply only to "importations," and thus to slaves, Luther
Martin contended that the wording was ambiguous enough to authorize a
duty on white immigrants (*ibid.*, III, 161, 210).

19. James Morton Smith, *Freedom's Fetters: The Alien and Sedition Laws
and American Civil Liberties* (Ithaca, N.Y., 1956), pp. 80-83; Ferrand, ed.,
Records, III, 376-79, 436-37. At the time of the Missouri controversy, Madison
insisted that "the term 'migration' . . . referred, exclusively, to a migration
or importation from other countries into the U. States," and added that the
Northwest Ordinance, which had been intended to restrict the markets for
African slaves, would probably not have been adopted if Congress had possessed the power to end the foreign slave trade (Gaillard Hunt, ed., *The Writings of James Madison* . . . [9 vols., New York, 1900-1910], IX, 5).

20. Farrand, ed., *Records*, III, 443-44. Walter Berns, in a detailed and
learned analysis of the migration clause, suggests duplicity on the part of Madison and others for later fostering the "traditional interpretation" that "such
persons" referred to white immigrants as well as slaves, and that the term
"migration" thus had no internal operation ("The Constitution and the Migration of Slaves," *Yale Law Journal*, LXXVIII [1968], 198-228). I disagree with
Berns's argument, though not with all his conclusions, for the following reasons: (1) He fails to consider the possibility that "such persons" could have
been thought to include white immigrants and also to refer to interstate "migration," especially in the original restrictive version proposed by the Committee
of Detail. (2) Nothing is proved by the expectation of some Northerners that
the clause would eventually put an end to slavery, for there was widespread
confusion of "slavery" with the "slave trade." Both American and British
abolitionists assumed that an end to slave imports would lead automatically to
the amelioration and gradual abolition of slavery. Berns offers no positive evidence that in 1787 anyone thought of the commerce clause, or of interstate
movement, as the key to general emancipation. In any event, the clause applied only to the states then existing. (3) Berns fails to distinguish the interstate slave trade from the interstate migration of slaves with their masters. In
fact, most slaves who moved westward did so with their masters, and one
could debate whether this constituted "commerce." (4) It is a bit misleading
to take the Northwest Ordinance as a sweeping precedent, since it did not affect the slaves already living in the Northwest. Though Congress re-enacted
the Ordinance, it also refused to adopt positive emancipation measures to give
force to the proscription against slavery. Moreover, for a time, the Ordinance
was interpreted in a way that allowed slaveholders to settle in Indiana and Illinois with their slaves. (5) Most important, Berns presupposes that in 1787
slavery was a declining institution and that "nearly everyone viewed slavery as
an evil which must and would be abolished as soon as practicable" (p. 214,
n. 52). Yet there is abundant evidence that in 1787 both the demand for
slaves and the number of slaveholders were steadily increasing, even in Virginia. The relative lack of controversy raised by the migration clause in South
Carolina, of which Berns makes much, simply shows that the most ardent defenders of slavery saw the Constitution as a strong bulwark for their peculiar
institution. The terms under which the southwestern territories were ceded to
the federal government suggest the clear expectation that slavery would ex-

pand westward without interference. One may agree that the language of Article I, Section 9, might reasonably be construed as granting Congress the power to prohibit the movement of any slaves into the territories or new states, and, after 1808, into the original states. But this construction necessarily turns on changing values and definitions, and above all, on a frank disavowal of slavery as a matter of public policy—since it would constitute a clear discrimination against slaveholding migrants. There is no reason to believe that the framers intended or could have agreed upon such a construction.

21. Robinson, *Slavery in the Structure of American Politics*, pp. 227-28.

22. Farrand, ed., *Records*, III, 334, 437; Elliot, ed., *Debates*, I, 123-24; II, 452; IV, 272-86.

• By the 1830s, Southern support for the abolition of slavery had generally disappeared. The growing pressures of abolitionist sentiment in the North and fears of slave uprisings in their own states led many Southerners to begin constructing an elaborate and belligerent ideological defense of Negro slavery. There were two pivotal episodes in the development of Southern sectional consciousness during the 1830's: the Nat Turner revolt in 1831 and the subsequent South Carolina Nullification Crisis. The brief but gory slave insurrection in Southampton County, Virginia, reinforced Southern fears of black violence and was partly responsible for defeat of a movement in the state for gradual abolition in 1831-32. Although, on its face, the Nullification Crisis involved a dispute over the tariff question between South Carolina and the federal government, William W. Freehling has shown in his book on the crisis, Prelude to Civil War, that the controversy exposed the growing anxieties throughout the South over possible Northern interference with the institution of slavery itself. The South Carolinian leader John C. Calhoun expressed the proslavery convictions held by most important Southerners of his generation when he declared in 1837 that "where two races of different origin, and distinguished by color and other physical differences, as well as intellectual, are brought together, the relation now existing in the slaveholding states between the two is, instead of an evil, a good—a positive good." During the three decades preceding the Civil War, as George M. Fredrickson shows in the following article, the South's leading thinkers went to enormous lengths to shore up their "positive-good," proslavery ideology.

Slavery and Race:
The Southern Dilemma

GEORGE M. FREDRICKSON

Prior to the 1830s, black subordination was the practice of white Americans, and the inferiority of the Negro was undoubtedly a common assumption, but open assertions of *permanent* inferiority were exceedingly rare. It took the assault of the abolitionists to unmask the cant about a theoretical human equality that coexisted with Negro slavery and racial discrimination and to force the practitioners of racial oppression to develop a theory that accorded with their behavior. Well before the rise of radical abolitionism, however, spokesmen for the lower South gave notice that they were prepared to defend slavery as an institution against any kind of attack that might develop. In the 1820s the leadership of the major cotton-producing states made it clear that a national colonizationists effort was unacceptable because in their view slavery was an essential and Constitutionally protected local institution which was of no concern of the Federal government or the non-slaveholding states. These apologists for black servitude characteristically answered the colonizations by agreeing with them that emancipation on the soil was unthinkable and then proceeding to point out not only that colonization was impractical as a program of Negro removal but also that its very agitation was a danger to the security of a slave society because the expectations it raised among blacks threatened to undermine the discipline of the plantation. A permanent and rigid slave system, it was argued, was both economically necessary in the rice- and cotton-growing areas and vital as a system of control for a potentially dangerous black population. Such a viewpoint soon triumphed in all the slaveholding states. In 1831 and 1832, the Virginia legislature debated a colonization proposal that might have opened the way to gradual emancipation, but its defeat marked the end of a

From Chapter 2, "Slavery and Race: The Southern Dilemma," *The Black Image In The White Mind* by George M. Fredrickson (New York: Harper & Row, Publishers, 1971), pp. 43-70. Copyright © 1971 by George M. Fredrickson. Reprinted by permission of Harper & Row, Publishers, Inc.

serious search, even in the upper South, for some way to set slavery on the path to extinction.[1]

After the Virginia debate, Professor Thomas R. Dew of William and Mary College, speaking for the victorious proslavery faction, set forth the most thorough and comprehensive justification of the institution that the South had yet produced. Dew's effort should properly be seen as reflecting a transitional stage in the proslavery argument. Since he was refuting the proponents of gradual emancipation and colonization who still thrived in western Virginia and not the new and radical abolitionists of the North, his arguments stressed practicality and expediency and, in a sense, did little more than help bring Virginia in line with the kind of proslavery sentiment already triumphant farther South. Much of his lengthy essay was devoted to showing that colonization was an impossible scheme because the natural increase of the black population would outrun any number that could possibly be colonized. His justification of slavery rested first of all on the contention that servitude had been a necessary stage of human progress and hence could not be regarded as evil in itself. He then went on to argue that the concrete circumstances of Southern life required the institution and that no set of abstract principles should be invoked to obscure the basic fact that the Negro was not prepared for freedom. Although this was fundamentally an extension of the kind of argument that had previously been the basis of the defense of slavery as "a necessary evil," Dew implied that such a practical adjustment to reality had no evil in it, and he raised expediency to the level of conservative principle when he cited Edmund Burke's dictum that "circumstances give in reality to every political principle its distinguishing color and discriminating effect."[2]

In his discussion of Negro character and prospects, Dew did not deviate forthrightly and insistently from traditional quasi-environmentalist assumptions about the nature of most racial differences. Although at the beginning of his essay he described Negroes as "differing from us in color and habits and vastly inferior in the scale of civilization," he did not deal consistently with the question whether this inferiority resulted from innate character or from the "habits" engendered by a long exposure to inhibiting circumstances. In his discussion of "obstacles to emancipation," Dew at one point provided an analysis not incompatible with the conservative environmentalism of the colonizationists. "The blacks," he wrote, "have now all the habits and feelings of slaves, the whites have those of masters; the prejudices are formed, and mere legislation cannot improve them. . . . Declare the Negroes of the South free tomorrow, and vain will be your decree until you have prepared them for it. . . . The law would make them freemen, and custom or prejudice, we care not which you call it, would degrade them to the condition of slaves." Such a prediction, he indicated, was merely an application of the rule that "each one should remain in society in the condition in which he has been born and trained, and not [try] to mount too fast without preparation."[3]

This ultraconservative principle could presumably have been applied to slaves or serfs of any race; and, as if to substantiate this inference, Dew went on to give as an example of premature emancipation the attempt to liberate the Polish peasants in the 1790s. But Dew could also describe black behavior as if it were predetermined by innate racial traits; for he contradicted his suggestion that Negro characteristics were simply acquired habits of servility by arguing, somewhat obscurely, that the supposed indolence of free blacks resulted from "an inherent and intrinsic cause." And when he asserted that "the free black will work *nowhere* except by compulsion," he decisively parted company with the colonizationists.[4] If Dew was a transitional figure in the general defense of slavery because he combined arguments from expediency with hints of a conservative, proslavery theory of society, he was equally transitional as a racial theorist, because of his vacillation between arguments for black inferiority drawn from a perception of the force of "habits," "customs," and "prejudices" and those suggesting that a permanency of racial type justified enslavement.

By the middle of the 1830s the full impact of the abolitionist argument had been felt in the South, and Dew's ambiguous treatment of the racial factor and his contention that slavery was sometimes justified by circumstances no longer provided Southern apologists with what they regarded as a fully adequate defense of the institution. The abolitionists' charge that slavery was inherently sinful was now met increasingly by the unequivocal claim that slavery was "a positive good." Furthermore their practical assertion of racial equality as something to be achieved in the United States and not through colonization inspired proslavery spokesmen to clarify their racial views and to assert, as a major part of their case, the unambiguous concept of inherent Negro inferiority.

South Carolinians led the way. In 1835 Governor George McDuffie told the South Carolina General Assembly that the Negroes were "destined by providence" for slavery and that this was made evident not only by the color of their skin but also by "the intellectual inferiority and natural improvidence of this race." They were, he indicated, "unfit for self-government of any kind," and "in all respects, physical, moral, and political, inferior to millions of the human race." McDuffie professed astonishment that anyone should "suppose it possible to reclaim the African race from their destiny" as slaves or subjects of some other form of absolute despotism.[5] The Charleston lawyer William Drayton said much the same thing the following year in a pamphlet attacking the abolitionists: "Personal observation must convince every candid man, that the negro is constitutionally indolent, voluptuous, and prone to vice; that his mind is heavy, dull, and unambitious; and that the doom that has made the African in all ages and countries, a slave—is the natural consequence of the inferiority of his character."[6] In 1837 John C. Calhoun made his famous defense of slavery before the Senate of the United States and showed how important racial doctrines really were in the new and militant defense of servitude which developed in the 1830s. "I hold that in the present state of civilization, where two races of different origin, and distinguished by color, and other physical differences, as well as intellectual, are brought together, the relation now existing in the slaveholding states between the two, is, instead of an evil, a good—a positive good."[7]

It was thus in tandem with the concept of slavery as "a positive good" that the doctrine of permanent black inferiority began its career as a rationale, first for slavery itself and later for postemancipation forms of racial oppression. The attitudes that underlay the belief that the Negro was doomed by nature itself to perpetual slavishness and subordination to the whites were not new, nor was the doctrine itself if considered as a popular belief that lacked intellectual respectability; but when asserted dogmatically and with an aura of philosophical authority by leading Southern spokesmen and their Northern supporters in the 1830s, it became, for the first time, the basis of a world view, an explicit ideology around which the beneficiaries of white supremacy could organize themselves and their thoughts.

The emergence of racist ideology in the United States was comparable in some respects to the rise of European conservative ideology, as described by Karl Mannheim in his essay on "Conservative Thought." Mannheim made a distinction between "traditionalism"—the emotional and relatively inarticulate tendency to hold on to established and inherited patterns of life—and "conservatism," which he saw as "conscious and reflective from the first, since it arises as a counter movement in conscious opposition to the highly organized, coherent, and systematic 'progressive' movement." This distinction is clearly analogous to one that can be drawn between racial prejudice as an emotional response to an enslaved and physically distinct group and the early form of ideological racism as a "conscious and reflective" attempt to develop, in response to an insistent egalitarianism, a world view based squarely and explicitly on the idea that whites are unalterably superior to blacks. As long as the traditional order was not threatened by radicalism, it required no elaborate theoretical defense. Or, as Gustave de Beaumont, Tocqueville's companion, put it in his novel, *Marie:* "As long as philanthropy on behalf of the Negroes resulted in nothing but useless declamation, the Americans tolerated it without difficulty; it mattered little to them that the equality of the Negroes should be proclaimed in theory, so long as in fact they remained inferior to the whites." But abolitionism, like Jacobinism, forced previously unarticulated assumptions to the level of defensive ideological conscious.[8]

The colonizationists may have stimulated an indirect and pragmatic defense of slavery as a regional necessity, but their occasional expressions of a theoretical racial egalitarianism had not forced their Southern opponents to proclaim vigorously that the Negro was inherently inferior and slavish, for the reason that proponents of colonization had not challenged the necessity or inevitability of black subservience as a fact of life in the United States. The abolitionist contention that Christianity and the Declaration of Independence not only affirmed equality in theory but cried out for its immediate implementation could not go similarly unanswered by the defenders of black subordination.

In their efforts to justify slavery as a necessary system of race relations the proslavery theorists of the 1830s and 1840s developed an arsenal of arguments for Negro inferiority which they repeated *ad nauseam.* Heavily emphasized was the historical case against the black man based on his supposed failure to develop a civilized way of life in Africa. As portrayed in proslavery writing, Africa was and always had been the scene of unmitigated savagery, cannibalism, devil worship, and licentiousness. Also advanced was an early form of the biological argument, based on real or imagined physiological and anatomical differences—especially in cranial characteristics and facial angles—which allegedly explained mental and physical inferiority. Finally there was the appeal to deep-seated white fears of widespread miscegenation, as proslavery theorists sought to deepen white anxieties by claiming that the abolition of slavery would lead to intermarriage and the degeneracy of the race. Although all these arguments had appeared earlier in fugitive or embryonic form, there is something startling about the rapidity with which they were brought together and organized in a rigid polemical pattern, once the defenders of slavery found themselves in a propaganda war with the abolitionists.

The basic racist case against the abolitionist assertion of equality sprang full blown—but without the authoritative "scientific" underpinning that would later give it greater respectability—in a pamphlet published in New York in 1833, entitled *Evidence Against the Views of the Abolitionists, Consisting of Physical and Moral Proofs of the Natural Inferiority of the Negroes.* In this extraordinary document a writer named Richard Colfax set forth in rudimentary form all the basic elements of the racist theory of Negro character. Colfax emphasized in particular a whole range of physical differences between whites and blacks which supposedly demonstrated inherent Negro inferiority. The Negro's facial angle, he contended, was "almost to a level with that of the brute"; hence "the acknowledged meanness of the Negro's intellect only coincides with the shape of his head." The lesson to be drawn from such data was that the black man's *"want of capacity to receive a complicated education renders it improper and impolitic that he should be allowed the privileges of citizenship in an enlightened country."* Since "the Negroes, whether physically or morally considered, are so inferior as to resemble the brute creation as nearly as they do the white species, . . . *no alteration of their present social condition would be productive of the least benefit to them,* inasmuch as no change of their nature can be expected to result therefrom." This unchangeability of the black character had been demonstrated historically, according to Colfax, because over a period of three or four thousand years Africans had had many opportunities to benefit from personal liberty and "their proximity to refined nations," but they had "never even *attempted* to raise themselves above their present equivocal station in the great zoological chain."[9]

The only element lacking in Colfax's racist argument was a full scientific explanation of the underlying *causes* of inequality. In the century that followed, theorists of racial inferiority would offer new and ingenious proofs or explanations for Colfax's assertions, but they would add very little to his general thesis.

As part of their effort to gain widespread support for such views, proslavery polemicists turned their attention to the free Negroes of the North, whom they presented not so much as a population degraded by white prejudice and color consciousness as one demonstrating its natural unfitness for freedom. When the census of 1840, which later proved to be inaccurate, revealed a very high rate of insanity among free Negroes as compared with slaves, they seized upon these statistics as evidence of the Negro's constitutional inability to function in a free society. In 1844 Calhoun, then Secretary of State, concluded that "the census and other authentic documents show that, in all instances in which the states have changed the former relation between the two races the African, instead of being improved, has become worse. They have been invariably sunk into vice and pauperism, accompanied by bodily and mental afflictions incident thereto—deafness, insanity and idiocy—to a degree without example. . . ."[10]

II

As the debate progressed, it became evident that Northern opponents of slavery could, if they chose, easily deflect the increasingly vexed question of biological differences by arguing that constitutional Negro deficiencies, even if they existed, provided no justification for slavery. On the contrary, they would only make it more sinful; for what could be more unchristian than exploitation of the weak by the strong? Owen Lovejoy, an abolitionist Congressman from Illinois and brother of the martyred editor Elijah P. Lovejoy, eloquently presented this point of view in 1860: "We may concede it as a matter of fact that [the Negro race] is inferior; but does it follow, therefore, that it is right to enslave a man simply because he is inferior? This, to me, is a most abhorrent doctrine. It could place the weak everywhere at the mercy of the strong; it would place the poor at the mercy of the rich; it would place those who are deficient in intellect at the mercy of those that are gifted in mental endowment. . . ."[11]

Many Southerners were themselves too strongly influenced by Christian and humanitarian values to let such an indictment stand. Their answer was that the slave was not only unfit for freedom but was ideally suited to slavery; for the Negro found happiness and fulfillment only when he had a white master. As one writer put it, Negro slaves are "the most cheerful and merry people we have among us."[12] For from the blacks' being "degraded," Southern apologists maintained that they were much better off in slavery than they had been in Africa. According to the South Carolina novelist William Gilmore

Simms, the Negro came from a continent where he was "a cannibal, destined . . . to eat his fellow, or be eaten by him." Southern slavery "brought him to a land in which he suffers no risk of life or limb other than that to which his owner is equally subjected," and had increased "his health and strength," improved "his physical symmetry and animal organization," elevated "his mind and morals," and given "him better and more certain food, better clothing, and more kind and valuable attendance when he is sick." It was no wonder, then, that he had developed a happy disposition.[13]

In promulgating the stereotype of the happy and contented bondsman, Southerners were doing more than simply putting out propaganda to counter the abolitionist image of the wretched slave. They were also seeking to put to rest their own nagging fears of slave rebellion. It was no accident that proslavery spokesmen in the Virginia legislature made much of the alleged contentment of the slaves; for the debate took place in the wake of the Nat Turner uprising of 1831, and servitude had come under attack as leading inevitably to black resistance. One of the proslavery members made it clear that the recent rebellion was a bizarre exception to the general pattern of master-slave relationships: "Our slave population is not only a happy one, but it is a contented, peaceful and harmless [one] . . . during all this time [the last sixty years] we have had one insurrection."[14]

The image of black violence and retribution, drawn not only from Nat Turner but from memories of what had occurred in Santo Domingo, continued to haunt the Southern imagination however. Insurrection panics were frequent after 1830, and for men who supposedly ruled over a docile population, Southern slaveowners were extraordinarily careful to maintain absolute control over their "people" and to quarantine them from any kind of outside influence that might inspire dissatisfaction with their condition. In moments of candor, Southerners admitted their suspicion that duplicity, opportunism, and potential rebelliousness lurked behind the mask of Negro affability.[15]

A concept of the duality or instability of Negro character was in fact one of the most important contributions made by Southern proslavery propagandists to the racist imagery that outlasted slavery. In its original protoracist form, this duality was the one set forth by Thomas R. Dew between the savage Negro of Africa and the "civilized" black slave. Dew maintained that no large-scale insurrections were likely "where the blacks are as much civilized as they are in the United States. Savages and Koromantyn slaves can commit such deeds, because their whole life and education have prepared them; but the Negro of the United States has imbibed the principles, sentiments, and the feelings of the whites; in one word, he is civilized. . . ."[16] But Dew's analysis implicitly conceded too much to environment; indeed it made the Negro character seem almost infinitely plastic. What, it might be asked, was to prevent blacks from soon becoming "civilized" up to the level of the whites and claiming equality with them? Later writers often qualified the notion that slavery "civilized" the Negro by asserting that innate racial traits limited his potential development to a more or less tenuous state of "semi-civilization," a conception which provided an unequivocal justification of permanent servitude.

According to this theory, the Negro was by nature a savage brute. Under slavery, however, he was "domesticated" or, to a limited degree, "civilized." Hence docility was not so much his natural character as an artificial creation of slavery. As long as the control of the master was firm and assured, the slave would be happy, loyal, and affectionate; but remove or weaken the authority of the master, and he would revert to type as a bloodthirsty savage. That many Southerners did not believe, even in theory, in Negro docility under *all* conditions came out most vividly in proslavery discussions of emancipation and its probable consequences. Servile war was often seen as the inevitable result of loosening the bonds of servitude. In the words of William Drayton, who drew on the example of Santo Domingo, "the madness which a sudden freedom from restraint begets—the overpowering burst of a long buried passion, the wild frenzy of revenge, and the savage lust for blood, all unite to give the warfare of liberated slaves, traits of cruelty and crime which nothing earthly can equal."[17] Drayton's suggestion that emancipation would bring a reversion to basic savage type was set forth more explicitly by a writer in *De Bow's Review*, who described as follows the consequences of liberating a large black population: ". . . the brutish propensities of the negro now unchecked, there remains no road for their full exercise . . . but in the slaughter of his white master, and through the slaughter, he strides (unless he himself be exterminated) to the full exercise of his *native barbarity and savageness*."[18] As proof of the Negro's inevitable "reversion to type" when freed, defenders of slavery pointed continually to the alleged "relapse into barbarism" which had taken place in Haiti, the British West Indies, and Liberia, once the domesticating influence of slavery had been removed.[19]

The notion that bestial savagery constituted the basic Negro character and that the loyal "Sambo" figure was a social product of slavery served to channel genuine fears and anxieties by suggesting a program of preventive action, while at the same time legitimizing a conditional "affection" for the Negro. As a slave he was lovable but as a freedman he would be a monster. This duality was expressed in its most extreme form by Dr. Samuel A. Cartwright of Louisiana, who wrote in 1861 that ". . . the negro must, from necessity, be the slave of man or the slave of Satan."[20]

There were, however, ambiguities in the concept of Negro "domestication" or "semi-civilization" under slavery. One involved the question of whether or not, in the far distant future, the slave's savage instincts might entirely disappear as the result of some quasi-Lamarckian process of evolution, a development which would presumably fit the Negro for a change of status. Many writers regarded this question as open and undecided; others fell into blatant self-contradiction when they confronted it. William Gilmore Simms, in setting forth a pro-slavery theory of human progress, described how the rise of peoples to civilized status had often involved the tutelage of slavery as a stage in their development. "It is possible that a time will come," he wrote, "when, taught by our schools, and made strong by our training, the negroes of the southern states may arrive at freedom." Later in the same paragraph, however, he rudely shut the door that he had tentatively opened: "I do not believe that [the Negro] will ever be other than a slave, or that he was made to be otherwise; but that he is designed as an implement in the hand of civilization always."[21] This view was given authoritative expression from the mid-1840s on by "ethnological" writers like Samuel Cartwright and Josiah Nott. From a narrowly proslavery perspective, however, the whole question was in effect academic, because even those apologists who accepted the possibility that blacks might someday be ready for freedom maintained that additional centuries of servitude would be required to transform the essential Negro character.[22]

A more significant ambiguity, one which led to an important cleavage, resulted from differences over exactly what Negro "domestication" meant in terms of the actual relationships between masters and slaves. One way of suggesting what was at issue is to ask whether the model for the ideal slave was taken from the realm of the subhuman, with the slave as a high type of domesticated animal to serve as the white man's tool like another beast of burden, or from the human family as

a "domestic" and domesticating institution, with the slave in the role
of a child, responding with human affection to a kindly master. This
ambiguity was related to an ambiguity about the nature of the plantation: was it a commercial enterprise with the blacks as a subhuman
labor force, or a small patriarchal society?

George Fitzhugh, writing in the 1850s, was the most eloquent
spokesman of the familial or paternalist view of slavery. For him, the
harsh, exploitative side of slavery disappeared almost entirely; the master became a "parent or guardian," and the slave a child who, on the
basis of a "common humanity," was admitted to "the family circle"[23]
and subjected to "family government." The view of Negro psychology
that sustained such a view was set forth by the Reverend H. N.
McTyeire in a typical example of the advice that clergymen of a certain type gave to slaveholders:

> The sympathies which have their range within the social sys-
> tem—the emotions which form the ordinary cement of social
> existence, are found in the negro, and they are to be taken into
> account, in dealing with him. The master who ignores them and
> proceeds on brute principles, will vex his own soul and render
> his servants worthless and wretched. Love and fear, a regard for
> public opinion, gratitude, shame, the conjugal, parental, and
> filial feelings, these must all be appealed to and cultivated."[24]

The very fact, however, that such advice had to be given suggests
that there was a contrary point of view. Paternalists emphasized the
reality of slave "gratitude" as a natural human emotion deriving from
kindly treatment; men with a different orientation thought differently.
This, for example, is how George S. Sawyer, a Louisiana slaveholder,
described the Negro character: "The very many instances of remarkable fidelity and attachment to their masters, a characteristic quite
common among them, are founded not so much upon any high intellectual and refined sentiment of gratitude, as upon instinctive impulse, possessed to an even higher degree by some of the canine
species."[25]

It was a short step from such an analogy to the argument that it
was more difficult to mistreat Negroes or to overwork them than
would be the case with whites; and some Southerners even concluded
that for most purposes a master could simply forget about the possibility that his charges had normal human sensibilities. Cartwright,
a Louisiana physician who had many years of practice on the planta-

tions of what was then the Southwest, maintained in 1843 that the Negro race "has a peculiar instinct protecting it against the abuses of arbitrary power"; for blacks could not be overworked and were comparatively insensitive to sufferings that would be unbearable to whites. But Cartwright did believe that there was such a thing as "mismanagement" of Negroes. In a later "medical" essay, he described various Negro "diseases" that resulted from it, including drapetomia (running away) and rascality. Since such afflictions stemmed from bad government or imperfect slavery, their source was not in the harshness of servitude but in the unnatural liberty permitted by ineffectual masters.[26] The comforting notion that slaves did not suffer, even from flagrant mistreatment, was given expression by a Southern lady novelist in 1860. She not only argued that Negroes could not be overworked but claimed that it was physically impossible for a master to knock a slave "senseless to the ground"—as he was so often knocked in abolitionist writings—because the Negro skull was so thick that such an effort would bruise or break a white man's fist.[27]

The supposed animal insensitivity of the Negro was also invoked as a basis for denying familial affection among slaves and thereby implicitly justifying the breakup of families. According to Thomas R. R. Cobb of Georgia, the Negro's "natural affections are not strong, and consequently he is cruel to his offspring, and suffers little by separation from them."[28] Sawyer went further and asserted that blacks are totally lacking in family feeling and that it is "lust and beastly cruelty" and not "emotions of parental and kindred attachment" that "glow in the negro's bosom."[29] Such opinions suggest that the kind of "hard" racism that manifest itself in the image of "the Negro as beast" did not originate in the era of segregation late in the nineteenth century but had its origins in the antebellum period, when it vied for supremacy in Southern propaganda with the "soft" image of the black slave as beloved child.

III

The South's fundamental conception of itself as a slaveholding society was unstable. In the intellectual context of the time, the notion of the slave as dependent or child implied one kind of social order; the view that he was essentially subhuman suggested another.

Seeing the Negro as basically human despite his inferiority was compatible in theory with his integration into a certain type of human society—one based on a frank and open recognition of a whole range of inequalities. One branch of proslavery thought took this tack —the theoretical defense of a social order in which slavery was part of a larger hierarchy maintained by a sense of mutual obligation between superiors and inferiors. This viewpoint was foreshadowed by Thomas R. Dew's dictum that everyone, white or black, should be content to remain in the social station "in which he has been born and bred," and that consequently it was as ill advised for planters to encourage white overseers to aspire to gentility by giving them access to the drawing room as it was to invite expectations of freedom from the slaves.[30] In a defense of slavery published in 1838, Chancellor William Harper of the University of South Carolina elaborated on this hierarchical concept when he answered the abolitionist charge that the slave was denied the possibility of intellectual improvement by attacking the very notion of a society based on equality of opportunity. "The slave receives," Harper wrote, "such instruction as qualifies him to discharge the duties of his particular station. The Creator did not intend that every human being should be highly cultivated, morally and intellectually." Then, hitting even more directly at the American egalitarian ideal, he added: ". . . if, as Providence has evidently decreed, there can be but a certain portion of intellectual excellence in any community, it is better that it should be *unequally* divided. It is better that a part should be fully and highly cultivated, and the rest utterly ignorant." As a matter of principle, the lower classes, regardless of race, should be subordinated and kept in ignorance. Following the logic of his argument, Harper contended that the misery and uncertainty of status which seemed endemic to the "laborious poor" of nonslaveholding societies could be readily relieved by the imposition of something like slavery.[31]

Out of this kind of reactionary thinking there evolved by the early 1850s the fully developed thesis that slavery was "a positive good," not only as a system of controlling an inferior race but, more basically, as a way of providing security to the laboring class of any society. George Fitzhugh carried this line of thought to its logical extreme when he attacked the fundamental assumptions of capitalism and democracy by arguing that the working class of advanced industrial countries like Great Britain would be better off under slavery. For Fitzhugh and other Southern defenders of a reactionary seigneurialism, the patriarchal plantation was the best model for society in general, because the cement of all enduring social relationships was the pattern of responsibility and dependence that existed in the family and on the idealized plantation. Their attack on "free society" was based on the claim that a lack of such relationships led inevitably to misery, anarchy, and revolution.[32]

Fitzhugh was aware that his whole reactionary social philosophy would be undermined if slavery were justified principally in terms of racial differences; hence in his writings of the mid-1850s, he was emphatic in his assertion that the South must be willing to defend slavery in general and not just for blacks. "The strongest argument against slavery, and all the prejudice against it," he wrote in 1857, "arise from the too great inferiority of race, which begets cruel and negligent treatment in the masters, who naturally feel little sympathy for ignorant, brutal savages. Inferiority of race is quite as good an argument against slavery as in its favor." "The whole history of the institution," he concluded, "shows that in giving up slavery in the abstract, we take the weakest position of defense that we could possibly select. We admit it to be wrong and then attempt to defend it in that peculiar form that has always been most odious to mankind."[33]

Fitzhugh's concern with this ideological problem suggested that many people in the South had not in fact taken his high ground and were trying to justify slavery on what he considered the narrow and treacherous basis of race alone. And he was right; for the view that slavery was rooted in the peculiar nature of the Negro rather than in ultraconservative concepts of society and government was a popular one. James D. B. De Bow, editor of *De Bow's Review*, a major source of proslavery doctrine, encouraged Fitzhugh's assault on a free society and liberal ideas, but he also opened his journal to the ethnological school and actively endorsed the views of men like Cartwright, Josiah C. Nott, and John H. Van Evrie who defended slavery almost exclusively on the basis of racist anthropology, arguing that the Negro was so radically inferior to the Caucasian that his destiny in America was either brute servitude or extermination. The Biblical curse of Ham could serve almost as well, and in the hands of writers like Matthew Estes and Josiah Priest, it became a judgment of God which placed the black man virtually beyond the pale of humanity.[34]

If Fitzhugh envisioned a seigneurial society based on the image of a patriarchal plantation, the militant racists implicitly or explicitly projected a democratic and egalitarian society for whites, denying that the blacks were, in any real sense at all, part of the human community. They were advocates of what the sociologist Pierre L. van den Berghe has called "*Herrenvolk* democracy." In his comparative study

of racism, van den Berghe has contrasted "*Herrenvolk* democracies"—
"regimes like those of the United States or South Africa that are democratic for the master race but tyrannical for the subordinate groups"
—with genuinely aristocratic multiracial societies like those of colonial
Latin America.[35] The conflict between a developing *Herrenvolk* ideology and an aristocratic or seigneurial philosophy theoretically incompatible with democracy served to divide the mind of the Old South.
To understand this conflict, one must recognize that Southerners
could mean two different things when they questioned the applica-
bility of the Declaration of Independence. They could reject the idea
of equality in general, like Chancellor Harper and Fitzhugh, or they
could reject simply the interpretation of it which included the Negro
as a man created equal to the whites. Those who embraced the second
option saw themselves as preserving the egalitarian philosophy as a
white racial prerogative. This latter view was stated succinctly by the
Alabama fire-eater William L. Yancey before a Northern audience in
1860: "Your fathers and my fathers built this government on two
ideas: the first is that the white race is the citizen, and the master race,
and the white man is the equal of every other white man. The second
idea is that the Negro is the inferior race."[36] In the same year, a writer
in the *Southern Literary Messenger* made a similar point in an historical analysis of slavery. Unlike the paternalists, he condemned ancient
slavery and medieval serfdom in principle, because under such systems "races richly endowed by nature, and designed for high and lofty
purposes, were kept from rising to their natural level." But all forms of
white servitude and subordination had fallen before "the progress of
truth, justice, and Christianity." Negro slavery, on the other hand, had
persisted because it was not really incompatible with the growth of liberty and equality.[37]

Southerners often went further and contended that Negro slavery
was not only compatible with white equality but was the very foundation of it. Governor Henry A. Wise of Virginia contended that true
equality could exist among whites only where black servitude existed.
"Break down slavery," he argued, "and you would with the same blow
destroy the great democratic principle of equality among men."[38] The
claim was frequently made that the white South had no recognized
social classes; that far from establishing an aristocracy of slaveholders,
as the abolitionists claimed, it put all white men, whether they owned
slaves or not, on a dead level. Thomas R. R. Cobb described the
lower-class whites of the South as having the sense of belonging "to

an elevated class": "It matters not that he is no slaveholder; he is not of the inferior race; he is a freeborn citizen. . . . The poorest meets the richest as an equal; sits at the table with him; salutes him as a neighbor; meets him at a public assembly, and stands on the same social platform."[39]

Such observations obviously reflected a social ideal radically at variance with the image of the South as a seigneurial or quasi-feudal society. The proponents of this view made racial consciousness the foundation and cement of Southern society and not an incidental aspect. It was carried to its logical extreme in the writings of Dr. John H. Van Evrie, a proslavery New York physician and editor whose views were widely hailed in the South. In the 1853 pamphlet version of his *Negroes and Negro "Slavery,"* which carried on the cover the enthusiastic endorsements of Jefferson Davis, J. D. B. De Bow, and other prominent Southern spokesmen, Van Evrie combined arguments for the biological inequality of the blacks with a vigorous attack on all past or present forms of class privilege and social hierarchy within homogeneous white societies. He denounced with particular emphasis the oppression of British peasants and laborers by an "aristocracy" that was not naturally superior to those it governed. Having condemned all forms of subordination of whites to other whites as "artificial" and unjust, Van Evrie then relegated the blacks to abject and perpetual servitude for one reason alone—because they constituted a permanently inferior biological species. He even attacked those proslavery writers who attempted "to defend Southern institutions by comparing the condition of the Negro with the condition of the British laborer," because "no comparison is allowable or possible":

> The Negro is governed by those *naturally* superior, and is in the *best* condition of any portion or branch of his race, while the British laborer, governed by those *naturally* his equals, and even sometimes his inferiors, is in the *worst* condition of any portion of *his* race. The first is secure in all the rights that nature gives him, the latter is *practically* denied all or nearly all of his—the first is protected and provided for by those the Creator has designed should govern him, the latter is kept in ignorance, brutalized, over worked and plundered by those who it is designed should only *govern themselves—one is a normal condition,* the other an *infamous usurpation.*[40]

The most famous and authoritative statement of the principle that hierarchical subordination should always be strictly reserved for inferior races appeared in Alexander H. Stephens's famous "Cornerstone Speech" of 1861, heralding the foundation of the Confederacy. "Many governments," said the newly elected Vice President of the Confederate States of America, "have been founded on the principles of subordination and serfdom of certain classes of the same race; *such were, and are in violation of the laws of nature.* Our system commits no such violation of nature's laws. With us, all the white race, however high or low, rich or poor, are equal in the eyes of the law. Not so with the Negro. Subordination is his place. He, by nature, or by the curse against Canaan, is fitted for that condition which he occupies in our system." As for the basis of the new Confederate government: "Its foundations are laid, its cornerstone rests upon the great truth that the Negro is not equal to the white man, that slavery—subordination to the superior race—is his natural or normal condition."[41]

IV

Empirically speaking, Southern slavery was *both* an example of slavery in general *and* a form of servitude strictly limited to a single and supposedly inferior race. Two qualities about his laborers were thus bound to impress themselves upon the slaveholder's consciousness—that they were slaves and that they were black. On an unreflective attitudinal level these two aspects of the situation could coexist, reinforcing each other by creating a disposition to defend slavery because it was simultaneously the basis of concrete economic and social privilege for a class of Southerners and the institutional underpinning for a psychologically satisfying sense of racial superiority. But, as we have seen, the attempt to develop a consistent philosophical defense of the institution led inevitably to efforts to derive the argument principally from one facet or the other. Emphasis on slavery per se as an organizing principle of society led to a genuinely reactionary and paternalistic theory of society; but if racial differentiation was seen as the heart of the matter, then the result, in the larger American ideological context, was "*Herrenvolk* democracy" or "egalitarian" racism.

The elaborate intellectual efforts of writers like Fitzhugh and Henry Hughes (the Mississippi "sociologist") to prove that the "ethnical qualification" in the South's system of labor was "accidental,"[42] can perhaps best be seen as an attempt to articulate the genuinely antidemocratic aspirations of an elite of large planters by legitimizing in the abstract the self-serving principle of aristocratic domination. There is undoubtedly some truth in Eugene Genovese's assertion that the master-slave relationship and the plantation environment tended by their very nature to produce a class with "an aristocratic, antibourgeois spirit with values and mores emphasizing family and status, a strong code of honor, and aspirations to luxury, ease, and accomplishment."[43] Fitzhugh, Hughes, and other aristocratic paternalists with similar if less highly developed views—men like Edmund Ruffin, William J. Grayson, and George Frederick Holmes—probably did express, in some sense, the deeper impulses of the South's upper class, "the logical outcome" of its social thinking.[44]

It is doubtful, however, that these aristocratic proslavery theorists produced a coherent world view that placed the South as a whole on the road to accepting a reactionary class ideology as opposed to a modern type of race ideology. First of all, these thinkers betrayed their own ambivalence by giving greater attention to racial inferiority as a justification of Southern slavery than their general theory actually required. Although Hughes had described the racial factor as an "accidental" element in the Southern labor system, he went on to argue at some length that subordination of the blacks in the South was essential to prevent amalgamation and preserve the purity of the white race; Edmund Ruffin combined universalist arguments for slavery with a full rendition of the historical thesis that blacks as a race had demonstrated a peculiar intellectual inferiority and incapacity for freedom; even Fitzhugh maintained that the inherent "childlike" character of the Negro was in itself a persuasive argument for his enslavement.[45]

Moreover, it is questionable that even an "ethnically qualified" argument for aristocracy and slavery as being good in themselves won very many adherents outside a circle of slaveholding intellectuals who seemed alienated to some extent from their society and were without a determining influence on Southern politics or the formation of public opinion. Some of these theorists severely limited their own influence by openly manifesting aristocratic revulsion to the values and practices that resulted from the extension of democratic procedures and attitudes during the Jacksonian period. Among the older paternalistic theorists, Ruffin and Grayson belonged to the group that William R. Taylor describes as "Southern mugwumps," men who had retreated from politics in the 1820s and 1830s, partly because of their temperamental and ideological opposition to the changing character of public life. It also is noteworthy that most of the paternalist ideologues were from Virginia and South Carolina, the most conservative Southern states. Their point of view was not so commonly expressed by the proslavery apologists of the newer and increasingly dominant Southwestern states, where a quasi-democratic ethos and a forthright emphasis on *"Herrenvolk"* solidarity were made evident.[46]

The overwhelming majority of antebellum Southerners, it should be recalled, either owned no slaves or were farmers who owned only a few. Although many undoubtedly aspired to become planters, there is little indication that they accepted a reactionary social philosophy or even understood it. On the contrary, most signs would suggest that for intraracial purposes they were fiercely democratic in their political and social thinking, strongly opposed to any formal recognition of the principle of aristocracy among whites. The reactionary elements of the planter class could not readily force their values on such a population, because political democracy in the Old South, and particularly in the Southwest, was no sham: universal white manhood suffrage existed in most states during the late antebellum period, and candidates closely identified with a "black belt" or planter interest were sometimes defeated in bitterly contested elections which revealed a vigorous two-party system and a high level of popular interest and participation. The "plain folk," mostly stiff-necked back-country farmers with their own frontier-type traditions, were not, despite their relative poverty, economically or socially dependent, in any full sense, on the planter elite; and with the extension of the suffrage in the 1830s this element acquired a political leverage that required some upper-class accommodation.[47]

In the end, therefore, the planter class, whatever its own inner feelings, endeavored to maintain its *de facto* hegemony by making a "democratic" appeal, one which took into account the beliefs, desires, and phobias of an enfranchised nonslaveholding majority. No successful Southern politician, whatever his ties to the "aristocracy," was able to talk like Fitzhugh and give theoretical sanction to the enslavement or subordination of whites. When politicians justified slavery, they almost invariably did so largely in terms of race; the nonslaveholders feared blacks as potential competitors and opposed emancipation as a threat to their own "equal" status as whites. Because of inherent limitations on their ability to rule as they saw fit, the dominant class had to be content with a public defense of slavery that contradicted any consistently aristocratic pretensions they may have had; for they recognized that efforts to sanction white servitude in the abstract might endanger black servitude as a concrete reality. The fundamental insecurity that made such an adjustment mandatory was re-

vealed by the hysterical reaction of Southern conservatives to the publication in 1857 of Hinton Rowan Helper's *The Impending Crisis of
the South,* an attack on the slave system from a lower-class white point
of view.[48] Not at all sure of the adherence of nonslaveholding whites
to slavery itself, much less to a reactionary view of its implications,
spokesmen for the planter class were generally willing to gain the
necessary support for their concrete interests on any platform that
would sanction them, even if it sacrificed their full ideological ambi-
tions. In the last analysis, therefore, *Herrenvolk* egalitarianism was the
dominant public ideology of the South, because it was the only one
likely to ensure a consensus.

Spokesmen for the class of large planters were able to endorse such
a doctrine without blatant hypocrisy because they themselves had
never denied that inferiority of race was *one* justification of slavery.
It has already been noted that Fitzhugh, who had tried harder than
anyone to confine racial differences within an ultraconservative social
perspective—as only one example of the manifold inequalities which
ought to be reflected in paternalistic institutions—had nevertheless always argued that the inherent characteristics of the Negro race made
its enslavement both natural and necessary. And at the very end of the
antebellum period, when the sectional conflict was approaching its climax, Fitzhugh himself put an increasing stress on the racial factor and
consented to an enlargement of the theoretical gap between the races.
Indeed, one of the most dramatic indications that the effort to develop
and promulgate a genuinely paternalistic world view was aborted by
concessions to racism and Negrophobia can be found in the shifting
emphasis in Ftzhugh's writings between 1857 and 1861. In 1857 Fitzhugh had warned against a defense of slavery that relied on "too great
inferiority of race." But in his 1859 article "Free Negroes in Hayti,"
he revealed his own growing interest in racial doctrines. Paying tribute
to "ethnology, a study almost neglected fifty years since," which had
now "been elevated to the dignity of a science," he went on to describe how Haitian blacks were "relapsing into their former savage
state." In support of the view that Haitian "degeneration" revealed
basic Negro traits, he cited Count Joseph Arthur de Gobineau, the father of modern European racism, whose book *The Moral and Intellectual Diversity of Races* was published in the United States in 1856.
But Fitzhugh still held back from an unequivocal endorsement of Gobineau's assertion that Negroes had an absolutely fixed and unchange-
able set of undesirable traits. He acknowledged that the Haitian ex-

perience demonstrated the current inability of the Negro to make progress under freedom but intimated that it was still an open question what might eventually be made of him under slavery.[49] In 1861, however, Fitzhugh announced his capitulation to extreme racism. In a review of Van Evrie's *Negroes and Negro "Slavery,"* in book form, Fitzhugh concluded that Van Evrie had provided

> demonstrative reasoning, demonstrative proof, that the negro is of a different species, physically, from the white man. He then shows that the habitudes, instincts, moral and intellectual qualities and capabilities of all animals are the universal and necessary concomitants (if not the consequences) of their physical conformation. . . . We maintain then, that without descending to moral reasoning or speculation, he has *demonstrated* that the negro is physically, morally, and intellectually a different being (from necessity) from the white man, and must ever so remain. . . .

Fitzhugh concluded that Van Evrie had "a new idea, a new and fruitful idea."[50]

When he yielded to the pressure of Negrophobic opinion and to a materialist racism that by his own earlier admission was incompatible with a paternalist concept of slavery, Fitzhugh demonstrated that the aristocratic slaveholder's philosophy had failed to capture the Southern mind. His new racial emphasis reflected his inability to convert the South to reactionary seigneurialism as an alternative to the extreme racist doctrines that were growing in popularity as the basis of the proslavery argument during the 1850s. As his own heightened interest in "ethnology" suggests, one of the factors behind this rise in the significance of anti-Negro thought was the growth, outside the South as well as within it, of a body of "scientific" opinion which seemed to give the racial emphasis such intellectual authority that there was an almost irresistible temptation to make it a principal weapon against proponents of emancipation and racial equality.

NOTES

1. On proslavery attitudes in the lower South in the 1820s, see William W. Freehling, *Prelude to Civil War: The Nullification Controversy in South Carolina, 1816–1836* (New York, 1966), Chapter III and pp. 122-128; and William Sumner Jenkins, *Pro-Slavery Thought in the Old South* (Chapel Hill, N. C., 1935), pp. 65-79. The best account of the Virginia debate is Joseph Clarke Robert, *The Road from Monticello: A Study of the Virginia Slavery Debate of 1832* (Durham, N. C., 1941).

2. "Professor Dew on Slavery," *The Pro-Slavery Argument* (Charleston, 1852), p. 355, and *passim*. Dew's essay was originally published as *Review of the Debate of the Virginia Legislature of 1813 and 1832* (Richmond, 1832).

3. *Ibid.*, pp. 287, 435-456.

4. *Ibid.*, pp. 437, 429-430. (The italics are mine.)

5. Speech before the General Assembly of South Carolina, as reprinted in *The Source Book of American History*, ed. Albert Bushnell Hart (New York, 1905), p. 245.

6. William Drayton, *The South Vindicated from the Treason and Fanaticism of the Northern Abolitionists* (Philadelphia, 1836), p. 232.

7. John C. Calhoun, *Works*, ed. Richard K. Crallé (New York, 1853–1857), II, 631.

8. Karl Mannheim, *Essays on Sociology and Social Psychology* (London, 1953), pp. 99 and 74-164, *passim*; Gustave de Beaumont, *Marie, or Slavery in the United States* (Stanford, Cal., 1958), p. 11. (First published in 1835.)

9. Richard H. Colfax, *Evidence Against the Views of the Abolitionists* . . . (New York, 1833), pp. 25-26, 30, and *passim*. In the late 1840s and 1850s, these arguments would be placed in a framework of respectable scientific theory by the "American School of ethnology" (see Chapter Three below). Subsequent to the publication of Colfax's *Evidence Against the Views of the Abolitionists*, the same historical and biological case against the Negro was presented, for example, in Drayton's *The South Vindicated* (1836); James Kirke Paulding's *Slavery in the United States* (New York, 1836); J. H. Guenebault's *Natural History of the Negro Race* (Charleston, 1837); The Reverend Josiah Priest's *Slavery, As It Relates to the Negro or African Race* (Albany, N. Y., 1843); Samuel A. Cartwright's *Essays, Being Inductions Drawn from the Baconian Philosophy* . . . (Vidalia, La., 1843); and Matthew Estes, *A Defense of Negro Slavery, As It Exists in the United States* (Montgomery, Ala., 1846).

10. John C. Calhoun, *Works*, V, 337. There are excellent discussions of the controversy over the census of 1840 in Leon F. Litwack, *North of Slavery: The Negro in the Free States, 1790–1860* (Chicago, 1961), pp. 40-46, and Norman Dain, *Concepts of Insanity in the United States, 1789–1865* (New Brunswick, N. J., 1964), pp. 104-108.

11. "The principle upon which slaveholding was sought to be justified in this country would, if carried out in the affairs of the universe," Lovejoy added, "transform Jehovah, the supreme, into an infinite juggernaut, rolling the huge wheels of his omnipotence, ankle deep, amid the crushed, and mangled, and bleeding bodies of human beings on the ground that he was infinitely superior, and that they were an inferior race." (Cited in the *Liberator*, April 26, 1860.)

12. William A. Smith, *Lectures on the Philosophy and Practice of Slavery* . . . (Nashville, 1856), pp. 223-224.

13. William Gilmore Simms, "The Morals of Slavery," *The Pro-Slavery Argument*, p. 273. (Originally published in *The Southern Literary Messenger* III [November, 1837], 641-657.)

14. From a speech of James Gholson of Brunswick County, in Robert, *Road from Monticello*, p. 67.

56   GEORGE M. FREDRICKSON

15. See Mary Boykin Chesnut, *A Diary from Dixie*, ed. Ben Ames Williams (Boston, 1949), p. 141, for a classic expression of Southern doubts about slave contentment and docility.

16. *Pre-Slavery Argument*, p. 463.

17. Drayton, *The South Vindicated*, p. 246.

18. "L. S. M.," review of John Campbell's *Negromania*, in *The Industrial Resources of the Southern and Western States*, ed. J. D. B. De Bow (New Orleans, 1852), II, 203. (The italics are mine.)

19. See for example, Thomas R. R. Cobb, *An Inquiry into the Law of Negro Slavery in the United States of America* (Philadelphia, 1858), pp. cxcvii, ccxxvii.

20. Dr. Samuel Cartwright, "Negro Freedom: An Impossibility under Nature's Laws," *De Bow's Review*, XXX (May–June, 1861), 651.

21. *Pro-Slavery Argument*, pp. 266-268.

22. For an example of the thesis that blacks would be ready "at some distant day" for "the privileges of civil liberty," see W. A. Smith, *Lectures on . . . Slavery* (1856), p. 246 and *passim*. By the time Smith wrote, however, this was clearly not the dominant view among proslavery apologists.

23. George Fitzhugh, *Sociology for the South; or, the Failure of Free Society* (Richmond, 1854), pp. 82-83, 105-107; *Cannibals All! or, Slaves Without Masters*, ed. C. Vann Woodward (Cambridge, Mass., 1960), p. 205. (First published in 1857.)

24. H. N. McTyeire, "Plantation Life–Duties and Responsibilities," *De Bow's Review*, XXIX (September, 1860), 361.

25. George S. Sawyer, *Southern Institutes; or, an Inquiry into the Origin and Early Prevalence of Slavery and the Slave Trade* (Philadelphia, 1858), p. 197.

26. Samuel A. Cartwright, *Essays*, p. 3, and "Diseases and Peculiarities of the Negro," in De Bow, ed., *Industrial Resources*, II, 318-324. For another expression of the view that the Negro, like the mule, could not be overworked, see Estes, *Defense of Negro Slavery*, pp. 78-80.

27. Mrs. Henry Schoolcraft, *The Black Gauntlet: A Tale of Plantation Life in South Carolina* (Philadelphia, 1860), pp. 49, 61.

28. Cobb, *Inquiry*, p. 39.

29. Sawyer, *Institutes*, p. 222.

30. *Pro-Slavery Argument*, p. 436.

31. "Harper on Slavery," *ibid.*, pp. 35-36, 49-50 (originally published as *Memoir on Slavery* [Charleston, 1838]).

32. Fitzhugh, *Sociology for the South* and *Cannibals All!*, *passim*. See also Henry Hughes, *Treatise on Sociology: Theoretical and Practical* (Philadelphia, 1854), for a different formulation of the same basic argument.

33. George Fitzhugh, "Southern Thought Again," *De Bow's Review*, XXIII (November, 1857), 451.

34. For more on De Bow and the ethnological school see Chapter Three, below. The virulently racist use of the curse of Ham was most strikingly manifested in Josiah Priest's *Slavery, As It Relates to the Negro* (1843), reissued as *Bible Defense of Slavery* . . . (Glasgow, Ky., 1852). See also Estes, *Defense of Negro Slavery*.

35. Pierre L. van den Berghe, *Race and Racism: A Comparative Perspective* (New York, 1967), pp. 17-18.

36. Extracts from a speech of Yancey in Boston, October 12, 1860, in the *Liberator*, October 26, 1860.

37. "The Negro Races," the *Southern Literary Messenger*, XXXI (July, 1860), 9-10.

38. Quoted in Jenkins, *Pro-Slavery Thought*, p. 190.

39. Cobb, *Inquiry*, p. 213. This statement of Cobb and those of several other prominent Southern spokesmen who made the same points are quoted in Jenkins, *Pro-Slavery Thought*, pp. 190-194.

40. John H. Van Evrie, pamphlet *Negroes and Negro "Slavery": The First an Inferior Race: The Latter Its Normal Condition* (Baltimore, 1853), pp. 30-31 and *passim*. Van Evrie's doctrines as elaborated in the later book of the same title will be discussed more extensively in Chapter Three as applications of the "scientific" racism that burgeoned in the North as well as in the South during the 1850s.

41. Henry Cleveland, *Alexander H. Stephens, In Public and Private; With Letters and Speeches, Before, During, and Since the War* (Philadelphia, 1866), pp. 722-723, 721. (The italics are mine.)

42. Hughes, *Treatise*, p. 42.

43. Eugene D. Genovese, *The Political Economy of Slavery: Studies in the Economy and Society of the Slave South* (New York, 1965), p. 28.

44. See Edmund Ruffin, *The Political Economy of Slavery* (1859); William J. Grayson, *The Hireling and the Slave* . . . (Charleston, 1856); and Robert L. Dabney, *A Defense of Virginia* . . . (New York, 1867). For a provocative discussion of Fitzhugh's thought as the natural outgrowth of the slaveholder's situation, see Part Two of Eugene Genovese's *The World the Slaveholders Made: Two Essays in Interpretation* (New York, 1969). For reasons that will become clear, however, I dissent from Genovese's thesis that the reactionary, consistently antidemocratic slaveholder's philosophy was the dominant world view that emerged from the antebellum South.

45. Hughes, *Treatise*, pp. 238-243; Ruffin, *Political Economy*, pp. 10-19; Fitzhugh, *Sociology for the South*, pp. 82-83, and *Cannibals All!*, p. 20.

46. William R. Taylor, *Cavalier and Yankee: The Old South and American National Character* (New York, 1961), pp. 55-65. Edmund Ruffin's eschewal of a public career in the face of "democratic" tendencies that he refused to accept is further documented in Avery O. Craven's *Edmund Ruffin, Southerner* (New York and London, 1932), pp. 39-43.

47. That the Old South experienced a "democratic revolution" (for whites only) during the Jacksonian period has been argued most effectively by Fletcher M. Green and Charles S. Sydnor (see Green, *Democracy in the Old South and Other Essays*, ed. J. Isaac Copeland [Nashville, 1969], pp. 65-86; and Sydnor, *The Development of Southern Sectionalism 1819–1848* [Baton Rouge, La., 1948], Chapter XII), and has been reiterated in Clement Eaton's *The Growth of Southern Civilization, 1790–1860* (New York, 1961), pp. 172-175, 308-309. These historians recognize that this "democratization" was largely political and did not in the end undermine the social and economic dominance of the planter class, but contend that it did force the elite to ad-

just to the new order because it impelled them to profess a "democratic" ideology and to work through democratic electoral processes. Green and Sydnor have probably overstated their thesis because they have paid too little attention to persistently conservative and aristocratic facets of Southern life. But recent historians of basically Marxist orientation, such as Eugene Genovese and Barrington Moore, Jr. (see Moore's *Social Origins of Dictatorship and Democracy: Lord and Peasant in the Making in the Modern World* [Boston, 1966], Chapter Three), have gone to the other extreme by overlooking almost entirely the fact that the Old South had even a limited democratic aspect. They seem to imply that the planters ruled pretty much like the hereditary aristocracy of a typical premodern and hierarchical agrarian society. It admittedly strains credulity to describe the Old South as having been in any profound sense democratic or egalitarian. There were immense inequalities not only between masters and slaves but also between rich planters and much of the nonslaveholding population. But it seems clear that the late antebellum Southern oligarchy lacked the aura of unquestioned legitimacy that surrounds an established seigneurial class with a privileged status recognized and accepted by the community as a whole.

48. This reaction is discussed in the introduction to Hinton Rowan Helper, *The Impending Crisis of the South: How to Meet It*, ed. George M. Fredrickson (Cambridge, Mass., 1968), pp. xv-xix.

49. George Fitzhugh, "Free Negroes in Hayti," *De Bow's Review*, XXVII (November, 1859), 527-549.

50. George Fitzhugh, "The Black and White Races of Men," *De Bow's Review*, XXX (April, 1861), 447.

II: SLAVES AND MASTERS

• During the first half of this century U. B. Phillips's writings on slavery were considered authoritative by most historians and definitive by many. Phillips, a white Southerner, produced classic historical defenses of slavery in American Negro Slavery (1918) and in Life and Labor in the Old South (1927). His research uncovered a wealth of important material, and, although more recent scholars have challenged his racist beliefs and his sympathetic attitude toward slavery, Phillips's writings remain important.

Kenneth M. Stampp published The Peculiar Institution in the mid-1950s. The work stands on its own, of course, both in methodology and in point of view, but there is no question that Stampp had U. B. Phillips very much in mind when he wrote his monograph on slavery in the United States. Stampp saw nothing benign, nothing ameliorative, nothing uplifting about slavery. He viewed the institution as a thoroughly cruel and brutal system of exploitation and social control. The following selection, from the chapter "To Make Them Stand in Fear," discusses some aspects of slavery which helped produce Stampp's moral outrage over Phillips's apologetics.

To Make Them Stand in Fear

KENNETH M. STAMPP

A realistic Arkansas slaveholder once addressed himself to the great problem of his class, "the management of Negroes," and bluntly concluded: "Now, I speak what I know, when I say it is like 'casting pearls before swine' to try to *persuade* a negro to work. He must be *made* to work, and should always be given to understand that if he fails to perform his duty he will be punished for it." Having tested the *"persuasion doctrine"* when he began planting, he warned all beginners that if they tried it they would surely fail.[1]

Most masters preferred the "persuasion doctrine" nevertheless. They would have been gratified if their slaves had willingly shown proper subordination and wholeheartedly responded to the incentives offered for efficient labor. They found, however, that some did not respond at all, and that others responded only intermittently. As a result, slaveholders were obliged to supplement the lure of rewards for good behavior with the threat of punishment for bad. One Virginian always assumed that slaves would "not labor at all except to avoid punishment," and would "never do more than just enough to save themselves from being punished." Fortunately, said a Georgian, punishment did not make the Negro revengeful as it did members of other races. Rather, it tended "to win his attachment and promote his happiness and well being." [2]

Without the power to punish, which the state conferred upon the master, bondage could not have existed. By comparison, all other techniques of control were of secondary importance. Jefferson Davis and a few others gave their bondsmen a hand in the chastisement of culprits. On Davis's Mississippi estate trusted slaves tried, convicted, and punished the violators of plantation law.[3] But this was an eccentric arrangement. Normally the master alone judged the seriousness of an offense and fixed the kind and amount of punishment to be administered.

From *The Peculiar Institution: Slavery in the Ante-Bellum South* by Kenneth M. Stampp (New York: Alfred A. Knopf, 1956), pp. 171-91. Copyright © 1956 by Kenneth M. Stampp. Reprinted by permission of Alfred A. Knopf, Inc.

Slaveholders devised a great variety of penalties. They demoted unfaithful domestics, foremen, and drivers to field labor. They denied passes to incorrigibles, or excluded them from participating in Saturday night dances. An Arkansas planter gave his bondsmen a dinner every Sunday and required those on the "punishment list" to wait on the others without getting any of the food themselves. Masters forced malingerers to work on Sundays and holidays and at night after the others had finished. They penalized them by confiscating the crops in their "truck patches," or by reducing the sums due them. They put them on short rations for a period of time, usually depriving them of their meat allowances. And they sold them away from their families and friends.

Some of the penalties were ingenious. A Maryland tobacco grower forced a hand to eat the worms he failed to pick off the tobacco leaves. A Mississippian gave a runaway a wretched time by requiring him to sit at the table and eat his evening meal with the white family. A Louisiana planter humiliated disobedient male field-hands by giving them "women's work" such as washing clothes, by dressing them in women's clothing, and by exhibiting them on a scaffold wearing a red flannel cap.[4]

A few slaveholders built private jails on their premises. They knew that close confinement during a working day was a punishment of dubious value, but they believed that it was effective during leisure hours. "Negroes are gregarious," explained a small planter, "they dread solitariness, and to be deprived from the little weekly dances and chitchat. They will work to death rather than be shut up." Accordingly, a Louisianian locked runaways in his jail from Saturday night until Monday morning. When he caught a cotton picker with a ten pound rock in his basket, he jailed him every night and holiday for five months.[5]

Others made use of public jails, paying the jailer a fee for the service. One South Carolinian put a runaway in solitary confinement in the Charleston workhouse; another had a slave "shut in a darkcell" in the same institution. A Georgia planter advised his overseer to take a disobedient slave "down to the Savannah jail, and give him prison discipline and by all means solitary confinement for 3 weeks, when he will be glad to get home again." [6]

The stocks were still a familiar piece of equipment on the plantations of the ante-bellum South. . . .

"Chains and irons," James H. Hammond correctly explained, were used chiefly to control and discipline runaways. "You will admit," he argued logically enough, "that if we pretend to own slaves, they must not be permitted to abscond whenever they see fit; and that if nothing else will prevent it these means must be resorted to." [7] Three entries in Hammond's diary, in 1844, indicated that he practiced what he preached. July 17: "Alonzo runaway with his irons on." July 30: "Alonzo came in with his irons off." July 31: ". . . re-ironed Alonzo."

Hammond was but one of many masters who gave critics of the peculiar institution a poignant symbol—the fettered slave. A Mississippian had his runaway Maria "Ironed with a shackle on each leg connected with a chain." When he caught Albert he "had an iron collar put on his neck"; on Woodson, a habitual runaway, he "put the ball and chain." A Kentuckian recalled seeing slaves in his state wearing iron collars, some of them with bells attached. The fetters, however, did not always accomplish their purpose, for numerous advertisements stated that fugitives wore these encumbrances when they escaped. For example, Peter, a Louisiana runaway, "Had on each foot when leaving, an iron ring, with a small chain attached to it." [8]

But the whip was the most common instrument of punishment— indeed, it was the emblem of the master's authority. Nearly every slaveholder used it, and few grown slaves escaped it entirely. Defenders of the institution conceded that corporal punishment was essential in certain situations; some were convinced that it was better than any other remedy. If slavery were right, argued an Arkansas planter, means had to be found to keep slaves in subjugation, "and my opinion is, the lash—not used murderously, as would-be philanthropists assert, is the most effectual." A Virginian agreed: "A great deal of whipping is not necessary; *some* is." [9]

The majority seemed to think that the certainty, and not the severity, of physical "correction" was what made it effective. While no offense could go unpunished, the number of lashes should be in proportion to the nature of the offense and the character of the offender. The master should control his temper. "Never inflict punishment when in a passion," advised a Louisiana slaveholder, "but wait until perfectly cool, and until it can be done rather in sorrow than in anger." Many urged, therefore, that time be permitted to elapse between the misdeed and the flogging. A Georgian required his driver to do the whipping so that his bondsmen would not think that it was "for the pleasure of punishing, rather than for the purpose of enforcing obedience." [10]

Planters who employed overseers often fixed the number of stripes they could inflict for each specific offense, or a maximum number whatever the offense. On Pierce Butler's Georgia plantation each driver could administer twelve lashes, the head driver thirty-six, and the overseer fifty. A South Carolinian instructed his overseer to ask permission before going beyond fifteen. "The highest punishment must not exceed 100 lashes in one day and to that extent only in extreme cases," wrote James H. Hammond. "In general 15 to 20 lashes will be a sufficient flogging." [11]

The significance of these numbers depended in part upon the kind of whip that was used. The "rawhide," or "cowskin," was a savage instrument requiring only a few strokes to provide a chastisement that a slave would not soon forget. A former bondsman remembered that it was made of about three feet of untanned ox hide, an inch thick at the butt end, and tapering to a point which made it "quite elastic and springy." [12]

Many slaveholders would not use the rawhide because it lacerated the skin. One recommended, instead, a leather strap, eighteen inches long and two and a half inches wide, fastened to a wooden handle. In Mississippi, according to a visitor, the whip in general use consisted of a "stout flexible stalk" covered with a tapering leather plait, about three and a half feet in length, which formed the lash. "To the end of the lash is attached a soft, dry, buckskin cracker, about three eights of an inch wide and ten or twelve inches long, which is the only part allowed to strike, in whipping on the bare skin. . . . When it is used by an experienced hand it makes a very loud report, and stings, or 'burns' the skin smartly, but does not bruise it." [13]

How frequently a master resorted to the whip depended upon his temperament and his methods of management. On some establishments long periods of time elapsed with relatively few whippings—until, as a rice planter explained, it seemed "as if the devil had got into" the hands, and for a time there was "a good deal of it." Or, occasionally, a normally amiable slave got out of hand and had to be flogged. "Had to whip my Man Willis for insolence to the overseer," wrote a Tennesseean. "This I done with much regret as he was never whipped before." [14]

On other establishments the whip was in constant use. The size of the estate may have had some relationship to the amount of whipping, but the disposition of the proprietor was decidedly more crucial. Small farmers, as well as large planters, often relied upon corporal punishment as their chief method of enforcing discipline. Southern women were sometimes equally prone to use the lash upon errant domestics.

Some overseers, upon assuming control, thought it wise to whip every hand on the plantation to let them know who was in command. Some masters used the lash as a form of incentive by flogging the last

slave out of his cabin in the morning.[15] Many used it to "break in" a
young slave and to "break the spirit" of an insubordinate older one.
"If the negro is humble and appears duly sensible of the impropriety
of his conduct, a very moderate chastisement will answer better than
a severe one," advised a planter. "If however, he is stubborn . . . a
slight punishment will only make bad worse." Slaves had to be flogged,
explained an Alabamian, until they manifested "submission and pen-
itence." [16]

In short, the infliction of stripes curbed many a bondsman who
could not be influenced by any other technique. Whipping had a dis-
piriting effect upon most of them. "Had to administer a little rod to
Bob this morning," reported a Virginian. "Have seen for more than 3
months I should have to humble him some, hope it may benefit
him." [17]

"To manage *negroes* without the exercise of too much passion, is
next to an impossibility. . . . I would therefore put you on your
guard, lest their provocations should on some occasions transport you
beyond the limits of decency and christian morality." The Reverend
Charles Pettigrew, of North Carolina, gave this advice to his sons
when he willed them his estate. John H. Cocke, of Virginia, cautioned
the overseer on his Bremo Plantation: "Most persons are liable to be
thrown into a passion by the improper conduct of those they have to
govern." After traveling through the South, Olmsted wondered
"whether humanity and the accumulation of wealth, the prosperity of
the master and the happiness and improvement of the subject, are not
in some degree incompatible." [18] Physical cruelty, as these observations suggest, was always a possible consequence of the master's power
to punish. Place an intemperate master over an ill-disposed slave, and
the possibility became a reality.

Not that a substantial number of slaveholders deliberately adopted
a policy of brutality. The great majority, in fact, preferred to use as
little violence as possible. Many small slaveholders, urban and rural,
who had close personal contacts with their bondsmen and knew them
as human beings, found it highly disagreeable to treat them un-
kindly. Large planters, in their instructions to overseers, frequently
prohibited barbarous punishments. Thomas Affleck's plantation record
book advised overseers that the "indiscriminate, constant and excessive
use of the whip" was "altogether unnecessary and inexcusable." A
Louisiana proprietor was very explicit on this point. In whipping a
slave the overseer was never to be "cruel or severe," though he could
repeat the whipping at intervals "until the most entire submission"

was achieved. "I object to having the skin cut, or my negroes marked in any way by the lash. . . . I will most certainly discharge any overseer for striking any of my negroes with a club or the butt of his whip." [19]

A master who gave some thought to his standing in the community certainly wished to avoid a reputation for inordinate cruelty. To be counted a true Southern Gentleman one had to be humane to his bondsmen, to exercise self-control in dealing with them, to know how to give commands without raising his voice. Plenty of masters possessed these qualities. A European visitor marveled at the patience, the "mild forbearance," some of them exhibited. It seemed that every slaveholder's temper was subjected to a discipline which either ruined or perfected it. And more than a few met the test with remarkable success.[20]

Many openly censured those who were guilty of inhumanity. A Georgian told a Northerner that the government of slaves was necessarily despotic, but that Southerners despised ruthless masters. A South Carolinian wrote in a published letter, "The overseer whose constant and only resort is to the lash . . . is a brute, and deserves the penitentiary." And a North Carolinian denounced a neighbor as a "*moral miasma*" because of the way he treated his slaves.[21]

Those who were destitute of humane instincts might still be restrained by the slave's economic worth. To injure by harsh punishment a prime field-hand valued at a thousand dollars or more was a costly indulgence. It may be, therefore, that rising slave prices encouraged a decline in the incidence of brutality.

But these restraints were not always enough. Some masters, made irascible by the endless irritations which were an inevitable part of owning slaves, were unmerciful in exercising their almost unlimited powers. Some were indifferent about their reputations among neighbors, or hoped to conceal the conditions that existed on their isolated estates. Some were as prodigal in the use of human chattels as they were in the use of other property. Neither law, nor social pressure, nor economic self-interest made Southern Gentlemen out of all slaveholders. As long as the peculiar institution survived, the master class contained a group of unfeeling men.

Few who knew southern slavery intimately denied that there existed within it an element of savagery. No apologist disputed the evidence published by Theodore Dwight Weld, the abolitionist, for he gathered it from southern newspapers and public records.[22] It is unnecessary, however, to turn to the abolitionists—or to former slaves—for proof. Daniel R. Hundley, a Southerner who admired and defended his section's institutions, agreed that the South was "no second paradise." He knew that slaves were "badly treated" on some estates, and that masters were sometimes unconcerned about it. Moreover, "he must be a very bold man who will deny that the overseers on many southern plantations, are cruel and unmercifully severe." [23] . . .

Southerners themselves having established the fact of cruelty, it only remains to estimate its extent and to examine its nature. Proslavery writers asserted that cases of cruelty were the rare exceptions to the general rule of humanity by which slaves were governed. Travelers in the South gave conflicting testimony. Abolitionists and ex-slaves insisted that cruelty was far more common than defenders of the institution would admit.

The exact truth will never be known, because surviving records are fragmentary and sometimes hint only vaguely at conditions. There is no way to discover what went on in the "voiceless solitudes" where no records were kept, or on hundreds of plantations where visitors were unwelcome and the proprietors were in residence only part of the year. (In 1860, several large planters in Rapides Parish, Louisiana, would not even permit the census takers to trespass upon their estates.) Even so, the public and private records that do survive suggest that, although the average slaveholder was not the inhuman brute described by the abolitionists, acts of cruelty were not as exceptional as proslavery writers claimed.

As a South Carolina judge sadly confessed, there were "men and women on earth who deserved no other name than *fiends*," for they seemed to delight in brutality.[24] No southern state required masters to be tested for their competence to rule slaves. Instead, they permitted slaves to fall willy-nilly into the hands of whoever inherited them or had the cash or credit to buy them. As a result, bondsmen were owned by persons of unsound minds, such as the South Carolinian who had his chattels "throw dirt upon [his] roof . . . to drive off witches." They were owned by a woman "unable to read or write, . . . scarcely able to count ten," legally incompetent to contract marriage.[25] They were owned by drunkards, such as Lilburne Lewis, of Livingston County, Kentucky, who once chopped a slave to bits with an ax; and by sadists, such as Madame Lalourie, of New Orleans, who tortured her slaves for her own amusement. It would be pointless to catalogue the atrocities committed by psychopaths.

Cruelty, unfortunately, was not limited to the mentally unbalanced. Men and women, otherwise "normal," were sometimes corrupted by the extraordinary power that slavery conferred upon them. Some made bondsmen the victims of their petulance. (The repentant wife of a Louisiana planter once wrote in her diary: "I feel badly got very angry and whipped Lavinia. O! for government over my temper." [26]) Others who were reasonably humane to most of their slaves made the ones who annoyed them beyond endurance the targets of their animosity. Still others who were merely irresponsible, rather than inherently brutal, made slaves the objects of their whims. In other words, masters were seldom consistent; they were apt to be indulgent or harsh depending upon their changing moods, or their feelings toward individual slaves. In truth, said one Southerner, "men of the right stamp to manage negroes are like Angels visits few and far between." [27]

Kindness was not a universal trait among small slaveholders, especially among those who were ambitious to climb the economic ladder. Both a shoemaker and a carpenter, each of whom owned a single slave, were guilty of atrocities.[28] Southern farmers with modest holdings were also, on occasion, capable of extreme cruelty toward slaves.

But brutality was more common on the large plantations. Overseers, almost all of whom were native-born Southerners, seldom felt any personal affection for the bondsmen they governed. Their inclination in most cases was to punish severely; if their employers prohibited severity, they ignored such instructions as often as not. Planters complained that it was difficult to find an overseer who would "condescend to take orders from his employer, and manage according to the system of another man." The typical overseer seemed to have little confidence in the use of incentives as a method of governing slaves; he had a decided preference for physical force.[29]

Illustrations of this problem sometimes found their way into the records of southern courts. Overseers sued masters for their wages when discharged for cruelty; masters sued overseers for injuring slave property; occasionally the state intervened to prosecute an overseer for killing or maiming a bondsman.[30] Most of these cases never reached the courts, as the planter dealt with the problem himself. An Alabamian discovered that he had found no solution even when he employed a relative to oversee. "I want you to distinctly understand me," he scolded, "withhold your rushing whipping and lashing—for I will not stand it any longer." A Louisiana planter, returning to his estate after a year's absence, related in his journal the "most terrible account of the severity [and] cruelty" of his overseer. At least twelve slaves had died from "negligence and ill treatment." Discharging this overseer and employing another, he was dismayed to find that the new one also "punished severely without discretion." [31]

A planter was often in a quandary when his overseer was both brutal and efficient. "I do not know whether I will keep Harris another year or not," a Mississippian told his wife. "He is a first rate manager except he is too cruel. I have had my feelings greatly shocked at some of his conduct." But he re-employed Harris after exacting from him a promise to be less harsh. Harris, he explained, made big crops, and he did not wish "to break it all up by getting a new manager."

A few years later this same planter, having transferred his operations to Arkansas, viewed the problem of slave management in a different light. While Harris was away on a month's leave of absence, the proprietor ran the estate himself. He found governing slaves to be a "pretty rough business" and waited impatiently for his overseer to return.[32]

Ordinarily the owner of a large plantation was realistic enough to know that controlling a gang of field-hands was at best a wretched business, and that a certain amount of savagery was inevitable. There seemed to be no other way to keep certain bondsmen under control. "Experience and observation have taught me that some negroes require a vast deal more punishment than others to be brought to a performance of their duties," wrote an Arkansas planter. And a Louisiana sugar planter assured his distressed wife that he would not sanction the admitted cruelty of his overseer unless there was "a *great* necessity for it." Indeed, he found the management of slaves "exceedingly disagreeable . . . under any and all circumstances." [33]

Although cruelty was endemic in all slaveholding communities, it was always most common in newly settled regions. Along the rough southern frontier thousands of ambitious men were trying swiftly to make their fortunes. They operated in a frantically competitive society which provided few rewards for the virtues of gentility and almost put a premium upon ruthlessness. In the eastern tobacco and rice districts brutality was unquestionably less prevalent in the nineteenth century than it had been during the colonial period. But in the Southwest only limited areas had developed a mellowed gentry as late as 1860. In the Alabama-Mississippi Black Belt, in the cotton and sugar parishes of Louisiana, along the Arkansas River, and in eastern Texas the master class included the "parvenus," the "cotton snobs," and the "Southern Yankees." If these planters failed to observe the code of the patrician, they apparently thought none the less of each other for it.

The hired slave stood the greatest chance of subjection to cruel punishments as well as to overwork. His employer, a Kentucky judge confessed, had no incentive to treat him kindly "except the mere feelings of humanity, which we have too much reason to believe in many instances . . . are too weak to stimulate the active virtue." [34] This was no exaggeration.

Southerners who were concerned about the welfare of slaves found it difficult to draw a sharp line between acts of cruelty and such measures of physical force as were an inextricable part of slavery. Since the line was necessarily arbitrary, slaveholders themselves disagreed about where it should be drawn. Was it barbarous to "correct" a slave by putting him in the stocks, or by forcing him to wear chains or an iron collar? How severely might a slave be flogged before the punishment became brutal? These were matters of personal taste.

But no master denied the propriety of giving a moderate whipping to a disobedient bondsman. During the seventeenth and eighteenth centuries the lash was used to punish free men as well as slaves. By mid-nineteenth century, however, it was seldom used upon any but slaves, because public opinion now considered it to be cruel. Why it was less cruel to whip a bondsman was a problem that troubled many sensitive masters. That they often had no choice as long as they owned slaves made their problem no easier to resolve. . . .

Beyond this were cases of pure brutality—cases of flogging that resulted in the crippling, maiming, or killing of slaves. An early nineteenth-century Charleston grand jury presented "as a serious evil the many instances of Negro Homicide" and condemned those who indulged their passions "in the barbarous treatment of slaves.[35] "Salting"—washing the cuts received from the whip with brine—was a harsh punishment inflicted upon the most obstinate bondsmen. Though all but a few deplored such brutality, slaveholders found themselves in a dilemma when nothing else could subdue a rebel.

If a master was too squeamish to undertake the rugged task of humbling a refractory bondsman, he might send him to a more calloused neighbor or to a professional "slave breaker." John Nevitt, a Mississippi planter not averse to the application of heroic remedies, received from another master a young chattel "for the purpose of punishing him for bad conduct." Frederick Douglass remembered a ruthless man in Maryland who had a reputation for being "a first rate hand at breaking young negroes"; some slaveholders found it beneficial to send their beginning hands to him for training.[36]

The branding of slaves was a widespread custom in colonial days; it was less common in the nineteenth century. But as late as 1838, a

72   KENNETH M. STAMPP

North Carolinian advertised that Betty, a fugitive, was recently
"burnt . . . with a hot iron on the left side of her face; I tried to
make the letter M." In 1848, a Kentuckian identified his runaway
Jane by a brand mark "on the breast something like L blotched." [87]
Mutilation as a form of punishment also declined without disappear-
ing entirely. A Louisiana jailer, in 1831, gave notice that he had a runaway in his custody: "He has been lately gelded, and is not yet well."
Another Louisianian recorded his disgust for a neighbor who had
"castrated 3 men of his." [88]

Some masters who were otherwise as humane as the peculiar institution would permit tolerated almost anything that might "cure"
habitual runaways. Andrew Jackson once offered fifty dollars reward for
the capture of a fugitive, "and ten dollars extra for every hundred
lashes any person will give him to the amount of three hundred.". . .
The tracking of runaways with dogs was no figment of abolitionist
imaginations; it was a common practice in all slave states, defended
and justified in the courts. Groups of slaveholders sometimes rode
through the swamps with their dogs and made the search for fugitives
a sport comparable to fox hunting. Others preferred to hire professional slave catchers who provided their own "Negro dogs.". . .

The dogs could give a fugitive a severe mauling if the owner was
willing to permit it. After a Mississippi master caught an escaped slave
he allowed his dogs to "bite him very severely." A Louisiana planter
"treed" a runaway and then "made the dogs pull him out of the tree,
Bit him very badly, think he will stay home awhile." On another
occasion his dogs tore a slave naked; he then "took him Home Before
the other negro[es] . . . and made the dogs give him another over
hauling." [89]

The angry mobs who dealt extra-legal justice to slaves accused of
serious crimes committed barbarities seldom matched by the most
brutal masters. . . .

Mobs all too frequently dealt with slaves accused of murder or rape.
They conducted their own trials or broke into jails or court rooms to
seize prisoners for summary execution. Their more fortunate victims
were hanged; the others were burned to death, sometimes in the presence of hundreds of bondsmen who were forced to attend the cere-
mony. . . .

The abolition of slavery, of course, did not bring to a close the
record of brutality in the South any more than it did elsewhere. But
it did make less tenable the argument that brutality was sometimes in
the public interest. And it did rescue many a master from the dilemma

he faced when his desire to be humane was compromised by the demands of proper discipline.

NOTES

1. *Southern Cultivator*, XVIII (1860), pp. 130-31, 239-40.
2. Olmsted, *Seaboard*, pp. 104-105; *Southern Cultivator*, XII (1854), p. 206.
3. Walter L. Fleming, "Jefferson Davis, the Negroes and the Negro Problem," *Sewanee Review*, XVI (1908), pp. 410-11.
4. John Thompson, *The Life of John Thompson, A Fugitive Slave* (Worcester, Mass., 1856), p. 18; Sydnor, *Slavery in Mississippi*, p. 89; Davis (ed.), *Diary of Bennet H. Barrow*, pp. 112, 154, 175.
5. *De Bow's Review*, XI (1851), p. 371; Davis (ed.), *Diary of Bennet H. Barrows*, pp. 165, 269.
6. Gaillard Plantation Journal, entry for May 22, 1849; Gavin Diary, entry for March 26, 1856; Phillips (ed.), *Plantation and Frontier*, II, pp. 31-32.
7. *De Bow's Review*, VII (1849), p. 500.
8. Nevitt Plantation Journal, entries for November 9, 1827; March 28, 1831; July 18, 1832; Coleman, *Slavery Times in Kentucky*, pp. 248-49; New Orleans *Picayune*, December 26, 1847.
9. *Southern Cultivator*, XVIII (1860), p. 239-40; *Southern Planter*, XII (1852), p. 107.
10. *De Bow's Review*, XXII (1857), pp. 376-79; *Southern Agriculturist*, IV (1831), p. 350.
11. Kemble, *Journal*, pp. 42-43; Phillips (ed.), *Plantation and Frontier*, I, pp. 116-22; Plantation Manual in Hammond Papers.
12. Douglass, *My Bondage*, p. 103.
13. *Southern Cultivator*, VII (1849), p. 135; [Ingraham], *South-West*, II, pp. 287-88.
14. Olmsted, *Seaboard*, pp. 438-39; Bills Diary, entry for March 30, 1860.
15. *Southern Cultivator*, II (1844), pp. 169-70; Davis, *Cotton Kingdom in Alabama*, pp. 54-55.
16. *Southern Cultivator*, VIII (1850), p. 164; William P. Gould Ms. Plantation Rules.
17. Adams Diary, entry for July 2, 1860.
18. Johnson, *Ante-Bellum North Carolina*, p. 496; John H. Cocke Ms. Plantation Rules, in N. F. Cabell Collection of Agricultural Papers; Olmsted, *Seaboard*, pp. 367-68.
19. *De Bow's Review*, XXII (1857), pp. 376-79.
20. Martineau, *Society in America*, II, pp. 109-10.
21. Lester B. Shippee (ed.), *Bishop Whipple's Southern Diary 1843–1844* (Minneapolis, 1937), pp. 31-32; *Southern Cultivator*, II (1844), p. 107; William S. Pettigrew to James C. Johnston, September 24, 1846, Pettigrew Family Papers.
22. Theodore Dwight Weld, *American Slavery As It Is: Testimony of a Thousand Witnesses* (New York, 1839).
23. Hundley, *Social Relations*, pp. 63-64, 187-88, 203-205.
24. Charleston *Courier*, May 14, 1847.
25. Catterall (ed.), *Judicial Cases*, II, pp. 336, 427.

26. Quoted in Taylor, "Negro Slavery in Louisiana," p. 254.

27. Moore Rawls to Lewis Thompson (n.d.), Lewis Thompson Papers.

28. New Orleans *Picayune*, March 16, 1858; Northup, *Twelve Years a Slave*, pp. 105-16.

29. *Southern Cultivator*, II (1844), p. 107; Bassett, *Plantation Overseer*, pp. 3-5.

30. Catterall (ed.), *Judicial Cases, passim*.

31. James P. Tarry to Samuel O. Wood, November 27, 1853; July 1, 1854, Samuel O. Wood Papers; Haller Nutt Ms. Journal of Araby Plantation, entries for November 1, 1843, *et seq*.

32. Gustavus A. Henry to his wife, December 12, 17, 1848; December 7, 1857, Henry Papers.

33. *Southern Cultivator*, XVIII (1860), p. 287; Sitterson, *Sugar Country*, p. 105.

34. Catterall (ed.), *Judicial Cases*, I, p. 284.

35. Henry, *Police Control*, pp. 67-68.

36. Nevitt Plantation Journal, entry for June 5, 1828; Douglas, *My Bondage*, p. 203; Sydnor, *Slavery in Mississippi*, pp. 69-70.

37. Johnson, *Ante-Bellum North Carolina*, pp. 493-94; Coleman, *Slavery Times in Kentucky*, pp. 248-49.

38. Taylor, "Slavery in Louisiana," p. 236; Davis (ed.), *Diary of Bennet H. Barrow*, pp. 173-74.

39. William Read to Samuel S. Downey, August 8, 1848, Downey Papers; Davis (ed.), *Diary of Bennet H. Barrow*, pp. 369-70, 376.

• In 1974, two scholars co-authored two volumes called Time on the Cross. Robert William Fogel, an economic historian, and Stanley L. Engerman, an economist, divided their work: a primary, first volume contains the text with some visual aids for "The Economics of American Negro Slavery"; a supplementary, second volume, "Evidence and Methods," contains source references and appendixes, as well as a discussion of "the technical, methodological, and theoretical bases" for their conclusion that slavery was not an inherently inefficient economic system. They did not, of course, defend the morality of enslavement or the social order it spawned. Their emphasis, however, was on assessing statistically the economic worth of the slave system for both master and slave.

Fogel and Engerman did not dismiss, but they certainly downplayed, the notion of continuous terror as the cement which held the slave system together. This view is well illustrated in "Punishment and Rewards," the first of two selections from Time on the Cross which follow.

The second excerpt from Fogel and Engerman, "Property Rights in Man," provides a good example of their general approach and outlook, as well as indicating the extent of their provocative—and for some, provoking—revisionism.

Punishment and Rewards

ROBERT WILLIAM FOGEL and

STANLEY L. ENGERMAN

The exploitative nature of slavery is most apparent in its system of punishment and rewards. Whipping was probably the most common punishment meted out against errant slaves. Other forms of punishment included the deprivation of various privileges (such as visits to town), confinement in stocks, incarceration, sale, branding, and the death penalty.

Whipping could be either a mild or a severe punishment, depending on how it was administered. Some whippings were so severe that they resulted in death. Indeed, in cases such as murder, the sentences of slaves who would otherwise have been executed were frequently converted to severe whipping, coupled with exportation to another state or a foreign country. For . . . by converting the death penalty to whipping and exportation, the state could recover a substantial part of the value of a slave that would have been lost through his execution. In other instances, whipping was as mildly applied as the corporal punishment normally practiced within families today.

Reliable data on the frequency of whipping is extremely sparse. The only systematic record of whipping now available for an extended period comes from the diary of Bennet Barrow, a Louisiana planter who believed that to spare the rod was to spoil the slave. His plantation numbered about 200 slaves, of whom about 120 were in the labor force. The record shows that over the course of two years a total of 160 whippings were administered, an average of 0.7 whippings per hand per year. About half the hands were not whipped at all during the period.

There was nothing exceptional about the use of whipping to enforce discipline among slaves until the beginning of the nineteenth century. It must be remembered that through the centuries whipping was considered a fully acceptable form of punishment, not merely for criminals but also for honest men or women who in some way shirked their duties. Whipping of wives, for example, was even sanctified in some versions of the Scripture. The Matthew's Bible, which preceded the King James version, told the husband, in a note at 1 Pet. 3, that if his wife was "not obedient and healpfull vnto hym endeuoureth to beate the feare of God into her heade, and that therby she maye be compelled to learne her duitie and do it." During the seventeenth and most of the eighteenth centuries whipping was commonly employed as a punishment in the North as well as in the South. Not until the end of the eighteenth century and the beginning of the nineteenth century did whipping rapidly fall from favor in the free states.

To attribute the continuation of whipping in the South to the maliciousness of masters is naïve. Although some masters were brutal, even sadistic, most were not. The overwhelming majority of the ex-slaves in the W.P.A. narratives who expressed themselves on the issue reported that their masters were good men. Such men worried about the proper role of whipping in a system of punishment and rewards. Some excluded it altogether. Most accepted it, but recognized that to be effective whipping had to be used with restraint and in a coolly calculated manner. Weston, for example, admonished his overseer not to impose punishment of any sort until twenty-four hours after the offense had been discovered. William J. Minor, a sugar planter, instructed his managers "not [to] cut the skin when punishing, nor punish in a passion." Many planters forbade the whipping of slaves except by them or in their presence. Others limited the number of lashes that could be administered without their permission.

The decline of whipping as an instrument of labor discipline outside of the South appears to have been heavily influenced by economic considerations. With the rise of capitalism, impersonal and indirect sanctions were increasingly substituted for direct, personal ones. The hiring of free workers in the marketplace provided managers of labor with a powerful new disciplinary weapon. Workers who were lazy, indifferent, or who otherwise shirked their duties could be fired—left to starve beyond the eyesight or expense of the employer. Interestingly enough, denial of food was rarely used to enforce discipline on slaves. For the illness and lethargy caused by malnutrition reduced the capacity of the slave to labor in the fields. Planters preferred whipping to incarceration because the lash did not generally lead to an extended loss of the slave's labor time. In other words, whipping persisted in the South because the cost of substituting hunger and incarceration for the lash was greater for the slaveowner than for the northern employer of free labor. When the laborer owns his own human capital, forms of punishment which impair or diminish the value of the capital are borne exclusively by him. Under slavery, the master desired forms of punishment which, while they imposed costs on the slave, did so with minimum impairment to the human capital which the master owned. Whipping generally fulfilled these conditions.

While whipping was an integral part of the system of punishment and rewards, it was not the totality of the system. What planters wanted was not sullen and discontented slaves who did just enough to keep from getting whipped. They wanted devoted, hard-working, responsible slaves who identified their fortunes with the fortunes of their masters. Planters sought to imbue slaves with a "Protestant" work ethic and to transform that ethic from a state of mind into a high level of production. "My negros have their name up in the neighbourhood," wrote Bennet Barrow, "for making more than any one else & they think Whatever they do is better than any body Else." Such an attitude could not be beaten into slaves. It had to be elicited.

Much of the managerial attention of planters was focused on the problem of motivating their hands. To achieve the desired response they developed a wide-ranging system of rewards. Some rewards were directed toward improving short-run performance. Included in this category were prizes for the individual or the gang with the best picking record on a given day or during a given week. The prizes were such items as clothing, tobacco, and whiskey; sometimes the prize was cash. Good immediate performance was also rewarded with unscheduled holidays or with trips to town on weekends. When slaves worked at times normally set aside for rest, they received extra pay—usually in cash and at the rate prevailing in the region for hired labor. Slaves who were performing well were permitted to work on their own account after normal hours at such tasks as making shingles or weaving baskets, articles which they could sell either to their masters or to farmers in the neighborhood.

Some rewards were directed at influencing behavior over periods of intermediate duration. The rewards in this category were usually paid at the end of the year. Year-end bonuses, given either in goods or cash, were frequently quite substantial. Bennet Barrow, for example, distributed gifts averaging between $15 and $20 per slave family in both 1839 and 1840. The amounts received by particular slaves were proportional to their performance. It should be noted that $20 was about a fifth of national per capita income in 1840. A bonus of the same relative magnitude today would be in the neighborhood of $1,000.

Masters also rewarded slaves who performed well with patches of land ranging up to a few acres for each family. Slaves grew marketable crops on these lands, the proceeds of which accrued to them. On the Texas plantation of Julian S. Devereux, slaves operating such land produced as much as two bales of cotton per patch. Devereux marketed their crop along with his own. In a good year some of the slaves earned in excess of $100 per annum for their families. Devereux set up accounts to which he credited the proceeds of the sales. Slaves drew on these accounts when they wanted cash or when they wanted Devereux to purchase clothing, pots, pans, tobacco, or similar goods for them.

Occasionally planters even devised elaborate schemes for profit sharing with their slaves. William Jemison, an Alabama planter, entered into the following agreement with his bondsmen.

> [Y]ou shall have two thirds of the corn and cotton made on the plantation and as much of the wheat as will reward you for the sowing it. I also furnish you with provisions for this year. When your crop is gathered, one third is to be set aside for me. You are then to pay your overseer his part and pay me what I furnish, clothe yourselves, pay your own taxes and doctor's fee with all expenses of the farm. You are to be no expense to me, but render to me one third of the produce and what I have loaned you. You have the use of the stock and plantation tools. You are to return them as good as they are and the plantation to be kept in good repair, and what clear money you make shall be divided equally amongst you in a fair proportion agreeable to the services rendered by each hand. There will be an account of all lost time kept, and those that earn most shall have most.

There was a third category of rewards. These were of a long-term nature, often requiring the lapse of a decade or more before they paid off. Thus, slaves had the opportunity to rise within the social and economic hierarchy that existed under bondage. Field hands could become artisans or drivers. Artisans could be allowed to move from the plantation to town where they would hire themselves out. Drivers could move up to the position of head driver or overseer. Climbing the economic ladder brought not only social status, and sometimes more freedom; it also had significant payoffs in better housing, better clothing, and cash bonuses.

Little attention has hitherto been paid to the manner in which planters selected the slaves who were to become the artisans and managers. In some cases boys were apprenticed to carpenters, blacksmiths, or some similar craftsmen when they were in their early teens, as was typically done with whites. For slaves, this appears to have been the exception rather than the rule. Analysis of occupational data derived from probate and plantation records reveals an unusual distribution of ages among slave artisans. Slaves in their twenties were substantially underrepresented, while slaves in their forties and fifties were overrepresented. This age pattern suggests that the selection of slaves for training in the crafts was frequently delayed until slaves reached their late twenties, or perhaps even into the thirties.

Normally this would be an uneconomical policy, since the earlier an investment is made in occupational training, the more years there are to reap the returns on that investment. Slavery altered this pattern by shifting the authority to determine occupational investments from the parents to the masters. In free societies, kinship is usually the primary basis for determining which members of the new generation are trained in skilled occupations. But the slaveholder lacked the vested interests of a parent. He could, therefore, treat entry into the skilled occupations as a prize that was to be claimed by the most deserving, regardless of family background. The extra effort put forth by young field hands who competed for these jobs appears to have more than offset the loss in returns due to the curtailed period over which the occupational investment was amortized. We do not mean to suggest that kinship played no role in the intergenerational transfer of skills among slaves. We merely wish to stress that its role was significantly reduced as compared with free society.

Another long-run reward was freedom through manumission. The chance of achieving this reward was, of course, quite low. Census data indicate that in 1850 the manumission rate was just 0.45 per thousand slaves. Manumission could be achieved either through the philanthropy of a master or through an agreement which permitted a slave to buy himself out. Sometimes gifts of freedom were bestowed while the master was still alive. More often it was a bequest set forth in a will. Self-purchase involved arrangements under which slaves were permitted to purchase themselves with money that they earned from work on their own account, or in the case of skilled urban slaves, by increasing the share of income which the artisan paid to his master. Some skilled slaves were able to accumulate enough capital to purchase their freedom within a decade. For others the period extended to two decades or more. Little information is currently available on the prices at which such transactions were concluded. It is not known whether slaves involved in self-purchase were generally forced to pay a price in excess of their market value.

From the foregoing it is clear that slaves did not all live at a uniform level of income. The elaborate system of rewards erected by planters introduced substantial variation in the slave standard of living. Much work remains to be done before it will be possible to reconstruct with reasonable accuracy the full range of the slave income distribution. It has been possible, however, to estimate the "basic income" of slaves in 1850. This, together with some fragmentary evidence on the higher incomes of slaves, will at least suggest the range of income variation that prevailed.

By "basic income" we mean the value of the food, clothing, shelter, and medical care furnished to slaves. The average value of the expenditure on these items for an adult male in 1850 was about $48.00. The most complete information on the extra earnings of field hands comes from several Texas plantations. The leading hands on these estates frequently earned between $40 and $110 per year above basic income through the sale of cotton and other products raised on their patches. This experience was not unique to Texas. On one Alabama plantation, eight hands produced cotton that earned them an average of $71 each, with the high man collecting $96. On still another plantation the average extra earnings of the thirteen top hands was $77. These scattered cases suggest that the ratio of high earnings to basic earnings among field hands was in the neighborhood of 2.5.

When the incomes of artisans are taken into account, the spread in slave earnings became still wider. The top incomes earned by craftsmen must have been several times basic income. This is implied by the high prices which artisans had to pay to buy themselves out. The average price of a prime-aged blacksmith was about $1,700 in 1850. Thus, a thirty-year-old man who was able to buy himself out in a decade probably earned in the neighborhood of $170 per year over subsistence. This suggests a ratio of artisan to basic income of about 4.5.

The highest annual figure we have been able to uncover for extra earnings by a field hand in a single year is $309. Aham, the Alabama slave whose sales of peaches, apples, and cotton yielded this sum, had accumulated enough capital over the years so that in 1860 he held notes on loans totaling over $2,400. The ratio of Aham's agricultural income to basic income is 7.4. If we assume that Aham earned 6 percent, or $144, on the loans, the ratio would rise to 10.4. The highest income above maintenance that we have found for an artisan is $500. In this case the ratio of earned to basic income is 11.4.

While the reward structure created much more room for upward mobility within the slave system than is usually supposed, the scope of opportunity should not be exaggerated. The highest levels of attainment were irrevocably foreclosed to slaves. The entrepreneurial talent obviously possessed by bondsmen such as Aham could not be used to catapult them into the stewardship of great businesses as long as they remained slaves. No slave, regardless of his gifts, could aspire to political position. No man of letters—there were slaves who acquired considerable erudition—could ever hold an appointment in the faculty of a southern university as long as he was a bondsman. The entrepreneurial genius had to settle for lingering in the shadow of the master on whose protection he was dependent. The man of letters could go no further than the position of tutor to the children of a benevolent and enlightened planter. It was on the talented, the upper crust of slave society, that deprivations of the peculiar institution hung most heavy. This, perhaps, explains why it was that the first to flee to northern lines as Yankee advances corroded the Rebel positions were not the ordinary field hands, but the drivers and the artisans. . . .

Property Rights in Man

ROBERT WILLIAM FOGEL and
STANLEY L. ENGERMAN

In recent years economists have extended the use of the concept of
capital beyond its usual application to machines, buildings, and other
inanimate objects. They have applied the concept of capital to the
wealth inherent in the capacity of human beings to perform labor,
calling such wealth "human capital." This extension of the concept
seemed odd at first because it was applied not to explain behavior in
nineteenth-century slave societies but in twentieth-century free societies. Nobody doubts that human beings were a form of capital in
slave society. Slaves who were traded commanded prices as specific
and well-defined as those on land, buildings, or machines. Since prices
of slaves varied by age, health, skill level, and geographic location, it
is clear that the vocational training of slaves or their relocation from
one region to another were just as much forms of investment as the
erection of a building or extension of a fence.

What made the application of the concept of human capital to free
societies seem odd is that free people are not traded in well-defined
markets and hence do not command market prices. However, the absence of explicit market prices on human beings does not mean that
free men do not actually have capital values, but only that the absence
of a trade in human beings usually prevents their capital values from
being made explicit. Legal recognition of the fact that free people
continue to have capital values takes place whenever courts grant cash
awards to the widows of men killed in industrial accidents. The
amount of such an award usually turns on a debate regarding the
capital value of the deceased at the time of his death.

Viewed in this light, the crucial difference between slave and free
society rests not *on the existence* of property rights in man, in human

From *Time on the Cross: The Economics of American Negro Slavery* by Robert William Fogel and Stanley L. Engerman (Boston: Little, Brown and
Company, 1974), pp. 232-46. Copyright © 1974 by Little, Brown and Company, Inc. Reprinted by permission of Little, Brown and Company. Edited by
permission of the authors.

capital, but on who may hold title to such property rights. Under freedom, each person holds title, more or less, to his own human capital. He is prevented by law from selling the title to this capital except for quite limited periods of time and then only under a very restricted set of conditions. Moreover, one generally cannot sell the title to the human capital of others, or if such sales are permitted (as in the cases of the contracts of movie and athletic stars, or as in the case of the parents or guardians of minors), the title is transferred only for relatively short intervals of time and under strictly defined limitations. In slave societies, however, a large number of individuals were permanently deprived of the title to their own human capital. Those who held the titles (the masters) were virtually unrestricted by law in the ability to sell them. And ownership of a female slave brought with it title, in perpetuity, to all her descendants.

How did the special way in which the antebellum South treated the matter of property rights in man affect the economic behavior of that society? What special economic advantage, if any, did the system of property rights which prevailed under slavery give the slaveowners? How did this system of property rights affect the real income of the masters, of slaves, of free Southerners, and of free Northerners? While these are not new questions, certain of the findings of the cliometricians suggest new answers. Two findings of particular importance are that:

    1. Economies of scale in southern agriculture were achieved exclusively with slave labor.
    2. While the urban demand for slave labor was quite elastic, the agricultural demand was very inelastic.

The first finding is not new. Olmsted realized that economies of scale were achieved only with slave labor, and specifically addressed himself to that question. Characteristically, Olmsted concluded that the failure of small free farmers to combine into large units through the medium of "a joint-stock cotton plantation" was due to their ignorance and lack of enterprise. But as we have seen, small free southern farmers were not bunglers. Nor were they lacking in enterprise. Many small free farmers became the masters of large slave plantations. If there had been no special advantage to slave labor, one would expect at least some of these enterprising individuals to have based their plantations on free labor. The fact that economies of scale were achieved exclusively with slave labor clearly indicates that in large-scale production some special advantage attached to the use of slaves.

Interestingly enough, there is no evidence that slaves possessed any special advantage or disadvantage for large-scale production in urban industries. While some large-scale factories were based exclusively on slave labor, others were based exclusively on free labor. Many urban firms, perhaps most, employed a combination of the two types of labor. For example, in the Tredegar Iron Works, the largest iron manufacturer in the South and the fourth largest in the nation, slaves sometimes made up as much as half of the labor force. The second finding—the relatively high urban elasticity of demand for slaves— means that in the urban context slaves and free laborers were quite good substitutes for each other. When the price of slaves rose relative to free wages, urban enterprises shifted away from the employment of slave labor and increased the employment of free labor. And when the prices of slaves fell relative to free wages, these urban enterprises shifted back into slave labor.

In agriculture, however, the demand for slaves was highly inelastic. This means that in the slave-using agricultural sector, free labor was a very poor substitute for slave labor. Variations in the ratio of slave prices to free wages had virtually no effect on the preferences of large plantations for slave labor. Even when slave prices rose quite sharply relative to free wages, the labor force of the large plantations remained overwhelmingly slave. Whatever special advantage attached to slave labor was, therefore, confined exclusively to the use of that labor in large-scale agricultural enterprises.

To identify the unique advantage of slaves to large-scale agricultural enterprises, it is necessary to make use of the economists' distinction between "pecuniary" and "nonpecuniary" income. Pecuniary income is tangible income of some sort, whether received in money or in kind. Pecuniary income enters into national income accounts and hence is also referred to as "measured" income. Nonpecuniary income is of an intangible nature and it is not measured in national income accounts. Nonpecuniary income can be either positive or negative. For example, it is generally thought that the nonpecuniary income earned by most members of the faculty of Harvard University is large and positive, since these faculty members usually prefer to stay at Harvard even when they have been offered much larger pecuniary incomes by other institutions. The difference between the pecuniary income actually received by professors at Harvard and what they could earn elsewhere is a first approximation of the value that these academics attach to the nonpecuniary benefits of being located at Harvard.

It is not necessary to belabor the point that for free men, work in gangs on plantations involved large nonpecuniary disadvantages. Nevertheless, it seems reasonable to suppose that if planters offered free laborers large enough pecuniary payments, they could have attracted a sufficient number of free laborers to run their plantations. How big a premium would they have had to offer to induce free agriculturalists to forego the tempo and life-style of small farms and to accept a much more intense, more highly regulated, more interdependent regimen? And did the plantations have the capacity to pay that premium? For as competitive firms, there was a well-defined upper limit to the premium that they could afford. The ceiling on the potential premium to free labor for plantation work was given by the increase in output that could be achieved through combining small-scale farms into large-scale farms. Thus, if a would-be planter tried to bribe a typical group of white farmers into forming a large-scale plantation based on gang labor, he would not be able to offer more than a 50 percent increase over what they were already earning through their labor on small farms. The failure of free small-scale farmers to combine into large-scale plantations is *prima facie* evidence that the nonpecuniary disadvantages of gang labor—and all that it entailed—were greater than 50 percent of the wages of free farm laborers.

It might be thought that the preceding argument implies that since slaves did work on plantations, the nonpecuniary disadvantages of gang labor to them was less than 50 percent of the wages of free labor. That conclusion would be warranted only if the conditions under which labor was elicited from slaves corresponded to those for free men. Obviously they did not. In general, the labor of free men could only be elicited through wage bargains. However, ownership of the human capital of blacks carried with it the right to use force to obtain labor. Ownership of the title to a slave gave a master the right to use whatever force was necessary—including such force as might eventuate in death—to compel his chattel to engage in the normal work routine of the plantation. From the master's viewpoint, the advantage of force, when *judiciously* applied, was that it produced desired behavior, in certain realms of activity, at a lower cost than could have been achieved through financial inducements. The analogy to the parental use of force today is striking. Parents often find that it is cheaper (easier) to *compel* children to go to bed at a given hour rather than to attempt to bribe them into doing so. But one should not leap from this analogy to the unwarranted conclusion that force necessarily resulted in the infantilization of mature slaves.

Force was not an incidental feature of slavery. Without force, the alienability of the title to the human capital of blacks would have been worthless, at least insofar as it affected the plantation's capacity to produce. For it was only by applying force that it was possible to get blacks to accept gang labor without having to pay a premium that was in excess of the gains from economies of scale. The validity of this contention is demonstrated by the experience of the immediate postemancipation period. After the slaves were freed, many planters attempted to reconstruct their work gangs on the basis of wage payments. But such attempts generally foundered, despite the fact the wages offered to freedmen exceeded the incomes they had received as slaves by more than 100 percent. Even at this premium, planters found it impossible to maintain the gang system once they were deprived of the right to apply force. Freedmen generally preferred renting land and farming it, usually for shares, to working in gangs, although the payments being offered for gang labor were more than 100 percent greater than the average earnings of freedmen through sharecropping. Thus whether one compares immediate postwar gang wages with income from sharecropping or prewar pecuniary payments, available evidence shows that the application of force made it possible to obtain labor from slaves at less than half the price that would have had to have been offered in the absence of force. The nonpecuniary disadvantage of gang labor was no less to blacks than to whites.

The special advantage of slavery for agricultural production, then, is that it was a very cheap way of "compensating" slaves for the nonpecuniary disadvantages of gang labor. This discovery makes it possible to explain why the advantage of slave labor was much less in urban industry than in agriculture. The nonpecuniary disadvantage of accepting the monotonous and intense routine of factories appears to have been offset by nonpecuniary benefits which both black and white workers attached to life in the cities. In other words, the net nonpecuniary disadvantage of work in urban industry was quite low, perhaps even negative. The scope of the benefits that could be obtained from the application of force was thus much more limited in urban industry than in plantation agriculture.

For a given amount of labor, there was an optimum amount of force—an amount that would make the total cost (cost of force plus the pecuniary payment to the slave) of procuring the desired labor a minimum. Planters worried about what that optimum was. They realized that there were limits on the extent to which force could be substituted for pecuniary payments, that if they resorted to too much force they would increase rather than reduce the cost of labor. That is why they generally restricted the amount of force that their overseers or drivers were permitted to impose on hands, why they felt it was necessary to give explicit instructions on when, how, and to what degree force could be applied.

It has been widely assumed that slaveholders employed force because it permitted them to push pecuniary payments to the subsistence level, or at least close to that level. This assumption is false. Odd as it may seem, the optimal combination of force and pecuniary income was one that left slaves on large plantations with *more* pecuniary income per capita than they would have earned if they had been free small farmers. The explanation of this paradoxical finding turns on the fact there were definite costs to the generation of force. After a certain point, the cost of obtaining an additional unit of labor with force became greater than the cost of obtaining it through pecuniary payments. To use the language of economists—there were rapidly diminishing returns to force. The analysis of the trade-off which faced planters in choosing between force and pecuniary payments is a complex but standard problem of economics. Because of its complexity we have relegated it to appendix B [see *Time on the Cross*, II, pp. 155-60], where it is shown that the average pecuniary income actually received by a prime field hand was roughly 15 percent greater than the income he would have received for his labor as a free agricultural worker. In other words, far from being kept at the brink of starvation, slaves actually shared in the gains from economies of scale—so far as purely pecuniary income was concerned. Slaves received approximately 20 percent of the increase in product attributable to large-scale operations.

This finding underscores the importance of the system of pecuniary incentives. It is not correct to say, as one leading historian did, that though pecuniary "rewards were much used," force was the "principal basis" for promoting the work of slaves. Pecuniary incentives were no more an incidental feature of slavery than force. Both were indispensable to the existence of the plantation system. The absence of either could have made the cost of production under the plantation system greater than the gains from large-scale production.

Planters recognized that both forms of economic inducement were essential, and they expected their managers to be adept at employing both. "Nothing," said the *Instructions to Managers* in a widely used plantation account book,

> is more important in the right government of negroes, than the feeling and deportment of the manager towards them. And whilst he must be strict and impartial in carrying out his rules amongst them, and in requiring the performance of their labor, 'tis but just and humane, when they have done their duty, to treat them with kindness, and even sometimes with indulgence. In all government rewards and encouragements are as necessary as punishment, and are often more effective. Notice, then: encourage and reward such as best perform their duties. Even a word of kindness, if judiciously used, will effect much. At other times respite from labor for a few hours of any day, or at the end of the week, may be granted, and when such loss of time will not materially affect the plantation operations; and at others, some additional allowances of provisions and indulgencies at the holydays, etc.
>
> The good opinion of a good master is always desired by his negroes, and the manager should, therefore, make it a point to report to the proprietor the names and characters of all those who are deserving on account of faithful attention to duty, that they may be further rewarded. . . .
>
> The object of all punishment should be, 1st, for correction to deter the offender from a repetition of an offence, from the fear of the like certain punishment; and, 2nd, for example to all others, shewing them that if they offend, they will likewise receive certain punishment. And these objects and ends of all just punishments can be better attained by the certainty than by the severity of punishment.
>
> Never fail, therefore, to notice the breach of an established rule, and be equally unfailing in punishing the offender justly, according to the nature and circumstance of the offence. Never inflict punishment when in a passion, nor threaten it; but wait until perfectly cool, and until it can be done rather with sorrow than in anger.

Olmsted repeatedly ran into examples of the heavy use made of pecuniary incentives by slaveholders and of the effectiveness of such incentives. On a sugar plantation in Louisiana he was surprised to find that slaves worked "with greater cheerfulness" during the grinding season than any other, although during this season they averaged eighteen hours of work per day. The reason, he discovered, was that at grinding time the hands were "better paid." In the Carolinas he reported that slaves on hire to fisheries as divers also revealed a surprising Protestant ethic. "What! slaves eager to work, and working cheerfully, earnestly, and skilfully?" The reason Olmsted, again reported, was that they were receiving extra pay for "skill" and "perseverance."

Olmsted was also aware of how high such extra pay could go. "One of the largest manufacturers [of tobacco in Virginia]," he said, in the course of trying to demonstrate how much dearer slave labor was than free labor, "informed me that he paid seldom less than $60 a year, and sometimes over $300, to each slave he used, in addition to the rent paid to their masters, which was from $100 to $150 a year." On a rice plantation in Georgia, Olmsted encountered a slave engineer who received "considerably higher wages, in fact [in the form of presents], than the white overseer."

On the issue of pecuniary incentives, however, as on so many others, Olmsted badly misinterpreted the evidence. In each of the foregoing instances, except the case in which he was arguing for the high real cost of slave labor, Olmsted treated the use of pecuniary incentives as an exception, employed only by "[m]en of sense" who had "discovered that when they desire to get extraordinary exertions from their slaves, it is better to offer them rewards than to whip them; to encourage them, rather than to drive them." Olmsted's preconceptions prevented him from realizing that pecuniary rewards were as integral a part of slavery as punishment.

Discovery of the relatively high average level of pecuniary payments to slaves not only calls into question the traditional interpretation of the incentive system, but also the traditional explanations for the relatively low incidence of rebellion on the part of slaves. The failure to recognize the flexible and many-faceted character of the slave system, and the widely held assumption that systematic employment of force precluded the use of pecuniary incentives in any significant way, have led historians to exaggerate the cruelty of slavery. This in turn led them to expect slaves to be pushed frequently, if not continuously, to the point of rebellion. The relative absence of rebellion thus posed a dilemma. In the attempt to resolve the dilemma, some historians have stressed the overwhelming odds against the success of attempts at rebellion, depicting, or suggesting, that the South was an armed camp.

Available evidence does not sustain this hypothesis. If physical power was the explanation for the absence of rebellion, one would expect to see government expenditures rise with the density of the slave population. Analysis of census data shows no such correlation. It might be argued that police power was supplied not by the state but by the planters themselves. If that were the case, one would expect to see the number of white males per plantation increase with plantation size. No such correlation exists. Regardless of the plantation size there were roughly six white persons per plantation—slightly over the average family size. On a plantation of one hundred slaves, the ratio of adult slaves to adult white males was roughly thirty to one. It strains credulity to believe that men armed with just pistols, if at all, could so cower slaves pushed to the point of rebellion that they would be unable to act against their oppressors. White planters and overseers were not supermen. Two or three strong, young slaves lurking behind some building surely could have disposed of a brutal overseer or planter, as sometimes happened, without anyone being the wiser as to the identity of the perpetrators of the deed.

Concern of planters with "abolitionist agitators" was not paranoia but hard-headed business. Planters were able to produce the needed force to maintain their system at exceedingly low costs. A small group of determined revolutionaries might well have pushed the cost of force to prohibitive levels. Similarly, the frequent discussions, in instructions to overseers, of the need for moderation in the application of force are not *prima facie* evidence of widespread brutality—proof that too much force was in fact being applied. As pointed out in chapter 4, overseers' instructions focused on the issues that planters considered most crucial to successful operations. That they would caution against the abuse of force is no more of a basis for assuming that slaves were generally treated cruelly by overseers than their instructions on feeding of livestock is proof that animals were being starved. Interestingly enough, the instructions reveal that the main fear of planters regarding the misuse of force was that it would raise costs, not by provoking general rebellion, but by leading to the flight of the individual slaves who were being abused.

One factor which undoubtedly reduced the cost of the force required to maintain the system of slavery was the ubiquity of racist attitudes among whites, and the embodiment of these attitudes in laws which severely reduced the value of freedom to blacks. For blacks, the alternative to slavery was not freedom but, as one scholar has put it, "quasi-freedom." This term applies to the North as well as to the South. In both sections of the country free blacks led a precarious existence. While northern Negroes were usually spared the threat of reinslavement because of infractions of the law, they were barred from testifying in ten states, prevented from assembling in two, and excluded from voting in ten. Illinois, the "Land of Lincoln," banned the migration of free Negroes into the state. Those who entered and stayed more than ten days were guilty of a "high misdemeanor." Data in the 1850 census suggest that the economic condition of the average free northern Negro may have been worse than that of the average free Negro in the South. A comparison between New York and New Orleans reveals that New York Negroes lived in more crowded housing, had a lower proportion of craftsmen, and less wealth per capita than free Negroes in New Orleans.

For blacks during the antebellum era, then, freedom and slavery were not separated by a sharp dividing line. One gradually shaded into the other. To some blacks, especially among the talented whose opportunities were most constricted by slavery, even quasi-freedom was worth nearly any price—and they risked everything for it. But for the average slave, who in any case expected his lot to be that of a laborer, the costs of revolution, or even flight, were not worth the gains of quasi-freedom—except under special circumstances such as the separation of a man from his wife or parents from their children.

That slaves received higher pecuniary incomes than they would have as free agricultural laborers does not mean that their real incomes were higher. For, as previously noted, there were large nonpecuniary disadvantages to the gang system, equal to at least $75 per year per adult male hand. Table 3 shows that for the southern slave population as a whole, gang labor imposed a nonpecuniary loss of at least $90,000,000. Against this very large loss, slaves received a relatively small pecuniary offset of $6,000,000. Thus their net loss was $84,000,000.

Although it may be surprising to some readers, the main gainers from the gang system were not slaveholders but consumers of cotton. Since cotton plantations had the characteristics of a competitive industry, all gains in productivity that did not go into the form of higher wages would normally have been passed on to consumers in the form of lower prices of cotton. Indeed, under normal circumstances, the extra profits to slaveholders which arose from the gang system would have been transitory. That they persisted was not due to any special behavior on the part of planters. It was due to the behavior of consumers of cotton whose demand for the fiber increased more rapidly than the labor force and total factor productivity. In this sense, even the extra profit of slaveholders was due to the behavior of consumers of cotton. . . . Of the total pecuniary gain from gang labor, consumers received nearly half, or $14,000,000, while slaveowners received about $10,000,000.

Slaves as a class, therefore, suffered a net loss in 1850 of at least $84,000,000 so that the rest of the world could benefit by $24,000,-000. (The use of the term "rest of the world" was deliberate. For most U.S. cotton was consumed not in the United States but abroad). It is of some interest to note that the pecuniary benefits of gang production were much more widely diffused than the losses suffered by slaves. For every slave working in the cotton fields, there were hundreds of consumers of cotton. This means that the average annual gain to a consumer was quite small. Indeed, for every dollar gained by a typical consumer of cotton cloth, there was a slave laboring somewhere under the hot southern sun who would lose at least $400.

• *At first, Time on the Cross bowled over reviewers (many of them quantifying historians or economists like Fogel and Engerman), but, even before all the accolades were in, a reaction took place. "Traditional" historians, and some cliometricians (economic historians who employ the statistical and computer arts), began publishing caveats, and then stronger critiques of Fogel and Engerman. The longest, and surely the most strongly worded attack came from social historian Herbert G. Gutman. To him, Time on the Cross (cited as T/C) and Fogel and Engerman (cited as F + E) were dead wrong. Gutman donned his Inspector Javert cape and stalked F + E page by page, appendix by appendix, table by table. The passages from Gutman on whipping, incentives and rewards, etc., follow closely the selections from T/C reprinted in this book.*

Slave Work Habits and the Protestant Ethic

HERBERT G. GUTMAN

F + E's [Robert William Fogel and Stanley L. Engerman's] most crucial arguments about the quality of slave labor and much of their least convincing evidence are found in a brief portion of chapter four entitled "Punishments, Rewards, and Expropriations." A short but controversial section, it has attracted the attention of nearly all reviewers and contains data essential to some of F + E's most startling conclusions.[1] It also uses evidence in ways that strikingly reveal the utter inadequacy of the old-fashioned model of slave society that tarnishes T/C [*Time on the Cross*]. David and Temin vigorously dispute the low rate of expropriation estimated by F + E, insisting

From *Slavery and the Numbers Game: A Critique of "Time on the Cross"* by Herbert G. Gutman (Urbana: University of Illinois Press, 1975), pp. 15-25, 34-35, 37-39. Copyright © 1975 by Herbert G. Gutman. Reprinted by permission of the author and University of Illinois Press.

that inaccurate estimates indicate a bias.[2] The focus here is different. It is on F + E's arguments and their use of evidence to show that enslaved Afro-Americans worked hard and diligently because they wanted to and because profit-maximizing owners skillfully mixed a few punishments with many rewards to encourage productive slave labor. We examine "punishments" and "rewards"—the positive and negative incentives used by slaveowners, especially planters, to improve slave labor and to increase productivity.[3] F + E do not deny that slaveowners used physical punishment, but they greatly minimize its significance in relation to the prevalence of positive labor incentives. The carrot counted more than the stick. . . .

Convinced that a system of positive planter-sponsored labor incentives existed, F + E also insist that most slaves responded positively to the rewards offered them. The very last paragraph in T/C emphasizes this point. A high level of slave productivity resulted in the production of cotton, tobacco, sugar, and rice. But the "spikes of racism" —that is, "myths"—hid this "fact" from contemporaries and later historians. Racist beliefs turned slave high achievers into Uncle Toms.[4] The biased beliefs of antislavery advocates and so-called neo-abolitionist historians kept hidden from the American people, and especially from black Americans, truths about how the ancestors of twentieth-century Afro-Americans had been transformed as slaves into nineteenth-century "economic" men and women. Sambo really was Horatio Alger with a black skin.

Evidence supporting such a transformation is not found in T/C. If such a transformation actually occurred, *that* would be a social fact of great importance in understanding the behavior and beliefs of enslaved Afro-Americans and of their emancipated descendants. But most of the evidence in T/C about this important conclusion is not impressive. Much of it is circumstantial; none of it is substantial; most of it is quite traditional; hardly any of it comes from new sources; and, when used, such sources are often imprecisely and sometimes wildly exaggerated. To transform means "to change something to a different form," a change "in appearance, condition, nature, or character." Transformation, therefore, is a social process and has to occur over time. Something happens to someone. Slaves are made into "efficient" workers. The F + E model, however, is static and ahistorical. F + E never consider who was being transformed. Because there is no discussion of who the slaves were and how well they worked at the beginning of this social process, it is hardly possible to describe a transformation. Instead of that kind of needed and useful analysis, important evidence—especially that dealing with punishments, rewards, and mobility—is so badly used that it casts considerable and disturbing doubt upon the entire argument.

SCANT EVIDENCE ON NEGATIVE LABOR INCENTIVES (OR SLAVE PUNISHMENTS)

Negative labor incentives, or punishments, are treated with a single and greatly misinterpreted quantitative example: Appendix C ("Misconduct and Punishments: 1840–1841") in Edwin Adams Davis, ed., *Plantation Life in the Florida Parishes of Louisiana, 1836–1846, as Reflected in the Diary of Bennet H. Barrow*.[5] The historian Davis apparently gathered cases of slave misconduct and punishment from the cotton planter Barrow's diary.[6] The Davis study contains one of the few easily accessible quantitative sources used by F + E. Cliometric theory is not needed to examine it. Analysis does not depend upon computer technology. Ordinary readers of T/C should examine these data, and draw their own conclusions about how accurately they have been used. My own analysis follows.

The Barrow punishment record serves to create a pseudostatistic that diminishes the importance of slave whippings. This record is the only evidence dealing with slave punishment, so it serves to trivialize planter-sponsored negative labor incentives. After a brief paragraph which tells that "whipping could be either a mild or a severe punishment" (an indisputable but hardly original generalization), a critical four-sentence paragraph based entirely on the Davis appendix follows: "Reliable data on the frequency of whipping is extremely sparse. The only systematic record of whipping now available for an extended period comes from the diary of Bennet Barrow, a Louisiana planter who believed that to spare the rod was to spoil the slave. His plantation numbered about 200 slaves, of whom about 120 were in the labor force. The record shows that over the course of two years a total of 160 whippings were administered, an average of 0.7 whippings per hand per year. About half the hands were not whipped at all during the period. . . ."[7]

The two brief paragraphs which follow the one quoted above do not enlarge upon these "findings" but examine whipping generally and offer some "comparative" observations.[8] The data drawn from the Barrow diary, then, are the only items of hard data dealing with negative labor incentives.

HOW THE HISTORIAN MEASURES THE FREQUENCY OF SLAVE WHIPPINGS

The sentence—"The record shows that over the course of two years a total of 160 whippings were administered, an average of 0.7 whippings per hand per year"—is examined first. Several questions come to mind. Is "0.7 whippings per hand per year" a useful average? Have the Barrow diary data and the appendices which accompany them been properly used? Have the right historical questions been asked of those data? It is assumed for the moment that Barrow owned 200 slaves, of whom about 120 were in the labor force. (It shall be seen below that each number—200 and 120—is wrong.) To report "an average of 0.7 whippings per hand per year" using these numbers is accurate. That is not, however, the significant average. The wrong question has been asked. The logic producing this average is socially flawed along with the inferences suggested by it. The same logic could just as easily calculate the average number of whippings per hand per week (0.013). It is known, for example, that "on average" 127 blacks were lynched every year between 1889 and 1899.[9] How does one assess that average? Assume that 6 million blacks lived in the United States in 1889 and that 127 of them were lynched. Is it useful to learn that "the record shows an average of 0.0003 lynchings per black per year so that about 99.9997 percent of blacks were not lynched in 1889?" An accurate average, that is a banal statistic. Lynching as a form of social control cannot be evaluated by dividing the number of blacks (or whites) lynched into the number of living blacks (or whites). The absolute number of lynchings in a given time period and whether that number rose or fell later in time are important numbers. They measure the changing frequency with which this particular instrument of social violence was used. It is then possible to study that instrument's relative significance.

The same is true with slave whippings. Southern law permitted slaveowners to punish their chattel, and most historians agree that whipping served as the most common form of physical punishment, figuring as a central device in imposing order over troublesome slaves and in revealing the source of authority in a slave society. The essential statistic, therefore, is not the average number of whippings per hand per year.[10] Whether by the week or the year, such an average does not measure the utility of the whip as an instrument of social and economic discipline. It is much more relevant to know how often the whip was used: on Plantation X with Y slaves in Z years, how frequently was the whip used? That information is available in the Davis volume. In 1840–1841, Barrow's slaves were whipped 160 times. A slave—"on average"—was whipped every 4.56 days. Three slaves were whipped every two weeks. Among them, sixty (37.5 percent) were females. A male was whipped once a week, and a female once every twelve days. Are these averages "small" or "large"? That depends. And it depends upon much more than whether one is a "neo-abolitionist" or a "quantitative" historian. These are quite high averages, and for good reason. If whipping is viewed primarily as an instrument of labor discipline and not as the mere exercise of arbitrary power (or cruelty), whipping three slaves every two weeks means that this instrument of physical discipline had an adequate social visibility among the enslaved. Slave men and women were whipped frequently enough—whatever the size of the unit of ownership—to reveal to them (and to us) that whipping regularly served Barrow as a negative instrument of labor discipline. Imagine reading the following argument:

> While whipping was an integral part of the system of punishment and rewards, it was not the totality of the system. What planters wanted was not sullen and discontented slaves who did just enough to keep from getting whipped. They wanted devoted, hard-working, responsible slaves who identified their fortunes with the fortunes of their masters. Planters sought to imbue slaves with a "Protestant" work ethic and to transform that ethic from a state of mind into a high level of production. . . . *Reliable data on the frequency of whipping is extremely sparse. The only systematic record of whipping now available comes from the diary of Bennet Barrow, a Louisiana planter who believed that to spare the rod was to spoil the slave. Over the course of two years, Barrow whipped a slave every 4.56 days. Women were whipped less frequently than men. On average, a male slave was whipped every 7.3 days and a female slave every 12.2 days.* [The "Protestant" work ethic] . . . could not be beaten into slaves. It had to be elicited.

A schoolboy would not take such an argument based on this evidence seriously. There is a *real* social difference between a slave being whipped every 4.56 days and "an average of 0.7 whippings per hand per year." And it rests on more than a mastery of long division.

CONSTRUCTING A WHIPPING TABLE

So far, it has been pointed out that F + E asked the wrong question. That error is common among historians. But F + E also have inaccurately used the Barrow diary and the accompanying appendices. "His [Barrow's] plantation," they write, "numbered about 200 slaves, of whom about 120 were in the labor force." Both numbers are wrong. Whipping data are available for 1840–1841, but the Davis volume, including the diary itself, does not tell how many slaves Barrow owned in 1840–1841. An "Inventory of the Estate of Bennet H. Barrow," printed as an appendix, gives by name and age the slaves he owned when he died. About 200 men, women, and children are listed. But Barrow died in 1854, fourteen years after the recorded whippings, and it appears that F + E assume that Barrow owned "about 200 slaves" in 1840–1841. No data in the Davis volume warrant that assumption. Additional appendices—birth (1835–1846) and death (1831–1845) lists (pp. 427-431)—show that slightly more than twice as many slaves were born as died in these years. Since Barrow apparently sold few slaves, these records suggest that he owned far fewer than 200 slaves in 1840–1841. F + E, therefore, measured the actual number of recorded whippings against a total slave population far in excess of its real size. As a result, the frequency with which *individual* slaves were whipped is greatly underestimated. (After the publication of the journal version of this review-essay, Professor William Scarborough of the University of Southern Mississippi kindly supplied me with the number of slaves Barrow owned in 1840, a statistic drawn from his own research into the 1840 federal manuscript census. That document reveals that Barrow owned 129 [not 200] slaves in 1840. F + E estimate that 90 Barrow slaves were not whipped; the actual number is closer to 19, a drop of about 80 percent. Their inaccurate reckoning shows that 1 out of 2.2 Barrow slaves escaped the whip. Actually, only 1 out of 6.7 was not whipped. The ages of the Barrow slaves in 1840 are not known, but if they fit the typical age distribution given by F + E, then 89 were at least ten years old. F + E tell that Barrow whipped 110 individual slaves. If all slaves at least ten years old were whipped one or more times, we still would have to account for 21 slaves [110 − 89 = 21]. These 21 slaves had to be children under the age of ten. That means that half of slave children under ten were whipped at least once. If Barrow did not whip children under the age of five, and if children under the age of ten were fairly evenly distributed, that means that every child aged five to nine probably was whipped one or more times in 1840–1841. F + E's argument about relative absence of negative labor incentives would have been greatly strengthened if they had assumed that Bennet Barrow never lived rather than that he owned "200" slaves in 1840.)

BARROW'S DIARY ENTRIES COMPARED TO THE WHIPPING LIST

The Barrow diary entries are just as valuable as the Davis whipping list.[11] There is some question whether the diary is complete.[12] The same volume also includes several valuable appendices and a sixty-seven-page essay on Barrow, his family, and his business, plantation, and social doings. Written in the Phillips tradition, the essay has some of the severe shortcomings characteristic of that genre but still contains much useful information. F + E rely heavily on the essay and Davis' list, "Misconduct and Punishments: 1840–1841," but for an unexplained reason none of the rich details describing plantation management and especially slave disciplining that stud the ten-year diary found their way into the pages of T/C. F + E possibly felt that this material was irrelevant to T/C's central themes. Extracts from the diary follow:[13]

1836
Dec. 26   House Jerry & Isreal chained during Christmas Jerry for general bad conduct—for a year and better—Isreal bad conduct during cotten picking season

1837
Sept. 4   . . . had a general Whiping frollick
Oct. 2   More Whiping to do this Fall than alltogether in three years owing to my D mean Overseer
Dec. 31   ran two of Uncle Bats negros off last night—for making a disturbance—no pass—broke my sword Cane over one of their skulls

1838
Jan. 23   my House Servants Jane Lavenia & E. Jim broke into my store room—and helped themselves verry liberally to every thing— . . . I Whiped [them] . . . worse than I ever Whiped any one before
Sept. 28   Dennis and Tom "*Beauf*" ran off on Wednesday— . . . if I can see either of them and have a gun at the time will let them have the contents of it . . .
Oct. 12   [Tom ran off again] will Whip him more than I ever Whip one, I think he deserves more—the second time he has done so this year . . .
Oct. 20   Whiped about half to day
Oct. 26   Whiped 8 or 10 for weight to day—those that pick least weights generally most trash . . .
Oct. 27   Dennis ran off yesterday—& after I had Whiped him

Nov. 2 Dennis came in sick on Tuesday—ran off again yesterday—without my ever seeing him—will carry my
Gun & small shot for him—I think I shall cure him
of his rascallity

Nov. 7 Dennis came in last night—had him fasted—attempted to Escape. ran as far as the creek but was
caught—the Ds rascal on the place

Dec. 30 Demps gave his wife Hetty a light cut or two & then
locked her up to prevent her going to the Frollick—I
reversed it turning her loose & fastning him

1839

Jan. 4 Whiped evry hand in the field this evening com-
mencing with the driver

April 27 My hands worked verry badly—so far general Whipping yesterday

July 19 Gave L. Dave a good Whipping for some of his rascallity intend chaining him & Jack nights & Sunday
till I think they are broke in—to behave

Sept. 9 Whiped G. Jerry & Dennis for their shirking

Sept. 30 Had G. Jerry T. Fill & Bts Nat up here washing all
yesterday as punishment—generally dirty & ragged

Oct. 2 Lewis still out. no doubt but he is down at Uncle
Bats Where his Father lives—which proves the im-
propiety of having slaves off the plantation

Oct. 3 told Dennis I intended to Whip him. [Dennis fled]
. . . started Jack after him—to give him $50 if he
catches him—I had rather a negro would do anything
Else than runaway. Dennis & his Brother Lewis &
G. Jerry the only ones that gives me any trouble to
make do their part

Oct. 4 Boy Lewis came in last night—gave him the worst
Whipping I ever gave any young negro. I predict he
will not runaway *soon*. Building a Jail for him Dennis
& Ginny Jerry—intend jailing them for Saturday
nights 'till Monday mornings

Oct. 13 Put Darcas in Jail last night for pretending to be
sick, repeatedly—the first one ever put in the Jail &
C Jerry

Oct. 20 Gave my negros about my lot the worst Whipping
they ever had

Oct. 23 Gave every cotten picker a Whipping last night for
trash & of late my driver has lost considerable authority with them

[Dec. 23 Dennis caught]

Dec. 24   intend exhibiting Dennis during Christmas on a scaffold in the middle of the Quarter & with a red Flannel Cap on

Dec. 25   Let Darcas out of Jail—Dennis confined in Jail

1840

Jan.   9   Darcas began to sherk again—let her out of Jail Christmas she promised to do well &c.

April 18   gave my driver a few licks this evening, not knowing Who had done bad work

April 19   had a general Whipping among the House ones & two Carters for stealing, &c.

July   5   had Jack rigged out this evening with red flanel on his years [*sic*] & a Feather in them & sheet on, "in the Quarter." every negro up. Made Alfred and Betsey ride him round the Quarter dismount and take a kiss, for quarreling. Jack & Lize, Frank & Fanney the same.

July 30   [The cook Lavenia had run away and was found] Lavenia thought she had been whipped unjustly owing to Jane (the Cook), let Lavenia give her a good *drubing,* &c.

Oct. 13   I think my hands have Picked cotton worse this year than in several years picked it verry trashy & not better weights nor as good as *common,* intend Whipping them *straght*

Oct. 15   am sattisfied the best plan is to give them every thing they require for their comfort and never that they will do without Whipping or some punishment

1841

Jan.   3   [Barrow gave the Negroes a dinner] and afterwards inspected their manners in the Ballroom several acted very rude as usual. put them in Jail

Aug. 16   Ginney Jerry has been sherking about ever since Began to pick cotten. after Whipping him yesterday told him if ever he dodged about from me again would certainly shoot him. this morning at Breakfast time Charles came & told me that Jerry was about to run off. took my Gun found him in the Bayou behind the Quarter, shot him in the thigh

Sept. 16   Ginney Jerry ran off Last Thursday to day a week, after being shot, Will shoot to kill him should I be fortunate enoughf [*sic*] to meet him, Will sell him &c.

Oct.   2   More hands attempting to sherk for two weeks past than I ever knew, Gave a number of them a good *floging*

1842

June 15 [Ginney Jerry ran away again] will shoot to kill him if an opportunity offers. . . . has not been touched this year, nor have I said a word to him, pray for a shot at him

Nov. 6 Friday night Jack Let Jerry slip for purpose of getting a pig thinking as Jerry was Jailed at night there would be no suspicion of him—for some reason told Alfred Jerry had a pig in his house A. went and found it as Jack thought. put him in Jail & in the stocks in the morning there was nothing of Jerry stocks Broke & door—no doubt some one turned him out—one concerned in the Pig—gave about a dozen severe Whipping in the Yard & all—Jack old Jenny & Darcas the most severe hand sawing

1844

Nov. 28 Whiped all my grown cotten pickers to day

Nov. 29 [Dennis ran off and was then caught] gave him the worst Whipping he ever had—& ducking

1845

May 27 [Darcas cut her husband with a hatchet in the hip] Very dangerous cut—will make her sick of the sight of a Hatchet as Long as she Lives

June 4 missed several of my young Hogs, found 8 or 10 Guilty, ducked & gave them a good thrashing, Mr. *Ginney* Jerry next morning Felt insulted at his treatment & put out, would give "freely" $100 to get a shot at him

Sept. 6 The negro hunters came this morning, Were not out long before we struck the trail of Ginny Jerry, ran and trailed for about a mile *treed* him, made the dogs pull him out of the tree, Bit him very badly, think he will stay home a while

Oct. 18 Fell quite unwell for two days past, effect of negro hunting

Oct. 27 Went with the negro Dogs to Hunt Ruffins runaways, & his small house boy Ed. ran off still out, 12 years of age—no Luck—negro dogs here—tired of them

Nov. 11   the negro dogs to Mrs Wades Quarter. . . . dogs
soon tore him naked, took him Home Before the
other negro & made the dogs give him another over
hauling, has been drawing a knife & Pistol on persons about Town

It is surprising that as rich a source as these diary entries was entirely neglected. It reveals much about the labor incentives Barrow
used with his slaves. More than once, for example, Barrow penned
suggestive diary notations such as "had a general Whiping frolick,"
"whiped about half to day," "general Whipping yesterday," "intend
Whipping them *straght*," "whiped all my grown cotten pickers to
day." None of these general whippings counted in the list of whippings. The diary, in fact, reveals that general whippings of productive
Barrow male and female slaves occurred quite regularly: there were at
least six collective whippings—1837, 1838, twice in 1839, 1840, and
1841—between 1837 and 1841. The diary also listed other punishments. In his fine dissertation on the slave family, Bobby Jones concluded that Barrow resorted to "practically every known form of
chastisement slaveholders used." Jones pointed out: "During his career, Barrow resorted to chains; extra work; whipping; humiliation,
such as making a man wear women's clothing and parade around the
quarters; imprisonment; stocks; 'raked several negro heads to day';
'staking out'; 'hand-sawing'; and dousing or ducking in water which
occurred in October and November." Jones figured that "hand-sawing"
probably meant "a beating administered with the toothed-edge of a
saw."[14] The diary extracts reprinted in these . . . pages include yet
other punishments, including the occasional shooting of a runaway. It
is not inappropriate to ask—especially in a study which assesses the
relative importance of slave physical punishments—why F + E failed
to weigh the full punishment record reported in the diary. That
source, after all, serves as the single piece of evidence on slave punishments.[15] . . .

NEGATIVE LABOR INCENTIVES AND THE UBIQUITOUS WORDS
"MORE" AND "MOST" IN T/C

We are finished for the moment with Bennet Barrow and his slaves,
but not yet with F + E on negative labor incentives. A brief paragraph
follows the "summary" of the Barrow whippings to remind the reader
once again that whipping was common in many places before the
nineteenth century—even quoting from what is called "the Matthew's
Bible," the English translation by John Rogers under the pseudonym

Thomas Matthew. The next paragraph "generalizes" about whipping and contains ten sentences which indicate that none of the evidence used is "quantitative." The sentences are numbered *seriatum:*

> [1] To attribute the continuation of whipping in the South to the maliciousness of masters is naïve. [2] Although *some* masters were brutal, even sadistic, *most* were not. [3] The *overwhelming majority* of the ex-slaves in the W.P.A. narratives who expressed themselves *on the issue* reported that their masters were *good men.* [4] *Such men* worried about the proper role of whipping in a system of punishment [sic] and rewards. [5] *Some* excluded it altogether. [6] *Most* accepted it, but recognized that to be effective whipping had to be used with restraint and in a coolly calculated manner. [7] Weston, *for example,* admonished his overseer not to impose punishment of any sort until twenty-four hours after the offense had been discovered. [8] William J. Minor, a sugar planter, instructed his managers "not [to] cut the skin when punishing, nor punish in a passion." [9] *Many* planters forbade the whipping of slaves except by them or in their presence. [10] *Others* limited the number of lashes that could be administered without their permission. [Italics added.][16]

Sentence 1 is left aside for the moment. The other nine sentences are a curious mode of argument in this work, mainly because the imprecision in language and the use of isolated examples (sentences 7 and 8) are styles of historical rhetoric and argument usually scorned by cliometricians when used by noncliometricians. How typical were Weston and Minor?[17] What methods were used to establish their typicality? Sentences 2, 5, 6, 9, and 10 contain favored imprecise quantitative words such as *some* and *most* (2, 5, and 6), *many* (9), and *others* (10). It is surprising to see how often such ambiguous words are used. It is, of course, difficult to generalize without using words meant to describe the presence or absence of regularities, and such words are essential to the social and economic historian. But neither volume one nor volume two of T/C contains any evidence indicating how F + E uncovered such regularities in planter behavior. Sentences 3 and 4—at least as written—do not bear at all on the question of planter patterns of punishment. The point under discussion is the regularity and frequency of slave punishment, not whether elderly former slaves, who were mostly between the ages of eight and twelve when the general emancipation occurred and, therefore, had probably never been beaten or whipped, felt their old owners to be "good" or "bad" men. Where, furthermore, is the evidence that the planters as a social class or group "*worried* about the *proper* role of whipping in a system of punishment and rewards" (italics added)? *Worry* has a fairly precise meaning, but *proper* is an ambiguous word. To worry means "to feel uneasy, or anxious; fret; torment oneself and suffer from disturbing thoughts." Did men like Bennet Barrow, William Minor, and Weston fret over the use of the whip and suffer disturbing thoughts? *Proper* has several meanings, and it is unclear which one is implied in this sentence. Do F + E mean that planters worried about how to adapt whipping to the purposes of enslavement? Do they mean that planters worried about conforming to established standards of behavior? Or do they mean that planters worried about whether or not whipping was right? These are quite different kinds of worries, and each has a social importance of its own. . . .

F + E ON THE ECONOMIC COST OF WHIPPING, AND JAMES HAMMOND
ON THE SOCIAL UTILITY OF WHIPPING:
THE INADEQUATE ECONOMIC "MODEL"

The brief discussion of whipping in T/C is followed by a still briefer discussion of other slave punishments. F + E soundly remind readers that whipping as an instrument of labor discipline declined "with the rise of capitalism" when "impersonal and indirect sanctions were increasingly substituted for direct, personal ones." Hiring labor in the marketplace "provided managers . . . with a powerful new disciplinary weapon." "Workers who were lazy . . . or who otherwise shirked their duties could be fired—left to starve beyond the eyesight or expense of the employer." These summary sentences hardly differ from the classic indictments of early capitalism. "Interestingly enough," F + E add, "denial of food was rarely used to enforce discipline on slaves. For the illness and lethargy caused by malnutrition reduced the capacity of the slave to labor in the fields." The jailing of slaves is mentioned, but only to be dismissed as a common form of slave punishment. Nothing, however, in these findings is new. Stampp, for example, insisted that cases "of deliberate stinting of rations were fortunately few," and that hardly any slaveholders "built private jails on their premises" because "they knew that close confinement during a working day was a punishment of dubious value."[18] F + E have not demolished yet another "myth" but simply confirmed (without adding new evidence) what is well known. Nevertheless, there is a need for more study about the relationship between control of the food supply, planter-sponsored labor incentives, and slave social behavior. Prolonged denial of food obviously causes malnutrition, just as prolonged overeating causes obesity. And that the "illness and lethargy caused by

malnutrition" impair labor efficiency is self-evident. But the social issue is not whether owners denied slaves food; it has rather to do with
how control of the food supply affected the life-chances and the behavior of slaves. The denial of a weekly meat ration on occasion did
not cause illness and malnutrition, but it served by example to make
clear that owners controlled the food supply. The presence of slave
gardens where slaves often grew foodstuffs for family consumption does
not alter the essential point. It simply makes it more complicated.
Slaves did not own these garden plots, and such places could be taken
from them. We need to study the relationship between control of the
food supply, social dominance, and labor efficiency.

Much more is involved in slave punishments than an "economic"
equation or an emphasis that does no more than stress the rational decisions of "economic man." F + E explain: "When the laborer owns
his own human capital, forms of punishment which impair or diminish
the value of that capital are borne exclusively by him. Under slavery,
the master desired forms of punishment which, while they imposed
costs on the slave, did so with minimum impairment to the human
capital which the master owned. Whipping generally fulfilled these
conditions." They write, "Whipping persisted in the South because
the cost of substituting hunger [sic] and incarceration for the lash was
greater for the slaveowner than for the northern employer of free labor."[19] So simple an "economic" explanation hardly does justice to
the complex motivations that shaped planter behavior. "Remember,"
the articulate pro-slavery advocate James Henry Hammond insisted,
"that on our estates we dispense with the whole machinery of public
police and public courts of justice. Thus we try, decide, and execute
the sentences, in thousands of cases, which in other countries would
go into the courts." Hardly a detached observer, Hammond was anxious to minimize the harshness implicit in master-slave relationships.
He wrote in answer to British critics of enslavement: "If a man steals
a pig in England, he is transported—torn from wife, children, parents,
and sent to the antipodes, infamous, and an outcast forever, though
probably he took from the superabundance of his neighbor to save the
lives of his famishing little ones. If one of our well-fed negroes, merely
for the sake of fresh meat, steals a pig, he gets perhaps forty stripes. . . .
Are our courts or yours the most humane? If Slavery were not in question, you would doubtless say ours is mistaken lenity. Perhaps it often
is; and slaves too lightly dealt with sometimes grow daring."

A South Carolina planter and lawyer who served in the United
States Senate and felt both northern free laborers and southern planta-

tion slaves "the very mudsills of society," Hammond had doubts about the social utility of whipping. "Stocks are rarely used by private individuals, and confinement still more seldom," said the planter, "though both are common punishments for whites, all the world over. I think they should be more frequently resorted to with slaves as substitutes for flogging, which I consider the most injurious and least efficacious mode of punishing them for serious offenses. It is not degrading, and unless excessive, occasions little pain. You may be a little astonished, after all the flourishes that have been made about 'cart whips,' &c., when I say flogging is not the most degrading punishment in the world."[20] How do we fit Hammond's plea that stocks and jails be used more frequently than the whip into a model of planter behavior which measures the utility of diverse punishments only by their "cost" to the planter in "labor time"? Hammond suggests the limitations of so cost-conscious a model when he writes that whipping was insufficiently "degrading." We are back to the meaning of words and to the inadequacies of the central F + E model. To degrade, according to the *Oxford English Dictionary,* means to lower in "rank, position, reputation, [and] character." Why did Hammond feel whipping to be the least effective mode of punishing especially troublesome slaves? It seems clear that the whip—at least in Hammond's estimation—did not have its intended social effect. It failed to lower the troublesome slave in "rank, position, [and] reputation." Rank, position, and reputation among whom? Hammond and his fellow planters? Or the enslaved themselves? Hammond surely meant the enslaved. And if that is so, it is imperative that in measuring the utility of whipping we understand how the enslaved interpreted the act of being whipped. On the Barrow plantation, at least, whipping did not deter misconduct. Barrow himself built a private jail. And the South Carolinian Hammond proposed that jails and stocks be used more commonly than the whip. Was it because the enslaved felt incarceration to be more degrading than whipping? And if so, why? A narrow economic calculus cannot explain so important a social distinction.

NOTES

1. T/C, I, pp. 144-153, 236-246.
2. David and Temin, "Slavery: The Progressive Institution?" as cited.
3. T/C, I, pp. 114-153; II, pp. 116-119.
4. *Ibid.,* pp. 263-264.
5. New York, 1943, pp. 431-440.
6. The entire volume includes several other useful appendices, such as a

brief but illuminating sketch of Barrow and his planter peers and Barrow's diary entries from 1836 to 1846, pp. 72-385.

7. T/C, I, p. 145.

8. A few sentences in volume two, p. 116, tell readers that "an adequate social history of whipping remains to be written" and that scattered historical writings indicate the persistence (despite a declining frequency) of whippings as a means of disciplining "members of the laboring classes" into the mid-nineteenth century in England, Russia, and even the American North. But what the British historian E. H. Carr calls the "economic whip" steadily replaced physical punishment in developing capitalist countries.

9. C. Vann Woodward, *Origins of the New South, 1877–1913* (1951), pp. 351-352.

10. Using the same data, interestingly, Eugene D. Genovese makes the same mistake. "Masters," he writes, "who were not slaves to their passions tried to hold corporal punishment to a minimum. The harsh Bennet H. Barrow of Louisiana used his whip more than most: his slaves averaged one whipping a month and many only once a year" (*Roll, Jordan, Roll* [1974], p. 64).

11. "The only systematic record of whipping now available for an extended period," write F + E, "comes from the diary of Bennett Barrow. . . ." The sentence more properly should read: "The only systematic record of whipping available to us for an extended period. . . ." F + E have not systematically searched plantation records for similar evidence. That much is clear from their list of sources. No one, to my knowledge, including F + E, has yet made a systematic search for such data. It is badly needed.

12. Some of the whippings listed in the Davis appendix, for example, are not found in the published diary.

13. Davis, *Plantation Life*, pp. 85-192 and 202-376, *passim*.

14. Bobby Jones, "A Cultural Middle Passage: Slave Marriage and Family in the Antebellum South," Ph.D. diss., University of North Carolina, 1965, pp. 57-58. This source is cited in the F + E bibliography so that if the authors missed such entries in examining the diary itself, they might have noticed them in reading this unusually important study.

15. The fact that this is the single piece of evidence used by F + E to deal with physical punishment does not deter the economist Peter Passell from concluding that "Fogel and Engerman find no . . . pattern of abuse." The "economic" findings in T/C do not surprise that reviewer, but "what is surprising is the general level of dignity accorded the slaves in other aspects of life" (Passell, review of T/C, *New York Times Book Review*, 28 April 1974, p. 4).

16. T/C, I, p. 146.

17. It may have been that Minor did not want the skin cut because it lowered the value of a slave in the market. Who wanted to purchase troublesome property? Hardly a detached source, the *New York Tribune* (10 March 1853) reported that whipping scars cut the sale price of an adult male slave from $750–$800 down to $460.

18. Stampp, *Peculiar Institution*, pp. 172, 289.

19. T/C, I, p. 147.

20. "Letters on Slavery," *Pro-Slavery Argument* (1852), pp. 119-135.

III: SLAVE CULTURE

• Eugene Genovese's Roll, Jordan, Roll, another of the major works on slavery and slave culture to appear in the 1970s, shared the 1975 Bancroft Prize with Fogel and Engerman's Time on the Cross. Roll, Jordan, Roll did not create so much controversy, however, receiving general acclaim—an unaccustomed situation for Genovese, a Marxist who had been involved in many of the historiographical battles, and some of the political battles, fought by American historians during the previous decade. In the early 1960s, Genovese began examining the economics and ideology of the slave-master class, concentrating on "the world the slaveholders made." Still, he appreciated that there are worlds within worlds. A good deal of Roll, Jordan, Roll treats the nature of the paternalistic master-slave relationship, but much of the book devotes attention to "the world the slaves made," to the fashioning of an American subculture. This creativeness within restricted spheres is nowhere better illustrated than in the importance of slave religion to the creation of slave culture, a subject which Genovese explores in depth and with analytic subtlety. The nature of black American Christianity —autonomous though not independent, subversive though not revolutionary—emerges from Genovese's synthesis, showing how slaves took what was useful and usable and transformed it into something satisfying and vital.

The Gospel in the Quarters

EUGENE D. GENOVESE

Whatever the religion of the masters, the slaves, when given a choice, overwhelmingly preferred the Baptists and secondarily the Methodists. By the 1850s the recruitment of blacks to the Episcopal Church in Virginia had virtually ceased.[1] In the South as a whole the Presbyterians had a small following, especially in the up country, and the Catholics scored some success in Louisiana. Melville J. Herskovits has advanced the provocative thesis that the slaves' preference for the Baptists reflected the continued strength of traditional West African religion. Noting the practice of total immersion, he has suggested a connection in the slaves' mind with the powerful river spirits in the West African religions; in particular, he thinks that enslaved priests from Dahomey must have provided leadership and continuity from Africa to Afro-America.[2] E. Franklin Frazier, who has led the attack on Herskovits's thesis, dismisses the argument on the grounds that enslavement and the slave trade had effectively destroyed the social basis of African religion among the blacks and that Herskovits's speculations hardly constitute evidence. He suggests, instead, that the slaves responded to the fiery style and uninhibited emotionalism of the frontier Baptist and Methodist preachers and that the Baptists had the additional advantage of a loose church structure to accommodate slaves more easily.[3] Although Frazier's views have come under withering fire for their extreme formulation of a break with the African past, he clearly has had the better of this particular argument. Herskovits's insistence on links between West African and Afro-American folk religion has merit, but it simply cannot be stretched to account for the slaves' preference for the Baptists. Arthur Huff Fauset has pointed out that the same blacks who chose the Baptists might have chosen the Methodists, the Baptists' hottest rivals in the plantation districts—and the Methodists'

From *Roll, Jordan, Roll: The World the Slaves Made* by Eugene D. Genovese (New York: Pantheon Books, 1974), pp. 232-55. Copyright © 1972, 1974 by Eugene D. Genovese. Reprinted by permission of Pantheon Books, a division of Random House, Inc.

greatest fun in life was ridiculing total immersion and adult baptism.[4]

Methodism, on the face of it, hardly seems a likely candidate for the affections of a high-spirited, life-loving people. Grim, humorless, breathing the fires of damnation—notwithstanding love feasts and some joyful hymns—it was more calculated to associate Jesus with discipline and order than with love. The slaves adjusted Methodism, as they adjusted every other creed, to their own way of life, and they transformed each in the process, as the ring shout may demonstrate. Once converted, the slaves had to stop dancing, for it was sinful. Dutifully, they stopped going to dances and went to the praise-house instead. What they did there looked like dancing to the white uninitiated and still looks like dancing to those who recognize the origin of the Charleston and several other popular dances. But no: it could not have been dancing. Dancing was sinful, and these slaves had been converted. They were not dancing; they were "shouting." Henry George Spaulding, a white Unitarian minister who visited Port Royal, South Carolina, with the United States Sanitary Commission during the war, left us a description of the ring shout, which he insisted was the "religious dance of the Negroes":

> Three or four, standing still, clapping their hands and beating time with their feet, commence singing in unison one of the peculiar shout melodies, while the others walk around in a ring, in single file, joining also in the song. Soon those in the ring leave off their singing, the others keeping it up the while with increased vigor, and strike into the shout step, observing most accurate time with the music. . . . They will often dance to the same song for twenty or thirty minutes. . . .[5]

Whatever Spaulding thought, the blacks convinced themselves that they did not dance the shout, for as everyone knows, you cross your feet when you dance; and since they did not tolerate crossing of feet, they clearly were not dancing.

The slaves' insistence on shouting harked back to Africa in both form and content. The style, which subsequently came to dominate American popular dancing in a variety of versions, could not have been more clearly African. The same might also be said about the insistence that the community worship God in a way that integrated the various forms of human expression—song, dance, and prayer, all with call-and-response, as parts of a single offering the beauty of which pays homage to God. This idea of beauty as deriving from the whole of human expression rather than from its separate manifestations, or even its artifacts, was not entirely new to the Christian tradition. It had originally been as much a part of Euro-Christian tradition as of African but had been lost during the Middle Ages and especially after the Reformation. Thomas Merton ends his study of the reform of the Roman Catholic liturgy: "One thing that is certain to come out of Africa is the revival of the ancient liturgical art of *the dance*, traditionally a problem to Western Christianity."[6]

The Methodists had in common with the Baptists certain features, beyond those mentioned by Frazier, that did appeal to the slaves. They had retained some interest in ameliorating plantation conditions; their congregations had long been racially mixed and never wholly accepted the white pressures to segregate; and above all, their preachers spoke plainly. Richard Allen, founder of the Bethel African Methodist Episcopal Church of Philadelphia and himself an ex-slave, explained: "I was confident that no religious sect or denomination would suit the capacity of the colored people so well as the Methodists, for the plain simple gospel suits best for any people, for the unlearned can understand, and the learned are sure to understand."[7] But the greatest advantage held by both Baptists and Methodists, with their particular strength in the countryside and in the cities respectively, was that they worked hard to reach the blacks and understood the need to enlist black preachers and "assistants" to work with them. Emotional appeal and organizational flexibility gave the Baptists the edge, but they might have thrown it away had they not undertaken the task of conversion with the vigor they did. The organizational flexibility of the Baptists provided a particularly good opportunity for the retention of magic and folk belief despite the theological strictures against them. Excommunications for backsliding into paganism occurred, but the loose methods of organization made surveillance difficult; and the black preachers found it easy to look the other way without incurring the wrath of a watchful hierarchy.

The Baptists' efforts to proselytize among slaves and their willingness to rely on, or at least not exclude, black preachers did not prove them less racist or more deeply concerned with the secular fate of the blacks than were others. Whatever advantage they may have derived from their early hostility to slavery and later concern with amelioration faded as the several southern churches closed ranks behind the single reform formula of confirming slavery as a normal condition for blacks and urging more humane treatment. During the last three decades of the antebellum period Baptists, Methodists, Presbyterians, and others accelerated, both by design and simply by taking the path of least resistance, the long-developing trend toward racial separation within the churches.[8]

Even during the eighteenth century a double push for separation had been taking place. Hostile whites steadily tried to push the blacks into separate congregations, especially where the black population was substantial, and blacks often moved to facilitate the split, partly because they felt uncomfortable and wished to practice their religion in their own way, and partly because they resented the inferior position into which they were being thrust within the white churches. For the blacks the move to separate was thus both a positive desire for independent cultural expression and a defense against racism.[9]

The rise of the independent black churches in Philadelphia and other cities of both North and South, often under the leadership of strong personalities, did make the task of the white segregationists all the easier.[10] At the same time the trend toward separation affected the plantation belt itself in less dramatic and less formal ways. By the end of the antebellum period most southern blacks who professed Christianity called themselves Baptists, and so they were. But they had become black Baptists—a category increasingly of their own making. The division had fateful consequences. Ulrich Bonnell Phillips clearly saw the negative implications for both black and white, but especially white: "In general, the less the cleavage of creed between master and man, the better for both, since every factor conducing to solidarity of sentiment was of advantage in promoting harmony and progress. When the planter went to sit under his rector while the slave stayed at home to hear an exhorter, just so much was lost in the sense of fellowship."[11] What Phillips did not wish to see was that the consequences for the slaves were not entirely negative, for separation helped them to widen the degree of autonomy they were steadily carving out of their oppressors' regime.[12]

On the plantations and farms the slaves met for services apart from the whites whenever they could. Weekly services on Sunday evenings were common. Where masters were indulgent, additional meetings might take place during the week, and where they were not, they might take place anyway. Masters and overseers often accepted the Sunday meetings but not the others, for the slaves would stay up much of the night praying, singing, and dancing. The next day being a workday, the meetings were bad for business.[13]

The slaves' religious meetings would be held in secret when their masters forbade all such; or when their masters forbade all except Sunday meetings; or when rumors of rebellion or disaffection led even indulgent masters to forbid them so as to protect the people from trigger-happy patrollers; or when the slaves wanted to make sure that no white would hear them. Only during insurrection scares or tense moments occasioned by political turmoil could the laws against such meetings be enforced. Too many planters did not want them enforced. They regarded their slaves as peaceful, respected their religious sensibilities, and considered such interference dangerous to plantation morale and productivity. Others agreed that the slaves presented no threat of rising and did not care about their meetings. Had the slaves been less determined, the regime probably would have been far more stringent; but so long as they avoided conspiracies and accepted harsh punishment as the price for getting caught by patrols, they raised the price of suppression much too high to make it seem worthwhile to planters with steady nerves.[14]

When the meetings had to be held in secret, the slaves confronted a security problem. They would announce the event by such devices as that of singing "Steal Away to Jesus" at work.[15] To protect the meeting itself, they had an infallible method. They would turn over a pot "to catch the sound" and keep it in the cabin or immediate area of the woods. Almost infallible: "Of course, sometimes they might happen to slip up on them on suspicion."[16] George P. Rawick suggests that the practice of turning over a pot probably had African origins, and John F. Szwed links it to rituals designed to sanctify the ground. The slaves' belief in its efficacy gave them additional confidence to brave the risks, and their success in avoiding detection led some whites to think that there might just be something to the pot technique.[17]

The desire of the slaves for religious privacy took a limited as well as a general form. Eliza Frances Andrews went down to the plantation praise-house after dinner one night to hear the slaves sing. "At their 'praise meetings,'" she commented, "they go through all sorts of motions in connection with their songs, but they won't give way to their wildest gesticulations or engage in their sacred dances before white people for fear of being laughed at."[18] But the slaves had no objection to pleasing curious whites when they expected an appreciative response. They took enormous pride in their singing and in the depth of their religious expression. They resisted being laughed at, but they responded to expressions of respect. Gus Feaster, an ex-slave from Union County, South Carolina, proudly told of such instances:

At night when the meeting done busted till next day was when the darkies really did have they freedom of spirit. As the wagon be creeping along in the late hours of moonlight, the darkies would raise a tune. Then the air soon be filled with the sweetest tune as us rid on home and sung all the old hymns that us loved. It was always some big black nigger with a deep bass voice like a frog that'd start up the tune. Then the other mens jine in, followed up by the fine little voices of the gals and the cracked voices of the old womens and the grannies. When us reach near the big house us soften down to a deep hum that the missus like! Sometimes she hist up the window and tell us sing "Swing Low, Sweet Chariot" for her and the visiting guests. That all us want to hear. Us open up, and the niggers near the big house that hadn't been to church would wake up and come out to the cabin door and jine in the refrain. From that we'd swing on into all the old spirituals that us love so well and that us knowed how to sing. Missus often 'low that her darkies could sing with heaven's inspiration.[19]

This pride, this self-respect, this astonishing confidence in their own spiritual quality, explain the slaves' willingness to spend so much of their day of leisure at prayer meetings. Often they would hear the white preacher or the master himself on Sunday morning, but the "real meetin' " and the "real preachin' " came later, among themselves.[20] Richard Carruthers, an ex-slave from Texas, explained another feature of the concern with prayer. "Us niggers," he said, "used to have a prayin' ground down in the hollow and some time we come out of the field, between eleven and twelve at night, scorchin' and burnin' up with nothin' to eat, and we wants to ask the good Lord to have mercy."[21]

The meetings gave the slaves strength derived from direct communion with God and each other. When not monitored, they allowed the message of promised deliverance to be heard. If the slaves had received false information or had been misled by the whites, they provided an opportunity for correction, as when the white preachers led them in prayers for the Confederacy, and their black preachers, in secret session, led them in prayers for the Union.[22] But above all, the meetings provided a sense of autonomy—of constituting not merely a community unto themselves but a community with leaders of their own choice.

The slaves' religious frenzy startled white onlookers, although few ever saw it fully unleashed. The more austere masters tried to curb it but usually had little success. Emoline Glasgow of South Carolina had a Methodist master who took one of his slaves to church and determined to keep him in line by bribery if necessary. He offered to give the slave a new pair of boots if he behaved himself. All went well until about the middle of the service, when the slave let go: "Boots or no boots, I gwine to shout today."[23] The slaves took their letting-go seriously and condemned those who simulated emotion. When the Catholic priests forbade shouting in Louisiana, Catherine Cornelius spoke for the slaves in insisting that "the angels shout in heaven" and in doggedly proclaiming, "The Lawd said you gotta shout if you want to be saved. That's in the Bible." Sincerity meant everything. Emma Fraser, an ex-slave from South Carolina, talked about her singing in church in the way that others talked about shouting. "But ef I sing an' it doan move me any, den dat a sin on de Holy Ghost; I be tell a lie on de Lord."[24] The frenzy, as W. E. B. Du Bois called it, brought the slaves together in a special kind of communion, which brought out the most individual expressions and yet disciplined the collective. The people protected each other against the excesses of their release and encouraged each other to shed inhibitions. Everyone responded according to his own spirit but ended in a spiritual union with everyone else.[25]

Possession appeared much less often among the slaves of the Old South than among those of Saint-Domingue or Brazil, where the practice of Vodûn and the rites of the African cults ran high. Yet ecstatic seizures, however defined, appeared frequently and submit to differing interpretations. Critics have recognized in them a form of hysteria, and Frantz Fanon even speaks of a kind of madness. Roger Bastide has suggested that they are vehicles by which repressed personalities surface in symbolic form. Many anthropologists, however, have remained skeptical of psychoanalytic explanations and have pointed out that no genuine schizophrenic could possibly adjust to the firm system of control that the rituals demand. No matter how wild and disorderly they look to the uninitiated, they are in fact tightly controlled; certain things must be done and others not done. They thus require, according to Alfred Métraux, social, not psychological, explanation. Yet, schizophrenia aside, a psychoanalytic explanation is compatible with a social one. The question may be left for experts, if any. Two things are clear. First, the slaves' wildest emotionalism, even when it passed into actual possession, formed part of a system of collective behavior, which the slaves themselves controlled. The slaves may have been driven wild with ecstasy when dancing during their services, but never so wild that their feet would cross without evoking sharp rebuke. And second, the slaves' behavior brought out a determination to assert their power and the freedom of their spirit, for, as Max Weber says, ecstasy may become an instrument of salvation or self-deification.[26]

If emotional fervor alone had distinguished black religion, the usual interpretations would take on greater credibility—that no great difference existed between the religion of the slaves and that of the lower-class whites who followed the frontier Baptist and Methodist preachers. The frequently heard assertion that the blacks merely copied the whites may be left aside as unworthy of discussion. If one must choose between the two separate tendencies, the view of Dr. Du Bois, according to which the style of the poor whites has been a "plain copy" of the style of the blacks, easily holds the field.[27] White and black responses reinforced each other, as they had to in an interracial setting. Their blending reflected a common frontier Christian character and no doubt contributed something toward bringing together two antagonistic peoples. But there were differences that illuminate the special quality of the black experience.

Neither a common body of belief—to the extent that it was in fact common—nor even common rites could guarantee a common spiritual experience. Rites reflect, and in turn reshape, the communities that practice them. Slaves and poorer rural whites (that is, small farmers and actual "poor whites") brought fundamentally different community settings to their common rites, and they therefore brought fundamentally different spiritual needs, responses, and values.[28] When slaves from small farms shared religious meetings and churchgoing with their white yeomen and poor white neighbors, they no doubt drew closer to their inner experience, but even then some distance was inevitable. For plantation blacks, the distance had to be much greater.

The blacks did not hide their disdain for white shouters, whom they regarded, as Dr. Du Bois did later, as a plain copy of themselves. Even in the early camp meetings the blacks notoriously outshouted the whites and stayed up singing and praying long after the whites had retired. They made up their own hymns, which drew protests from orthodox whites because they were their own and because they came too close to sounding like plantation jubilee melodies.[29] Viewing a meeting in Georgia, which attracted even more blacks than whites, Olmsted observed: "The Negroes kept their place during all the tumult; there may have been a sympathetic groan or exclamation uttered by one or two of them, but generally they expressed only the interest of curiosity. . . . There was generally a self-satisfied smile upon their faces; and I have no doubt they felt they could do it with a great deal more energy and abandon, if they were called upon."[30] Beneath the similarities and differences of style lay a divergence of meanings, including some divergence in the very meaning of God.

The slaves drew their call-and-response pattern from their African heritage, however important the reinforcing elements from the Europeans. Europeans had also used something like a song-style of preaching and responding, which had somewhat different qualities. Blacks and whites in the South performed in distinct ways. The content of the white responses to a preacher—undoubtedly with many exceptions—consisted of "Amens" and the like. The whites cheered their preacher on or let him know they were moved. The preacher needed that response, craved it, even demanded it. But the black preacher had to evoke it, not for his own satisfaction, subjectively important as that may have been, but because without it the service had no relationship to God.[31] This difference in style betrayed a difference in theological tendency. The whites were fundamentalists to the core, the blacks only apparently so. Both preached the Bible in fiery style, but as the Reverend Henry H. Mitchell suggests, the whites were fiery mad, while the blacks were fiery glad.[32] Or as Martin Ruffin, an ex-slave from Texas, said of a black preacher, Sam Jones, he "preached Hell-fire and judgment like the white preachers."[33]

While the religion of the slaves, as everyone saw, exhibited joy much as the religion of their African forebears had, who in his right mind would say the same thing of the religion of the whites? W. J. Cash writes of white southern religion:

What our Southerner required . . . was a faith as simple and emotional as himself. A faith to draw men together in hordes, to terrify them with Apocalyptic rhetoric, to cast them into the pit, rescue them, and at last bring them shouting back into the fold of Grace. . . . The God demanded was an anthropomorphic God—the Jehovah of the Old Testament: a God who might be seen, a God who *had* been seen. A passionate, whimsical tyrant to be trembled before, but whose favor was the sweeter for that. A personal God, a God for the individualist, a God whose representatives were not silken priests but preachers risen from the people themselves.

What was demanded here, in other words, was the God and

the faith of the Methodists and the Baptists and the Presbyterians.[34]

Cash fails to note that the blacks identified with the same churches and turned them into something rather different.

Olmsted's description of that white hellfire preacher in action before a congregation of lower-class whites says a great deal:

> The preliminary devotional exercises—a Scripture reading, singing, and painfully irreverential and meaningless harangues nominally addressed to the Deity, but really to the audience—being concluded, the sermon was commenced by reading a text, with which, however, it had, so far as I could discover, no further association. Without often being violent in his manner, the speaker nearly all the time cried aloud at the utmost stretch of his voice, as if calling to some one a long distance off; . . . and as he was gifted with a strong imagination, and possessed of a good deal of dramatic power, he kept the attention of the people very well. There was no argument upon any point that the congregation were likely to have much difference of opinion upon, nor any special connection between one sentence and another; yet there was a constant, sly, sectarian skirmishing, and a frequently recurring cannonade upon French infidelity and socialism, and several crushing charges upon Fourier, the Pope of Rome, Tom Paine, Voltaire, "Roosu," and Jo Smith. . . . He had the habit of frequently repeating a phrase, or of bringing forward the same idea in a slightly different form, a great many times. The following passage, of which I took notes, presents an example of this, followed by one of the best instances of his dramatic talent that occurred. He was leaning far over the desk, with his arm stretched forward, gesticulating violently, yelling at the highest key, and catching breath with an effort:
>
> "A—ah! why don't you come to Christ? ah! what's the reason? ah! Is it because he was of *lowly birth*? ah! Is that it? *Is it* because he was born in a manger? ah! Is it because he was of a humble origin? ah! Is it because he was lowly born? a-ha! . . . Perhaps you don't like the messenger—is that the reason? I'm the Ambassador of the great and glorious King; it's his invitation, 'taint mine. You mustn't mind me. I ain't no account. Suppose a ragged, insignificant little boy should come running in here and tell you, 'Mister, your house's a-fire!' would you mind the ragged, insignificant little boy, and refuse to listen to him, because he didn't look respectable?"[35]

It is not easy to imagine a black preacher's wanting to know if his slave congregation despised Jesus for being poor and not looking respectable. Time and again, the message of the black preachers turned precisely on the low earthly station of the Son of God.

Dr. Mitchell draws for us a sharp distinction between southern black and white uses of the Bible. "A Black preacher," he notes, "is more likely to say, 'Didn't He say it!' than to be officious about what 'the Word of God declares!'" For the blacks the Bible provides an inexhaustible store of good advice for a proper life; it does not usually provide an unchanging body of doctrine, as with the white fundamentalists. Hence, biblical figures must come alive, must be present, must somehow provide a historical example for modern application. Black religion eschews bibliolatry and does not have a strong anti-intellectual bias.[36] Those who might suspect that Dr. Mitchell is being carried into romantic exaggeration might note that social scientists who have closely studied black religious behavior in the South have unearthed materials that lend firm support to his analysis.[37] At issue, therefore, are the slaves' notions of heaven, hell, sin, and soul.

White Methodist and Baptist preachers ripped each other up in theological debates all over the South and did not let up when singly preaching to the slaves. The slaves turned out to cheer them on. Olmsted, after remarking that Baptist and Methodist preachers spent much of their time denouncing each other's doctrines, added, "The negroes are represented to have a great taste for theological controversy."[38] Eliza Frances Andrews described a Methodist slave in Georgia who had a staunch Baptist master: "They used to have some high old religious discussions together."[39]

The slaves' penchant for theological disputation ought neither to be dismissed as a ridiculous spectacle nor accepted at face value. There is nothing ridiculous in the idea of illiterate field hands' trying to follow an argument about God, for He was ever-present in their lives, even if they did respond more readily to evidence of spiritual motivation in the preacher than they did to his argument. Then too, the white Baptist and Methodist preachers had learned to translate the most difficult points of theology into unadorned English for their frontier congregations. If they could not make themselves understood to the slaves, it was usually for reasons other than their inability to speak plain English. But neither should the slaves' reaction be taken straight, first, because the theological questions that most interested them were of a different order, and second, because they had too high a sense of humor not to respond to a good show when they saw one.

The Baptist churches in the South ran the gamut from Calvinism to Arminianism, but the powerful tendency, especially in the rougher terrain of the Mississippi Valley, took extreme predestinarian ground. Now, Regular Baptists who talk like John Calvin on the fate of man present something of a puzzle. The accepted and plausible, if somewhat impish, explanation is that the free-will polemics of the rough-and-tumble Methodists drove their Baptist adversaries further and further into extreme formulations of their standpoint. So far did one wing go that its famous two-seed doctrine, according to which Eve produced two seeds only one of which originated with God, has quite sensibly been classified by some scholars as thinly disguised Manichaeanism.[40] Yet, predestinarian doctrine did not appear in black religion. In part, the explanation may lie in a greater attention to preaching among the slaves by the free-will Baptists and those who glided over the issue. But the deeper reason must be sought in the slaves' own inclinations. Only rarely did orthodox Calvinism come from the mouths of black preachers, and even in those cases its uses remain in doubt. In 1793, a black preacher upset Harry Toulmin by preaching Calvinist doctrine, but the point he was making in his excellent sermon was the equality of man before God.[41] The slave quarters provided poor ground for predestinarianism. When slaves and ex-slaves insisted that God had foreordained everything, they usually meant that even slavery had an appropriate place in His eternal design. And at that, their reaction could turn bitter. In Wilkinson County, Mississippi, an old slave gravedigger, accompanied by a young helper, asked a white stranger a question:

"Massa, may I ask you something?"
"Ask what you please."
"Can you 'splain how it happened in the fust place, that the white folks got the start of the black folks, so as to make dem slaves and do all de work?"
The younger helper, fearing the white man's wrath, broke in: "Uncle Pete, it's no use talking. It's fo'ordained. The Bible tells you that. The Lord fo'ordained the Nigger to work, and the white man to boss."
"Dat's so. Dat's so. But if dat's so, then God's no fair man!"[42]

Since predestination leaves no room for magic, its attraction for people whose religious sensibility retained the features of folk origin was almost nonexistent. No socially deprived lower class has found it easy to warm to Calvinist theology. As Keith Thomas writes:

The doctrine of providence was always less likely to appeal to those at the bottom end of the social scale than the rival doctrine of luck. For the believer in luck can account for his misfortune without jeopardizing his self-esteem. The concept of luck explains any apparent discrepancy between merit and reward and thus helps to reconcile men to the environment in which they live.[43]

The slaves stayed close to their conjurers, and the preachers who could reach them knew enough not to force the issue.

For the slaves, salvation came through an uneasy combination of free will and faith—faith in God and faith in each other—because faith meant love. An old preacher, who had been a slave in South Carolina, remarked, "Brother, you has to have faith in your fellow man befo' you has faith in de lawd."[44] The spirituals vibrated with the message: God will deliver us if we have faith in Him. And they emphasized the idea of collective deliverance of the slaves as a people by their choice of such heroes as Moses, Jonah, and Daniel.[45] The slaves' attachment to the doctrine of salvation by faith, their ability to turn the most serious matters to good-humored advantage, and their inexhaustible penchant for puttin' on Ole Massa all appeared in an incident described by Olmsted. A formally pious slave was plaguing his master by his persistence in undefined immorality. The master asked a minister to intercede and try to appeal to the slave's religious nature. As Olmsted told it:

The clergyman did so, and endeavored to bring the terrors of the law to bear upon his conscience. "Look yeah, massa," said the backslider, "don't de Scriptur say, 'Dem who believes an' is baptize shall be save'?" "Certainly," the clergyman answered; and went on to explain and expound the passage: but directly the slave interrupted him again.

"Jus you tell me now, massa, don't de good book say dese word: 'Dem as believes and is baptize, shall be save'; want to know dat."

"Yes, but . . ."

"Das all I want to know, sar; wat's de use o' talkin' to me. You ain't a going to make me bleve wat de blessed Lord says, ain't so, not ef you tries forever."

The clergyman again attempted to explain. . . . "De Scriptur say, if a man believe and be baptize he *shall* be save. Now, massa minister, I *done* believe and I *done* baptize, and I *shall be save* suah—Dere's no use talkin', sar."[46]

According to the scriptural defense of slavery, which commanded enormous attention throughout the white South during the forties and fifties, the enslavement of the blacks by the whites fulfilled the biblical curse on Ham, much as for the Russian londlords the curse had fallen on their serfs. Japheth's predicted dwelling in the tents of Shem accounted for the expropriation of the Indians' lands, and the enforced service of blacks to whites took care of the sons of Ham. The suggestion that in time Ethiopia would stretch out her hands to God caused some misgivings, but not many. "Panola," as a planter from Mississippi signed himself in the agricultural journals, nicely took care of any qualms. Was Ethiopia ready to stretch out her hand to God? No. How did he know? "Niggers are too *high* for that."[47] The imagery extended even to militant black sources and appears, for example, although with a quite different meaning, in David Walker's famous *Appeal to the Colored Citizens of the World.*

Despite a few hints to the contrary, the slaves did not view their predicament as punishment for the collective sin of black people. No amount of white propaganda could bring them to accept such an idea. Occasionally, blacks spoke of slavery as a punishment for sin, but even then the precise meaning remained vague. The stark assertion of the white preachers that blacks suffered from the sin of Ham had few if any echoes in the quarters. When Eli Coleman, an ex-slave from Kentucky, spoke of blacks' being under God's curse and therefore in a living hell, he insisted that their great problem was lack of higher vocational and educational skills.[48] Rarely if ever has the transition from John Calvin to Adam Smith been so tightly telescoped. Charity Moore remembered her father's interpretation of the Bible and original sin. The story is charming enough, but its finale demands attention. Adam, it seems, had been so frightened by his sin that he turned white. The rest of the story she "disremembered."[49] Another version, by Ezra Adams, who had been a plowhand on a South Carolina slave plantation, took a plainly secular turn: Adam sinned by taking what did not belong to him. "If what Adam done back yonder," he explained, "would happen now, he would be guilty of crime. Dat's how 'ciety names sin." Thus black preachers invoked parables to demonstrate that God could make good come from evil; that there was good in the most errant brother and sister; and, by implication, that He was bringing good to His enslaved people whose conditions rather than themselves were evil.[50]

For the slaves, sin meant wrongdoing—injustice to others and violation of accepted moral codes. Their otherworldly idea of Heaven shared its place with a this-worldly idea that stressed freedom and a community of love for one's brothers and sisters; little room remained for a theology based on original sin. Hence, black theology largely ignored the one doctrine that might have reconciled the slaves to their bondage on a spiritual plane.

Original sin does not appear in African religions, and the problem of freedom and order therefore assumes radically different forms. Without such a doctrine the delicate balance between the two tips toward the claims of the collective against those of the individual. Much as the doctrine of original sin reflects the class divisions in Western society, whatever its deeper insight into human nature, it also creates greater possibilities for individual freedom, particularly since the cause of individual freedom has historically been inseparable from the use of private property. When the Christian faith took its stand on the doctrine of original sin, it constructed a defense of the individual personality on which the most secularized ideologies of liberalism came to be built. But Christianity's world-shaking achievement also rested on guilt and self-contempt, without which its doctrine of freedom could not have been theologically and socially disciplined. This particular tension between freedom and order provided the driving force of Western culture, as well as the basis for its pessimism.

The African legacy to Afro-America—that celebrated joy in life which is so often denigrated or explained away—represented a life-affirming faith that stressed shame and minimized guilt. Enslavement might be shameful and an expression of weakness, but it could not easily produce a sense of guilt—of getting what you deserved and of being punished for having offended God. Christianity might have transformed the slaves into the slavish robots of Nietzsche's polemic or the Sambos of Stanley Elkins's model, if they had not virtually reshaped it to fit their own psychic needs and their own sensibility.

The ambiguity of the slaves' Heaven and of the limitations on their idea of sin had roots in African ideas of the Soul. Again, it is not possible to know to what extent they stubbornly clung to African ideas and to what extent plantation slave conditions recreated certain patterns of thought. But, clearly, no sharp break occurred. Their life as slaves in the New World, even after conversion to Christianity, did not destroy the traditional sensibility. Newbell Niles Puckett, in his study of folk beliefs among southern blacks during the twentieth century, pointedly insists that their idea of the Soul comes close to traditional African ideas. In some cases he finds "a definite belief in a *kra* or dream-soul," according to which a dream becomes the actual experience of the dreamer's Soul wandering into another world.[51]

A more significant question concerns the relationship of the Soul to the natural order. In the classical Christian tradition man is unique; he alone has a Soul, which establishes his claims to freedom as a matter of responsibility before God. Even in Calvinist theology, in which man's Soul is predestined to salvation or damnation, man himself chose not to obey God in the first place. African ideas place man himself and therefore his Soul within nature. Reincarnation and the return of spirits to the world of the living may occur. Man's Soul is one spirit among many, for all things are infused with spirits. Man himself is one of many material hosts. For traditional Africans, like many non-Christian peoples elsewhere, the Soul came to mean the inner life—the quintessential experience of which matter was merely the form. Thus the Soul, crystallized in a man's shadow, could be detached from his person. Hence, spirits wandered in this world.[52]

The theology of the black preachers made peace with folk ideas of the Soul when it slid over the meaning of Heaven. In so doing, it strengthened the slaves' sense of belonging to the world and of being promised deliverance through faith in Jesus Christ. The compromise was effected on Christian ground, but it necessarily had to reduce that very otherworldliness on which classical Christian individualism in general and antinomianism in particular had arisen. This adjustment entailed sacrifice of considerable revolutionary power.

The idea that the slaves' repeated references to Heaven prove their religious orientation to have been primarily otherworldly rests on a narrow reading of their complex thought. The most obvious function of a concern with Heaven among preachers to the slaves would appear to have been a determination to reconcile them to their lot and turn their attention to an ideal realm. The sermons of black preachers, not to mention white, often centered on this theme. E. S. Abdy heard a slave preacher in Kentucky in 1834 and described him and his performance: "He was about sixty years of age—shrewd and sensible, and, as far as I could judge from some of his observations, a very religious man. What he said upon the duty of submission to his lot here, and his reliance on Divine justice hereafter would have done no discredit to the best educated white."[53] Yet, such messages contain much ambiguity, and so did the very language and delivery of those who spoke them.

Miles Mark Fisher, in a provocative, controversial, but often strained study of the slave songs, vigorously denies that the slaves had any understanding of or interest in the immortality of the Soul. The part of his interpretation that evokes most querulousness is his insistence that Africa played the central role in slave consciousness and that references to Heaven in the spirituals should be understood as meaning Africa or other earthly places of refuge. He does not prove this part of his case, but he does suggest a deep ambiguity in the slaves' apparently otherworldly references.[54]

The slaves' concern with Heaven cannot be interpreted as escapism, especially since, as Howard Thurman and Lawrence Levine point out, a rigid separation of the sacred and the secular had no place in the slaves' view of the world.[55] The several meanings of Heaven in the spirituals must therefore be seen as one—as a necessary and intrinsic ambiguity that reflects a view of the world in which the spiritual and the material merge. No choice need be made between this-worldly and otherworldly interpretations of the song sung by slaves in Mississippi:

> But some ob dese days my time will come,
> I'll year dat bugle, I'll year dat drum,
> I'll see dem armies, marchin' along,
> I'll lif' my head an' jine der song.[56]

Or of "Didn't My Lord Deliver Daniel," or of "Joshua Fit de Battle ob Jericho," or of "Oh, Mary, Don't You Weep," or of "Go Down, Moses." They do not necessarily refer to deliverance in this world or in the other, for they might easily mean either or both. But either way or both ways, they did imply the immanence of God's justice here or hereafter, as He sees fit to bestow it. In this sense, the spirituals were, as Dr. Du Bois himself suggested, "Sorrow Songs" that transcended their sorrow and became hymns of joy.

> Through all the sorrow of the Sorrow Songs there breathes a hope—a faith in the ultimate justice of things. The minor cadences of despair change often to triumph and calm confidence. Sometimes it is faith in life, sometimes a faith in death, sometimes assurances of boundless justice in some fair world beyond. But whichever it is, the meaning is always clear: that sometime, somewhere, men will judge men by their souls and not by their skins.[57]

The slaves' talent for improvisation, as well as their deep religious conviction, drew expressions of wonder and admiration from almost everyone who heard them sing. The boatmen of Georgia and South Carolina and of the Mississippi River received the most attention and drew the most comment, but the common field hands of the Cotton belt did not lag far behind in performance. The words "wild" and "weird" recurred among white observers, from the abolitionists to the slaveholders to the merely curious. Harriet Beecher Stowe heard Sojourner Truth sing "There Is a Holy City" and remarked, "Sojourner, singing this hymn seemed to impersonate the fervor of Ethiopia, wild, savage, hunted of all nations, but burning after God in her tropic heart and stretching her scarred hands towards the glory to be revealed."[58] Eliza Frances Andrews, listening to the slaves on her plantation singing at a praise-meeting, called their songs "mostly a sort of weird chant that makes me feel all out of myself when I hear it way in the night, too far off to catch the words."[59]

Asked how the songs originated, a black man replied:

> I'll tell you; it's dis way. My master call me up and order me a short peck of corn and a hundred lash. My friends see it and is sorry for me. When dey come to de praise meeting dat night dey sing about it. Some's very good singers and know how; and dey work it in, work it in, you know; till dey get it right; and dat's de way.[60]

In 1845, J. Kennard wrote in *Knickerbocker Magazine:*

> Who are the true rulers? The Negro poets to be sure. Do they not set the fashion, and give laws to the public taste? Let one of them, in the swamps of Carolina, compose a new song, and it no sooner reaches the ear of a white amateur, than it is written down, amended (that is, almost spoilt), printed and then put upon a course of rapid dissemination, to cease only with the utmost bounds of Anglo-Saxondom, perhaps with the world. Meanwhile, the poor author digs away with his hoe, utterly ignorant of his greatness.[61]

T. S. Eliot observed:

> When a poet's mind is perfectly equipped for its work, it is constantly amalgamating disparate experience; the ordinary man's experience is chaotic, irregular, fragmentary. The latter falls in love, or reads Spinoza, and these two experiences have nothing to do with each other, or with the noise of the type-

writer or the smell of cooking; in the mind of the poet these experiences are always forming new wholes.[62]

It is doubtful that, by this standard, the world has ever seen so many
poets whose minds were "perfectly equipped" simultaneously at work
to produce so powerful a synthesis of sacred and secular themes.

Alexander K. Farrar, a planter in Adams County, Mississippi, provided an illuminating illustration of the slaves' understanding of
Heaven and its worldly uses. Some slaves had committed murder and
had been sentenced to hang. A public display was in order, he thought,
for too many slaves believed that the punishment for murder would
be transportation, and they had to be disabused. Farrar urged that the
bodies be exhibited to the slaves but strongly opposed a public hanging. "If the Negroes are brought out in public to be hung," he explained, "and they get up and talk out that they have got religion and
are ready to go home to heaven, etc etc.—it will have a bad effect upon
the other Negroes."[63]

In its blandest and most accommodationist forms, the orientation
of oppressed classes toward an afterlife contains important elements
of political judgment that help to counteract the pressures for dehumanization and despair and contribute toward the formation of class
consciousness. If the lower classes cannot claim to be much, the idea
of Heaven, with its equality before God, gives them a strong sense of
what they are destined to become. It thereby introduces a sense of
worth and reduces the stature of the powerful men of the world. The
emphasis on Heaven metamorphoses from the otherworldly into the
inner-worldly and creates its own ground for dissent in this world.[64]
The other side of this lower-class concern with Heaven is its vision of
Hell—the afterlife appropriate to the oppressor. Of the Methodists'
influence on the British working class, E. P. Thompson writes: "Faith
in a life to come served not only as a consolation to the poor but also
as some emotional compensation for present sufferings and grievances:
it was possible not only to imagine the 'reward' of the humble but
also to enjoy some revenge upon their oppressors, by imagining their
torments to come."[65] This sense of a revenge to come always carried
with it the thrust of a political quiescence accompanied by vicarious
thrills. Its positive political significance remained only a tendency. By
sharpening a sense of class justice it prepared the way for explosive
hostility, should circumstances present an opportunity for aggressive
action.

In less dramatic ways, the slaves manipulated the idea of Heaven both defensively and offensively. It could become a vehicle for a sarcastic judgment of the masters, as it did for Andrew Moss of Georgia: "De white folks what owned slaves thought that when dey go to Heaven de colored folks would be dere to wait on 'em."[66] One theme that recurs is love for each other. The slaves viewed Heaven as a place of reconciliation with each other; only sometimes did they view it as a place of reconciliation with whites. Annie Laurie Broiderick, a white woman from a slaveholding family in Vicksburg, Mississippi, recalled the activities of the Methodist slaves. "During their protracted meetings," she wrote, "after becoming pious, they would work themselves into a frenzy, and begin their shouting by walking up to each other, taking and shaking the hand with words, 'I hope to meet you in heaven. . . .' "[67] Anne Bell, an ex-slave from South Carolina, made the same point in her own way: "Does I believe in 'ligion? What else good for colored folks? I ask you if dere ain't a heaven, what's colored folks got to look forward to? They can't git anywhere down here. De only joy they can have here is servin' and lovin'; us can git dat in 'ligion but dere is a limit to de nigger in everything else."[68]

Fanny Kemble's three-year-old daughter confronted the maid: "Mary, some persons are free and some are not." No reply. "I am a free person. I say, I am a free person, Mary—do you know that?" Acknowledgment: "Yes, missus." Relentless child: "Some persons are free and some are not—do you know that, Mary?" Reply: "Yes, missus, *here*; I know it is so here, in this world."[69]

Did the slaves sing of God's Heaven and a life beyond this life? Or of a return to Africa? Or of a Heaven that was anywhere they would be free? Or of an undefined state in which they could love each other without fear? On any given occasion they did any one of these; probably, in most instances they did all at once. Men and women who dare to dream of deliverance from suffering rarely fit their dreams into neat packages.

Black eschatology emerges more clearly from the slaves' treatment of Moses and Jesus. The slaves did not draw a sharp line between them but merged them into the image of a single deliverer, at once this-worldly and otherworldly. Colonel Higginson said that their heads held a jumple of Jewish biblical history and that they associated Moses with all great historical events, including the most recent. After the war black preachers took the political stump to tell the freedmen in South Carolina that the Republican gubernatorial candidate, Franklin J. Moses, was none other than the man himself, who had come to lead them to the Promised Land. All across the South blacks insisted that they had seen Mr. Linkum visit their locality as part of his work of deliverance.

The image of Moses, the this-worldly leader of his people out of bondage, and Jesus, the otherworldly Redeemer, blended into a pervasive theme of deliverance. A former house slave, who considered himself superior to the field hands, admitted praying with them. "Well, yes'm," he explained, "we would pray the Lord to deliver us." Eliza Frances Andrews waxed indignant over the freedmen's adulation for the abolitionist who had come to teach them during the Union occupation. They think he is Jesus Christ, she protested. "Anyhow," she paraphrased them, "he has done more for them than Jesus Christ ever did." The Reverend C. C. Jones observed that the few remaining Muslim slaves on the Georgia coast identified Muhammed with Jesus, and he might have added, therefore with Moses too.[70]

The variety of uses to which the slaves put Moses may be glimpsed in two comments by ex-slaves. Savilla Burrell of South Carolina said:

> Young Marse Sam Still got killed in de Civil War. Old Marse live on. I went to see him in his last days and I set by him and kept de flies off while dere. I see the lines of sorrow had plowed on dat old face and I 'membered he'd been a captain on hoss back in dat war. It come into my 'membrance de song of Moses; "de Lord had triumphed glorily and de hoss and his rider have been throwed into de sea."[71]

And George Briggs, also from South Carolina, himself an old preacher, commented: "Man learns right smart from Exodus 'bout how to lead. . . . Moses still de strongest impression dat we has as rulers. God gits His-self into de heads of men dat He wants to rule and He don't tell nobody else nothing 'bout it neither."[72] The great heroes of the spirituals, even when Jesus' name appears, often turn out to be the deliverers of the people as a whole in this world.[73]

The slaves had a special and central place for Jesus, but a place that whites had difficulty recognizing. Julius Lester has given us, with a few short strokes, a convincing reading. The slaves, he writes, "fashioned their own kind of Christianity, which they turned to for strength in the constant times of need. In the Old Testament story of the enslavement of the Hebrews by the Egyptians, they found their own story. In the figure of Jesus Christ, they found someone who had suffered as they suffered, someone who understood, someone who offered them rest from their suffering."[74] Moses had become Jesus, and Jesus, Moses; and with their union the two aspects of the slaves' religious quest—collective deliverance as a people and redemption from their terrible personal sufferings—had become one through the mediation of that imaginative power so beautifully manifested in the spirituals.

If Jesus had suffered as they had suffered, if He had in fact died to relieve their suffering, He necessarily took on an aspect apart from the Moses figure. "The death of the savior," writes Max Weber, "may be viewed as a means of mollifying the wrath of god, before whom the savior appears as an intercessor for men. . . ."[75] He therefore assumed a double aspect for the slaves, much as Moses did in a somewhat different way. In this sense the slaves were no more "confused" than are those who would accept the Trinity as a single manifestation of a monotheist's God and yet insist on preserving the identities and discrete meanings of the Father, the Son, and the Holy Ghost.

Jesus was closer to them than Moses, as He has so often been to the poor, by virtue of the low earthly station the Son of God chose as His own. In the words of G. G. Coulton:

> Gibbon sneers at Tertullian's boast that a Christian mechanic could give an answer to problems which had puzzled the wisest heads of antiquity. But is not Gibbon's criticism a dangerous half-truth? From a wider point of view, must we not count it a real step forward in civilization that the artisan should seriously attempt to answer these questions at all? Christianity certainly brought in a new spirit; and the spirit is all-important. The belief in a crucified carpenter—the conviction that the highest triumph may be gotten of the completest earthly failure—did, as a matter of fact, take more men out of themselves, and took them further out of themselves than anything else since the dawn of history.[76]

Appropriately, Christianity spread across the Mediterranean basin, not as a religion of slaves, but primarily as a religion of artisans. In time, the Roman ruling class did everything in its power to impose it on the slaves in order to reconcile them to their lot and point them toward otherworldly concerns. When the black slaves of the New World made it their own, they transformed it into a religion of resistance—not often of revolutionary defiance, but of a spiritual resistance that accepted the limits of the politically possible. Paul Radin observes that whereas the whites asked Jesus for forgiveness, the blacks primarily asked for recognition.[77] The slaves' assimilation of Moses to Jesus represented a vital mechanism for that transformation.

However politically radical the historical Jesus may have been and however subversive some may wish to understand the New Testament as being, Christian revolutionaries have always had a hard time explaining away the Epistles of Paul and too much else. Sooner or later, usually sooner, they have summoned the God of Wrath of the Old Testament. For black slaves who were determined to resist the powers that be and yet powerless to defy them openly, who looked longingly toward delivery from bondage and yet had little thirst or opportunity for vengeance, who sought spiritual redemption in Heaven and yet could not ignore their need for bodily redemption in this world, the assimilation of Moses to Jesus provided the way to reconcile all contradictions. Moses, once become Jesus, had his dangerous message muted, and the gloomy implications of the forty years in the wilderness could be forgotten. Jesus, once become Moses, underwent a transubstantiation that carried with it the promise of this-worldly salvation without suicidal adventures. The assimilation solved the problem of how to achieve spiritual freedom, retain faith in earthly deliverance, instill a spirit of pride and love in each other, and make peace with a political reality within which revolutionary solutions no longer had much prospect.

It bridged another painful gap as well. At the risk of oversimplification, the God of the Old Testament may be taken as a national deity—Lord of the Chosen People and God of Wrath—and the God of the New Testament may be taken as the first projected Lord of the entire human community and a God of Love. Then the slaves' "confusion" appears as a necessary, if not firmly consistent, response to their objective position in white America. It allowed them to preserve, in muted form, a sense of being God's special children and yet allowed them to accept, or at least not deny, the whites, whose lives were so intimately bound up with their own as brothers in Christ. An ex-slave said, "The love of God is beyond understanding. It makes you love everybody."[78] For people who, even as slaves, were creating an incipient nation within a nation, it would be difficult to imagine a more satisfactory solution.

NOTES

1. Scarborough, ed., *Diary of Edmund Ruffin*, Feb. 20, 1859, (I, 284).
2. Herskovits, *Myth of the Negro Past*, pp. 232-234.
3. The ultimate complexity of the problem is suggested by the parallel suc-

cess of fundamentalist sects among colonial peoples. See Worsley, *Trumpet Shall Sound*, p. 235.

4. Arthur Huff Fauset, *Black Gods of the Metropolis: Negro Religious Cults of the Urban North* (Philadelphia, 1971), pp. 101-102.

5. Henry George Spaulding, "Negro 'Shouts' and Shout Songs," in Bernard Katz, ed., *The Social Implications of Early Negro Music in the United States* (New York, 1969), pp. 4-5. Also G. G. Johnson, *Social History of the Sea Islands*, pp. 150-151; James Weldon Johnson, *The Book of American Negro Spirituals* (New York, 1925), pp. 33-34; Courlander, *Negro Folk Music*, pp. 194-195; Kiser, *Sea Island to City*, p. 79.

6. Thomas Merton, *Seasons of Celebration: Meditations on the Cycle of Liturgical Feasts* (New York, 1965), p. 248. The place of the dance in the Afro-American cult known as Voodoo is discussed by John Q. Anderson, "The New Orleans Voodoo Ritual Dance and Its Twentieth Century Survivals," *Southern Folklore Quarterly* (Dec., 1960), 135-143.

7. Richard Allen, quoted in Eileen Southern, *The Music of Black Americans: A History* (New York, 1971), p. 87.

8. In North Carolina the Methodists worked harder than the Baptists among the slaves and recruited more widely. See Bassett, *Slavery in the State of North Carolina*, Ch. 3. Also J. M. King, *South Carolina Baptists*, pp. 127-129; Parkinson, "Religious Instruction of Slaves," unpubl. M.A. thesis, University of North Carolina, 1948, p. 52; Everett Dick, *The Dixie Frontier: A Social History of the Southern Frontier from the First Transmontane Beginnings to the Civil War* (New York, 1964), p. 188; Posey, *Baptist Church in the Lower Mississippi Valley*, pp. 89-93; Quarles, *Negro in the Making of America*, p. 58; and in general, Carter G. Woodson, *The History of the Negro Church* (Washington, D.C., 1921).

9. R. B. Semple, *History of the Rise and Progress of the Baptists in Virginia* (Richmond, Va., 1810), p. 101; Robert, *Road from Monticello*, p. 7; C. P. Patterson, *Negro in Tennessee*, p. 20; J. G. Taylor, *Negro Slavery in Louisiana*, p. 138; William L. Richter, "Slavery in Ante-bellum Baton Rouge, 1820–1860," LH, X (Spring, 1969), 125-146; Swint, ed., *Dear Ones at Home*, p. 125; Gaston Hugh Wamble, "Negroes and Missouri Protestant Churches Before and After the Civil War," Mo.H.R., LXI (April, 1967), 321-347. The experience in Canada is instructive, for there too blacks established their own churches; see Robin W. Winks, *The Blacks in Canada: A History* (New Haven, Conn., 1971), pp. 53, 71. For some interesting reflections by white ministers on the question of racial separation, see Whitefoord Smith, Memorandum, July 18, 1849; also July 23, 1849; Hanson Diary, March 30, 1860.

10. Wade, *Slavery in the Cities*, pp. 83, 161-162, 167-168; also Benjamin Elizah Mays and Joseph William Nicholson, *The Negro's Church* (New York, 1969), p. 3; Benjamin Elizah Mays, *The Negro's God as Reflected in His Literature* (New York, 1969), pp. 30-65; Walter H. Brooks, "Evolution of the Negro Baptist Church," JNH, VII (Jan., 1922), 11-22; Christopher Rush, *A Short History of the Rise and Progress of the African Episcopal Church in America* (New York, 1843), esp. pp. 18, 60-61, 91, for efforts in the North and relations with white churches.

11. Phillips, *American Negro Slavery*, p. 321; cf. C. C. Jones, *Religious Instruction*, pp. 90-91.

12. See E. U. Essien-Udom, *Black Nationalism: A Search for an Identity in America* (New York, 1964), pp. 31, 37-38.

13. Olmsted, *Back Country*, p. 93.

14. South Carolina had as good a police system as any and also a no-nonsense tradition in matters of social control, yet the laws were enforced only during times of stress. See Henry, *Police Control of the Slave*, pp. 133-141.

15. Rawick, ed., *Texas Narr.*, V (4), 198.

16. Fisk University, *Unwritten History of Slavery*, p. 87.

17. Rawick, *Sundown to Sunup* pp. 41 ff.; John F. Szwed in personal correspondence. Also, Rawick, ed., *Indiana Narr.*, VI (2), 98.

18. E. F. Andrews, *War-Time Journal of a Georgia Girl*, Feb. 12, 1865 (p. 89).

19. Botkin, ed., *Lay My Burden Down*, p. 146.

20. Yetman, ed., *Life Under the "Peculiar Institution,"* p. 13 (testimony of Lucretia Alexander of Arkansas).

21. *Ibid.*, p. 53.

22. Rawick, ed., *Texas Narr.*, IV (1), 11; *Ark. Narr.*, IX (4), 254; *Mo. Narr.*, XI, 305.

23. Rawick, ed., *S.C. Narr.*, II (2), 135.

24. Saxon *et al.*, *Gumbo Ya-Ya*, p. 242; Rawick, ed., *S.C. Narr.* II (2), 87.

25. Some elite house slaves, free Negroes, and urban slaves—by no means all and probably not the majority—were quite uncomfortable in these circumstances and preferred to pray in the "white" manner. See, e.g., Mary Sharpe to C. C. Jones, June 2, 1856, in Myers, ed., *Children of Pride*; Mrs. Smith Journal, 1793, p. 22; Olmsted, *Seaboard*, p. 405.

26. Max Weber, *The Sociology of Religion* (trans. Ephraim Fischoffs; Boston, 1964), p. 157. On spirit possession in Brazil see Warren, "The Negro and Religion in Brazil," *Race*, VI (Jan., 1965), esp. p. 201; in Haiti, Métraux, *Voodoo in Haiti*, pp. 120-122; also Roger Bastide, *Sociologie et psychoanalyse* (Paris, 1950), p. 252; H. U. Beier, "The Egungen Cult Among the Yorubas," *Présence Africaine*, Nos. 17-18 (Feb.–May, 1958), pp. 33-36; Georges Balandier, *Ambiguous Africa: Cultures in Collision* (trans. Helen Weaver; New York, 1965), pp. 46-47; Worsley, *Trumpet Shall Sound*, p. 61; Norbeck, *Religion in Primitive Society*, pp. 99, 100.

27. Du Bois, *Souls of Black Folk*, p. 142.

28. See the illuminating discussion by Evans-Pritchard, *Theories of Primitive Religion*, p. 46, and his analysis of Radin's views on p. 247.

29. For a good summary discussion see Southern, *Music of Black Americans*, p. 96.

30. Olmsted, *Seaboard*, p. 460.

31. On the African origins of the call-and-response pattern in the spirituals see esp. Alan Lomax, "The Homogeneity of African–Afro-American Musical Style," in Norman E. Whitten and John F. Szwed, eds., *Afro-American Anthropology: Contemporary Perspectives on Theory and Research* (New York, 1970), Ch. 9, and his other stimulating writings. Also John W. Work, *American Negro Songs and Spirituals* (New York, 1940), p. 9; John J. Szwed, "Afro-American Musical Adaptation," *Journal of American Folklore* (Mar., 1969), 219-228; Charles W. Joyner, *Folk Song in South Carolina* (Columbia, S.C.,

1971), pp. 6, 71; and the general discussion of slave songs, stories, and folk-lore in Blassingame, *Slave Community*, Ch. 1 and pp. 57 ff. The Rev. Henry H. Mitchell has pointed out that shouting and the like among lower-class southern whites and Pentecostals provide an important link between the white and black variants of Christianity and ought to be valued as such; see *Black Preaching* (Philadelpphia, 1970), p. 101.

32. Mitchell, *Black Preaching*, p. 50.
33. Rawick, ed., *Texas Narr.*, V (3), 266.
34. Cash, *Mind of the South*, p. 58.
35. Olmsted, *Seaboard*, pp. 455-457.
36. Mitchell, *Black Preaching*, pp. 49-50, 101, 112-113, 133.
37. See, e.g., Puckett, *Folk Beliefs*, p. 535; Powdermaker, *After Freedom*, pp. 246, 260-261.
38. Olmsted, *Seaboard*, p. 123.
39. E. F. Andrews, *War-Time Journal of a Georgia Girl*, June 28, 1865 (p. 321).
40. Posey, *Baptist Church in the Lower Mississippi Valley*, pp. 70-71.
41. Toulmin, *Western Country in 1793*, p. 30.
42. See, e.g., Keckley, *Behind the Scenes*, p. xii, for a combination of these tendencies. The graveyard incident is from Sydnor, *Slavery in Mississippi*, pp. 251-252.
43. K. Thomas, *Religion and the Decline of Magic*, p. 111.
44. Rawick, ed., *S.C. Narr.*, II (1), 93.
45. See the perceptive analysis of Lawrence Levine, "Slave Songs and Slave Consciousness," in Hareven, ed., *Anonymous Americans*, pp. 118-121. For the continued strength of this doctrine see St. Clair Drake and Horace R. Cayton, *Black Metropolis: A Study of Negro Life in a Northern City* (2 vols.; New York, 1962), II, 615-616; Raymond Julius Jones, *A Comparative Study of Religious Cult Behavior Among Negroes, with Special Reference to Emotional Group Conditioning Factors* (Washington, D.C., n.d.).
46. Olmsted, *Seaboard*, pp. 123-124.
47. For an account of the polemic over the meaning of the curse in relation to the condition of Africa, see Eugene D. Genovese, "A Georgia Slaveholder Looks at Africa," *GHQ*, LI (June, 1967), 189.
48. Rawick, ed., *Texas Narr.*, IV (1), 239; also *Ala. Narr.*, VI (1), 5, 336.
49. Rawick, ed., *S.C. Narr.*, III (3), 205-207.
50. *Ibid.*, II (1), 7. For the good-from-evil preaching see J. G. Williams, *"De Ole Plantation"* (Charleston, S.C., 1895), p. 12; Rawick, ed., *Ga. Narr.*, XII (1), 296.
51. Puckett, *Folk Beliefs*, p. 110; cf. K. A. Busia, "The Ashanti," in Forde, ed., *African Worlds*, p. 197; Eva L. R. Meyerowitz, "Concepts of the Soul Among the Akan of the Gold Coast," *Africa*, XXI (Jan., 1951), 24-31.
52. See Clifford Geertz, *The Religion of Java* (New York, 1960), p. 232; Paulson, *Old Estonian Folk Religion*, pp. 22, 166; Mbiti, *African Religions and Philosophy*, Chs. 5-6.
53. Abdy, *Journal of Residence and Tour*, II, 292.
54. Miles Mark Fisher, *Negro Slave Songs in the United States* (Ithaca, N.Y., 1953), pp. 71-72; also pp. 137, 146, 156. The conversion account in Fisk

University, *God Struck Me Dead*, p. 84, would appear to support Dr. Fisher's interpretation. We may recall that many recent black movements deny or minimize an afterlife; see Essien-Udom, *Black Nationalism*, pp. 153 ff., 251; and Cleage, *Black Messiah*.

55. Howard Thurman, *The Negro Spiritual Speaks of Life and Death* (New York, 1947), pp. 17, 27-28, 38, 51; Levine, "Slave Songs and Slave Consciousness," p. 114. Also Mbiti, *African Religions and Philosophy*, p. 4 and Ch. 14.

56. Wharton, *Negro in Mississippi*, p. 20.

57. Du Bois, *Souls of Black Folk*, p. 189; also *The Gift of Black Folk: The Negroes in the Making of America* (New York, 1970), Ch. 7; Mays, *Negro's God*, p. 21. Geroid Tanquary Robinson has cited the Russian peasants' songs of resistance and compared them to the spirituals; see *Rural Russia Under the Old Regime*, p. 48.

58. Harriett Beecher Stowe, quoted in Charles H. Nichols, *Many Thousand Gone: The Ex-slaves' Account of Their Bondage and Their Freedom* (Leiden, 1963), pp. 99.

59. E. F. Andrews, *War-Time Journal of a Georgia Girl*, Feb. 12, 1865 (p. 91). See also the reaction in *Journal of Charlotte Forten*, p. 203.

60. James Miller McKim, "Negro Songs," in Katz, ed., *Social Implications of Early Negro Music*, p. 2. See also Alvan Sanborn, ed., *Reminiscences of Richard Lathers* (New York, 1907), p. 5; Trollope, *Domestic Manners of the Americans*, p. 299.

61. J. Kennard, quoted in Southern, *Music of Black Americans*, p. 103.

62. T. S. Eliot, "The Metaphysical Poets," *Selected Essays* (London, 1936), pp. 286-287.

63. Alexander K. Farrar to W. B. Foules, Dec. 6, 1857, in the Farrar Papers.

64. See the stimulating discussion by Weber, *Sociology of Religion*, pp. 106-108.

65. E. P. Thompson, *Making of the English Working Class*, p. 34.

66. Yetman, ed., *Life Under the "Peculiar Institution,"* p. 232.

67. Broidrick, "A Recollection of Thirty Years Ago" (ms.); cf. Hatcher, *John Jasper*, p. 177.

68. Rawick, ed., *S.C. Narr.*, II (1), 53-54.

69. Kemble, *Journal*, p. 22.

70. Higginson, *Army Life*, p. 27; Rawick, ed., *S.C. Narr.*, III (4), 159; Botkin, ed., *Lay My Burden Down*, pp. 16 ff.; Fisk University, *Unwritten History of Slavery*, p. 112; E. F. Andrews, *War-Time Journal of a Georgia Girl* (July 21, 1865), p. 339; C. C. Jones, *Religious Instruction*, p. 26. For an alternative interpretation of Jesus, as well as of the other theological questions discussed in this section, see James H. Cone, *The Spirituals and the Blues* (New York, 1972).

71. Rawick, ed., *S.C. Narr.*, II (1), 151.

72. *Iibid.*, II (1), 91, also p. 151.

73. See the analysis of Levine, "Slave Songs and Slave Consciousness," p. 121; see also Fisher, *Negro Slave Songs*, for a different interpretation that is nonetheless compatible with Levine's.

74. Lester, *To Be a Slave*, p. 79. As Powdermaker says, the slaves, deprived

of their African history, seized the biblical history of the Jews and made it their own; *After Freedom*, pp. 231-232.

75. Weber, *Sociology of Religion*, p. 185.

76. G. G. Coulton, *Ten Medieval Studies* (Cambridge, 1930), pp. 190-191.

77. See Paul Radin's introduction to Fisk University, *God Struck Me Dead*, p. viii.

78. Fisk University, *God Struck Me Dead*, p. 61.

• Because written records do not often bring us accurately into the world of the slave cabins, historians have begun to exploit a variety of nonliterary sources that do. Such tools, according to Orlando Patterson, are "material remains, Afro-American Creole languages and oral traditions, including transcribed folk tales, folk songs, and the like." Examining one of the most important of the slaves' means of expression, the folk song, Lawrence Levine finds a sense of African identity and a considerable artistic achievement, both unlikely attributes of a defeated, childlike people. The songs, in fact, often provided an "acceptable outlet for complaints about slavery and hopes for freedom." Slaveholders often boasted of the singing of their property. Clearly, they enjoyed it far more than they understood it.

Slave Songs and Slave Consciousness

LAWRENCE W. LEVINE

Negroes in the United States, both during and after slavery, were anything but inarticulate. They sang songs, told stories, played verbal
games, listened and responded to sermons, and expressed their aspirations, fears, and values through the medium of an oral tradition that
had characterized the West African cultures from which their ancestors had come. By largely ignoring this tradition, much of which has
been preserved, historians have rendered an articulate people historically inarticulate, and have allowed the record of their consciousness to
go unexplored.

Having worked my way carefully through thousands of Negro songs,
folktales, jokes, and games, I am painfully aware of the problems inherent in the use of such materials. They are difficult, often impossible, to date with any precision. Their geographical distribution is usually unclear. They were collected belatedly, most frequently by men
and women who had little understanding of the culture from which
they sprang, and little scruple about altering or suppressing them. Such
major collectors as John Lomax, Howard Odum, and Newman White
all admitted openly that many of the songs they collected were "un-
printable" by the moral standards which guided them and presumably
their readers. But historians have overcome imperfect records before.
They have learned how to deal with altered documents, with consciously or unconsciously biased firsthand accounts, with manuscript
collections that were deposited in archives only after being filtered
through the overprotective hands of fearful relatives, and with the
comparative lack of contemporary sources and the need to use their
materials retrospectively. The challenge presented by the materials of
folk and popular culture is neither totally unique nor insurmountable.

In this essay I want to illustrate the possible use of materials of this
kind by discussing the contribution that an understanding of Negro

songs can make to the recent debate over slave personality. In the process I will discuss several aspects of the literature and problems related to the use of slave songs.

The subject of Negro music in slavery has produced a large and varied literature, little of which has been devoted to questions of meaning and function. The one major exception is Miles Mark Fisher's 1953 study, *Negro Slave Songs in the United States*, which attempts to get at the essence of slave life through an analysis of slave songs. Unfortunately, Fisher's rich insights are too often marred by his rather loose scholarly standards, and despite its continuing value his study is in many respects an example of how *not* to use Negro songs. Asserting, correctly, that the words of slave songs "show both accidental and intentional errors of transmission," Fisher changes the words almost at will to fit his own image of their pristine form. Arguing persuasively that "transplanted Negroes continued to promote their own culture by music," Fisher makes their songs part of an "African cult" which he simply wills into existence. Maintaining (again, I think, correctly), that "slave songs preserved in joyful strains the adjustment which Negroes made to their living conditions within the United States," Fisher traces the major patterns of that adjustment by arbitrarily dating these songs, apparently unperturbed by the almost total lack of evidence pertaining to the origin and introduction of individual slave songs.[1]

Fisher aside, most other major studies of slave music have focused almost entirely upon musical structure and origin. This latter question especially has given rise to a long and heated debate.[2] The earliest collectors and students of slave music were impressed by how different that music was from anything familiar to them. Following a visit to the Sea Islands in 1862, Lucy McKim despaired of being able "to express the entire character of these negro ballads by mere musical notes and signs. The odd turns made in the throat; and that curious rhythmic effect produced by single voices chiming in at different irregular intervals, seem almost as impossible to place on score, as the singing of birds, or the tones of an Aeolian Harp."[3] Although some of these early collectors maintained, as did W. F. Allen in 1865, that much of the slave's music "might no doubt be traced to tunes which they have heard from the whites, and transformed to their own use, . . . their music . . . is rather European than African in its character,"[4] they more often stressed the distinctiveness of the Negro's music and attributed it to racial characteristics, African origins, and indigenous developments resulting from the slave's unique experience in the New World.

This tradition, which has had many influential twentieth-century adherents,[5] was increasingly challenged in the early decades of this century. Such scholars as Newman White, Guy Johnson, and George Pullen Jackson argued that the earlier school lacked a comparative grounding in Anglo-American folk song. Comparing Negro spirituals with Methodist and Baptist evangelical religious music of the late eighteenth and early nineteenth centuries, White, Johnson, and Jackson found similarities in words, subject matter, tunes, and musical structure.[6] Although they tended to exaggerate both qualitatively and quantitively the degrees of similarity, their comparisons were often a persuasive and important corrective to the work of their predecessors. But their studies were inevitably weakened by their ethnocentric assumption that similarities alone settled the argument over origins. Never could they contemplate the possibility that the direction of cultural diffusion might have been from black to white as well as the other way. In fact, insofar as white evangelical music departed from traditional Protestant hymnology and embodied or approached the complex rhythmic structure, the percussive qualities, the polymeter, the syncopation, the emphasis on overlapping call and response patterns that characterized Negro music both in West Africa and the New World, the possibility that it was influenced by slaves who attended and joined in the singing at religious meetings is quite high.

These scholars tended to use the similarities between black and white religious music to deny the significance of slave songs in still another way. Newman White, for example, argued that since white evangelical hymns also used such expressions as "freedom," the "Promised Land," and the "Egyptian Bondage," "without thought of other than spiritual meaning," these images when they occurred in Negro spirituals could not have been symbolic "of the Negro's longing for physical freedom."[7] The familiar process by which different cultural groups can derive varied meanings from identical images is enough to cast doubt on the logic of White's argument.[8] In the case of white and black religious music, however, the problem may be much less complex, since it is quite possible that the similar images in the songs of both groups in fact served similar purposes. Many of those whites who flocked to the camp meetings of the Methodists and Baptists were themselves on the social and economic margins of their society, and had psychic and emotional needs which, qualitatively, may not have been vastly different from those of black slaves. Interestingly, George Pullen Jackson, in his attempt to prove the white origin of Negro spirituals, makes exactly this point:

"I may mention in closing the chief remaining argument of the die-hards for the Negro source of the Negro spirituals. . . . How could any, the argument runs, but a natively musical and sorely oppressed race create such beautiful things as 'Swing Low,' 'Steal Away,' and 'Deep River'? . . . But were not the whites of the mountains and the hard-scrabble hill country also 'musical and oppressed'? . . . Yes, these whites were musical, and oppressed too. If their condition was any more tolerable than that of the Negroes, one certainly does not get that impression from any of their songs of release and escape."[9]

If this is true, the presence of similar images in white music would merely heighten rather than detract from the significance of these images in Negro songs. Clearly, the function and meaning of white religious music during the late eighteenth and early nineteenth centuries demands far more attention than it has received. In the interim, we must be wary of allowing the mere fact of similarities to deter us from attempting to comprehend the cultural dynamics of slave music.

Contemporary scholars, tending to transcend the more simplistic lines of the old debate, have focused upon the process of syncretism to explain the development of Negro music in the United States. The rich West African musical tradition common to almost all of the specific cultures from which Negro slaves came, the comparative cultural isolation in which large numbers of slaves lived, the tolerance and even encouragement which their white masters accorded to their musical activities, and the fact that, for all its differences, nothing in the European musical tradition with which they came into contact in America was totally alien to their own traditions—all these were conducive to a situation which allowed the slaves to retain a good deal of the integrity of their own musical heritage while fusing to it compatible elements of Anglo-American music. Slaves often took over entire white hymns and folk songs, as White and Jackson maintained, but altered them significantly in terms of words, musical structure, and especially performance before making them their own. The result was a hybrid with a strong African base.[10]

One of the more interesting aspects of this debate over origins is that no one engaged in it, not even advocates of the white derivation theory, denied that the slaves possessed their own distinctive music. Newman White took particular pains to point out again and again that the notion that Negro song is purely an imitation of the white man's music "is fully as unjust and inaccurate, in the final analysis, as the

Negro's assumption that his folk-song is entirely original." He observed that in the slaves' separate religious meetings they were free to do as they would with the music they first learned from the whites, with the result that their spirituals became "the greatest single outlet for the expression of the Negro folk-mind."[11] Similarly, George Pullen Jackson, after admitting that he could find no white parallels for over two-thirds of the existing Negro spirituals, reasoned that these were produced by Negro singers in true folk fashion "by endless singing of heard tunes and by endless, inevitable and concomitant singing differentiation." Going even further, Jackson asserted that the lack of deep roots in Anglo-American culture left the black man "even freer than the white man to make songs over unconsciously as he sang . . . the free play has resulted in the very large number of songs which, though formed primarily in the white man's moulds, have lost all recognizable relationship to known individual white-sung melodic entities."[12] This debate over origins indicates clearly that a belief in the direct continuity of African musical traditions or in the process of syncretism is not a necessary prerequisite to the conclusion that the Negro slaves' music was their own, regardless of where they received the components out of which it was fashioned; a conclusion which is crucial to any attempt to utilize these songs as an aid in reconstructing the slaves' consciousness.

Equally important is the process by which slave songs were created and transmitted. When James McKim asked a freedman on the Sea Islands during the Civil War where the slaves got their songs, the answer was eloquently simple: "Dey make em, sah."[13] Precisely *how* they made them worried and fascinated Thomas Wentworth Higginson, who became familiar with slave music through the singing of the black Union soldiers in his Civil War regiment. Were their songs, he wondered, a "conscious and definite" product of "some leading mind," or did they grow "by gradual accretion, in an almost unconscious way"? A freedman rowing Higginson and some of his troops between the Sea Islands helped to resolve the problem when he described a spiritual which he had a hand in creating:

> Once we boys went for some rice and de nigger-driver he keep a-callin' on us; and I say, "O de ole nigger-driver!" Den anudder said, "Fust ting my mammy tole me was, notin' so bad as nigger-driver." Den I made a sing, just puttin' a word, and den anudder word.

He then began to sing his song:

> O, de ole nigger-driver!
> O, gwine away!
> Fust ting my mammy tell me,
> O, gwine away!
>
> Tell me 'bout de nigger-driver,
> O, gwine away!
> Nigger-driver second devil,
> O, gwine away!

Higginson's black soldiers, after a moment's hesitation, joined in the singing of a song they had never heard before as if they had long been familiar with it. "I saw," Higginson concluded, "how easily a new 'sing' took root among them."[14]

This spontaneity, this sense of almost instantaneous community which so impressed Higginson, constitutes a central element in every account of slave singing. The English musician Henry Russell, who lived in the United States in the 1830's, was forcibly struck by the ease with which a slave congregation in Vicksburg, Mississippi, took a "fine old psalm tune" and, by suddenly and spontaneously accelerating the tempo, transformed it "into a kind of negro melody."[15] "Us old heads," an ex-slave told Jeanette Robinson Murphy, "use ter make 'em up on de spurn of de moment. Notes is good enough for you people, but us likes a mixtery." Her account of the creation of a spiritual is typical and important:

> We'd all be at the "prayer house" de Lord's day, and de white preacher he'd splain de word and read whar Esekial done say—
>
> Dry bones gwine ter lib ergin.
>
> And, honey, de Lord would come a-shinin' thoo dem pages and revive dis ole nigger's heart, and I'd jump up dar and den and holler and shout and sing and pat, and dey would all cotch de words and I'd sing it to some ole shout song I'd heard 'em sing from Africa, and dey'd all take it up and keep at it, and keep a-addin' to it, and den it would be a spiritual.[16]

This "internal" account has been verified again and again by the descriptions of observers, many of whom were witnessing not slave services but religious meetings of rural southern Negroes long after emancipation. The essential continuity of the Negro folk process in the more isolated sections of the rural South through the early decades of the twentieth century makes these accounts relevant for the slave period as well. Natalie Curtis Burlin, whose collection of spirituals is musically the most accurate one we have, and who had a long and close acquaintance with Negro music, never lost her sense of awe at the process by which these songs were molded. On a hot July Sunday in rural Virginia, she sat in a Negro meeting house listening to the preacher deliver his prayer, interrupted now and then by an "O Lord!" or "Amen, Amen" from the congregation.

> Minutes passed, long minutes of strange intensity. The mutterings, the ejaculations, grew louder, more dramatic, till suddenly I felt the creative thrill dart through the people like an electric vibration, that same half-audible hum arose,—emotion was gathering atmospherically as clouds gather—and then, up from the depths of some "sinner's" remorse and imploring came a pitiful little plea, a real "moan," sobbed in musical cadence. From somewhere in that bowed gathering another voice improvised a response: the plea sounded again, louder this time and more impassioned; then other voices joined in the answer, shaping it into a musical phrase; and so, before our ears, as one might say, from this molten metal of music a new song was smithied out, composed then and there by no one in particular and by everyone in general.[17]

Clifton Furness has given us an even more graphic description. During a visit to an isolated South Carolina plantation in 1926, he attended a prayer meeting held in the old slave cabins. The preacher began his reading of the Scriptures slowly, then increased his tempo and emotional fervor, assuring his flock that "Gawd's lightnin' gwine strike! Gawd's thunder swaller de ert!"

> Gradually moaning became audible in the shadowy corners where the women sat. Some patted their bundled babies in time to the flow of the words, and began swaying backward and forward. Several men moved their feet alternately, in strange syncopation. A rhythm was born, almost without reference to the words that were being spoken by the preacher. It seemed to take shape almost visibly, and grow. I was gripped with the feeling of a mass-intelligence, a self-conscious entity, gradually informing the crowd and taking possession of every mind there, including my own.

In the midst of this increasing intensity, a black man sitting directly in front of Furness, his head bowed, his body swaying, his feet patting up and down, suddenly cried out: "Git right—sodger! Git right—sodger! Git right—wit Gawd!"

> Instantly the crowd took it up, moulding a melody out of half-formed familiar phrases based upon a spiritual tune, hummed here and there among the crowd. A distinct melodic outline became more and more prominent, shaping itself around the central theme of the words, "Git right, sodger!"
> Scraps of other words and tunes were flung into the medley of sound by individual singers from time to time, but the general trend was carried on by a deep undercurrent, which appeared to be stronger than the mind of any individual present, for it bore the mass of improvised harmony and rhythms into the most effective climax of incremental repetition that I have ever heard. I felt as if some conscious plan or purpose were carrying us along, call it mob-mind, communal composition, or what you will.[18]

Shortly after the Civil War, Elizabeth Kilham witnessed a similar scene among the freedmen, and described it in terms almost identical to those used by observers many years later. "A fog seemed to fill the church," she wrote, ". . . an invisible power seemed to hold us in its iron grasp; . . . A few moments more, and I think we should have shrieked in unison with the crowd."[19]

These accounts and others like them make it clear that spirituals both during and after slavery were the product of an improvisational communal consciousness. They were not, as some observers thought, totally new creations, but were forged out of many preexisting bits of old songs mixed together with snatches of new tunes and lyrics and fit into a fairly traditional but never wholly static metrical pattern. They were, to answer Higginson's question, *simultaneously* the result of individual and mass creativity. They were products of that folk process which has been called "communal re-creation," through which older songs are constantly recreated into essentially new entities.[20] Anyone who has read through large numbers of Negro songs is familiar with this process. Identical or slightly varied stanzas appear in song after song; identical tunes are made to accommodate completely different sets of lyrics; the same song appears in different collections in widely varied forms. In 1845 a traveler observed that the only permanent elements in Negro song were the music and the chorus. "The blacks themselves leave out old stanzas, and introduce new ones at pleasure. Travelling through the South, you may, in passing from Virginia to

Louisiana, hear the same tune a hundred times, but seldom the same words accompanying it."[21] Another observer noted in 1870 that during a single religious meeting the freedmen would often sing the words of one spiritual to several different tunes, and then take a tune that particularly pleased them and fit the words of several different songs to it.[22] Slave songs, then, were never static; at no time did Negroes create a "final" version of any spiritual. Always the community felt free to alter and recreate them.

The two facts that I have attempted to establish thus far—that slave music, regardless of its origins, was a distinctive cultural form, and that it was created or constantly recreated through a communal process—are essential if one is to justify the use of these songs as keys to slave consciousness. But these facts in themselves say a good deal about the nature and quality of slave life and personality. That black slaves could create and continually recreate songs marked by the poetic beauty, the emotional intensity, the rich imagery which characterized the spirituals —songs which even one of the most devout proponents of the white man's origins school admits are "the most impressive religious folk songs in our language"[23]—should be enough to make us seriously question recent theories which conceive of slavery as a closed system which destroyed the vitality of the Negro and left him a dependent child. For all of its horrors, slavery was never so complete a system of psychic assault that it prevented the slaves from carving out independent cultural forms. It never pervaded all of the interstices of their minds and their culture, and in those gaps they were able to create an independent art form and a distinctive voice. If North American slavery eroded the African's linguistic and institutional life, if it prevented him from preserving and developing his rich heritage of graphic and plastic art, it nevertheless allowed him to continue and to develop the patterns of verbal art which were so central to his past culture. Historians have not yet come to terms with what the continuance of the oral tradition meant to blacks in slavery.

In Africa, songs, tales, proverbs, and verbal games served the dual function of not only preserving communal values and solidarity, but also of providing occasions for the individual to transcend, at least symbolically, the inevitable restrictions of his environment and his society by permitting him to express deeply held feelings which he ordinarily was not allowed to verbalize. Among the Ashanti and the Dahomeans, for example, periods were set aside when the inhabitants were encouraged to gather together and, through the medium of song, dance, and

tales, to openly express their feelings about each other. The psychological release this afforded seems to have been well understood. "You
know that everyone has a *sunsum* (soul) that may get hurt or knocked
about or become sick, and so make the body ill," an Ashanti high
priest explained to the English anthropologist R. S. Rattray:

> Very often . . . ill health is caused by the evil and the hate that
> another has in his head against you. Again, you too may have
> hatred in your head against another, because of something that
> person has done to you, and that, too, causes your *sunsum* to fret
> and become sick. Our forbears knew this to be the case, and so
> they ordained a time, once every year, when every man and
> woman, free man and slave, should have freedom to speak out
> just what was in their head, to tell their neighbours just what
> they thought of them, and of their actions, and not only their
> neighbours, but also the king or chief. When a man has spoken
> freely thus, he will feel his *sunsum* cool and quieted, and the
> *sunsum* of the other person against whom he has now openly
> spoken will be quieted also.

Utilization of verbal art for this purpose was widespread throughout
Africa, and was not confined to those ceremonial occasions when one
could directly state one's feelings. Through innuendo, metaphor, and
circumlocution, Africans could utilize their songs as outlets for individual release without disturbing communal solidarity.[24]

There is abundant internal evidence that the verbal art of the slaves
in the United States served many of these traditional functions. Just
as the process by which the spirituals were created allowed for simultaneous individual and communal creativity, so their very structure
provided simultaneous outlets for individual and communal expression.
The overriding antiphonal structure of the spirituals—the call and response pattern which Negroes brought with them from Africa and
which was reinforced by the relatively similar white practice of "lining
out" hymns—placed the individual in continual dialogue with his community, allowing him at one and the same time to preserve his voice as
a distinct entity and to blend it with those of his fellows. Here again
slave music confronts us with evidence which indicates that however
seriously the slave system may have diminished the strong sense of
community that had bound Africans together, it never totally destroyed it or left the individual atomized and emotionally and psychi-
cally defenseless before his white masters. In fact, the form and structure of slave music presented the slave with a potential outlet for his

individual feelings even while it continually drew him back into the communal presence and permitted him the comfort of basking in the warmth of the shared assumptions of those around him.

Those "shared assumptions" can be further examined by an analysis of the content of slave songs. Our preoccupation in recent years with the degree to which the slaves actually resembled the "Sambo" image held by their white masters has obscured the fact that the slaves developed images of their own which must be consulted and studied before any discussion of slave personality can be meaningful. The image of the trickster, who through cunning and unscrupulousness prevails over his more powerful antagonists, pervades slave tales. The trickster figure is rarely encountered in the slave's religious songs, though its presence is sometimes felt in the slave's many allusions to his narrow escapes from the devil.

> *The Devil's mad and I'm glad,*
> *He lost the soul he thought he had.*[25]

> *Ole Satan toss a ball at me.*
> *O me no weary yet . . .*

> *Him tink de ball would hit my soul.*
> *O me no weary yet . . .*

> *De ball for hell and I for heaven.*
> *O me no weary yet . . .*[26]

> *Ole Satan thought he had a mighty aim;*
> *He missed my soul and caught my sins.*
> *Cry Amen, cry Amen, cry Amen to God!*

> *He took my sins upon his back;*
> *Went muttering and grumbling down to hell.*
> *Cry Amen, cry Amen, cry Amen to God!*[27]

The single most persistent image the slave songs contain, however, is that of the chosen people. The vast majority of the spirituals identify the singers as "de people dat is born of God," "We are the people of God," "we are de people of de Lord," "I really do believe I'm a child of God," "I'm a child ob God, wid my soul sot free," "I'm born of God, I know I am." Nor is there ever any doubt that "To the promised land I'm bound to go," "I walk de heavenly road," "Heav'n shall-a be my home," "I gwine to meet my Saviour," "I seek my Lord and I find Him," "I'll hear the trumpet sound/In that morning."[28]

The force of this image cannot be diminished by the observation that similar images were present in the religious singing of white evangelical churches during the first half of the nineteenth century. White Americans could be expected to sing of triumph and salvation, given their long-standing heritage of the idea of a chosen people which was reinforced in this era by the belief in inevitable progress and manifest destiny, the spread-eagle oratory, the bombastic folklore, and, paradoxically, the deep insecurities concomitant with the tasks of taming a continent and developing an identity. But for this same message to be expressed by Negro slaves who were told endlessly that they were members of the lowliest of races *is* significant. It offers an insight into the kinds of barriers the slaves had available to them against the internalization of the stereotyped images their masters held and attempted consciously and unconsciously to foist upon them.

The question of the chosen people image leads directly into the larger problem of what role religion played in the songs of the slave. Writing in 1862, James McKim noted that the songs of the Sea Island freedmen "are all religious, barcaroles and all. I speak without exception. So far as I heard or was told of their singing, it was all religious." Others who worked with recently emancipated slaves recorded the same experience, and Colonel Higginson reported that he rarely heard his troops sing a profane or vulgar song. With a few exceptions, "all had a religious motive."[29] In spite of this testimony, there can be little doubt that the slaves sang nonreligious songs. In 1774, an English visitor to the United States, after his first encounter with slave music, wrote in his journal: "In their songs they generally relate the usage they have received from their Masters or Mistresses in a very satirical stile and manner."[30] Songs fitting this description can be found in the nineteenth-century narratives of fugitive slaves. Harriet Jacobs recorded that during the Christmas season the slaves would ridicule stingy whites by singing:

> Poor Massa, so dey say;
> Down in de heel, so dey say;
> Got no money, so dey say;
> God A'mighty bress you, so dey say.[31]

"Once in a while among a mass of nonsense and wild frolic," Frederick Douglass noted, "a sharp hit was given to the meanness of slaveholders."

> *We raise de wheat,*
> *Dey gib us de corn;*
> *We bake de bread,*
> *Dey gib us de crust;*
> *We sif de meal,*
> *Dey gib us de huss;*
> *We peal de meat,*
> *Dey gib us de skin;*
> *And dat's de way*
> *Dey take us in;*
> *We skim de pot,*
> *Dey gib us de liquor,*
> *And say dat's good enough for nigger.*[32]

Both of these songs are in the African tradition of utilizing song to by-pass both internal and external censors and give vent to feelings which could be expressed in no other form. Nonreligious songs were not limited to the slave's relations with his masters, however, as these rowing songs, collected by contemporary white observers, indicate:

> *We are going down to Georgia, boys,*
> *Aye, aye.*
> *To see the pretty girls, boys,*
> *Yoe, yoe.*
> *We'll give 'em a pint of brandy, boys,*
> *Aye, aye.*
> *And a hearty kiss, besides, boys,*
> *Yoe, yoe.*[33]

> *Jenny shake her toe at me,*
> *Jenny gone away;*
> *Jenny shake her toe at me,*
> *Jenny gone away.*
> *Hurrah! Miss Susy, oh!*
> *Jenny gone away;*
> *Hurrah! Miss Susy, oh!*
> *Jenny gone away.*[34]

The variety of nonreligious songs in the slave's repertory was wide. There were songs of in-group and out-group satire, songs of nostalgia, nonsense songs, songs of play and work and love. Nevertheless, our total stock of these songs is very small. It is possible to add to these by incorporating such post-bellum secular songs which have an authentic slavery ring to them as "De Blue-Tail Fly," with its ill-concealed satisfaction at the death of a master, or the ubiquitous

My ole Mistiss promise me,
W'en she died, she'd set me free,
She lived so long dat 'er head got bal',
An' she give out'n de notion a dyin' at all.[35]

The number can be further expanded by following Constance Rourke's suggestion that we attempt to disentangle elements of Negro origin from those of white creation in the "Ethiopian melodies" of the white minstrel shows, many of which were similar to the songs I have just quoted.[36] Either of these possibilities, however, forces the historian to work with sources far more potentially spurious than those with which he normally is comfortable.

Spirituals, on the other hand, for all the problems associated with their being filtered through white hands before they were published, and despite the many errors in transcription that inevitably occurred, constitute a much more satisfactory source. They were collected by the hundreds directly from slaves and freedmen during the Civil War and the decades immediately following, and although they came from widely different geographical areas they share a common structure and content, which seems to have been characteristic of Negro music wherever slavery existed in the United States. It is possible that we have a greater number of religious than nonreligious songs because slaves were more willing to sing these ostensibly innocent songs to white collectors who in turn were more anxious to record them, since they fit easily with their positive and negative images of the Negro. But I would argue that the vast preponderance of spirituals over any other sort of slave music, rather than being merely the result of accident or error, is instead an accurate reflection of slave culture during the ante-bellum period. Whatever songs the slaves may have sung before their wholesale conversion to Christianity in the late eighteenth and early nineteenth centuries, by the latter century spirituals were quantitatively and qualitatively their most significant musical creation. In this form of expression slaves found a medium which resembled in many important ways the world view they had brought with them from Africa, and afforded them the possibility of both adapting to and transcending their situation.

It is significant that the most common form of slave music we know of is sacred song. I use the term "sacred" not in its present usage as something antithetical to the secular world; neither the slaves nor their African forebears ever drew modernity's clear line between the sacred and the secular. The uses to which spirituals were put are an unmistakable indication of this. They were not sung solely or even primarily in churches or praise houses, but were used as rowing songs, field songs, work songs, and social songs. On the Sea Islands during the Civil War, Lucy McKim heard the spiritual "Poor Rosy" sung in a wide variety of contexts and tempos.

> On the water, the oars dip "Poor Rosy" to an even andante; a stout boy and girl at the hominy-mill will make the same "Poor Rosy" fly, to keep up with the whirling stone; and in the evening, after the day's work is done, "Heab'n shall-a be my home" [the final line of each stanza] peals up slowly and mournfully from the distant quarters.[37]

For the slaves, then, songs of God and the mythic heroes of their religion were not confined to any specific time or place, but were appropriate to almost every situation. It is in this sense that I use the concept sacred—not to signify a rejection of the present world but to describe the process of incorporating within this world all the elements of the divine. The religious historian Mircea Eliade, whose definition of sacred has shaped my own, has maintained that for men in traditional societies religion is a means of extending the world spatially upward so that communication with the other world becomes ritually possible, and extending it temporally backward so that the paradigmatic acts of the gods and mythical ancestors can be continually re-enacted and indefinitely recoverable. By creating sacred time and space, man can perpetually live in the presence of his gods, can hold on to the certainty that within one's own lifetime "rebirth" is continually possible, and can impose order on the chaos of the universe. "Life," as Eliade puts it, "is lived on a twofold plane; it takes its course as human existence and, at the same time, shares in a trans-human life, that of the cosmos or the gods."[38]

This notion of sacredness gets at the essence of the spirituals, and through them at the essence of the slave's world view. Denied the possibility of achieving an adjustment to the external world of the antebellum South which involved meaningful forms of personal integration, attainment of status, and feelings of individual worth that all human beings crave and need, the slaves created a new world by transcending the narrow confines of the one in which they were forced to live. They extended the boundaries of their restrictive universe backward until it fused with the world of the Old Testament, and upward until it became one with the world beyond. The spirituals are the record of a people who found the status, the harmony, the values, the order they needed to survive by internally creating an expanded universe, by literally willing themselves reborn. In this respect I agree with the anthropologist Paul Radin that

> The ante-bellum Negro was not converted to God. He converted God to himself. In the Christian God he found a fixed point and he needed a fixed point, for both within and outside of himself, he could see only vacillation and endless shifting. . . . There was no other safety for people faced on all sides by doubt and the threat of personal disintegration, by the thwarting of instincts and the annihilation of values.[39]

The confinement of much of the slave's new world to dreams and fantasies does not free us from the historical obligation of examining its contours, weighing its implications for the development of the slave's psychic and emotional structure, and eschewing the kind of facile reasoning that leads Professor Elkins to imply that, since the slaves had no alternatives open to them, their fantasy life was "limited to catfish and watermelons."[40] Their spirituals indicate clearly that there *were* alternatives open to them—alternatives which they themselves fashioned out of the fusion of their African heritage and their new religion—and that their fantasy life was so rich and so important to them that it demands understanding if we are even to begin to comprehend their inner world.

The God the slaves sang of was neither remote nor abstract, but as intimate, personal, and immediate as the gods of Africa had been. "O when I talk I talk wid God," "Mass Jesus is my bosom friend," "I'm goin' to walk with [talk with, live with, see] King Jesus by myself, by myself," were refrains that echoed through the spirituals.[41]

> *In de mornin' when I rise,*
>   *Tell my Jesus huddy [howdy] oh,*
> *I wash my hands in de mornin' glory,*
>   *Tell my Jesus huddy oh.*[42]

> *Gwine to argue wid de Father and chatter wid de son,*
> *The last trumpet shall sound, I'll be there.*
> *Gwine talk 'bout de bright world dey des' come from.*
> *The last trumpet shall sound, I'll be there.*[43]

> *Gwine to write to Massa Jesus,*
> *To send some Valiant soldier*
> *To turn back Pharaoh's army, Hallelu!*[44]

The heroes of the Scriptures—"Sister Mary," "Brudder Jonah," "Brudder Moses," "Brudder Daniel"—were greeted with similar intimacy and immediacy. In the world of the spirituals, it was not the masters and mistresses but God and Jesus and the entire pantheon of Old Testament figures who set the standards, established the precedents, and defined the values; who, in short, constituted the "significant others." The world described by the slave songs was a black world in which no reference was ever made to any white contemporaries. The salve's positive reference group was composed entirely of his own peers: his mother, father, sister, brother, uncles, aunts, preacher, fellow "sinners" and "mourners" of whom he sang endlessly, to whom he sent messages via the dying, and with whom he was reunited joyfully in the next world.

The same sense of sacred time and space which shaped the slave's portraits of his gods and heroes also made his visions of the past and future immediate and compelling. Descriptions of the Crucifixion communicate a sense of the actual presence of the singers: "Dey pierced Him in the side . . . Dey nail Him to de cross . . . Dey rivet His feet . . . Dey hanged him high . . . Dey stretch Him wide. . . ."

Oh sometimes it causes me to tremble,–tremble,–tremble,
Were you there when they crucified my Lord?[45]

The Slave's "shout"—that counterclockwise, shuffling dance which frequently occurred after the religious service and lasted long into the night—often became a medium through which the ecstatic dancers were transformed into actual participants in historic actions: Joshua's army marching around the walls of Jericho, the children of Israel following Moses out of Egypt.[46]

The thin line between time dimensions is nowhere better illustrated than in the slave's visions of the future, which were, of course, a direct negation of his present. Among the most striking spirituals are those which pile detail upon detail in describing the Day of Judgment: "You'll see de world on fire . . . see de element a meltin', . . . see the stars a fallin' . . . see the moon a bleedin' . . . see the forked lightning, . . . Hear the rumblin' thunder . . . see the righteous marching, . . . see my Jesus coming . . . ," and the world to come where "Dere's no sun to burn you . . . no hard trials . . . no whips a crackin' . . . no stormy weather . . . no tribulation . . . no evildoers . . . All is gladness in de Kingdom."[47] This vividness was matched by the slave's certainty that he would partake of the triumph of judgment and the joys of the new world:

> Dere's room enough, room enough, room enough in de heaven,
>   my Lord
> Room enough, room enough, I can't stay behind.[48]

Continually, the slaves sang of reaching out beyond the world that confined them, of seeing Jesus "in de wilderness," of praying "in de lonesome valley," of breathing in the freedom of the mountain peaks:

> Did yo' ever
> Stan' on mountun,
> Wash yo' han's
> In a cloud?[49]

Continually, they held out the possibility of imminent rebirth; "I look at de worl' an' de worl' look new, . . . I look at my hands an' they look so too . . . I looked at my feet, my feet was too."[50]

These possibilities, these certainties were not surprising. The religious revivals which swept large numbers of slaves into the Christian fold in the late eighteenth and early nineteenth centuries were based upon a *practical* (not necessarily theological) Armianism: God would save all who believed in Him; Salvation was there for all to take hold of if they would. The effects of this message upon the slaves who were exposed to and converted by it have been passed over too easily by historians. Those effects are illustrated graphically in the spirituals which were the products of these revivals and which continued to spread the evangelical word long after the revivals had passed into history.

The religious music of the slaves is almost devoid of feelings of depravity or unworthiness, but is rather, as I have tried to show, pervaded by a sense of change, transcendence, ultimate justice, and personal worth. The spirituals have been referred to as "sorrow songs," and in some respects they were. The slaves sang of "rollin' thro' an unfriendly world," of being "a-trouble in de mind," of living in a world which was a "howling wilderness," "a hell to me," of feeling like a "motherless child," "a po' little orphan chile in de worl'," a "home-e-less child," of fearing that "Trouble will bury me down.' "[51]

But these feelings were rarely pervasive or permanent; almost always they were overshadowed by a triumphant note of affirmation. Even so despairing a wail as "Nobody Knows the Trouble I've Had" could suddenly have its mood transformed by lines like: "One morning I was a-walking down, . . . Saw some berries a-hanging down, . . . I pick de berry and I suck de juice, . . . Just as sweet as de honey in de comb."[52] Similarly, amid the deep sorrow of "Sometimes I feel like a Motherless chile," sudden release could come with the lines: "Sometimes I feel like/A eagle in de air. . . . Spread my wings an/Fly, fly, fly."[53] Slaves spent little time singing of the horrors of hell or damnation. Their songs of the Devil, quoted earlier, pictured a harsh but almost semicomic figure (often, one suspects, a surrogate for the white man), over whom they triumphed with reassuring regularity. For all their inevitable sadness, slave songs were characterized more by a feeling of confidence than of despair. There was confidence that contemporary power relationships were not immutable: "Did not old Pharaoh get lost, get lost, get lost, . . . get lost in the Red Sea?"; confidence in the possibilities of instantaneous change: "Jesus make de dumb to speak. . . . Jesus make de cripple walk. . . . Jesus give de blind his sight. . . . Jesus do most anything"; confidence in the rewards of persistence: "Keep a' inching along like a poor inch-worm,/ Jesus will come by'nd bye"; confidence that nothing could stand in the way of the justice they would receive: "You kin hender me here, but you can't do it dah," "O no man, no man, no man can hinder me"; confidence in the prospects of the future: "We'll walk de golden streets/Of de New Jerusalem." Religion, the slaves sang, "is good for anything, . . . Religion make you happy, . . . Religion gib me patience . . . O member, get Religion . . . Religion is so sweet."[54]

The slaves often pursued the "sweetness" of their religion in the face of many obstacles. Becky Ilsey, who was 16 when she was emancipated, recalled many years later:

> 'Fo' de war when we'd have a meetin' at night, wuz mos' always 'way in de woods or de bushes some whar so de white folks couldn't hear, an' when dey'd sing a spiritual an' de spirit 'gin to shout some de elders would go 'mongst de folks an' put dey han' over dey mouf an' some times put a clof in dey mouf an' say: "Spirit don talk so loud or de patterol break us up." You know dey had white patterols what went 'roun' at night to see de niggers didn't cut up no devilment, an' den de meetin' would break up an' some would go to one house an' some to er nudder an' dey would groan er w'ile, den go home.[55]

Elizabeth Ross Hite testified that although she and her fellow slaves on a Louisiana plantation were Catholics, "lots didn't like that 'ligion."

We used to hide behind some bricks and hold church ourselves.
You see the Catholic preachers from France wouldn't let us
shout, and the Lawd done said you gotta shout if you want to be
saved. That's in the Bible.

Sometimes we held church all night long, 'til way in the
mornin'. We burned some grease in a can for the preacher to see
the Bible by. . . .

See, our master didn't like us to have much 'ligion, said it
made us lag in our work. He jest wanted us to be Catholicses
on Sunday and go to mass and not study 'bout nothin' like that
on week days. He didn't want us shoutin' and moanin' all day'-
long, but you gotta shout and you gotta moan if you wants to be
saved.[56]

The slaves clearly craved the affirmation and promise of their religion. It would be a mistake, however, to see this urge as exclusively
otherworldly. When Thomas Wentworth Higginson observed that the
spirituals exhibited "nothing but patience for this life,—nothing but
triumph in the next," he, and later observers who elaborated upon this
judgment, were indulging in hyperbole. Although Jesus was ubiquitous in the spirituals, it was not invariably the Jesus of the New Testament of whom the slaves sang, but frequently a Jesus transformed into
an Old Testament warrior: "Mass' Jesus" who engaged in personal
combat with the Devil; "King Jesus" seated on a milk-white horse with
sword and shield in hand. "Ride on, King Jesus," "Ride on, conquer-
ing King," "The God I serve is a man of war," the slaves sang.[57] This
transformation of Jesus is symptomatic of the slaves' selectivity in
choosing those parts of the Bible which were to serve as the basis of
their religious consciousness. Howard Thurman, a Negro minister
who as a boy had the duty of reading the Bible to his grandmother,
was perplexed by her refusal to allow him to read from the Epistles of
Paul.

When at length I asked the reason, she told me that during the
days of slavery, the minister (white) on the plantation was always preaching from the Pauline letters—"Slaves, be obedient to
your masters," etc. "I vowed to myself," she said, "that if freedom ever came and I learned to read, I would never read that
part of the Bible!"[58]

Nor, apparently, did this part of the Scriptures ever constitute a
vital element in slave songs or sermons. The emphasis of the spirituals,
as Higginson himself noted, was upon the Old Testament and the ex-

ploits of the Hebrew children.[59] It is important that Daniel and David and Joshua and Jonah and Moses and Noah, all of whom fill the lines of the spirituals, were delivered in *this* world and delivered in ways which struck the imagination of the slaves. Over and over their songs dwelt upon the spectacle of the Red Sea opening to allow the Hebrew slaves past before inundating the mighty armies of the Pharaoh. They lingered delightedly upon the image of little David humbling the great Goliath with a stone—a pretechnological victory which post-bellum Negroes were to expand upon in their songs of John Henry. They retold in endless variation the stories of the blind and humbled Samson bringing down the mansions of his conquerors; of the ridiculed Noah patiently building the ark which would deliver him from the doom of a mocking world; of the timid Jonah attaining freedom from his confinement through faith. The similarity of these tales to the situation of the slave was too clear for him not to see it; too clear for us to believe that the songs had no worldly content for the black man in bondage. "O my Lord delivered Daniel," the slaves observed, and responded logically: "O why not deliver me, too?"

> *He delivered Daniel from de lion's den,*
> *Jonah from de belly ob de whale,*
> *And de Hebrew children from de fiery furnace,*
> *And why not every man?*[60]

These lines state as clearly as anything can the manner in which the sacred world of the slaves was able to fuse the precedents of the past, the conditions of the present, and the promise of the future into one connected reality. In this respect there was always a latent and symbolic element of protest in the slave's religious songs which frequently became overt and explicit. Frederick Douglass asserted that for him and many of his fellow slaves the song, "O Canaan, sweet Canaan,/I am bound for the land of Canaan," symbolized "something more than a hope of reaching heaven. We meant to reach the *North*, and the North was our Canaan," and he wrote that the lines of another spiritual, "Run to Jesus, shun the danger,/I don't expect to stay much longer here," had a double meaning which first suggested to him the thought of escaping from slavery.[61] Similarly, when the black troops in Higginson's regiment sang:

> *We'll soon be free, [three times]*
> *When de Lord will call us home.*

a young drummer boy explained to him, "Dey think *de Lord* mean for say *de Yankees*."[62] Nor is there any reason to doubt that slaves could have used their songs as a means of secret communication. An ex-slave told Lydia Parrish that when he and his fellow slaves "suspicioned" that one of their number was telling tales to the driver, they would sing lines like the following while working in the field:

> O Judyas he wuz a 'ceitful man
> He went an' betray a mos' innocen' man.
> Fo' thirty pieces a silver dat it wuz done
> He went in de woods an' e' self he hung.[63]

And it is possible, as many writers have argued, that such spirituals as the commonly heard "Steal away, steal away, steal away to Jesus!" were used as explicit calls to secret meetings.

But it is not necessary to invest the spirituals with a secular function only at the price of divesting them of their religious content, as Miles Mark Fisher has done.[64] While we may make such clear-cut distinctions, I have tried to show that the slaves did not. For them religion never constituted a simple escape from this world, because their conception of the world was more expansive than modern man's. Nowhere is this better illustrated than during the Civil War itself. While the war gave rise to such new spirituals as "Before I'd be a slave/I'd be buried in my grave,/And go home to my Lord and be saved!" or the popular "Many thousand Go," with its jubilant rejection of all the facets of slave life—"No more peck o' corn for me, . . . No more driver's lash for me, . . . No more pint o' salt for me, . . . No more hundred lash for me, . . . No more mistress' call for me"[65]—the important thing was not that large numbers of slaves now could create new songs which openly expressed their views of slavery; that was to be expected. More significant was the ease with which their old songs fit their new situation. With so much of their inspiration drawn from the events of the Old Testament and the Book of Revelation, the slaves had long sung of wars, of battles, of the Army of the Lord, of Soldiers of the Cross, of trumpets summoning the faithful, of vanquishing the hosts of evil. These songs especially were, as Higginson put it, "available for camp purposes with very little strain upon their symbolism." "We'll cross de mighty river," his troops sang while marching or rowing,

> We'll cross de danger water, . . .
> O Pharaoh's army drownded!
> My army cross over.

"O blow your trumpet, Gabriel," they sang,

> *Blow your trumpet louder;*
> *And I want dat trumpet to blow me home*
> *To my new Jerusalem.*

But they also found their less overtly militant songs quite as appropriate to warfare. Their most popular and effective marching song was:

> *Jesus call you, Go in de wilderness,*
> *Go in de wilderness, go in de wilderness,*
> *Jesus call you. Go in de wilderness*
> *To wait upon de Lord.*[66]

Black Union soldiers found it no more incongruous to accompany their fight for freedom with the sacred songs of their bondage than they had found it inappropriate as slaves to sing their spirituals while picking cotton or shucking corn. Their religious songs, like their religion itself, was of this world as well as the next.

Slave songs by themselves, of course, do not present us with a definitive key to the life and mind of the slave. They have to be seen within the context of the slave's situation and examined alongside such other cultural materials as folk tales. But slave songs do indicate the need to rethink a number of assumptions that have shaped recent interpretations of slavery, such as the assumption that because slavery eroded the linguistic and institutional side of African life it wiped out almost all the more fundamental aspects of African culture. Culture, certainly, is more than merely the sum total of institutions and language. It is also expressed by something less tangible, which the anthropologist Robert Redfield has called "style of life." Peoples as different as the Lapp and the Bedouin, Redfield has argued, with diverse languages, religions, customs, and institutions, may still share an emphasis on certain virtues and ideals, certain manners of independence and hospitality, general ways of looking upon the world, which give them a similar life style.[67] This argument applies to the West African cultures from which the slaves came. Though they varied widely in language, institutions, gods, and familial patterns, they shared a fundamental outlook toward the past, present, and future and common means of cultural expression which could well have constituted the basis of a sense of community and identity capable of surviving the impact of slavery.

Slave songs present us with abundant evidence that in the structure of their music and dance, in the uses to which music was put, in the survival of the oral tradition, in the retention of such practices as spirit possession which often accompanied the creation of spirituals, and in the ways in which the slaves expressed their new religion, important elements of their shared African heritage remained alive not just as quaint cultural vestiges but as vitally creative elements of slave culture. This could never have happened if slavery was, as Professor Elkins maintains, a system which so completely closed in around the slave, so totally penetrated his personality structure as to infantalize him and reduce him to a kind of *tabula rasa* upon which the white man could write what he chose.[68]

Slave songs provide us with the beginnings of a very different kind of hypothesis: that the preliterate, premodern Africans, with their sacred world view, were so imperfectly acculturated into the secular American society into which they were thrust, were so completely denied access to the ideology and dreams which formed the core of the consciousness of other Americans, that they were forced to fall back upon the only cultural frames of reference that made any sense to them and gave them any feeling of security. I use the word "forced" advisedly. Even if the slaves had had the opportunity to enter fully into the life of the larger society, they might still have chosen to retain and perpetuate certain elements of their African heritage. But the point is that they really had no choice. True acculturation was denied to most slaves. The alternatives were either to remain in a state of cultural limbo, divested of the old cultural patterns but not allowed to adopt those of their new homeland—which in the long run is no alternative at all—or to cling to as many as possible of the old ways of thinking and acting. The slaves' oral tradition, their music, and their religious outlook served this latter function and constituted a cultural refuge at least potentially capable of protecting their personalities from some of the worst ravages of the slave system.

The argument of Professors Tannenbaum and Elkins that the Protestant churches in the United States did not act as a buffer between the slave and his master is persuasive enough, but it betrays a modern preoccupation with purely institutional arrangements.[69] Religion is more than an institution, and because Protestant churches failed to protect the slave's inner being from the incursions of the slave system, it does not follow that the spiritual message of Protestantism failed as well. Slave songs are a testament to the ways in which Christianity provided slaves with the precedents, heroes, and future promise that allowed them to transcend the purely temporal bonds of the Peculiar Institution.

Historians have frequently failed to perceive the full importance of this because they have not taken the slave's religiosity seriously enough. A people cannot create a music as forceful and striking as slave music out of a mere uninternalized anodyne. Those who have argued that Negroes did not oppose slavery in any meaningful way are writing from a modern, political context. What they really mean is that the slaves found no *political* means to oppose slavery. But slaves, to borrow Professor Hobsbawm's term, were prepolitical beings in a prepolitical situation.[70] Within their frame of reference there were other—and from the point of view of personality development, not necessarily less effective—means of escape and opposition. If mid-twentieth-century historians have difficulty perceiving the sacred universe created by slaves as a serious alternative to the societal system created by southern slaveholders, the problem may be the historians' and not the slaves'.

Above all, the study of slave songs forces the historian to move out of his own culture, in which music plays a peripheral role, and offers him the opportunity to understand the ways in which black slaves were able to perpetuate much of the centrality and functional importance that music had for their African ancestors. In the concluding lines of his perceptive study of primitive song, C. M. Bowra has written:

> Primitive song is indispensable to those who practice it. . . . they cannot do without song, which both formulates and answers their nagging questions, enables them to pursue action with zest and confidence, brings them into touch with gods and spirits, and makes them feel less strange in the natural world. . . . it gives to them a solid centre in what otherwise would be almost chaos, and a continuity in their being, which would too easily dissolve before the calls of the implacable present . . . through its words men, who might otherwise give in to the malice of circumstances, find their old powers revived or new powers stirring in them, and through these life itself is sustained and renewed and fulfilled.[71]

This, I think, sums up concisely the function of song for the slave. Without a general understanding of that function, without a specific understanding of the content and meaning of slave song, there can be no full comprehension of the effects of slavery upon the slave or the meaning of the society from which slaves emerged at emancipation.

168   LAWRENCE W. LEVINE

NOTES

An earlier version of this essay was presented as a paper at the American Historical Association meetings on December 28, 1969. I am indebted to the two commentators on that occasion, Professors J. Saunders Redding and Mike Thelwell, and to my colleagues Nathan I. Huggins, Robert Middlekauff, and Kenneth M. Stampp for their penetrating criticisms and suggestions.

1. Miles Mark Fisher, *Negro Slave Songs in the United States* (New York, 1963, orig. pub. 1953), 14, 39, 132, and *passim*.

2. The contours of this debate are judiciously outlined in D. K. Wilgus, *Anglo-American Folksong Scholarship Since 1898* (New Brunswick, 1959), App. One, "The Negro-White Spirituals."

3. Lucy McKim, "Songs of the Port Royal Contrabands," *Dwight's Journal of Music*, XXII (November 8, 1862), 255.

4. W. F. Allen, "The Negro Dialect," *The Nation*, I (December 14, 1865), 744-745.

5. See, for instance, Henry Edward Krehbiel, *Afro-American Folksongs* (New York, 1963, orig. pub. 1914); James Wesley Work, *Folk Song of the American Negro* (Nashville, 1915); James Weldon Johnson, *The Book of American Negro Spirituals* (New York, 1925), and *The Second Book of Negro Spirituals* (New York, 1926); Lydia Parrish, *Slave Songs of the Georgia Sea Islands* (Hatboro, Penna., 1965, orig. pub. 1942); LeRoi Jones, *Blues People* (New York, 1963).

6. Newman I. White, *American Negro Folk-Songs* (Hatboro, Penna., 1965, orig. pub. 1928); Guy B. Johnson, *Folk Culture on St. Helena Island, South Carolina* (Chapel Hill, 1930); George Pullen Jackson, *White and Negro Spirituals* (New York, 1943).

7. White, *American Negro Folk-Songs*, 11-13.

8. Professor John William Ward gives an excellent example of this process in his discussion of the different meanings which the newspapers of the United States, France, and India attributed to Charles Lindbergh's flight across the Atlantic in 1927. See "Lindbergh, Dos Passos, and History," in Ward, *Red, White, and Blue* (New York, 1969), 55.

9. George Pullen Jackson, "The Genesis of the Negro Spiritual," *The American Mercury*, XXVI (June 1932), 248.

10. Richard Alan Waterman, "African Influence on the Music of the Americas," in Sol Tax (ed.), *Acculturation in the Americas: Proceedings and Selected Papers of the XXIXth International Congress of Americanists* (Chicago, 1952), 207-218; Wilgus, *Anglo-American Folksong Scholarship Since 1898*, 363-364; Melville H. Herskovits, "Patterns of Negro Music" (pamphlet, no publisher, no date); Gilbert Chase, *America's Music* (New York, 1966), Chap. 12; Alan P. Merriam, "African Music," in William R. Bascom and Melville J. Herskovits (eds.), *Continuity and Change in African Cultures* (Chicago, 1959), 76-80.

11. White, *American Negro Folk-Songs*, 29, 55.

12. Jackson, *White and Negro Spirituals*, 266-267.

13. James Miller McKim, "Negro Songs," *Dwight's Journal of Music*, XXI (August 9, 1862), 149.

14. Thomas Wentworth Higginson, *Army Life in a Black Regiment* (Beacan Press edition, Boston, 1962, orig. pub. 1869), 218-219.

15. Henry Russell, *Cheer! Boys, Cheer!*, 84-85, quoted in Chase, *America's Music*, 235-236.

16. Jeanette Robinson Murphy, "The Survival of African Music in America," *Popular Science Monthly*, 55 (1899), 660-672, reprinted in Bruce Jackson (ed.), *The Negro and His Folklore in Nineteenth-Century Periodicals* (Austin, 1967), 328.

17. Natalie Curtis Burlin, "Negro Music at Birth," *Musical Quarterly*, V (January 1919), 88. For Mrs. Burlin's excellent reproductions of Negro folk songs and spirituals, see her *Negro Folk-Songs* (New York, 1918-1919), Vol. I-IV.

18. Clifton Joseph Furness, "Communal Music Among Arabians and Negroes," *Musical Quarterly*, XVI (January 1930), 49-51.

19. Elizabeth Kilham, "Sketches in Color: IV," *Putnam's Monthly*, XV (March 1870), 304-311, reprinted in Jackson, *The Negro and His Folklore in Nineteenth-Century Periodicals*, 127-128.

20. Bruno Nettl, *Folk and Traditional Music of the Western Continents* (Englewood Cliffs, 1965), 4-5; Chase, *America's Music*, 241-243.

21. J. K., Jr., "Who Are Our National Poets?," *Knickerbocker Magazine*, 26 (October 1845), 336, quoted in Dena J. Epstein, "Slave Music in the United States Before 1860: A Survey of Sources (Part I)," *Music Library Association Notes*, XX (Spring 1963), 208.

22. Elizabeth Kilham, "Sketches in Color: IV," *Putnam's Monthly*, XV (March 1870), 304-311, reprinted in Jackson, *The Negro and His Folklore in Nineteenth-Century Periodicals*, 129.

23. White, *American Negro Folk-Songs*, 57.

24. Alan P. Merriam, "Music and the Dance," in Robert Lystad (ed.), *The African World: A Survey of Social Research* (New York, 1965), 452-468; William Bascom "Folklore and Literature," in *Ibid.*, 469-488; R. S. Rattray, *Ashanti* (Oxford 1923), Chap. XV; Melville Herskovits, "Freudian Mechanisms in Primitive Negro Psychology, in E. E. Evans-Pritchard *et al.* (eds.), *Essays Presented to C. G. Seligman* (London, 1934), 75-84; Alan P. Merriam, "African Music," in Bascom and Herskovits, *Continuity and Change in African Cultures*, 49-86.

25. William Francis Allen, Charles Pickard Ware, and Lucy McKim Garrison, compilers, *Slave Songs of the United States* (New York, 1867, Oak Publications ed., 1965), 164-165.

26. *Ibid.*, 43.

27. Harriet Jacobs, *Incidents in the Life of a Slave Girl* (Boston, 1861), 109.

28. Lines like these could be quoted endlessly. For the specific ones cited, see the songs in the following collections: Higginson, *Army Life in a Black Regiment*, 206, 216-217; Allen *et al.*, *Slave Songs of the United States*, 33-34, 44, 106-108, 131, 160-161; Thomas P. Fenner, compiler, *Religious Folk Songs of the Negro as Sung on the Plantations* (Hampton, Virginia, 1909, orig. pub. 1874), 10-11, 48; J. B. T. Marsh, *The Story of the Jubilee Singers; With Their Songs* (Boston, 1880), 136, 167, 178.

29. McKim, "Negro Songs," 148; H. G. Spaulding, "Under the Palmetto," *Continental Monthly*, IV (1863), 188-203, reprinted in Jackson, *The Negro and His Folklore in Nineteenth-Century Periodicals*, 72; Allen, "The Negro Dialect," 744-745; Higginson, *Army Life in a Black Regiment*, 220-221.

30. *Journal of Nicholas Cresswell, 1774–1777* (New York, 1934), 17-19, quoted in Epstein, *Music Library Association Notes*, XX (Spring 1963), 201.

31. Jacobs, *Incidents in the Life of a Slave Girl*, 180.

32. *Life and Times of Frederick Douglass* (rev. ed., 1892, Collier Books Edition, 1962), 146-147.

33. John Lambert, *Travels Through Canada and the United States of North America in the Years, 1806–1807 and 1808* (London, 1814), II, 253-254, quoted in Dena J. Epstein, "Slave Music in the United States Before 1860: A Survey of Sources (Part 2)," *Music Library Association Notes*, XX (Summer 1963), 377.

34. Frances Anne Kemble, *Journal of a Residence on a Georgian Plantation in 1838–1839* (New York, 1863), 128.

35. For versions of these songs, see Dorothy Scarborough, *On the Trail of Negro Folk-Songs* (Cambridge, 1925), 194, 201-203, 223-225, and Thomas W. Talley, *Negro Folk Rhymes* (New York, 1922), 25-26. Talley claims that the majority of the songs in his large and valuable collection "were sung by Negro fathers and mothers in the dark days of American slavery to their children who listened with eyes as large as saucers and drank them down with mouths wide open," but offers no clue as to why he feels that songs collected for the most part in the twentieth century were slave songs.

36. Constance Rourke, *The Roots of American Culture and Other Essays* (New York, 1942), 262-274. Newman White, on the contrary, has argued that although the earliest minstrel songs were Negro derived, they soon went their own way and that less than ten per cent of them were genuinely Negro. Nevertheless, these white songs "got back to the plantation, largely spurious as they were and were undoubtedly among those which the plantation-owners encouraged the Negroes to sing. They persist, to-day in isolated stanzas and lines, among the songs handed down by plantation Negroes . . ." White, *American Negro Folk-Songs*, 7-10 and Appendix IV. There are probably valid elements in both theses. A similarly complex relationship between genuine Negro folk creations and their more commercialized partly white influenced imitations was to take place in the blues of the twentieth century.

37. McKim, "Songs of the Port Royal Contrabands," 255.

38. Mircea Eliade, *The Sacred and the Profane* (New York, 1961), Chaps. 2, 4, and *passim*. For the similarity of Eliade's concept to the world view of West Africa, see W. E. Abraham, *The Mind of Africa* (London, 1962), Chap. 2, and R. S. Rattray, *Religion and Art in Ashanti* (Oxford, 1927).

39. Paul Radin, "Status, Phantasy, and the Christian Dogma," in Social Science Institute, Fisk University, *God Struck Me Dead: Religious Conversion Experiences and Autobiographies of Negro Ex-Slaves* (Nashville, 1945, unpublished typescript).

40. Stanley Elkins, *Slavery* (Chicago, 1959), 136.

41. Allen *et al.*, *Slave Songs of the United States*, 33-34, 105; William E. Barton, *Old Plantation Hymns: A Collection of Hitherto Unpublished Melodies of the Slave and the Freedmen* (Boston, 1899), 30.

42. Allen *et al.*, *Slave Songs of the United States*, 47.

43. Barton, *Old Plantation Hymns*, 19.

44. Marsh, *The Story of the Jubilee Singers*, 132.

45. Fenner, *Religious Folk Songs of the Negro*, 162; E. A. McIlhenny, *Befo' De War Spirituals: Words and Melodies* (Boston, 1933), 39.

46. Barton, *Old Plantation Hymns*, 15; Howard W. Odum and Guy B. Johnson, *The Negro And His Songs* (Hatboro, Penn., 1964, orig. pub. 1925), 33-34; for a vivid description of the "shout" see *The Nation*, May 30, 1867, 432-433; see also Parrish, *Slave Songs of the Georgia Sea Islands*, Chap. III.

47. For examples of songs of this nature, see Fenner, *Religious Folk Songs of the Negro*, 8, 63-65; Marsh, *The Story of the Jubilee Singers*, 240-241; Higginson, *Army Life in a Black Regiment*, 205; Allen *et al.*, *Slave Songs of the United States*, 91, 100; Burlin, *Negro Folk-Songs*, I, 37-42.

48. Allen *et al.*, *Slave Songs of the United States*, 32-33.

49. *Ibid.*, 30-31; Burlin, *Negro Folk-Songs*, II, 8-9; Fenner, *Religious Folk Songs of the Negro*, 12.

50. Allen *et al.*, *Slave Songs of the United States*, 128-129; Fenner, *Religious Folk Songs of the Negro*, 127; Barton, *Old Plantation Hymns*, 26.

51. Allen *et al.*, *Slave Songs of the United States*, 70, 102-103, 147; Barton, *Old Plantation Hymns*, 9, 17-18, 24; Marsh, *The Story of the Jubilee Singers*, 133, 167; Odum and Johnson, *The Negro And His Songs*, 35.

52. Allen *et al.*, *Slave Songs of the United States*, 102-103.

53. Mary Allen Grissom, compiler, *The Negro Sings A New Heaven* (Chapel Hill, 1930), 73.

54. Marsh, *The Story of the Jubilee Singers*, 179, 186; Allen *et al.*, *Slave Songs of the United States*, 40-41, 44, 146; Barton, *Old Plantation Hymns*, 30.

55. McIlhenny, *Befo' De War Spirituals*, 31.

56. *Gumbo Ya-Ya: A Collection of Louisiana Folk Tales*, compiled by Lyle Saxon, Edward Dreyer, and Robert Tallant from materials gathered by workers of the WPA, Louisiana Writer's Project (Boston, 1945), 242.

57. For examples, see Allen *et al.*, *Slave Songs of the United States*, 40-41, 82, 97, 106-108; Marsh, *The Story of the Jubilee Singers*, 168, 203; Burlin, *Negro Folk-Songs*, II, 8-9; Howard Thurman, *Deep River* (New York, 1945), 19-21.

58. Thurman, *Deep River*, 16-17.

59. Higginson, *Army Life in a Black Regiment*, 202-205. Many of those northerners who came to the South to "uplift" the freedmen were deeply disturbed at the Old Testament emphasis of their religion. H. G. Spaulding complained that the exslaves needed to be introduced to "the light and warmth of the Gospel," and reported that a Union army officer told him: "Those people had enough of the Old Testament thrown at their heads under slavery. Now give them the glorious utterances and practical teachings of the Great Master." Spaulding, "Under the Palmetto," reprinted in Jackson, *The Negro and His Folklore in Nineteenth-Century Periodicals*, 66.

60. Allen *et al.*, *Slave Songs of the United States*, 148; Fenner, *Religious Folk Songs of the Negro*, 21; Marsh, *The Story of the Jubilee Singers*, 134-135; McIlhenny, *Befo' De War Spirituals*, 248-249.

61. *Life and Times of Frederick Douglass*, 159-160; Marsh, *The Story of the Jubilee Singers*, 188.

172 LAWRENCE W. LEVINE

62. Higginson, *Army Life in a Black Regiment*, 217.

63. Parrish, *Slave Songs of the Georgia Sea Islands*, 247.

64. "Actually, not one spiritual in its primary form reflected interest in anything other than a full life here and now." Fisher, *Negro Slave Songs in the United States*, 137.

65. Barton, *Old Plantation Hymns*, 25; Allen *et al.*, *Slave Songs of the United States*, 94; McKim, "Negro Songs," 149.

66. Higginson, *Army Life in a Black Regiment*, 201-202, 211-212.

67. Robert Redfield, *The Primitive World and Its Transformations* (Ithaca, 1953), 51-53.

68. Elkins, *Slavery*, Chap. III.

69. *Ibid.*, Chap. II; Frank Tannenbaum, *Slave and Citizen* (New York, 1946).

70. E. J. Hobsbawm, *Primitive Rebels* (New York, 1959), Chap. I.

71. C. M. Bowra, *Primitive Song* (London, 1962), 285-286.

• *We last met Herbert G. Gutman on the trail of Messrs. Fogel and Engerman. Since that sortie, Gutman has published a major work of his own, The Black Family in Slavery and Freedom, 1750–1925. In it he argues for the durability and importance of the slave family. Gutman's is the most weighty of several works contradicting the belief that frequent separation of slaves rendered the black family a weak and tenuous institution. Here, Gutman uses the records of a South Carolina plantation to maintain that slaves were generally monogamous and that they had a strong consciousness of family, as well as close ties with grandparents, aunts and uncles, and cousins. He also includes significant observations about the moral code governing slave family life and about some of the taboos.*

Because She Was My Cousin

HERBERT G. GUTMAN

A single South Carolina slave birth register, which makes clear the extent of familial and kin networks among Afro-American slaves and shows that their development depended primarily upon the adaptive capacities of several closely related slave generations, is reason to put aside mimetic theories of Afro-American slave culture and to describe instead how common slave sexual, marital, familial, and social choices were shaped by a neglected cumulative slave experience. In this small South Carolina slave community, most children lived with two parents, and most adults lived in long-lasting marriages. Children were frequently given the names of blood kin from outside the immediate

From *The Black Family in Slavery and Freedom, 1750–1925* by Herbert G. Gutman (New York: Pantheon Books, 1976), pp. 45-47, 50-52, 61-68, 79-83, 88-93. Copyright © 1976 by Herbert G. Gutman. Reprinted by permission of Pantheon Books, a division of Random House, Inc.

family, and the rules that shaped slave marriage were very different from the rules that existed among the largest resident South Carolina plantation owners. Our interest is in how these common practices developed among the slaves and in what in their experiences sustained them, because that is the only way to begin to comprehend the familial arrangements and moral and social beliefs found among ex-slaves in 1864, 1865, and 1866. . . .

The social and cultural practices of the slaves living on the South Carolina Good Hope plantation do not require that much be known about their owner. Slaves on other large plantations with very different owners and very different experiences . . . behaved similarly to the Good Hope slaves. These Santee River cotton-plantation slaves, furthermore, were not supervised by a resident owner. Their owner, Joseph Heatly Dulles, the son of an immigrant British hardware merchant who had sided with the British during the War of Independence, was born in 1795, grew up in Charleston, graduated from Yale, and spent nearly his entire adult life in Philadelphia. The owner of a plantation about sixty miles northeast of Charleston, Dulles died in Philadelphia, aged eighty-one. He was a direct forebear of John Foster and Allen Dulles, corporate lawyers and appointed public servants who figured prominently in reshaping mid-twentieth-century American society.[1]

How a cumulative slave experience affected the beliefs and behavior of the Good Hope slaves is learned from a plantation birth register, which regularly recorded four demographic items about each newborn slave child: its date of birth, its given name, and the given names, when known, of both parents.[2] Most plantation whites who recorded slave births rarely listed a father's name, a social and business convention that rested upon the belief that because a slave child's status followed that of its mother, the father's name did not have to be recorded. Because it listed most fathers' names, and also because of its relative completeness and the length of time it covered, the Good Hope birth register is an unusual historical document. The first recorded birth occurred in Africa in 1760 and the last ninety-seven years later, three years before Abraham Lincoln's election to the presidency. Listing the names of at least six blacks born in eighteenth-century Africa and twelve others not yet ten years old when the Civil War started, the birth register included more than two hundred slave men, women, and children and covered nearly the entire formative Afro-American experience: birth in Africa, enslavement, South Carolina

plantation slavery, the development of an adaptive slave culture, emancipation, and finally life as legally free men and women.

In 1857, when the last recorded slave birth occurred, 175 men, women,
and children made up the Good Hope slave community and nearly
all were linked together by blood and marital ties that reached back
into the eighteenth century. Children up to the age of ten were about
one-third of the community, and about 10 percent of the slaves were
men and women at least fifty years old. One hundred fifty-four children had been born between 1820 and 1857. About one in five died,
mostly before their first birthday. None of the rest lived alone. Eleven
had matured and married; the others lived either with one parent or,
more commonly, with both parents. Twenty-eight immediate families
made up this slave community. A widowed parent headed two families; three others contained childless couples; the rest each had in
them a mother, a father, and their children. All but a few husbands
and wives were close to each other in age. Eleven slaves, ten of them
at least fifty years old, lived alone.

Kin networks linked slaves born in different generations, slaves
listed as members of separate immediate families, and slaves living
alone. A few examples illustrate the intensity of these ties:

—In 1857, Patty, Captain, and Flora lived alone. Patty, born
a mainland North American slave before her future owner's father Joseph Dulles left Ireland to become a Charleston merchant
and an American slaveowner, was the oldest Good Hope slave
and died in that year. Three generations of blood descendants
survived her. An African by birth, the widower Captain was sur-
rounded by married children and grandchildren. In 1857, his
oldest grandson, Charles, was twenty-one and his youngest, Ze-
kiel, a year old. The widowed Flora lived in the same community as her married sons Dick and Mike, their wives, four grandchildren, six married half brothers and half sisters, and twenty
nephews and nieces.
—By 1857, Prince and Elsy, husband and wife for thirty
years, had three married daughters (a fourth daughter had died
in infancy), seven grandchildren, and twenty-nine nieces and
nephews. Prince was Patty's son, and his younger married sister
Clarinda and brother Primus lived in the community with their
spouses and children.
—Phoebe and Cuffee headed single-parent households. It had
not always been so. Cuffee and Gadsey had been husband and

wife for at least twenty-three years. She had apparently died. Cuffee did not remarry. In 1857, he lived with two grown sons; his other children had married, and at least ten grandchildren and a great-grandchild lived in the community. Probably widowed, Phoebe was still living with five of her nine children. Jack had been the father of the first four; Tom the father of the rest. Phoebe's oldest daughter was married and had the same given name as Phoebe's mother. . . .

—Two young and as yet unmarried mothers lived with their families of origin. The twenty-one-year-old Betty and her two-year-old daughter Leah lived with Betty's father, Burge, and his second wife, Rose. Betty had been named for her paternal grandmother. The seventeen-year-old Gadsey and her two-year-old daughter, Betsey, lived with Gadsey's mother, Duck, and her husband, Jake. Gadsey was not Jake's daughter; she had been born when Duck was living with Wilson.

Similar familial and kin connections existed among plantation slaves over the entire South in the 1840s and the 1850s. And the slaves living in the Good Hope community were typical in other ways of plantation blacks. The age at which a woman had a first child, the size of completed families, and the length of marriages in the Good Hope slave community hardly differed in other plantation communities.

—Good Hope slave women bore a first child at an early age. The ages of twenty-three women whose first children were born between 1824 and 1856 are known: they had a first child at a median age of 19.6 years. The average age differed insignificantly. Three were not yet sixteen, and fourteen were between seventeen and twenty. Two each were aged twenty-one, twenty-two, and twenty-four.[3] Adequate data on the age of southern white women at the birth of a first child are as yet unavailable; hence the similarities between slave and free white women remain unknown. But these South Carolina slave mothers were far younger at the birth of a first child than European women at that time. Peter Laslett finds that the average age at which seventeenth- and eighteenth-century Englishwomen married was twenty-four, and Pierre Goubert fixes the average age of eighteenth-century Frenchwomen at the birth of a first child at between twenty-six and twenty-seven. The only estimate available to us relating free American women to slaves—that of Moncure D. Conway, a Virginia slaveholder who became an antislavery critic—compared southern slave and free white women in the

early 1860s and concluded that "the period of maternity is has-
tened, the average youth of negro mothers being nearly three
years earlier than that of the free race."[4]

—Good Hope children grew up in large families. Among
those born between 1800 and 1849, only one in seven had fewer
than three siblings, and slightly more than half had seven or
more siblings. Family size increased over time. Twenty-three
women had a first child between 1820 and 1849, and not all
had completed their families by 1857. About four in five had at
least four children; ten women had at least seven children.

—Good Hope children also knew their parents well because
most married couples lived in long-lasting unions. The ages of
twenty-three of the twenty-six fathers living with their wives or
their wives and children in 1857 are known. Among those aged
twenty-five to thirty-four, the typical marriage in 1857 had
lasted at least seven years, and for men aged thirty-two to forty-
four at least thirteen years. July, for example, was thirty-eight
years old in 1857, and he and Nancy had been married for at
least sixteen years. Six of the nine men forty-five and older had
lived with the same wife for at least twenty years. Sambo was
not typical of these older men; born in 1811, he was not listed
in the birth register as a father until his forty-fourth year, when
he and Lena had a child. Lena's first husband, William, had
died of fever in 1851 and left her with their infant son, William. The boy's paternal great-grandfather had been a slave
named William. Sambo and Lena named their first-born daughter for Sambo's older sister Nancy. Unlike Sambo, other elderly
men had nearly all lived in long marriages, lasting on the average
at least twenty-four years. Gabriel and Abram each had lived
with their wives at least thirty-four years.[5]

The community that the Good Hope slaves lived in by 1857 casts
fresh light on slave, not owner, belief and behavior. The Good Hope
absentee owners did not break up slave marriages, but in itself that
does not explain Good Hope slave belief and behavior, because other
slaves in less fortunate plantation settings behaved similarly. Examination of the full birth register indicates why the slaves themselves—
denied the security of legal marriages and subjected to the severe
external pressures associated with ownership—sustained lasting marriages and the slave social beliefs and practices associated with them.
The North Carolina Supreme Court Justice who wrote in 1853 that
"our law requires no solemnity or form in regard to the marriage of
slaves, and whether they 'take up' with each other by express permis-

sion of their owners, or from a mere impulse of nature, in obedience to the command 'multiply and replenish the earth,' cannot, in the contemplation of the law, make any sort of difference" spoke a legal truth. But the judge, like most nineteenth-century Americans, confused law and culture and therefore had no understanding of why slaves who married outside the law often lived together for many years. That fact and much else are learned about Afro-American slaves by reorganizing the birth register, which listed slave births in chronological order, into separate families grouped in generations that are fixed by the date of a first child's birth in each family. . . .[6]

We are not yet finished with the South Carolina Good Hope slaves and will return later in this chapter to see what in their experiences sustained the behavior so far observed among them. But the presence of prenuptial intercourse among them first deserves close examination. Two reasons, among others, dictate that detour. Prenuptial intercourse was common among other slaves, too, and no aspect of slave behavior has been more greatly misunderstood than slave sexual mores and practices. "Many of the plantations," the historian John Blassingame writes as late as 1973, "were so large that it was impossible for masters to supervise both the labor and the sex lives of their slaves. Sexual morality, often imperfectly taught (or violated by whites with impunity), drifted through a heavy veil of ignorance to the quarters. Consequently, for a majority of slaves, sex was a natural urge frequently fulfilled by casual liaisons." The misunderstanding on which such analysis rests is not a new one. Prenuptial intercourse among slaves was noticed and misunderstood by most non-slave contemporaries, too. Such behavior had been relatively common in the society in which the parents and grandparents of mid-nineteenth-century observers of the slaves had lived but was later harshly censured by a shifting moral code. Many mid-nineteenth-century observers believed that prenuptial intercourse was evidence of the absence of sexual standards and even indicated "savage," or "natural," behavior. Pro- and antislavery biases and mid-nineteenth-century Victorian beliefs, such as the belief that marriage and hence the "family" required positive legal and contractual sanction to be "real," that "sex" had to be subordinated absolutely to marriage, and that sexual "restraint" (the "ideal of chastity") had to be imposed upon all inferior and dependent classes and races distorted the perceptions of most observers. Articulate defenders of slavery like T. R. R. Cobb, James Henry Hammond, Chancellor Harper, William Grayson, and Robert Toombs considered prenuptial intercourse among slaves justification for racial and class domination. Cobb blamed it on the "natural lewdness of the negro." The *Southern Literary Messenger* said whites had found Africans "*naked* savage[s], prone to the unrestrained indulgence of sensual appetite," and that enslavement slowly "awakened" a "sense of shame" among them. Toombs and others discovered that "fewer children are born out of wedlock among slaves than in the capitals of the two most civilized countries of Europe—Austria and France." According to Hammond, an 1842 parliamentary report proved that among Britain's factory population "illicit sexual intercourse . . . seems to prevail universally in an early period of life." Grayson admitted that young female slaves were "loose in their conduct" but hardly different from "hired laborers." Sexual restraint, Harper explained, was "painful," involved a "constant effort to struggle against the strongest impulses," and depended upon a "refined and intellectual nature." The "great mass of mankind" could only "supply . . . their natural and physical wants." A "large . . . proportion" of slave women, said Harper, "set little value on chastity"; "a woman's having been a mother is very seldom indeed an objection to her being made a wife."[7]

The fullest record of northern observation of slave sexual behavior is found among the witnesses, mostly whites familiar with the South Carolina Sea Island blacks, before the American Freedmen's Inquiry Commission in 1863, a record that emphasized the absence of slave sexual norms and confused prenuptial intercourse with "licentiousness."[8] The Commission entirely ignored, perhaps even consciously suppressed, this testimony in its published reports. A few witnesses, like General Rufus Saxton's aide-de-camp E. W. Hooper, said the slaves "appreciate [chastity] . . . thoroughly." But most agreed with Saxton, the Sea Island military commander, that "the [slave] system . . . destroyed that feeling," that masters "never inculcated it," and that women were "paid . . . a premium to breed as fast as possible." Saxton said women bore children at a "very young age," "often [at] fourteen." Henry Judd believed prenuptial intercourse "universal." "Before marriage," said James Redpath, who spent the early war years with Kansas slaves, there was "no such thing" as chastity. Richard Hinton, who had been with the Missouri slaves, "never heard of one" fifteen- or sixteen-year-old slave girl who had not "copulated with somebody." The most important testimony came from two former slaves; both described widespread prenuptial intercourse. Then about forty years old, Harry McMillan had been born in Georgia but grown

up a Beaufort, South Carolina, slave. Asked if "colored women have a
great deal of sexual passion" and "all go out with men," McMillan
replied, "Yes, sir, there is a great idea of that. I do not think you will
find four out of a hundred that do not; they begin at fifteen or sixteen." The well-known Robert Smalls was even more explicit:

> QUESTION: Have not colored women a good deal of sexual pas-
> sion?
> ANSWER: Yes, sir.
> QUESTION: Are they not carried away by their passions to have
> intercourse with men?
> ANSWER: Yes, sir, but very few lawful married women are car-
> ried away if their husbands take care of them.
> QUESTION: How is it with young women?
> ANSWER: They are very wild and run around a good deal.

Asked "what proportion" had "sexual intercourse before marriage,"
Smalls answered, "The majority do, but they do not consider this intercourse an evil thing. . . ."[9]
   That many slaves distinguished between prenuptial intercourse and
"licentiousness" and believed prenuptial intercourse and pregnancy
compatible with settled marriage escaped the notice of all but a few
observers. A visit to the Sea Islands in 1863 convinced the Yankee
journalist Charles Nordhoff that "indiscriminate intercourse" did not
exist among slave women "to any great extent." Young women, however, were "not eminently chaste." Angered by a British journalist who
condemned black plantation women for not being "vestal virgins,"
Mary Chesnut confided in her Civil War diary that Virginia and
South Carolina slave women "have a chance here that women have
nowhere else. They can redeem themselves—the 'impropers' can. They
can marry decently, and nothing is remembered against these colored
ladies." A Yazoo, Mississippi, owner explained to Frederick Olmsted:
"They don't very often get married for good . . . without trying each
other out, as they say, for two or three weeks, to see how they are
going to like each other." (Eighty years later, an ex-slave called such
behavior "a make-out.") Harriet Beecher Stowe learned from a southern white correspondent that after a South Carolina woman's husband
was sold to Florida she had to take a new spouse and agreed to what
appears to have been a trial marriage, explaining later that "we lib
along two year—he watchin my ways and I watchin his ways."[10]
   Despite their cultural-bound moralism, observers like Chesnut, the

Yazoo owner, and Nordhoff were describing aspects of the sexual and social behavior disclosed by the Good Hope slaves, who demonstrated that prenuptial intercourse and settled marriage were compatible. Their behavior, which distinguished their norms from the prevalent Victorian ones, closely resembled practices found in many other premodern cultures. In 1833, for example, the British physician Peter Gaskell said that "sexual intercourse was almost universal prior to marriage in the [English] agricultural districts," but that "it existed only between parties where a tacit understanding had all the weight of obligation—and that was that marriage be the result." "The moral, customary, and legal rules of most human communities," Bronislaw Malinowski observed a century later, ". . . dissociate the two sides of procreation, that is sex and parenthood." In these cultures, marriage did not mean the "licensing of sexual intercourse but rather the licensing of parenthood." Prenuptial intercourse often served as "a method of arranging marriage by trial and error." Malinowski illustrated such practices by referring to the German peasant "trial night," observing that such courting practices occurred commonly in many premodern cultures and were not "licentious." "The same view," he wrote, "is taken by the savage Melanesian, by the West African, by the Bantu, and by the North American Indian." (He could have added the Good Hope and many other Afro-American slaves to his list.) Their behavior also demonstrated that "sexual repression is as rigid and definite as sexual license is clear and proscriptive" in all cultures, and that "regulated forms of nonconjugal intercourse" were not "subversive of marriage." The 1880 and 1900 federal manuscript censuses revealed the persistence among southern blacks of prenuptial intercourse, the birth of a child prior to a marriage, and bridal pregnancy. These same sources, however, also show that relatively few young black mothers headed single-parent households. That was also so among the Good Hope slaves. All women who became mothers before 1855, including those who had children by more than one man and even those whose first children had "unknown" fathers, spent most of their adult lives in settled unions, behavior which suggests that many slaves viewed prenuptial intercourse as a prelude to a settled marriage. If a permanent marriage had not been the expected norm, there should have been many more unmarried mothers under the age of thirty among the Good Hope slaves (and later among mothers listed in the pages of the 1880 and 1900 federal manuscript censuses).[11]

The acceptance of a slave norm that placed great emphasis upon a settled union and the belief that prenuptial pregnancy should be followed by marriage did not mean, of course, that all slaves behaved accordingly. "Sometimes," one old ex-slave recalled, "they would slip there and sleep with the woman and wouldn't marry them at all." Another ex-slave said, "Some of them had children for them what wasn't married to you. No, they would do nothing; they were glad of it. They would be glad to have them little bastards; brag about it." Competing values existed among the slaves, as among their owners and other peoples. In describing his 1828 marriage, the former North Carolina slave Lunsford Lane made it plain that he wanted no part of bridal pregnancy: "When we had been married nine months and one day, we were blessed with a son." Charles Nordhoff met an unhappily married Sea Islander in 1863 who had lived secretly with a younger woman for more than a year. She was about to bear his child, and he was "extremely anxious to marry her before the child is born." The man's slave wife consented to the separation. A plantation white noted in his 1854 diary: "The girl Martha, the wife of Willis, is delivered of a Daughter this morning—she has been married only two months. Her mother says 'she makes quick work of it' and seems distressed. I comfort her, by telling her such things often happen with the first born, but never afterwards." The young woman's mother worried more about her daughter's behavior than did the young woman's owner. But the owner also revealed that slave marriage "often" followed pregnancy. Mary Kindred, a former Texas slave, remembered a "l'il song" her grandmother had sung:

> One mornin' in May,
> I spies a beautiful dandy,
> A-rakin' way of de hay.
> I asks her to marry.
> She say, scornful, "No!"
> But befo' six months roll by
> Her apron strings wouldn't tie.
> She wrote me a letter
> She marry me then,
> I say, no, no, my gal, not I.

Another ex-slave said, "When I was a girl if you walked with a girl who had a baby we would be cut all to pieces. We wouldn't be allowed to speak to her."[12]

Despite the fact that some slaves everywhere rejected the dominant norm, marriage followed most prenuptial slave pregnancies. "If you fooled up a girl with a arm full of you," said an elderly male ex-slave, "you had to take care of her." Men who refused to marry such women may even have repudiated common norms and thereby won such women communal favor or special concern, an attitude that very much troubled Yankee missionaries and teachers among the wartime Sea Islanders. "It was held no shame for a girl to bear a child under any circumstances," said the journalist Nordhoff, and it dismayed Austa French to find that unmarried mothers were not ostracized. "There is no great gulf between them and the poor, as there is with the voluntary fallen," complained French. Such beliefs so upset one Island Yankee superintendent that he distributed a "very simple" outfit of clothing to the mothers of newborn children but only if they were married. Older women approached the teacher Elizabeth Botume "many times" to ask support for young unmarried mothers, behavior which conformed to their belief system. They once sought help for "poor sick Cumber," an unmarried woman who had suffered much in childbirth and was "bad off." They gave "united testimony," said Botume, aware that "we would have nothing to do with one like her." Botume sent a bundle of clothing, explaining that "their readiness to help the poor erring girl made me ashamed." Time and again, Botume heard the "touching appeals of these poor, ignorant, tender-hearted women for their down-fallen sisters." She finally rejected the plea of the old nurse Aunt Judy, hoping to make "this case an example." Aunt Judy heard Botume out and replied very slowly in a manner that splendidly illustrates what Eric Wolf calls the "ritual pantomime of dependence": "That's so, ma'am. You knows best. You *mus'* be right, fur you'na kin read the Bible, an' so you mus' know best. But I has to go now to the gal, poor creeter! Them wimmins is waitin' on me. . . ." Botume understood herself as well as she understood Aunt Judy, admitting that "her thanks and praise were really humiliating." She gave in, once more sending clothing and groceries. "All day," Botume remembered, "her words were in my mind. 'You *mus'* know best.' What did I know, that I should sit in judgment?" (Botume was unjust to herself. She had the rare capacity among those who had contact with slaves before and after their emancipation to learn from them—even about herself.) [13]

Fidelity was expected from slave men and women after marriage. "If a woman loses her husband," Robert Smalls told the American Freedmen's Inquiry Commission in 1863, "she mourns for him and will not marry for a year and a half unless she is driven to it by want and must have somebody to help her." Aggressive slave husbands guarded their wives. Henry Gladney said his South Carolina father ("Bill de Giant") "didn't 'low other slave men to look at my mammy." A North Carolina Supreme Court Justice observed in 1853 that "as a general rule" slaves "respect the exclusive rights of fellow-slaves who are married." Violence, even murder, sometimes followed suspected or actual infidelity. Tackett killed Daniel in 1819 or 1820, following a dispute over Daniel's North Carolina free black wife, Lotty. When Samuel and Mima, the parents of five children, quarreled and split up, another slave moved in with Mima. Samuel killed him. Years later, John, another North Carolina slave, murdered Ship-man, with whom John's wife Flora had allegedly engaged in "adulterous intercourse." Just before the Civil War, Alfred killed the Missis-sippi overseer Coleman after learning that Coleman "had forced [his wife] to submit to sexual intercourse with him." The Georgia slave Samuel Adams left his wife after she bore a mulatto child, and the Texas slave Harry Pope ended his marriage to Sarah Lucy because she had "a child by another negro." Edward Pierce, who superintended the Yankee Sea Island missionary enterprise, had an urgent call from the black Cato, whose son-in-law Alex had driven Cato's daughter from their cabin. The couple had been married eight or nine years, and Alex believed that Rose's newborn child was not his own. He broke up her bedstead, threw it out of doors, "bundled up all her things [and] . . . threatened to kill the first man who interfered with him in 'his own house.' " Other Sea Islanders complained when Yankee soldiers and civilians tried to "seduce their wives" or when their wives revealed "unfaithfulness" by "going with officers and soldiers." The Yankee magistrate and plantation superintendent Elbridge Gerry Dudley had a visit from a mulatto woman and her "full-blooded black" husband. "Both [were] smart people," recollected Dudley. "She complained that he treated her badly, not with violence, however, and wanted to know what she should do." Her husband's first wife and three children had been sold from him, and he and a second wife had ended voluntarily an unsatisfactory marriage. His third wife had her first child by him before a white physician married the couple. Now, the husband complained, she "went out with some clerks in the Provost Marshal's office." (Dudley later learned that the man's allegations were accurate and advised the woman to "go and live with her mother.") Fidelity was also expected of married men. A Sea Islander caused a stir by taking a new wife, and when the couple came forward to marry in a missionary church, his mother rose and protested, "I take Becca (the second wife) in dis han' and carry her to punishment, an' Sarah in dis han' an' carry her to Christ." Decades later, Zora Hurston described conjuration beliefs and practices among Florida blacks meant to restrain men from engaging in extramarital intercourse. A practice by one woman supposedly prevented her husband from having an erection while with other women. "Tings we lub," a South Carolina slave woman said, "we don't like anybody else hab 'em. . . . What I hide behind de curtain now, I can't hide behind de curtain when I stand before God—de whole world know it den." Mary Chesnut summed up these beliefs. "Negro women are married," said Chesnut, "and after marriage behave as well as other people." "Bad men," she went on, "are hated here as elsewhere."[14] . . .

Reproducing the slave labor force required only the simple *biological* dyad "mother and child." The *social* dyads "husband and wife" and "father and child" were not essential. Neither was the completed nuclear family. But many owners, who did little to discourage prenuptial intercourse among their slaves, nevertheless encouraged the formation of completed slave families. Some did so for moral reasons, and others did so for economic reasons that had much more to do with the production of commercial crops and the performance of other unskilled and skilled tasks than with the reproduction of the labor force. Slave women mostly counted in the calculations of their owners as mothers, and slave men counted mostly as laborers. Although the reproduction of the labor force did not require the existence of completed slave families, maintenance of labor discipline did. Only those slaves who lived in affective familial groupings (and especially the greatly prized slave husband and father) could respond to indirect and direct incentives that exploited their familial bonds. Monetary rewards based on family labor (such as the slave garden plot) and incentive payments for "extra" work balanced the threat of the sale of relatives and especially of grown children. A husband and father might work harder to get extra rations for his children, to earn cash to purchase a luxury item for his wife, or to prevent his children from being sold.

Ideologues among the slaveowners mixed Christian obligation and economic reality in emphasizing the utility of "family government" among the slaves. The Baptist cleric Holland McTyeire urged owners to encourage slave marriages and to divide slaves "into families." It paid to "gratify the *home feeling* of the servant."

> Local as well as family associations, thus cast about him, are
> strong yet pleasing cords binding him to his master. His welfare
> is so involved in the order of things that he would not for any
> consideration have it disturbed. He is made happier and safer;
> put beyond discontent, or temptations to rebellion and abduc-
> tion; for he gains nothing in comparison with what he loses. His
> comforts cannot be removed with him, and he will stay with
> them.

A cotton plantation overseer near Natchez made the same point differently. Those runaway men who outwitted the dogs, he told Frederick Olmsted, "almost always kept in the neighborhood, because they
did not like to go where they could not sometimes get back and see
their families. . . . [T]hey would come round their quarters to see
their families and to get food, and as soon as he knew it, he would
find their tracks and put the dogs on again. . . ."[15]

Pressures within the slave system encouraged early childbirth among
slave women, but patterns of sexual behavior among slaves, particularly
women, disclose that slaves made difficult choices, often beyond the
master's influence. "Old Buford," said an elderly Tennessee ex-slave,
"his darkies had chillun by him, and mammy wouldn't do it; and I've
seen him take a paddle with holes in it and beat her." "Some of
them," another Tennessee woman remembered, "thought it was an
honor to have the marsa, but I didn't want no white foolin' with me."
The worst whipping John Finnelly recollected from his slave childhood
"was give to Clarinda; she hit massa with de hoe 'cause he try to 'fere
with her and she try stop him." In an 1865 Georgia divorce trial, the
ex-slave Louisa supported her old owner's complaint that the white
woman's husband had slept with slave women. She had resisted his
advances: once she slept with the white children; another time, she
"nailed up the windows of her house." When he got into her room
once, she "blew up the light to keep him off her, and he would blow
it out." The white persisted and even offered her "two dollars to feel
her titties." Occasional reports in southern medical journals and elsewhere described how slave women made yet other choices involving
abortive and contraceptive practices.[16] Among Good Hope women
who had a first child by one man and later settled into an enduring
relationship with a second man, sometimes several years passed before
the birth of a second child. It is hard to believe that during that time
they practiced sexual abstinence. Nancy, for example, had a first child

by Tony in 1829. A second child, the first of seven fathered by Burge over a seventeen-year period, was born to her in 1836. Lettice's first child was born in 1848 by a man whose name is unknown, and she gave birth to the first of two children by Major six years later. The recollections by elderly ex-slaves suggest yet other choices made by slave adults. A few—nearly all women and nearly always interviewed by blacks—said their parents withheld sexual information from them as young teen-agers. Some learned about menstruation after the fact. ("When it first come on," remembered an elderly woman, "I ran to the branch trying to make it stop. . . . But it didn't bother me. I was trying to stop it for I didn't know whether I was going to get a killing for it or not. I didn't know what it was.") Others said they were "most grown befo' we knowed a thing 'bout man and woman." Some children learned from their mothers that babies were born in "hollow logs" (or that "Aunt Sarah brought the babies"). Adult reproductive functions became known to some only upon marriage. A few described a modified trundle bed that hid parental lovemaking from them, and the South Carolina ex-slave Jacob Stroyer detailed efforts to maintain privacy and even to keep grown siblings apart. Cabins "were built so as to contain two families," and Stroyer remembered how the slaves coped with overcrowding:

> Some had partitions, while others had none. When there were not partitions each family would fit up his own part as he could, sometimes they got old boards and nailed them up, stuffing the cracks with old rags; when they could not get boards they hung up old clothes. When the family increased, the children all slept together, both boys and girls, until either got married, then a part of another cabin was assigned to the one that was married, but the rest would have to remain with their mother and father as they did when children unless they could get with some of their relatives or friends who had small families. . . . [T]he young men slept in the apartment known as the kitchen and the young women slept in the room with their mother and father.

Such decisions reveal the presence of sociosexual standards that affected the choices made by slaves. . . .[17]

The strength and pervasiveness of slave exogamous beliefs is indicated by their persistence over time on the Good Hope, by their presence among other plantation slaves as will be seen in . . . yet other evidence. In 1828, Mississippi blacks, their number unknown but most if not all of them probably slaves, posed the following question to a local Baptist Association: "Is it gospel for a Baptist Church to hold members in fellowship who have married relations nearer than Cousins?" It remains unclear whether they were concerned about the practices of fellow-slaves or white church members, but it is their concern over the relationship between church membership and marital rules that is important. A secular work song recollected by the ex-slave Allen Parker is entirely unambiguous in its meaning:

> Sally's in de garden siftin' sand,
> And all she want is a honey man.
> De reason why I wouldn't marry,
> Because she was my cousin.

> O, row de boat ashore, hey, hey,
> Sally's in de garden siftin' sand.

Neither Parker nor the unknown Mississippi blacks were Good Hope slaves, and that is what makes this evidence so important. In the 1930s, the aged Phillis Thomas, who had been a slave child in Texas, recollected yet another song that emphasized exogamous slave mores:

> Herodias go down to de river one day,
> Want to know what John Baptist have to say.
> John spoke de words at de risk of he life,
> Not lawful to marry you brudder's wife.

Two children of slave parents who had ended up in Arkansas—Lizzie Johnson and Cora Horton—told federal interviewers similar stories about how sale had inadvertently resulted in marriages that violated the primary incest taboo shared by slaves and nonslaves. Lizzie Johnson's Holly Springs, Mississippi, parents had known a man who "married a woman after freedom and found out she was his mother." He had been sold from her when an infant. "They quit," Johnson said, "and he married ag'in. He had a scar on his thigh she recollected. The scar was right there when he was grown. That brought up more talk and they traced him up to be her own boy." Cora Horton's slave parents had come to Arkansas from Georgia via Tennessee, and she heard a similar story from her grandmother. "I don't think these people were held accountable for that, do you?" she asked the interviewer. Cora Horton's people and those of these other women grew up far from the South Carolina Good Hope plantation. Taboos rooted in exogamous beliefs had traveled with slaves in the forced migration that carried hundreds of thousands of blacks from the Upper to the Lower South.[18]

Although rules defining the choice of marital partners existed among slaves and their owners, the Good Hope slaves had not copied the first-cousin marriage taboo from their owners. That is proved by the simple fact that no such taboo existed among the South Carolina planters. Drawing from the 1860 federal manuscript census, Chalmers Gaston Davidson has sketched a collective portrait of the 440 South Carolina men and women (all but forty born in that state) who owned at least one hundred slaves. "They were most amazingly inter-wed," concludes Davidson, "the marriages of cousins being almost the rule rather than the exception. . . . Nor was this a sectional phe-nomenon. The Gists of up-country Union, the Mobleys of Fairfield, the Ellerbes of Chesterfield, and the Westons and Adamses of Lower Richland were altogether as inbred by 1860 as were the Fripps of St. Helena's Parish, the Jenkins-Townsend-Seabrook clan of Edisto Island, or the Maners, Roberts, and Lawtons of St. Peters. The separate septs of Allston, Heyward, and Porcher apparently expected and were ex-pected to marry only within their circle of blood or bond." Intensive endogamy—blood-cousin marriage actually increased in importance over time—also existed among eighteenth-century Prince George's County, Maryland, slaveowning whites, a pattern uncovered by Allen Kulikoff. Slaveowners there were marrying close blood kin at the height of the African slave trade to the mainland North American colonies, a finding showing that marital rules among slaves and their owners had independent histories. But marriage and kinship among eighteenth- and early-nineteenth-century southern whites need far more study before it can be argued that exogamous rules among the slaves either had their roots in an adaptive Afro-American culture or drew directly upon antecedent West African beliefs and practices.[19] Such study may show, for example, that owners who married blood cousins violated a taboo enforced by other whites so that slaves and nonslave-owning whites shared common marital rules. That would mean that slaves did not differ from "whites" but that whites differed among themselves. Evidence of this kind, however, would not be proof that early slave generations had "copied" common nonslave marital rules. In West Africa, marriage between "relatives of legally estab-lished affiliation" was "forbidden as incestuous," and descent lines were traced in part to "ensure that no common affiliation" stood "in the way" of marriage. A detailed study of mid-twentieth-century African marriage patterns furthermore shows that "individual choice is limited by prohibitions against marriage with related persons, the extent of which varies from tribe to tribe but is nearly always much wider than in the western world." But little is yet known about eighteenth-century African marital practices. When studied, they, too, promise to reveal the presence of diverse but effective marital rules. The sources of the marital taboos among the Good Hope and other slaves, of course, cannot be inferred from twentieth-century evidence. But their origin counts for far less than the fact that they existed with no legal sanction and no known "white" models and were just as active in the 1850s as in earlier decades.[20]

Exogamous rules reveal much more than the cultural boundaries for selecting marital partners. "The rule of exogamy," the anthropologist A. R. Radcliffe-Brown points out, "is a way of giving institutional recognition to the bond of kinship" and serves as "part of the machinery for establishing and maintaining a wide-ranging kinship system." "A system of kinship and marriage," Radcliffe-Brown also writes, "can be looked at as an arrangement which enables people to live together and co-operate with one another in an orderly social life." It "links persons together by convergence of interest and sentiment and . . . controls and limits those conflicts that are always possible as a result of divergence of sentiment or interest." Particularly observant contemporaries noticed such enlarged Afro-American slave kin groups. "It was months before I learned their family relations," said the teacher Elizabeth Botume of the South Carolina Sea Island slaves. "The terms 'bubber' for brother and 'titty' for sister, with 'nanna' for mother and 'mother' for grandmother, and 'father' for all the leaders in church and society, were so generally used I was forced to believe that they all belonged to one immense family." Among the same slaves "the common name for relative is parent," observed Laura M. Towne; "they use this word for the whole family even to cousins." "Parents," Robert Smalls agreed, "mean relations in general; the same that they mean when they say 'family.'" (That "parents mean relations in general" may be a clue to the socialization of slave children in enlarged kin groups, a subject that deserves detailed study.)[21]

Smalls, Towne, and a few others described ties between kin in different immediate families. "The country people," said Smalls, "regard their relations more than the city people; they often walk fifteen miles on a Saturday night to see a cousin." Towne agreed: "Their affection extends to the whole family. If a cousin is in want, they admit the claim." Other observers of the wartime Sea Islanders noticed binding ties between members of different immediate families.

Such observations filled the illuminating diary of the black Philadelphia schoolteacher Charlotte Forten. An unidentified plantation superintendent, who, together with four other whites, lived among blacks on one of the islands, reported that following a threatened Confederate invasion the whites tried to "force the men of color to leave their families." But the men refused, put "the old people and children in little canoes," and paddled the canoes to places that concealed them. Another time, a young Parris Island man took a St. Helena's Island wife. "The two really loved each other," the journalist Nordhoff learned from John Zacchos, a Greek and a former Cincinnati teacher who labored as the Parris Island Superintendent of Freedmen. But the woman remained attached to her family of origin and was pulled in opposite directions. "They were married in regular form," said Nordhoff, "but after living some weeks with her husband the girl returned one day to her father's house and there remained." Her parents encouraged her to stay with them. A "number of young fellows" accompanied her husband by boat to St. Helena's Island and helped spirit the young wife away. A "bloody" quarrel threatened. Zacchos intervened, heard arguments on both sides, explained that the woman had willingly married her husband and still loved him, said her parents had "no more claim on their daughter," and ordered that the couple "live together." Zacchos followed conventional rules, but the husband saw that his solution pained his wife and therefore left the final decision with her. Nordhoff summarized her words: "I your wife, Sam; I love you; I love my fader and mudder, too; in de spring and in harvest, when de hard work is in de field, I come live wid you; when no hard work to do in de field, den I go home and you come live wid me." "Public opinion," said Nordhoff, "sustained the girl." Her husband accepted the proposal; hers was a "reasonable" arrangement.[22]

Such observations by contemporaries were unusual, partly because of distorted beliefs about the slaves and partly because the slaves hid many of their beliefs from whites. The Georgia slaveholder Charles C. Jones, who believed that slaves had "little *family government*" because most slave "parents are not qualified," admitted that whites "live and die in the midst of negroes and know comparatively little of their real character" because they were "one thing before whites, and another before their own color. Deception toward the former is characteristic of them, whether bond or free. . . . It is a habit—a long established custom, which descends from generation to generation." When Robert Smalls was asked whether "the masters know any thing of their secret life," the ex-slave replied in 1863, "No, sir, one life they show their masters and another they don't show."[23]

NOTES

1. In 1834, Mrs. Anne Heatly Lovell willed the Good Hope plantation to her nephew Joseph Dulles. His sister was married then to the South Carolina congressman Langdon Cheves. Their father, Joseph Dulles, had left Ireland in about 1777 and settled in Charleston to become a hardware merchant. He married Sophia Heatly and prospered, owning ten slaves in 1790 and serving later in that decade as the Charleston Commissioner of Streets and Lamps. He moved to Philadelphia in 1810 but maintained business connections with his South Carolina enterprises, and at his death in 1818 lived on Philadelphia's fashionable Walnut Street and owned two Charleston house lots, other Charleston real estate, and 753 acres in the Colleton district. His wife was descended from the early-eighteenth-century South Carolina Heatly family, which had settled in what became Saint Matthew's Parish. The younger Joseph Dulles inherited the Good Hope plantation from his mother's sister, an enterprise that specialized in the production of Santee, or long-staple "black-seed," cotton. I am indebted to Mrs. Granville T. Prior, the director of the South Carolina Historical Society, for making much of this information available. See also Samuel G. Stoney, *The Dulles Family in South Carolina* (1955), 1-14.

2. Good Hope Plantation Birth Register, 1760–1857, mss. copy, South Carolina Historical Society, Charleston, S.C. I am indebted to Stanley Engerman for bringing this unusually important document to my attention.

3. The median age of fathers at the birth of a first child was older than that of mothers. The ages of nineteen out of twenty-four are known: their median age was twenty-three. Only two were under twenty, and one of them was fourteen.

4. Peter Laslett, *The World We Have Lost* (1965), 82-83; Pierre Goubert, "Legitimate Fecundity and Infant Mortality in France during the Eighteenth Century: A Comparison," *Daedelus*, 98 (Spring 1968), 593-603; Moncure Conway, *Testimonies Concerning Slavery*, second edition (1865), 20.

5. South Carolina did not require former slaves to register their marriages and reveal how long they had lived together as husband and wife. But we can speculate about what the Good Hope slaves would have reported if it had. In 1857, twenty-two Good Hope couples had lived in marriages ranging from four to thirty-four years, and to these older unions are added new ones formed by slaves unmarried in 1857. About twenty such marriages would have occurred between 1857 and 1866. In registering marriages in 1866, the former Good Hope slaves would have reported lengthy slave marriages in nearly similar proportions to those actually registered by former Virginia and North Carolina slaves. About one in four would have been married between ten and nineteen years and the same percentage for twenty or more years. Such similarities suggest far more than that the Virginia and North Carolina registrants had good memories and had not falsified the length of their earlier marriages. They would also indicate that slaves did not have to share spatial and temporal ex-

periences with the Good Hope slaves in order to carry long marriages into freedom. A contrast between the Rockbridge County registrants and the Good Hope slaves illustrates this point. Only nine Rockbridge whites in 1860 owned thirty or more slaves; one owned between fifty and sixty-nine. About 12 percent of Rockbridge slaves lived on such places. Three in four belonged to whites owning fewer than twenty slaves. Rockbridge blacks therefore could not have shared a common historical experience with the Good Hope slaves. In 1866, one hundred thirty Rockbridge males aged forty and older registered slave marriages. Seven in ten had lived with a wife for at least twenty years. Fourteen Good Hope men of the same age would have registered marriages in 1866, twelve of whom had lived with a slave wife at least twenty years. Long slave marriages did not depend upon the presence of supportive kin networks on a single large plantation. Such kin networks existed among the Good Hope slaves. They could not have existed among most Rockbridge County slaves.

6. *Alvany (a free woman of color) v. Powell*, 1 Jones Esq. 35, December 1853, printed in Helen T. Catterall, *Judicial Cases Concerning American Slavery and the Negro* (1926–37), II, 179-80. See M. G. Smith, "Social Structure in the British Caribbean About 1820," *Social and Economic Studies*, I (1953), 71-72, for an opposite argument. "As property," Smith observes, "slaves were prohibited from forming legal relationships or marriages which would interfere with and restrict their owner's property rights." This is a correct statement, but it does not follow from it that "slaves lacked any generally accepted mode of establishing permanent mating relationships outside of legally recognized marriage among themselves" and that the "mating of slaves was typically unstable." An opposite but neglected argument is found in Melville J. Herskovits, *The Myth of the Negro Past* (1941), 139. Herskovits does not deny that enslavement "gave a certain instability to the marriage tie"; no one can deny that fact. But he realizes that "many" slaves "who lived out their lives on the same plantation were able to establish and maintain families." "It is far from certain," Herskovits added, "that undisturbed matings have not been lost sight of in the appeal of the more dramatic separations that did occur in large numbers."

7. John W. Blassingame, *The Slave Community: Plantation Life in the Antebellum South* (1972), 82; T. R. R. Cobb, *Law of Slavery* (1858), ccix-ccxx; Toombs 1856 speech printed in A. H. Stephens, *A Constitutional View of the Late War* I (1868), 641-43; *Pro-Slavery Argument* (1852), 41, 44-45; *Southern Literary Messenger*, I (1844), 329-39, 470-80; *DeBow's Review*, 28 (1860), 52.

8. For other contemporary observations about slave sexual behavior, see *Facts Concerning the Freedmen. Their Capacities, and Their Destinies. Collected and Published by the Emancipation League* (Boston, 1863), 3-12; "Interview with J. R. Roudanez," in James MacKaye, *The Mastership and Its Fruits* (1864), 4-6. See also Charles Lyell, *A Second Visit to the United States of North America* I (1849), 271-73. Lyell's wife came to know an Alabama woman who had raised "a colored girl" to be "modest and well behaved." The young slave woman became the mother of "a mulatto child." "The mistress," Lyell reported, "reproached her very severely for her misconduct, and the girl at first took the rebuke much to heart; but having gone home one day to visit her mother, a native African, she returned, saying that her parent had assured

her she had done nothing wrong, and had no reason to be ashamed." Lyell felt this to be evidence of "the loose code of morality which the Africans have inherited from their parents."

9. Testimony before the American Freedmen's Inquiry Commission, 1863, file 2 (pp. 4-5), file 3 (pp. 4-7, 42-43, 63-64, 70, 85, 100-105, 125-26, 160, 223-24), file 8 (p. 28), Letters Received, Office of the Adjutant General, 1861–1870, Main Series, Reels 200 and 201, National Archives.

10. Charles Nordhoff, "Freedmen of South Carolina," in Frank Moore, ed., *Papers of the Day #1* (1863), 21-24; Mary B. Chesnut, A *Diary from Dixie* (1949), 121-23; F. L. Olmsted, *Journey in the Back Country* (1863), 113-14, 153-55; Harriet Beecher Stowe, *Key to Uncle Tom's Cabin* (1854), 298-301; *American Slave, South Carolina Narratives*, III, iv, 208-9.

11. Peter Gaskell, *Manufacturing Population of England* (1833), quoted Margaret Hewitt, *Wives and Mothers in Victorian England* (1958), 54; Bronislaw Malinowski, "Parenthood—the Basis of Social Structure," in V. F. Calverton and Samuel D. Schmalhausen, eds., *New Generation* (1930), 129-43; *id.*, *Sex and Repression in Savage Society* (1927), 195.

12. *Unwritten History* . . . (*Fisk*), 1-6, 67-69, 77-79, 123-27, 153-54; *American Slave, Texas Narratives*, IV, i, 62-65, *South Carolina Narratives*, II, ii, 200-203; 1854 diary notation quoted in Bobby Frank Jones, "A Cultural Middle Passage: Slave Marriage and Family in the Antebellum South," unpublished Ph.D. dissertation, University of North Carolina, 1965, 169; Lunsford Lane, *Narrative of Lunsford Lane* (1842), 11; Nordhoff, "Freedmen of the South," in Frank Moore, ed., *Papers of the Day #1*, 23-24.

13. Botume, *First Days Amongst the Contrabands* (1893), 125-27, 162-167; Nordhoff, "Freedmen of the South," 21-24; Austa French, *Slavery in South Carolina* (1863), 180-87, 190-91.

14. Alvany (a *free woman of color*) v. *Powell*, 1 Jones Esq. 35, December 1853, printed in Catterall, *Judicial Cases Concerning Slavery*, II, 179-80; *State v. Tackett*, 1 Hawks 210-22, December 1820; *State v. Samuel, a slave*, 2 Devereux and Battle's Law, 177-185, December 1836; *State v. John, a slave*, 8 Iredell 330-39, June 1848; *Alfred, a slave v. The State of Mississippi*, 37 Miss. 296-99, October 1859; *Samuel Adams v. William Adams*, 36 Ga. 236-37, June 1867; *Timmons v. Lacy*, 30 Texas 126, April 1867; *American Slave, South Carolina Narratives*, II, i, 13-16, ii, 129-33; testimony of Robert Smalls, A. D. Smith and E. G. Dudley, American Freedmen's Inquiry Commission, 1863, file 3, Office of the Adjutant General, Letters Received, Main Series, 1861–1870, Reel 200, National Archives; *Letters from Port Royal* (1906), ed. E. W. Pearson, 86-87; Zora Hurston, "Hoodoo in America," *Journal of American Folklore*, 44 (October–December 1931), 391, 400-401; Stowe, *Key to Uncle Tom's Cabin* (1854), 298-301; Chesnut, *Diary from Dixie*, 122. See also *Smith, a slave, v. The State*, 9 Ala. 990-98, June 1846; *William v. The State*, 33 Ga. Supp. 85-94, March 1864; Johnson, *Ante-bellum North Carolina: A Social History*, 538-39; Johnston, *Race Relations in Virginia*, 305-6.

15. Frederic Bancroft, *Slave Trading in the Old South* (1931), 74-75, 79-86; *Proslavery Argument* (1852), 40-44, 368; *American Cotton Planter*, I, n.s., 295, II, 331, III, 76; Olmsted, *Seaboard States* (1857), 280; J. C. Reed, *The Brother's War* (1905), 48-49, 156, 334, 432; J. S. Bassett, *Plantation Overseer* (1925), 21-22, 260-61; Phillips, *American Negro Slavery* (1918), 85-86;

Phillips, ed., *Plantation Documents* (1909), I, 179; W. K. Scarborough, *The Overseer: Plantation Management in the Old South* (1966), 68-70, 91-92, 97; W. D. Postell, *The Health of Slaves on Southern Plantations* (1951), 111, 119; Thomas W. Knox, *Camp-Fire and Cotton-Field: Southern Adventures in Time of War* (1865), 355-359; *Southern Cultivator*, V (1847), 142-43, VI (1848), 120, XVI (1858), 273-74, 319; J. W. DuBose, "Recollections . . ." *Alabama History Quarterly*, I (Spring 1930), 65-66; *DeBow's Review*, XVIII (1855), 715 XX (1856), 656, XXII (1857), 44, XXVIII (1860), 52-53.

16. The Hancock County, Georgia, physician E. M. Pendleton reported in 1849 that among his patients "abortion and miscarriage" occurred much more frequently among slave than free white women. The cause was either "slave labor" ("exposure, violent exercise, &c.") or, "as the planters believe, [that] the blacks are possessed of a secret by which they destroy the fetus at an early stage of gestation." "All country practitioners," he added, "are aware of the frequent complaints of planters" about the "unnatural tendency in the African female to destroy her offspring." "Whole families of women," he went on, "fail to have any children." The same doctor mentioned "several domestic remedies calculated to produce this effect" but was unsure that slave women knew of them. A much more detailed report of similar practices came from the Murfreesboro, Tennessee, physician John T. Morgan in a paper read before the Rutherford County Medical Society in May 1860. Morgan told that some slave women tried "to effect an abortion or to derange menstruation" by "medicine," "violent exercise," and "external and internal manipulation." Another physician had dealt with a slave woman who stuffed "a roll of rags about two or three inches long and as hard as a stick" into her vagina, but Morgan found it "a very rare thing for negroes to resort to mechanical means to effect an abortion, probably less than white women, on account of their ignorance." Instead, "the remedies mostly used by the negroes to procure abortion" were "the infusion or decoction of tansy, rue, roots and seed of the cotton plant, pennyroyal, cedar gum, and camphor, either in gum or spirits." These are medically questionable as successful emmenagogues; it was their use, not their value, that reveals most about the Tennessee slave women. "Old women" found rue "more effectual than tansy to procure abortion." But rue was not widely cultivated. Single tansy was "more generally known" as an abortifacient and was "being commonly cultivated in our gardens." Cotton plant roots, moreover, were "habitually and effectively resorted to by the slaves of the South for producing abortion." "They think," said Morgan, "it acts in this way without injury to the general health." He himself had not known of a case involving a brew made of cotton root but said another Tennessee doctor had found it "a most excellent emmenagogue in his practice—more so than any remedy he has ever tried." Morgan doubted the effectiveness of camphor as a stimulant to miscarriage but explained:

> From the extent it is employed it must effect something. It is employed extensively as a preventive of conception; . . . they take it just before or after menstruation, in quantities sufficient to produce a little nervousness for two or three days; when it has effect they consider themselves safe. . . . A good many women who are not fruitful after the first

birth, use camphor freely, and I have frequently detected its use in this way by the effect of secretions.

A Nashville medical journal summarized the discussion that Morgan's paper provoked among its auditors. One doctor blamed barrenness on "the want of attention and care of negro women" and "the exposure to which they are subject as field hands." Another blamed the slaves. He told of an owner who had kept between four and six slave women of "the proper age to breed" for twenty-five years and that "only two children had been born on the place at full term." The white sold a suspect couple but that did not end "the frequent abortions." Neither did the purchase of new slaves. "Every [new] conception was aborted by the fourth month." The slaves finally admitted that they took "medicine," and showed their owner "the weed which was their favorite remedy." That same physician learned from another owner about an "old negro woman" who supplied "the remedy" to his slaves and had been "instrumental in all . . . the abortions on his place."

In the 1870s, the Bostonian George Stetson attributed the alleged decline in the southern black population to "the root of the cotton plant," "known to all negro women as a powerful emmenagogue, . . . everywhere obtainable . . . [and] extensively used." Half a century later, Newbell Niles Puckett talked with three southern blacks who described medicinal and magical efforts to prevent conception or to induce abortion, including swallowing gunpowder mixed with sweet milk or just "nine bird-shot," drinking separate mixtures of "black haw roots" and bluestone with "red shank" roots followed by the juice of dog-fennel root, and a teaspoonful of turpentine each morning for nine consecutive days. A vaginal douche made from a tea brewed from cockleburr roots mixed with bluestone was intended to induce menstruation and wash out the fetus. Abortive devices also included a yarn string saturated with turpentine and worn around the waist for nine days. Other magical methods included the woman's keeping a copper coin or brass pin under her tongue during coitus, holding "perfectly motionless during coitus," and turning on her left side immediately "after the act." Even later than Puckett, the sociologist Hylan Lewis learned from elderly North Carolina blacks about such birth control devices as "a brew from an unknown root gotten from the woods, a brew from the roots of a cotton plant, and a brew from green coffee." The published edition of the Frank Brown Collection of North Carolina Folklore indicates that North Carolina whites as well as blacks believed that pregnancy could be "arrested by a strong tea made by boiling cotton roots," and that among Ozark whites "cotton roots mixed with tansy," pennyroyal, turpentine, and camomile and cedarberry tea were believed to induce abortion. Certain Pennsylvania and Illinois whites also believed that camphor and turpentine affected respectively pregnancy and conception. Much remains to be learned about such beliefs and practices among Afro-American slaves and emancipated blacks, but even this scattered evidence suggests that they were widespread among rural southern whites and even some rural northern whites, as well as among slaves.

Nothing much is yet known about the presence of nineteenth-century birth-control devices among the slaves or their owners and other southern whites. Hints that some whites and even blacks used such devices are found in the testimony of Richard Hinton and James Redpath before the American Freedmen's Inquiry Commission in 1863. Both men were northern abolitionists and hardly objective witnesses. Neither offered direct evidence. Hinton testified that a slave was ordered by his dead owner's wife "to sleep with her, and he did regularly." "He said," Hinton added, that the widow "procured some of these French articles that are used to prevent the consequences of sexual intercourse." Redpath believed that sexual relations were more common between white women and black men than most contemporaries realized. One example he cited involved a "prominent" white Mobile woman who gave birth to a mulatto child soon after her marriage. According to Redpath, the woman and her mulatto servant regularly had intercourse, including on her wedding day. "She had taken no precaution on that occasion," he said. E. M. Pendleton, "On the Susceptibility of the Caucasian and African Races to the Different Classes of Diseases," *Southern Medical and Surgical Journal* (1849), reprinted in *Southern Medical Reports*, II (1849), 338; John H. Morgan, "An Essay on the Production of Abortion Among Our Negro Population," *Nashville Journal of Medicine and Surgery*, XIX (August 1860), 117-123. Evidence of plantation-slave infanticide is found in F. M. Green, ed., *Ferry Plantation Journal, Jan. 4, 1838-Jan. 15, 1839* (1961), 25-26, and R. M. Myers, ed., *The Children of Pride* (1972), 527-28, 532-33, 544. Various southern rural abortifacts are detailed in George Stetson, *The Southern Negro as He Is* (1877), 20; N. N. Puckett, *Folk Beliefs of the Southern Negro* (1926), 331-32; Hylan Lewis, *Blackways of Kent* (1955), 91; *Frank Brown Collection of North Carolina Folklore*, VI (1961), 6-7. Hinton's and Redpath's testimonies are in American Freedmen's Inquiry Commission, 1863, files 8 and 9, Letters Received, Office of the Adjutant General, Main Series, 1861–1870, Reel 201, National Archives. For a denial of infanticide, see J. W. Alvord, Savannah, 13 Jan. 1870, to O. O. Howard, in JWA, *Letters from the South Relating to the Condition of the Freedmen Addressed to Major General O. O. Howard* (1870), 8.

17. *Odom v. Odom*, 36 Ga. 286-320, June 1867; *American Slave, South Carolina Narratives*, II, ii, 11-26, 166-70, 200-203, III, iii, 17-19; *Texas Narratives*, IV, ii, 35-40, V, iv, 190-94; *Arkansas Narratives*, IX, ix, 9-13; *Unwritten History (Fisk)*, 1-6, 55-58, 67-69, 77-79, 103-8, 141-51; *Negro in Virginia* (WPA), 89; Jacob Stroyer, *Sketches of My Life in the South* (1879), 8-12, 31-33.

18. Union, Miss., Baptist Association, *Minutes*, 1828 (Natchez, 1828), 6, cited in Kenneth K. Bailey, "Protestantism and Afro-Americans in the Old South: Another Look," *Journal of Southern History*, XLI (November 1975), 457; Allen Parker, *Recollections of Slavery Times* (1885), 66-67; *American Slave, Texas Narratives*, V, iv, 92-94; *Arkansas Narratives*, IX, iii, 318-22, iv, 102-3. See also the interview with Tom Cox in *Negro in Virginia* (WPA), 85-86. For a marriage that may have violated the primary incest taboo, see Emily Blackman, Okolona, Miss., 1 May 1867, to the editor, *Pennsylvania Freedmen's Bulletin* (June 1867), 7. She knew an ex-slave family from Alabama in which "the present wife is the daughter of the first one, both being here, and often at school together, with the husband on pleasant terms, the latter always making of his first wife as his 'mother-in-law.' "

19. Marital rules remain little studied. But Bernard Farber has found evidence of marriage between close blood kin in late eighteenth-century Salem,

Massachusetts, where "first-cousin marriage . . . facilitated the creation of alliances and partnerships in business and politics." Farber finds similar ties among Salem artisans and their wives. Endogamy in a developing economy that did not yet know the private corporation as a legal device for accumulating and consolidating wealth may have been a cultural practice shared by aspiring and established Yankee merchants and Carolina cavaliers. Our understanding of the importance of family and kinship ("the world of cousinship") in ordering antebellum southern white society is vastly enlarged in Bertram Wyatt-Brown's brilliant essay, "The Ideal Typology and Antebellum Southern History: A Testing of a New Approach," *Societas*, V (Winter 1975), 1-29.

It is also possible that endogamous marriages occurred among relatively privileged antebellum free Negroes. According to E. H. Fitchett, the tiny free colored Charleston elite was a "class-conscious group" whose "behavior was a replica of that class in white society which they aspired to be like." The St. Phillip's Church marriage book showed "a considerable number of marriages among families who were either business partners or who were identified with the same social and fraternal organizations." "Usage and expectation" meant that mate selection was "made from in-group members." Fitchett did not indicate whether such marriages involved blood kin. John Blassingame's study of postbellum. New Orleans blacks describes "a great deal of intermarriage" among "upper-class Negroes." But he does not discuss kin marriage. It may yet turn out that the small but significant amounts of real and personal wealth accumulated by these free black elites encouraged marital alliances more like those of white planters than those of black slaves.

See Bernard Farber, "Family and Community Structure: Salem in 1800," in Michael Gordon, ed., *The American Family in Socio-Historical Perspective* (1973), 100-110; E. H. Fitchett, "The Traditions of the Free Negro in Charleston, South Carolina," *Journal of Negro History*, XXV (1940), 139-42; John Blassingame, *Black New Orleans*, 1860–1880 (1973), 161-62.

20. Herskovits, *Myth of the Negro Past*, 64; L. P. Mair, "African Marriage and Social Change," in Arthur Phillips, ed., *Survey of African Marriage and Family Life*, part I (1953), 4; Chalmers Gaston Davidson, *The Last Foray, The South Carolina Planters of 1860: A Sociological Study* (1971), 5-6; I am indebted to Mr. Kulikoff for showing me portions of his fine study, as yet unpublished. He finds that, between 1730 and 1790, 42 percent of white Prince George's County marriages for which records exist were between persons closely related by blood or marriage. The percentages of cousin marriages increased: from 12.5 percent in 1730–1760 to 21.3 percent in 1760–1790. Some cousin marriages involved second cousins, but most were between first cousins.

A single instance has been found where slaveowners talked of prohibiting marriages between cousins. In 1856, the Virginia planter Thomas Jefferson Massie argued that only slaves "unconnected by blood" should be allowed "to pair off," fearing that kin-related marriages would make the slaves "little better than the monkeys of their native land." (Quoted in Phillips, *Life and Labor in the Old South*, 238-39.) V. Alton Moody suggested that "some" Louisiana sugar planters "strictly prohibited" slave cousin marriages. "Planters themselves," said Moody, "would marry cousins, but their negroes were too valuable to be permitted to degenerate." No evidence accompanied this assertion. (V. Alton Moody, "Slavery on Louisiana Sugar Plantations," *Louisiana Historical Quarterly*, VII [1924].)

21. A. R. Radcliffe-Brown, "Introduction," in A. R. Radcliffe-Brown and Daryll Forde, eds., *African Systems of Kinship and Marriage* (1950), 3, 66-67; Elizabeth Botume, *First Days Amongst the Contrabands*, 48; testimony of Laura Towne and Robert Smalls, 1863, American Freedmen's Inquiry Commission, Office of the Adjutant General, Letters Received, Main Series, 1861–1870, file 3, pp. 65, 105, 108-9, Reel 200, National Archives.

22. Testimony of Smalls and Towne as cited in footnote 27; *Journal of Charlotte Forten*, ed. Ray A. Billington (1953), *passim* and especially 142-46; unnamed superintendent, quoted in J. M. McKim, 24 July 1862, to the editor, *Liberator*, 8 Aug. 1862; Nordhoff, "Freedmen of the South," in Moore, ed., *Papers of the Day #1* (1863), 23-24.

23. Jones, *Religious Instruction of the Negroes in the United States* (1842), 110-11; testimony of Robert Smalls, 1863, American Freedmen's Inquiry Commission, Office of the Adjutant General, Letters Received, Main Series, 1861–1870, file 3, pp. 65, 105, 108-9, Reel 200, National Archives.

IV: SLAVE PERSONALITY

• *The following selection presents Stanley M. Elkins's influential analysis of the mechanisms used by American slaveholders to produce infantile behavior among their Negro bondsmen. It also discusses his controversial concentration-camp analogy. The student should remember that Elkins is attempting only to describe the "Sambo"-like characteristics* which he associates with the role playing expected of American Negro slaves; he is not in any sense expressing his approval *of the concept, whatever its validity as an explanation of slave personality.*

Slavery and Negro Personality

STANLEY M. ELKINS

PERSONALITY TYPES AND STEREOTYPES

. . . It will be assumed that there were elements in the very structure of the plantation system—its "closed" character—that could sustain infantilism as a normal feature of behavior. These elements, having less to do with "cruelty" per se than simply with the sanctions of authority, were effective and pervasive enough to require that such infantilism be characterized as something much more basic than mere "accommodations." It will be assumed that the sanctions of the system were in themselves sufficient to produce a recognizable personality type.[1]

It should be understood that to identify a social type in this sense is still to generalize on a fairly crude level—and to insist for a limited purpose on the legitimacy of such generalizing is by no means to deny that, on more refined levels, a great profusion of individual types might have been observed in slave society. Nor need it be claimed that the "Sambo" type, even in the relatively crude sense employed here, was a

From A *Problem in American Institutional and Intellectual Life* by Stanley M. Elkins (Chicago: University of Chicago Press, 1976), pp. 86-89, 115-39. Copyright © 1976 by University of Chicago Press. Reprinted by permission of University of Chicago Press.

universal type. It was, however, a plantation type, and a plantation existence embraced well over half the slave population.[2] Two kinds of material will be used in the effort to picture the mechanisms whereby this adjustment to absolute power—an adjustment whose end product included infantile features of behavior—may have been effected. One is drawn from the theoretical knowledge presently available in social psychology, and the other, in the form of an analogy, is derived from some of the data that have come out of the German concentration camps. It is recognized in most theory that social behavior is regulated in some general way by adjustment to symbols of authority—however diversely "authority" may be defined either in theory or in culture itself—and that such adjustment is closely related to the very formation of personality. A corollary would be, of course, that the more diverse those symbols of authority may be, the greater is the permissible variety of adjustment to them—and the wider the margin of individuality, consequently, in the development of the self. The question here has to do with the wideness or narrowness of that margin on the antebellum plantation.

The other body of material, involving an experience undergone by several million men and women in the concentration camps of our own time, contains certain items of relevance to the problem here being considered. The experience was analogous to that of slavery and was one in which wide-scale instances of infantilization were observed. The material is sufficiently detailed, and sufficiently documented by men who not only took part in the experience itself but who were versed in the use of psychological theory for analyzing it, that the advantages of drawing upon such data for purposes of analogy seem to outweigh the possible risks.

The introduction of this second body of material must to a certain extent govern the theoretical strategy itself. It has been recognized both implicitly and explicitly that the psychic impact and effects of the concentration-camp experience were not anticipated in existing theory and that consequently such theory would require some major supplementation.[3] It might be added, parenthetically, that almost any published discussion of this modern Inferno, no matter how learned, demonstrates how "theory," operating at such a level of shared human experience, tends to shed much of its technical trappings and to take on an almost literary quality. The experience showed, in any event, that infantile personality features could be induced in a relatively short time among large numbers of adult human beings coming from very diverse backgrounds. The particular strain which was thus placed upon prior theory consisted in the need to make room not only for the cultural and environmental sanctions that sustain personality (which in a sense Freudian theory already had) but also for a virtually unanticipated problem: actual change in the personality of masses of adults. It forced a reappraisal and new appreciation of how completely and effectively prior cultural sanctions for behavior and personality could be detached to make way for new and different sanctions, and of how adjustments could be made by individuals to a species of authority vastly different from any previously known. The revelation for theory was the process of detachment.

These cues, accordingly, will guide the argument on Negro slavery. Several million people were detached with a peculiar effectiveness from a great variety of cultural backgrounds in Africa—a detachment operating with infinitely more effectiveness upon those brought to North America than upon those who came to Latin America. It was achieved partly by the shock experience inherent in the very mode of procurement but more specifically by the type of authority-system to which they were introduced and to which they had to adjust for physical and psychic survival. The new adjustment, to absolute power in a closed system, involved infantilization, and the detachment was so complete that little trace of prior (and thus alternative) cultural sanctions for behavior and personality remained for the descendants of the first generation. For them, adjustment to clear and omnipresent authority could be more or less automatic—as much so, or as little, as it is for anyone whose adjustment to a social system begins at birth and to whom that system represents normality. We do not know how generally a full adjustment was made by the first generation of fresh slaves from Africa. But we do know—from a modern experience—that such an adjustment is possible, not only within the same generation but within two or three years. This proved possible for people in a full state of complex civilization, for men and women who were not black and not savages. . . .

THREE THEORIES OF PERSONALITY

The immense revelation for psychology in the concentration-camp literature has been the discovery of how elements of dramatic personality change could be brought about in masses of individuals. And yet it is not proper that the crude fact of "change" alone should dominate the conceptual image with which one emerges from this problem. "Change" per se, change that does not go beyond itself, is productive of nothing; it leaves only destruction, shock, and howling bedlam behind it unless some future basis of stability and order lies waiting to guarantee it and give it reality. So it is with the human psyche, which is apparently capable of making terms with a state other than liberty as we know it. The very dramatic features of the process just described may upset the nicety of this point. There is the related danger, moreover, of unduly stressing the individual psychology of the problem at the expense of its social psychology.

These hazards might be minimized by maintaining a conceptual distinction between two phases of the group experience. The process of detachment from prior standards of behavior and value is one of them, and is doubtless the more striking, but there must be another one. That such detachment can, by extension, involve the whole scope of an individual's culture is an implication for which the vocabulary of individual psychology was caught somewhat unawares. Fluctuations in the state of the individual psyche could formerly be dealt with, or so it seemed, while taking for granted the more or less static nature of social organization, and with a minimum of reference to its features. That such organization might itself become an important variable was therefore a possibility not highly developed in theory, focused as theory was upon individual case histories to the invariable minimization of social and cultural setting. The other phase of the experience should be considered as the "stability" side of the problem, that phase which stabilized what the "shock" phase only opened the way for. This was essentially a process of adjustment to a standard of social normality, though in this case a drastic readjustment and compressed within a very short time—a process which under typical conditions of individual and group existence is supposed to begin at birth and last a lifetime and be transmitted in many and diffuse ways from generation to generation. The adjustment is assumed to be slow and organic, and it normally is. Its numerous aspects extend much beyond psychology; those aspects have in the past been treated at great leisure within the rich provinces not only of psychology but of history, sociology, and literature as well. What rearrangement and compression of those provinces may be needed to accommodate a mass experience that not only involved profound individual shock but also required rapid assimilation to a drastically different form of social organization, can hardly be known. But perhaps the most conservative beginning may be made with existing psychological theory.

The theoretical system whose terminology was orthodox for most of the Europeans who have written about the camps was that of Freud. It was necessary for them to do a certain amount of improvising, since the scheme's existing framework provided only the narrowest leeway for dealing with such radical concepts as out-and-out change in personality. This was due to two kinds of limitations which the Freudian vocabulary places upon the notion of the "self." One is that the superego—that part of the self involved in social relationships, social values, expectations of others, and so on—is conceived as only a small and highly refined part of the "total" self. The other is the assumption that the content and character of the superego is laid down in childhood and undergoes relatively little basic alteration thereafter.[4] Yet a Freudian diagnosis of the concentration-camp inmate—whose social self, or superego, did appear to change and who seemed basically changed thereby—is, given these limitations, still possible. Elie Cohen, whose analysis is the most thorough of these, specifically states that "the superego acquired new values in a concentration camp."[5] The old values, according to Dr. Cohen, were first silenced by the shocks which produced "acute depersonalization" (the subject-object split: "It is not the real 'me' who is undergoing this"), and by the powerful drives of hunger and survival. Old values, thus set aside, could be replaced by new ones. It was a process made possible by "infantile regression"—regression to a previous condition of childlike dependency in which parental prohibitions once more became all-powerful and in which parental judgments might once more be internalized. In this way a new "father-image," personified in the SS guard, came into being. That the prisoner's identification with the SS could be so positive is explained by still another mechanism: the principle of "identification with the aggressor." "A child," as Anna Freud writes, "interjects some characteristic of an anxiety-object and so assimilates an anxiety-experience which he has just undergone. . . . By impersonating the aggressor, assuming his attributes or imitating his aggression, the child transforms himself from the person threatened into the person who makes the threat."[6] In short, the child's only "defense" in the presence of a cruel, all-powerful father is the psychic defense of identification.

Now one could, still retaining the Freudian language, represent all this in somewhat less cumbersome terms by a slight modification of the metaphor. It could simply be said that under great stress the superego, like a bucket, is violently emptied of content and acquires, in a radically changed setting, new content. It would thus not be necessary to postulate a literal "regression" to childhood in order for this to occur. Something of the sort is suggested by Leo Alexander. "The

psychiatrist stands in amazement," he writes, "before the thoroughness and completeness with which this perversion of essential superego
values was accomplished in adults . . . [and] it may be that the
decisive importance of childhood and youth in the formation of
[these] values may have been overrated by psychiatrists in a society in
which allegiance to these values in normal adult life was taken too
much for granted because of the stability, religiousness, legality, and
security of the 19th Century and early 20th Century society." [7]

A second theoretical scheme is better prepared for crisis and more
closely geared to social environment than the Freudian adaptation indicated above, and it may consequently be more suitable for accommo-
dating not only the concentration-camp experience but also the more
general problem of plantation slave personality. This is the "interpersonal theory" developed by the late Harry Stack Sullivan. One may
view this body of work as the response to a peculiarly American set of
needs. The system of Freud, so aptly designed for a European society
the stability of whose institutional and status relationships could always to a large extent be taken for granted, turns out to be less clearly
adapted to the culture of the United States. The American psychiatrist
has had to deal with individuals in a culture where the diffuse, shifting, and often uncertain quality of such relationships has always been
more pronounced than in Europe. He has come to appreciate the extent to which these relationships actually support the individual's
psychic balance—the full extent, that is, to which the self is "social"
in its nature. Thus a psychology whose terms are flexible enough to
permit altering social relationships to make actual differences in character structure would be a psychology especially promising for dealing
with the present problem.[8]

Sullivan's great contribution was to offer a concept whereby the
really critical determinants of personality might be isolated for purposes of observation. Out of the hopelessly immense totality of "influences" which in one way or another go to make up the personality,
or "self," Sullivan designated one—the estimations and expectations
of others—as the one promising to unlock the most secrets. He then
made a second elimination: the *majority* of "others" in one's existence
may for theoretical purposes be neglected; what counts is who the
significant others are. Here, "significant others" [9] may be understood
very crudely to mean those individuals who hold, or seem to hold, the
keys to security in one's own personal situation, whatever its nature.
Now as to the psychic processes whereby these "significant others"
become an actual part of the personality, it may be said that the very

sense of "self" first emerges in connection with anxiety about the attitudes of the most important persons in one's life (initially, the mother, father, and their surrogates—persons of more or less absolute authority), and automatic attempts are set in motion to adjust to these attitudes. In this way their approval, their disapproval, their estimates and appraisals, and indeed a whole range of their expectations become as it were internalized, and are reflected in one's very character. Of course as one "grows up," one acquires more and more significant others whose attitudes are diffuse and may indeed compete, and thus "significance," in Sullivan's sense, becomes subtler and less easy to define. The personality exfoliates; it takes on traits of distinction and, as we say, "individuality." The impact of particular significant others is less dramatic than in early life. But the pattern is a continuing one; new significant others do still appear, and theoretically it is conceivable that even in mature life the personality might be visibly affected by the arrival of such a one—supposing that this new significant other were vested with sufficient authority and power. In any event there are possibilities for fluidity and actual change inherent in this concept which earlier schemes have lacked.

The purest form of the process is to be observed in the development of children, not so much because of their "immaturity" as such (though their plasticity is great and the imprint of early experience goes deep), but rather because for them there are fewer significant others. For this reason—because the pattern is simpler and more easily controlled—much of Sullivan's attention was devoted to what happens in childhood. In any case let us say that unlike the adult, the child, being drastically limited in the selection of significant others, must operate in a "closed system."

Such are the elements which make for order and balance in the normal self: "significant others" plus "anxiety" in a special sense—conceived with not simply disruptive but also guiding, warning functions.[10] The structure of "interpersonal" theory thus has considerable room in it for conceptions of guided change—change for either beneficent or malevolent ends. One technique for managing such change would of course be the orthodox one of psychoanalysis; another, the actual changing of significant others.[11] Patrick Mullahy, a leading exponent of Sullivan, believes that in group therapy much is possible along these lines.[12] A demonic test of the whole hypothesis is available in the concentration camp.

Consider the camp prisoner—not the one who fell by the wayside but the one who was eventually to survive; consider the ways in which he was forced to adjust to the one significant other which he now had —the SS guard, who held absolute dominion over every aspect of his life. The very shock of his introduction was perfectly designed to dramatize this fact; he was brutally maltreated ("as by a cruel father"); the shadow of resistance would bring instant death. Daily life in the camp, with its fear and tensions, taught over and over the lesson of absolute power. It prepared the personality for a drastic shift in standards. It crushed whatever anxieties might have been drawn from prior standards; such standards had become meaningless. It focused the prisoner's attention constantly on the moods, attitudes, and standards of the only man who mattered. A truly childlike situation was thus created: utter and abject dependency on one, or on a rigidly limited few, significant others. All the conditions which in normal life would give the individual leeway—which allowed him to defend himself against a new and hostile significant other, no matter how powerful—were absent in the camp. No competition of significant others was possible; the prisoner's comrades for practical purposes were helpless to assist him.[13] He had no degree of independence, no lines to the outside, in any matter. Everything, every vital concern, focused on the SS: food, warmth, security, freedom from pain, all depended on the omnipotent significant other, all had to be worked out within the closed system. Nowhere was there a shred of privacy; everything one did was subject to SS supervision. The pressure was never absent. It is thus no wonder that the prisoners should become "as children." It is no wonder that their obedience became unquestioning, that they did not revolt, that they could not "hate" their masters. Their masters' attitudes had become *internalized* as a part of their very selves; those attitudes and standards now dominated all others that they had. They had, indeed, been "changed."

There still exists a third conceptual framework within which these phenomena may be considered. It is to be found in the growing field of "role psychology." This psychology is not at all incompatible with interpersonal theory; the two might easily be fitted into the same system.[14] But it might be strategically desirable, for several reasons, to segregate them for purposes of discussion. One such reason is the extraordinary degree to which role psychology shifts the focus of attention upon the individual's cultural and institutional environment rather than upon his "self." At the same time it gives us a manageable concept—that of "role"—for mediating between the two. As a mechanism, the role enables us to isolate the unique contribution of culture and institutions toward maintaining the psychic balance of the individual. In it, we see formalized for the individual a range of choices in models of behavior and expression, each with its particular style, quality, and attributes. The relationship between the "role" and the "self," though not yet clear, is intimate; it is at least possible at certain levels of inquiry to look upon the individual as the variable and upon the roles extended him as the stable factor.[15] We thus have a potentially durable link between individual psychology and the study of culture. It might even be said, inasmuch as its key term is directly borrowed from the theater, that role psychology offers in workable form the long-awaited connection—apparently missed by Ernest Jones in his *Hamlet* study—between the insights of the classical dramatists and those of the contemporary social theorist.[16] But be that as it may, for our present problem, the concentration camp, it suggests the most flexible account of how the ex-prisoners may have succeeded in resuming their places in normal life.

Let us note certain of the leading terms.[17] A "social role" is definable in its simplest sense as the behavior expected of persons specifically located in specific social groups.[18] A distinction is kept between "expectations" and "behavior;" the expectations of a role (embodied in the "script") theoretically exist in advance and are defined by the organization, the institution, or by society at large. Behavior (the "performance") refers to the manner in which the role is played. Another distinction involves roles which are "pervasive" and those which are "limited." A pervasive role is extensive in scope ("female citizen") and not only influences but also sets bounds upon the other sorts of roles available to the individual ("mother," "nurse," but not "husband," "soldier"); a limited role ("purchaser," "patient") is transitory and intermittent. A further concept is that of "role clarity." Some roles are more specifically defined than others; their impact upon performance (and, indeed, upon the personality of the performer) depends on the clarity of their definition. Finally, it is asserted that those roles which carry with them the clearest and most automatic rewards and punishments are those which will be (as it were) most "artistically" played.

What sorts of things might this explain? It might illuminate the process whereby the child develops his personality in terms not only of the roles which his parents offer him but of those which he "picks up" elsewhere and tries on. It could show how society, in its coercive character, lays down patterns of behavior with which it expects the individual to comply. It suggests the way in which society, now turning its benevolent face to the individual, tenders him alternatives and defines for him the style appropriate to their fulfilment. It provides us with a further term for the definition of personality itself: there appears an extent to which we can say that personality is actually made up of the roles which the individual plays.[19] And here, once more assuming "change" to be possible, we have in certain ways the least cumbersome terms for plotting its course.

The application of the model to the concentration camp should be simple and obvious. What was expected of the man entering the role of camp prisoner was laid down for him upon arrival:

> Here you are not in a penitentiary or prison but in a place of instruction. Order and discipline are here the highest law. If you ever want to see freedom again, you must submit to a severe training. . . . But woe to those who do not obey our iron discipline. Our methods are thorough! Here there is no compromise and no mercy. The slightest resistance will be ruthlessly suppressed. Here we sweep with an iron broom! [20]

Expectation and performance must coincide exactly; the lines were to be read literally; the missing of a single cue meant extinction. The role was pervasive; it vetoed any other role and smashed all prior ones. "Role clarity"—the clarity here was blinding; its definition was burned into the prisoner by every detail of his existence:

> In normal life the adult enjoys a certain measure of independence; within the limits set by society he has a considerable measure of liberty. Nobody orders him when and what to eat, where to take up his residence or what to wear, neither to take his rest on Sunday nor when to have his bath, nor when to go to bed. He is not beaten during his work, he need not ask permission to go to the W.C., he is not continually kept on the run, he does not feel that the work he is doing is silly or childish, he is not confined behind barbed wire, he is not counted twice a day or more, he is not left unprotected against the actions of his fellow citizens, he looks after his family and the education of his children.
>
> How altogether different was the life of the concentration-camp prisoner! What to do during each part of the day was arranged for him, and decisions were made about him from which there was no appeal. He was impotent and suffered from bed-wetting, and because of his chronic diarrhea he soiled his underwear. . . . The dependence of the prisoner on the SS . . . may be compared to the dependence of children on their parents. . . .[21]

The impact of this role, coinciding as it does in a hundred ways with that of the child, has already been observed. Its rewards were brutally simple—life rather than death; its punishments were automatic. By the survivors it was—it had to be—a role *well played*.

Nor was it simple, upon liberation, to shed the role. Many of the inmates, to be sure, did have prior roles which they could resume, former significant others to whom they might reorient themselves, a repressed superego which might once more be resurrected. To this extent they were not "lost souls." But to the extent that their entire personalities, their total selves, had been involved in this experience, to the extent that old arrangements had been disrupted, that society itself had been overturned while they had been away, a "return" was fraught with innumerable obstacles.[22]

It is hoped that the very hideousness of a special example of slavery has not disqualified it as a test for certain features of a far milder and more benevolent form of slavery. But it should still be possible to say, with regard to the individuals who lived as slaves within the respective systems, that just as on one level there is every difference between a wretched childhood and a carefree one, there are, for other purposes, limited features which the one may be said to have shared with the other.

Both were closed systems from which all standards based on prior connections had been effectively detached. A working adjustment to either system required a childlike conformity, a limited choice of "significant others." Cruelty per se cannot be considered the primary key to this; of far greater importance was the simple "closedness" of the system, in which all lines of authority descended from the master and in which alternative social bases that might have supported alternative standards were systematically suppressed.[23] The individual, consequently, for his very psychic security, had to picture his master in some way as the "good father," [24] even when, as in the concentration camp, it made no sense at all.[25] But why should it not have made sense for many a simple plantation Negro whose master did exhibit, in all the ways that could be expected, the features of the good father who was really "good"? If the concentration camp could produce in two or three years the results that it did, one wonders how much more pervasive must have been those attitudes, expectations, and values which had, certainly, their benovolent side and which were accepted and transmitted over generations.

For the Negro child, in particular, the plantation offered no really satisfactory father-image other than the master. The "real" father was virtually without authority over his child, since discipline, parental responsibility, and control of rewards and punishments all rested in other hands; the slave father could not even protect the mother of his children except by appealing directly to the master. Indeed, the mother's own role loomed far larger for the slave child than did that of the father. She controlled those few activities—household care, preparation of food, and rearing of children—that were left to the slave family. For that matter, the very etiquette of plantation life removed even the honorific attributes of fatherhood from the Negro male, who was addressed as "boy"—until, when the vigorous years of his prime were past, he was allowed to assume the title of "uncle."

From the master's viewpoint, slaves had been defined in law as property, and the master's power over his property must be absolute. But then this property was still human property. These slaves might never be quite as human as *he* was, but still there were certain standards that could be laid down for their behavior: obedience, fidelity, humility, docility, cheerfulness, and so on. Industry and diligence would of course be demanded, but a final element in the master's situation would undoubtedly qualify that expectation. Absolute power for him meant absolute dependency for the slave—the dependency not of the developing child but of the perpetual child. For the master, the role most aptly fitting such a relationship would naturally be that of the father. As a father he could be either harsh or kind, as he chose, but as a *wise* father he would have, we may suspect, a sense of the limits of his situation. He must be ready to cope with *all* the qualities of the child, exasperating as well as ingratiating. He might conceivably have to expect in this child—besides his loyalty, docility, humility, cheerfulness, and (under supervision) his diligence—such additional qualities as irresponsibility, playfulness, silliness, laziness, and quite possibly) tendencies to lying and stealing. Should the entire prediction prove accurate, the result would be something resembling "Sambo."

The social and psychological sanctions of role-playing may in the last analysis prove to be the most satisfactory of the several approaches to Sambo, for, without doubt, of all the roles in American life that of Sambo was by far the most pervasive. The outlines of the role might be sketched in by crude necessity, but what of the finer shades? The sanctions against overstepping it were bleak enough,[26] but the rewards —the sweet applause, as it were, for performing it with sincerity and feeling—were something to be appreciated on quite another level. The law, untuned to the deeper harmonies, could command the player to be present for the occasion, and the whip might even warn against his missing the grosser cues, but could those things really insure the performance that melted all hearts? Yet there was many and many a performance, and the audiences (whose standards were high) appear to have been for the most part well pleased. They were actually viewing their own masterpiece. Much labor had been lavished upon this chef d'oeuvre, the most genial resources of Southern society had been available for the work; touch after touch had been applied throughout the years, and the result—embodied not in the unfeeling law but in the richest layers of Southern lore—had been the product of an exquisitely rounded collective creativity. And indeed, in a sense that somehow transcended the merely ironic, it was a labor of love. "I love the simple and unadulterated slave, with his geniality, his mirth, his swagger, and his nonsense," wrote Edward Pollard. "I love to look upon his countenance shining with content and grease; I love to study his affectionate heart; I love to mark that peculiarity in him, which beneath all his buffoonery exhibits him as a creature of the tenderest sensibilities, mingling his joys and his sorrows with those of his master's home."[27] Love, even on those terms, was surely no inconsequential reward.

But what were the terms? The Negro was to be a child forever. "The Negro . . . in his true nature, is always a boy, let him be ever so old. . . ."[28] "He is . . . a dependent upon the white race; dependent for guidance and direction even to the procurement of his most indispensable necessaries. Apart from this protection he has the helplessness of a child—without foresight, without faculty of contrivance, without thrift of any kind."[29] Not only was he a child; he was a happy child. Few Southern writers failed to describe with obvious fondness the bubbling gaiety of a plantation holiday or the perpetual good humor that seemed to mark the Negro character, the good humor of an everlasting childhood.

The role, of course, must have been rather harder for the earliest generations of slaves to learn. "Accommodation," according to John Dollard, "involves the renunciation of protest or aggression against undesirable conditions of life and the organization of the character so that protest does not appear, but acceptance does. It may come to pass in the end that the unwelcome force is idealized, that one identifies with it and takes it into the personality; it sometimes even happens that what is at first resented and feared is finally loved."[30]

Might the process, on the other hand, be reversed? It is hard to imagine its being reversed overnight. The same role might still be played in the years after slavery—we are told that it was[31]—and yet it was played to more vulgar audiences with cruder standards, who paid much less for what they saw. The lines might be repeated more and more mechanically, with less and less conviction; the incentives to perfection could become hazy and blurred, and the excellent old piece could degenerate over time into low farce. There could come a point, conceivably, with the old zest gone, that it was no longer worth the candle. The day might come at last when it dawned on a man's full waking consciousness that he had really grown up, that he was, after all, only playing a part.

MECHANISMS OF RESISTANCE TO ABSOLUTE POWER

One might say a great deal more than has been said here about mass behavior and mass manifestations of personality, and the picture would still amount to little more than a grotesque cartoon of humanity were not some recognition given to the ineffable difference made in any social system by men and women possessing what is recognized, any-where and at any time, simply as character. With that, one arrives at something too qualitatively fine to come very much within the crude categories of the present discussion; but although it is impossible to generalize with any proper justice about the incidence of "character" in its moral, irreducible, individual sense, it may still be possible to con-clude with a note or two on the social conditions, the breadth or narrow-ness of their compass, within which character can find expression.

Why should it be, turning once more to Latin America, that there one finds no Sambo, no social tradition, that is, in which slaves were defined by virtually complete consensus as children incapable of being trusted with the full privileges of freedom and adulthood? There, the system surely had its brutalities. The slaves arriving there from Africa had also undergone the capture, the sale, the Middle Passage. They too had been uprooted from a prior culture, from a life very different from the one in which they now found themselves. There, however, the system was not closed.

Here again the concentration camp, paradoxically enough, can be instructive. There were in the camps a very small minority of the sur-vivors who had undergone an experience different in crucial ways from that of the others, an experience which protected them from the full impact of the closed system. These people, mainly by virtue of wretched little jobs in the camp administration which offered them a minute measure of privilege, were able to carry on "underground" activities. In a practical sense the actual operations of such "under-grounds" as were possible may seem to us unheroic and limited; stealing blankets; "organizing" a few bandages, a little medicine, from the camp hospital; black market arrangements with a guard for a bit of extra food and protection for oneself and one's comrades; the circulation of news; and other such apparently trifling activities. But for the psychological balance of those involved, such activities were vital; they made possible a fundamentally different adjustment to the camp. To a prisoner so engaged, there were others who mattered, who gave real point to his existence—the SS was no longer the *only* one. Conversely, the role of the child was not the only one he played. He could take initiative; he could give as well as receive protection; he did things which had meaning in adult terms. He had, in short, alternative roles; this was a fact which made such a prisoner's transition from his old life to that of the camp less agonizing and destructive; those very prisoners, moreover, appear to have been the ones who could, upon liberation, resume normal lives most easily. It is, in fact, these people—not those of the ranks—who have described the camps to us.[82]

It was just such a difference—indeed, a much greater one—that separated the typical slave in Latin America from the typical slave in the United States. Though he too had experienced the Middle Passage, he was entering a society where alternatives were significantly more diverse than those awaiting his kinsman in North America. Concerned in some sense with his status were distinct and at certain points competing institutions. This involved multiple and often competing "significant others." His master was, of course, clearly the chief one—but not the only one. There could, in fact, be a considerable number: the friar who boarded his ship to examine his conscience, the confessor; the priest who made the rounds and who might report irregularities in treatment to the *procurador*; the zealous Jesuit quick to resent a master's intrusion upon such sacred matters as marriage and worship (a resentment of no small consequence to the master); the local magistrate, with his eye on the king's official protector of slaves, who would find himself in trouble were the laws too widely evaded; the king's informer who received one-third of the fines. For the slave the result was a certain latitude; the lines did not all converge on one man; the slave's personality, accordingly, did not have to focus on a single role. He was, true enough primarily a slave. Yet he might in fact perform multiple roles. He could be a husband and a father (for the American slave these roles had virtually no meaning); open to him also were such activities as artisan, peddler, petty merchant, truck gardener (the law reserved to him the necessary time and a share of the proceeds, but such arrangements were against the law for Sambo); he could be a communicant in the church, a member of a religious fraternity [33] (roles guaranteed by the most powerful institution in Latin America—comparable privileges in the American South depended on a master's pleasure). These roles were all legitimized and protected *outside* the plantation; they offered a diversity of channels for the development of personality. Not only did the individual have multiple roles open to him as a slave, but the very nature of these roles made possible a certain range of aspirations should he some day become free. He could have a fantasy-life not limited to catfish and watermelons; it was within his conception to become a priest, an independent farmer, a successful merchant, a military officer.[34] The slave could actually—to an extent quite unthinkable in the United States—conceive of himself *as a rebel*. Bloody slave revolts, actual wars, took place in Latin America; nothing on this order occurred in the United States.[35] But even without a rebellion, society here had a network of customary arrangements, rooted in antiquity, which made possible at many points a smooth transition of status from slave to free and which provided much social space for the exfoliation of individual character.

To the typical slave on the ante-bellum plantation in the United States, society of course offered no such alternatives. But that is hardly to say that something of an "underground"—something rather more, indeed, than an underground—could not exist in Southern slave society. And there were those in it who hardly fitted the picture of "Sambo."

The American slave system, compared with that of Latin America, was closed and circumscribed, but, like all social systems, its arrangements were less perfect in practice than they appeared to be in theory. It was possible for significant numbers of slaves, in varying degrees, to escape the full impact of the system and its coercions upon personality. The house servant, the urban mechanic, the slave who arranged his own employment and paid his master a stipulated sum each week, were all figuratively members of the "underground." Even among those working on large plantations, the skilled craftsman or the responsible slave foreman had a measure of independence not shared by his simpler brethren. Even the single slave family owned by a small farmer had a status much closer to that of house servants than to that of plantation labor gang. For all such people there was a margin of space denied to the majority; the system's authority-structure claimed their bodies but not quite their souls.

Out of such groups an individual as complex and as highly developed as William Johnson, the Natchez barber, might emerge. Johnson's diary reveals a personality that one recognizes instantly as a type—but a type whose values came from a sector of society very different from that which formed Sambo. Johnson is the young man on the make, the ambitious free-enterpriser of American legend. He began life as a slave, was manumitted at the age of eleven, and rose from a poor apprentice barber to become one of the wealthiest and most influential Negroes in ante-bellum Mississippi. He was respected by white and black alike, and counted among his friends some of the leading public men of the state.[36]

It is of great interest to note that although the danger of slave revolts (like Communist conspiracies in our own day) was much overrated by touchy Southerners; the revolts that actually did occur were in no instance planned by plantation laborers but rather by Negroes whose qualities of leadership were developed well outside the full coercions of the plantation authority-system. Gabriel, who led the revolt of 1800, was a blacksmith who lived a few miles outside Richmond; Denmark Vesey, leading spirit of the 1822 plot at Charleston, was a freed Negro artisan who had been born in Africa and served several years aboard a slavetrading vessel; and Nat Turner, the Virginia slave who fomented the massacre of 1831, was a literate preacher of recognized intelligence. Of the plots that have been convincingly substantiated (whether they came to anything or not), the majority originated in urban centers.[37]

For a time during Reconstruction, a Negro elite of sorts did emerge in the South. Many of its members were Northern Negroes, but the Southern ex-slaves who also comprised it seem in general to have emerged from the categories just indicated. Vernon Wharton, writing of Mississippi, says:

> A large portion of the minor Negro leaders were preachers, lawyers, or teachers from the free states or from Canada. Their education and their independent attitude gained for them immediate favor and leadership. Of the natives who became their rivals, the majority had been urban slaves, blacksmiths, carpenters, clerks, or waiters in hotels and boarding houses; a few of them had been favored body-servants of affluent whites.[38]

The William Johnsons and Denmark Veseys have been accorded, though belatedly, their due honor. They are, indeed, all too easily identified, thanks to the system that enabled them as individuals to be so conspicuous and so exceptional and, as members of a group, so few.

NOTES

1. The line between "accommodation" (as conscious hypocrisy) and behavior inextricable from basic personality, though the line certainly exists, is

anything but a clear and simple matter of choice. There is reason to think that the one grades into the other, and vice versa, with considerable subtlety. In this connection, the most satisfactory theoretical mediating term between deliberate role-playing and "natural" role-playing might be found in role-psychology.

2. Although the majority of Southern slaveholders were not planters, the majority of slaves were owned by a planter minority. "Considerably more than half of them lived on plantation units of more than twenty slaves, and one-fourth lived on units of more than fifty. That the majority of slaves belonged to members of the planter class, and not to those who operated small farms with a single slave family, is a fact of crucial importance concerning the nature of bondage in the ante-bellum South." Stampp, *Peculiar Institution*, p. 31.

3. See esp. below, . . . n. 7.

4. "For just as the ego is a modified portion of the id as a result of contact with the outer world, the super-ego represents a modified portion of the ego, formed through experiences absorbed from the parents, especially from the father. The super-ego is the highest evolution attainable by man, and consists of a precipitate of all prohibitions and inhibitions, all the rules of conduct which are impressed on the child by his parents and by parental substitutes. The feeling of *conscience* depends altogether on the development of the super-ego." A. A. Brill, Introduction to *The Basic Writings of Sigmund Freud* (New York: Modern Library, 1938), pp. 12-13. "Its relation to the ego is not exhausted by the precept: 'You *ought to be* such and such (like your father); it also comprises the prohibition: 'You *must not be* such and such (like your father); that is, you may not do all that he does; many things are his prerogative.'" Sigmund Freud, *The Ego and the Id* (London: Hogarth Press, 1947), pp. 44-45. ". . . and here we have that higher nature, in this ego-ideal or super-ego, the representative of our relation to our parents. When we were little children we knew these higher natures, we admired them and feared them; and later we took them into ourselves." *Ibid.*, p. 47. "As a child grows up, the office of father is carried on by masters and by others in authority; the power of their injunctions and prohibitions remains vested in the ego-ideal and continues, in the form of conscience, to exercise the censorship of morals. The tension between the demands of conscience and the actual attainments of the ego is experienced as a sense of guilt. Social feelings rest on the foundation of identification with others, on the basis of an ego-ideal in common with them." *Ibid.*, p. 49.

5. *Human Behavior*, p. 136.

6. Anna Freud, *The Ego and the Mechanisms of Defence* (London: Hogarth Press, 1948), p. 121. "In some illustrative case reports, Clara Thompson stresses the vicious circle put in motion by this defense-mechanism. The stronger the need for identification, the more a person loses himself in his omnipotent enemy—the more helpless he becomes. The more helpless he feels, the stronger the identification, and—we may add—the more likely it is that he tries even to surpass the aggressiveness of his aggressor. This may explain the almost unbelievable phenomenon that prisoner-superiors sometimes acted more brutally than did members of the SS. . . Identification with the aggressor represented the final stage of passive adaptation. It was a means of defense of a rather paradoxical nature: survival through surrender; protection against the fear of the enemy—by becoming part of him; overcoming helplessness—by re-

gressing to childish dependence." Bluhm, "How Did They Survive?" pp. 24-25.

7. Leo Alexander, "War Crimes: Their Social-Psychological Aspects," *American Journal of Psychiatry*, CV (September, 1948), 173. "The super-ego structure is . . . in peril whenever these established guiding forces weaken or are in the process of being undermined, shifted, or perverted, and becomes itself open to undermining, shifting, or perversion even in adult life—a fact which is probably more important than we have been aware of heretofore." *Ibid.*, p. 175.

8. My use of Sullivan here does not imply a willingness to regard his work as a "refutation" to that of Freud, or even as an adequate substitute for it in all other situations. It lacks the imaginative scope which in Freud makes possible so great a range of cultural connections; in it we miss Freud's effort to deal as scientifically as possible with an infinite array of psychological and cultural phenomena; the fragmentary nature of Sullivan's work, its limited scope, its cloudy presentation, all present us with obstacles not to be surmounted overnight. This might well change as his ideas are elaborated and refined. But meanwhile it would be too much to ask that all connections be broken with the staggering amount of work already done on Freudian models.

9. Sullivan refined this concept from the earlier notion of the "generalized other" formulated by George Herbert Mead. "The organized community or social group [Mead wrote] which gives to the individual his unity of self may be called 'the generalized other.' The attitude of the generalized other is the attitude of the whole community. Thus, for example, in the case of such a social group as a ball team, the team is the generalized other in so far as it enters—as an organized process or social activity—into the experience of any one of the individual members of it." George H. Mead, *Mind, Self and Society: From the Standpoint of a Social Behaviorist* (Chicago: University of Chicago Press, 1934), p. 154.

10. The technical term, in Sullivan's terminology, for the mechanism represented by these two elements functioning in combination, is the individual's "self-dynamism." David Riesman has refined this concept; he has, with his "inner-directed, other-directed" polarity, considered the possibility of different kinds of "self-dynamisms." The self-dynamism which functions with reference to specific aims and which is formed and set early in life is characterized as the "gyroscope." On the other hand the self-dynamism which must function in a cultural situation of constantly shifting significant others and which must constantly adjust to them is pictured as the "radar." See *The Lonely Crowd, passim*. The principles summarized in this and the preceding paragraphs are to be found most clearly set forth in Harry Stack Sullivan, *Conceptions of Modern Psychiatry* (Washington: William Alanson White Psychiatric Foundation, 1945). Sullivan's relationship to the general development of theory is assessed in Patrick Mullahy, *Oedipus Myth and Complex: A Review of Psychoanalytic Theory* (New York: Hermitage House, 1948).

11. Actually, one of the chief functions of psychoanalysis as it has been practiced from the beginning is simply given more explicit recognition here. The psychiatrist who helps the patient exhibit to himself attitudes and feelings systematically repressed—or "selectively ignored"—becomes in the process a new and trusted significant other.

12. "Indeed . . . when the whole Sullivanian conception of the effect of significant others upon the origin and stability of self-conceptions is pushed

farther, really revolutionary vistas of guided personality emerge. If the maintenance of certain characteristic patterns of interpersonal behavior depends upon
their support by significant others, then to alter the composition of any person's
community of significant others is the most direct and drastic way of altering
his 'personality.' This can be done. Indeed, it is being done, with impressive
results, by the many types of therapeutic groups, or quasi-families of significant
new others, which have come up in the past few years." Patrick Mullahy (ed.),
The Contributions of Harry Stack Sullivan (New York: Hermitage House,
1952), p. 193.

13. It should be noted that there were certain important exceptions. . . .

14. An outstanding instance of authorities who are exponents of both is
of that of H. H. Gerth and C. Wright Mills, whose study *Character and Social
Structure* ranges very widely in both interpersonal theory and role psychology
and uses them interchangeably.

15. Conceptually, the purest illustration of this notion might be seen in such
an analogy as the following. Sarah Bernhardt, playing in *Phèdre,* enacted a role
which had not altered since it was set down by Racine two centuries before
her time, and she was neither the first woman who spoke those lines, nor was
she the last. Nor, indeed, was *Phèdre* her only triumph. Such was Bernhardt's
genius, such was her infinite plasticity, that she moved from immutable role to
immutable role in the classic drama, making of each, as critic and theatergoer
alike agreed, a masterpiece. Now Bernhardt herself is gone, yet the lines remain, waiting to be transfigured by some new genius.

16. In the resources of dramatic literature a variety of insights may await the
"social scientist" equipped with both the imagination and the conceptual tools
for exploiting them, and the emergence of role-psychology may represent the
most promising step yet taken in this direction. A previous area of contact has
been in the realm of Freudian psychology, but this has never been a very
natural or comfortable meeting ground for either the analyst or the literary
critic. For example, in Shakespeare's *Hamlet* there is the problem, both
psychological and dramatic, of Hamlet's inability to kill his uncle. Dr. Ernest
Jones (in *Hamlet and Oedipus*) reduces all the play's tensions to a single
Freudian complex. It should be at once more "scientific" and more "literary,"
however, to consider the problem in terms of role-conflict (Hamlet as prince,
son, nephew, lover, etc., has multiple roles which keep getting in the way of
one another). Francis Fergusson, though he uses other terminology, in effect
does this in his *Ideal of a Theater.*

17. In this paragraph I duplicate and paraphrase material from Eugene and
Ruth Hartley, *Fundamentals of Social Psychology* (New York: Knopf, 1952),
chap. xvi. See also David C. McClelland, *Personality* (New York: Sloane,
1951), pp. 289-332. Both these books are, strictly speaking, "texts," but this
point could be misleading, inasmuch as the whole subject is one not normally
studied at an "elementary" level anywhere. At the same time a highly successful effort has been made in each of these works to formulate the role concept
with clarity and simplicity, and this makes their formulations peculiarly relevant
to the empirical facts of the present problem. It may be that the very simplicity
of the roles in both the plantation and concentration-camp settings accounts
for this coincidence. Another reason why I am inclined to put a special premium
on simplicity here is my conviction that the role concept has a range of
"literary" overtones, potentially exploitable in realms other than psychology.

For a recent general statement, see Theodore R. Sarbin, "Role Theory," *Handbook of Social Psychology*, I, 223-58.

18. Hartley, *Fundamentals of Social Psychology*, p. 485.

19. "Personality development is not exclusively a matter of socialization. Rather, it represents the organism's more or less integrated way of adapting to *all* the influences that come its way—both inner and outer influences, both social and nonsocial ones. Social influences, however, are essential to human personality, and socialization accounts for a very great deal of personality development.

"From this point of view it would not be surprising to find that many personality disturbances represent some sort of breakdown or reversal of the socialization process." Theodore M. Newcomb, *Social Psychology* (New York: Dryden Press, 1950), p. 475.

20. Quoted in Leon Szalet, *Experiment "E"* (New York: Didier, 1945), p. 138.

21. Cohen, *Human Behavior*, pp. 173-74.

22. Theodore Newcomb is the only non-Freudian coming to my attention who has considered the concentration camp in the terms of social psychology. He draws analogies between the ex-inmates' problems of readjustment and those of returning prisoners of war. "With the return of large numbers of British prisoners of war . . . from German and Japanese camps, toward the end of World War II, it soon became apparent that thousands of them were having serious difficulties of readjustment. It was first assumed that they were victims of war neuroses. But this assumption had to be abandoned when it was discovered that their symptoms were in most cases not those of the commonly recognized neuroses. Most of the men having difficulty, moreover, did not have the kinds of personalities which would have predisposed them to neurotic disorders. Psychiatrists then began to wonder whether their disturbances represented only a temporary phase of the men's return to civilian life. But the difficulties were neither temporary nor 'self-correcting.' 'Even when men had been back for 18 months or even longer, serious and persistent difficulties were reported in something like one-third of the men.' . . . All in all . . . the authors were led to the conclusion that the returning war prisoner's troubles did not lie entirely within himself. They represented the strains and stresses of becoming *re*socialized in a culture which was not only different from what it had been but was radically different from that to which the men had become accustomed during their years of capture." "When a deliberate attempt is made to change the personality, as in psychotherapy, success brings with it changes in role patterns. When the role perscriptions are changed—as for . . . concentration-camp inmates—personality changes also occur. When forcible changes in role prescriptions are removed, the degree to which the previous personality is 'resumed' depends upon the degree to which the individual finds it possible to resume his earlier role patterns." Newcomb, *Social Psychology*, pp. 476-77, 482.

Social workers faced with the task of rehabilitating former concentration-camp prisoners rapidly discovered that sympathy and understanding were not enough. The normal superego values of many of the prisoners had been so thoroughly smashed that adult standards of behavior for them were quite out of the question. Their behavior, indeed, was often most childlike. They made extreme demands, based not on actual physical needs but rather on the fear that they might be left out, or that others might receive more than they. Those who regained their equilibrium most quickly were the ones who were able to begin new lives in social environments that provided clear limits, precise standards, steady goals, and specific roles to play. Adjustment was not easy, however, even for the most fortunate. On the collective farms of Israel, for example, it was understood that former concentration-camp inmates would be "unable to control their greed for food" for a number of months. During that time, concern for their neighbors' sensibilities was more than one could expect. Paul Friedman, "The Road Back for the DP's" *Commentary*, VI (December, 1948), 502-10; Eva Rosenfeld, "Institutional Change in Israeli Collectives" (Ph.D. diss., Columbia University, 1952), p. 278.

23. The experience of American prisoners taken by the Chinese during the Korean War seems to indicate that profound changes in behavior and values, if not in basic personality itself, can be effected without the use of physical torture or extreme deprivation. The Chinese were able to get large numbers of Americans to act as informers and to co-operate in numerous ways in the effort to indoctrinate all the prisoners with Communist propaganda. The technique contained two key elements. One was that all formal and informal authority structures within the group were systematically destroyed; this was done by isolating officers, non-commissioned officers, and any enlisted men who gave indications of leadership capacities. The other element involved the continual emphasizing of the captors' power and influence by judicious manipulation of petty rewards and punishments and by subtle hints of the greater rewards and more severe punishments (repatriation or non-repatriation) that rested with the pleasure of those in authority. See Edgar H. Schein, "Some Observations on Chinese Methods of Handling Prisoners of War," *Public Opinion Quarterly*, XX (Spring, 1956), 321-27.

24. In a system as tightly closed as the plantation or the concentration camp, the slave's or prisoner's position of absolute dependency virtually compels him to see the authority-figure as somehow really "good." Indeed, all the evil in his life may flow from this man—but then so also must everything of any value. Here is the seat of the only "good" he knows, and to maintain his psychic balance he must persuade himself that the good is in some way dominant. A threat to this illusion is thus in a real sense a threat to his very existence. It is a common experience among social workers dealing with neglected and maltreated children to have a child desperately insist on his love for a cruel and brutal parent and beg that he be allowed to remain with that parent. The most dramatic feature of this situation is the cruelty which it involves, but the mechanism which inspires the devotion is not the cruelty of the parent but rather the abnormal dependency of the child. A classic example of this mechanism in operation may be seen in the case of Varvara Petrovna, mother of Ivan Turgenev. Mme Turgenev "ruled over her serfs with a rod of iron." She demanded utter obedience and total submission. The slightest infraction of her rules brought the most severe punishment: "A maid who did not offer her a cup of tea in the proper manner was sent off to some remote village and perhaps separated from her family forever; gardeners who failed to prevent the plucking of a tulip in one of the flower beds before the house were ordered to be flogged; a servant whom she suspected of a mutinous disposition was sent off to Siberia." Her family and her most devoted servants were treated in much the same manner. "Indeed," wrote Varvara Zhitova, the

adopted daughter of Mme Turgenev, "those who loved her and were most devoted to her suffered most of all." Yet in spite of her brutality she was adored by the very people she tyrannized. David Magarshack describes how once when thrashing her eldest son she nearly fainted with sadistic excitement, whereupon "little Nicholas, forgetting his punishment, bawled at the top of his voice: 'Water! Water for mummy!' " Mme Zhitova, who knew Mme Turgenev's cruelty intimately and was herself the constant victim of her tyranny, wrote: "In spite of this, I loved her passionately, and when I was, though rarely, separated from her, I felt lonely and unhappy." Even Mme Turgenev's maid Agatha, whose children were sent to another village, when still infants so that Agatha might devote all her time to her mistress, could say years later, "Yes, she caused me much grief. I suffered much from her, but all the same I loved her! She was a real lady!" V. Zhitova, *The Turgenev Family*, trans. A. S. Mills (London: Havill Press, 1954), p. 25; David Magarshack, *Turgenev: A Life* (New York: Grove, 1954), pp. 14, 16, 22.

25. Bruno Bettelheim tells us of the fantastic efforts of the old prisoners to believe in the benevolence of the officers of the SS. "They insisted that these officers [hid] behind their rough surface a feeling of justice and propriety; he, or they, were supposed to be genuinely interested in the prisoners and even trying, in a small way, to help them. Since nothing of these supposed feelings and efforts ever became apparent, it was explained that he hid them so effectively because otherwise he would not be able to help the prisoners. The eagerness of these prisoners to find reasons for their claims was pitiful. A whole legend was woven around the fact that of two officers inspecting a barrack one had cleaned his shoes from mud before entering. He probably did it automatically, but it was interpreted as a rebuff of the other officer and a clear demonstration of how he felt about the concentration camp." Bettelheim, "Individual and Mass Behavior," p. 451.

26. Professor Stampp, in a chapter called "To Make Them Stand in Fear," describes the planter's resources for dealing with a recalcitrant slave. *Peculiar Institution*, pp. 141-91.

27. Edward A. Pollard, *Black Diamonds Gathered in the Darkey Homes of the South* (New York: Pudney & Russel, 1859), p. 58.

28. *Ibid.*, p. viii.

29. John Pendleton Kennedy, *Swallow Barn* (Philadelphia: Carey & Lea, 1832).

30. John Dollard, *Caste and Class in a Southern Town* (2nd ed.; New York: Harper, 1949), p. 255. The lore of "accommodation," taken just in itself, is very rich and is, needless to say, morally very complex. It suggests a delicate psychological balance. On the one hand, as the Dollard citation above implies, accommodation is fraught with dangers for the personalities of those who engage in it. On the other hand, as Bruno Bettelheim has reminded me, this involves a principle that goes well beyond American Negro society and is to be found deeply imbedded in European traditions: the principle of how the powerless can manipuate the powerful through aggressive stupidity, literal-mindedness, servile fawning, and irresponsibility. In this sense the immovably stupid "Good Soldier Schweik" and the fawning Negro in Richard Wright's *Black Boy* who allowed the white man to kick him for a quarter partake of the same tradition. Each has a technique whereby he can in a real sense exploit his powerful superiors, feel contempt for them, and suffer in the process no

great damage to his own pride. Jewish lore, as is well known, teems with this sort of thing. There was much of it also in the traditional relationships between peasants and nobles in central Europe.

Still, all this required the existence of some sort of alternative forces for moral and psychological orientation. The problem of the Negro in slavery times involved the virtual absence of such forces. It was with the end of slavery, presumably, that they would first begin to present themselves in generally usable form—a man's neighbors, the Loyal Leagues, white politicians, and so on. It would be in these circumstances that the essentially intermediate technique of accommodation could be used as a protective device beneath which a more independent personality might develop.

31. Even Negro officeholders during Reconstruction, according to Francis B. Simkins, "were known to observe carefully the etiquette of the Southern caste system." "New Viewpoints of Southern Reconstruction," *Journal of Southern History*, V (February, 1939), 52.

32. Virtually all the ex-prisoners whose writing I have made use of were men and women who had certain privileges (as clerks, physicians, and the like) in the camps. Many of the same persons were also active in the "underground" and could offer some measure of leadership and support for others. That is to say, both the objectivity necessary for making useful observations and the latitude enabling one to exercise some leadership were made possible by a certain degree of protection not available to the rank and file.

I should add, however, that a notable exception was the case of Bruno Bettelheim, who throughout the period of his detention had no privileged position of any kind which could afford him what I am calling an "alternative role" to play. And yet I do not think that it would be stretching the point too far to insist that he did in fact have such a role, one which was literally self-created: that of the scientific observer. In him, the scientist's objectivity, his feeling for clinical detail and sense of personal detachment, amounted virtually to a passion. It would not be fair, however, to expect such a degree of personal autonomy as this in other cases, except for a very few. I am told, for instance, that the behavior of many members of this "underground" toward their fellow prisoners was itself by no means above moral reproach. The depths to which the system could corrupt a man, it must be remembered, were profound.

33. See Tannenbaum, *Slave and Citizen*, pp. 64-65.

34. *Ibid.*, pp. 4 ff., 56-57, 90-93; see also Johnston, *Negro in the New World*, p. 90.

35. Compared with the countless uprisings of the Brazilian Negroes, the slave revolts in our own country appear rather desperate and futile. Only three emerge as worthy of any note, and their seriousness—even when described by a sympathetic historian like Herbert Aptheker—depends largely on the supposed plans of the rebels rather than on the things they actually did. The best organized of such "revolts," those of Vesey and Gabriel, were easily suppressed, while the most dramatic of them—the Nat Turner Rebellion—was characterized by little more than aimless butchery. The Brazilian revolts, on the other hand, were marked by imagination and a sense of direction, and they often involved large-scale military operations. One is impressed both by their scope and their variety. They range from the legendary Palmares Republic of the seventeenth century (a Negro state organized by escaped slaves and successfully defended for over fifty years), to the bloody revolts of the Moslem Negroes of Bahia

which, between 1807 and 1835, five times paralyzed a substantial portion of Brazil. Many such wars were launched from the *quilombos* (fortified villages built deep in the jungles by escaped slaves to defend themselves from re-capture); there were also the popular rebellions in which th Negroes of an entire area would take part. One is immediately struck by the heroic stature of the Negro leaders: no allowances of any sort need be made for them; they are impressive from any point of view. Arthur Ramos has described a number of them, including Zambi, a fabulous figure of the Palmares Republic; Luiza Mahin, mother of the Negro poet Luiz Gama and "one of the most outstand-leaders of the 1835 insurrection"; and Manoel Francisco dos Anjos Fereira, whose followers in the *Balaiada* (a movement which drew its name from "Baliao," his own nickname) held the *entire province of* Maranhão for three years. Their brilliance, gallantry, and warlike accomplishments give to their histories an almost legendary quality. On the other hand, one could not begin to think of Nat Turner in such a connection. See Ramos, *The Negro in Brazil*, pp. 24-53; Herbert Aptheker, *American Negro Slave Revolts* (New York: Columbia University, 1943, *passim*.

36. See William R. Hogan and Edwin A. Davis (eds.), *William Johnson's Natchez: The Ante-Bellum Diary of a Free Negro* (Baton Rouge: Louisiana State University Press, 1951), esp. pp. 1-64.

37. Aptheker, *American Negro Slave Revolts*, pp. 220, 268-69, 295-96, and *passim*.

38. Vernon L. Wharton, *The Negro in Mississippi, 1865–1890* (Chapel Hill: University of North Carolina Press, 1942), p. 164.

*Since 1959, when Stanley M. Elkins first published his con-
troversial views on slavery and Negro personality and offered
the concentration-camp analogy, there have been many
critiques of the work. One of the most cogent is by Kenneth
M. Stampp, author of the influential volume The Peculiar Institution (1956). Stampp rejects the Elkins view, but, at
the same time, applies some of the categories and psychological theories and hypotheses employed by Elkins to reach conclusions which, if not diametrically opposed, differ substantially from those presented by Elkins. Students can decide for
themselves whether or not the "Sambo thesis" has been
hoisted on its own petard.*

Rebels and Sambos

KENNETH M. STAMPP

I think it is safe to say that no historical scholar has ever been altogether satisfied with his sources. Whatever the subject of his investigation, whether he is concerned with the remote or recent past, the
available records never tell him all he would like to know—never permit
more than a partical reconstruction of any historical event. Under the
best of circumstances the historian is obliged to write about men he
has never known from scattered, fragmentary, and often censored
records that leave many crucial questions unanswered.

Historians who investigate the subject of slavery in the antebellum
South confront this problem in one of its more exasperating forms;
and they find it most acute when they inquire, as some have done in
recent years, about the behavior of slaves, about their relationships
with the master class, and about their personalities. There are, to be
sure, problems of conceptualization as well as of research, for explana-

From "Rebels and Sambos: The Search for the Negro's Personality in Slavery"
by Kenneth M. Stampp, *Journal of Southern History* 37 (August 1971): 367-
92. Copyright © 1971 by the Southern Historical Association. Reprinted by
permission of the managing editor.

tions of broad patterns of slave behavior, if such exist, must be based
on one or another theory of personality development. Nevertheless,
whatever methodological or conceptual strategies a historian may
devise, his search for answers to questions concerning slave behavior
and personality must begin with the accumulation of a reasonable
amount of empirical data. It is this urgent need for data that introduces at the outset the problem of limited sources.

What we know about slaves and their masters we have learned
mostly from the business records, diaries, letters, memoirs, and autobiographies of slaveholders; from travelers' observations; from contemporary newspapers and periodicals; and from various government
documents, including court records. Direct evidence from the slaves
themselves is hopelessly inadequate. Well over 90 percent of them
were illiterate, and even the small literate minority seldom found an
opportunity to write or speak with candor. Travelers in the South
occasionally interviewed slaves; in the 1850s Benjamin Drew, a white
New England abolitionist, interviewed a group of fugitives who had
settled in Canada;[1] and a few ex-slaves left autobiographies of varying
quality. But I know of not a single slave diary; and letters written by
slaves are rare. For more than sixty years after emancipation, no one
made a systematic attempt to record the narratives of former slaves.
Three belated efforts in the 1920s and 1930s appear to have come too
late to be of much value to historians, though the narratives are of
considerable interest to folklorists.[2] Historians have no doubt failed
to make as much use of the Negro's oral tradition of songs and folklore
as they should; but this material, as a source for slavery, also presents
problems. Among other things, the songs and folklore are ever
changing; and, since the collections were made for the most part
after slavery, we can seldom be sure that what they contain are true
expressions of the slaves.[3]

Inevitably, then, our knowledge of the life and behavior of American Negroes in slavery comes mainly from the testimony of white
observers. The letters written by slaves were usually written to white
men; the slave autobiographies were often dictated to and written
by white men; and the early collections of slave songs and folklore
were put together by white men, who may well have missed the
nuances in this often subtle material. In short, the ubiquitous white
man, as master, editor, traveler, politician, and amanuensis, stands
forever between slave and historian, telling the historian how the
slave was treated, how he behaved, what he thought, and what sort

of personality he had. However imaginative the historian may be, he will always have trouble breaking through this barrier, and he will always be handicapped by the paucity of firsthand testimony from the slaves themselves.

This being the case, it is hardly surprising that historians who have studied the behavior and personality of the Negro in slavery have failed to agree on the meaning of the evidence and have left many problems unsolved. Indeed, two of the books that address themselves directly and explicitly to this problem—Herbert Aptheker's *American Negro Slave Revolts*[4] and Stanley M. Elkins's *Slavery*[5]—arrive at opposite conclusions. Aptheker, whose purpose is to depict "in realistic terms the response of the American Negro to his bondage," found "that discontent and rebelliousness were not only exceedingly common, but, indeed, characteristic of American Negro slaves."[6] Elkins, focusing more narrowly on plantation field hands, suggests that characteristically they were not rebels but Sambos, with personalities very much as they were described in southern lore:

> Sambo, the typical plantation slave, was docide but irresponsible, loyal but lazy, humble but chronically given to lying and stealing; his behavior was full of infantile silliness and his talk inflated with childish exaggeration. His relationship with his master was one of utter dependence and childlike attachment: it was indeed this child-like quality that was the very key to his being.[7]

These two portraits of the southern slave, one as the discontented rebel, the other as the passive Sambo, are worth examining, because together they define the two extremes—the outer limits—of possible slave behavior.

Of the two portraits, Aptheker's is the easier to evaluate. From his empirical research, mostly in newspapers and government documents, he claims to have uncovered approximately 250 revolts and conspiracies, each involving a minimum of ten slaves and having the winning of freedom as its apparent goal.[8] He makes no attempt to explain slave behavior with any personality theory; but implicit throughout the book is an assumption that when a mass of people are as brutally exploited as the southern slaves, discontent and rebelliousness against the ruling class are bound to be endemic.

We are indebted to Aptheker for providing a useful corrective to the view, still prevalent when his book was published in 1943, that the slaves were almost uniformly contented. He presents detailed accounts of a few rebellions and of a number of authentic conspiracies; but above all he shows how persistent the *fear* of rebellion was among white southerners and how frequently insurrection panics drove them to near hysteria. However, the book has three major shortcomings. First, it fails to use sources critically; second, it argues beyond the evidence; and, third, it does not distinguish between slave discontent, which was probably widespread, and slave rebelliousness, which was only sporadic and always local. A more accurate title for this book would be *American Negro Slave Revolts, Conspiracies, and Rumors of Conspiracies,* for it is the last of these things that most of the book is really about.

An example of Aptheker's misinterpretation of his data can be found in the twelve pages devoted to the years 1835–1842, which follow a chapter on the Nat Turner Rebellion. He begins by declaring that "The year 1835 witnessed the reopening of this never-long interrupted drama of the organized struggle of an enslaved people to throw off their yoke." Then, presenting his evidence year by year, he tells us of rumors that "began to fly around," of plots that "were overheard," of reports of "what appears to have been a bona filde conspiracy," and of whisperings of "large-scale conspiracies." Aptheker then relates that after 1842 the "remainder of the forties were relatively quiet years." But his own evidence indicates that in the history of slave insurrections, except for the usual budget of rumors and alarms, the year 1835–1842 were also quiet ones.[9] Clearly, though revealing much about the anxieties of white masters, he has failed to establish his thesis that rebelliousness was characteristic of American Negro slaves.

Elkins, in a decidedly more influential counterhypothesis, offers the placid and contented Sambo as the typical plantation slave. He is concerned almost entirely with describing and explaining Sambo's personality and behavior rather than with offering empirical evidence of his existence. He disposes of the problem of evidence in two sentences: "The picture [of Sambo] has far too many circumstantial details, its hues have been stroked in by too many different brushes, for it be denounced as counterfeit. Too much folk-knowledge, too much plantation literature, too much of the Negro's own lore, have gone into its making to entitle one in good conscience to condemn it as 'conspiracy.'" Beyond this, at several points, Elkins simply tells his readers that the widespread existence of Sambo "will be assumed," or will be "taken for granted," and then proceeds to his explanation.[10]

Since the Elkins thesis is familiar, I will only summarize the three chief points of his strategy, which are (1) his use of comparative history, (2) his use of personality theory, and (3) his use of analogy. Elkins argues, first of all, that the Negro with a Sambo-type personality was not a universal product of slavery in the Americas but, because of certain unique conditions, a peculiar product of slavery in the United States. The principal differences between North American and Latin American slavery, he believes, were the latter's relatively greater flexibility and openness, the far greater opportunities it gave the Negro to escape into free society, and the presence of not one but several centers of authority: church and state as well as slave master. In the antebellum South slavery grew unchecked by church or state; its form was dictated by the needs of the planter capitalists; and state laws treated the slave essentially as property, thus depriving him of his identity as a human being. Southern slavery operated as a "closed system" in which the slaves had only limited contacts with free society and little hope of becoming part of it. It was this closed system that produced Sambo.[11]

Second, to explain how southern slavery had this devastating effect on the Negro, Elkins utilizes some of the literature on personality theory. Using Freud, he points to the impossibility of a "meaningful relationship between fathers and sons" and to the difficulty of becoming a man without "acceptable male models to pattern yourself after."[12] But he relies chiefly on a blend of certain aspects of the interpersonal theory of Harry Stack Sullivan and of role psychology. Sullivan maintains that personality can be studied only as it manifests itself in interpersonal relations,[13] and he stresses the manner in which personality is formed in relationships with so-called "significant others" —that is, with those in positions of authority or otherwise capable of enhancing or endangering one's security. Out of anxiety concerning the attitudes of these significant others a person learns to behave in ways that meet their expectations. Eventually, some of this behavior is internalized and becomes part of the personality. Role psychology emphasizes the roles, or models of behavior, that are extended to individuals throughout their lives by organizations, or by groups, or by society at large.[14] There are rewards for playing the expected role well and penalties for playing it badly or not at all. How well an individual plays a role depends in part on his skill, on his motivation, on his "role knowledge," and on "role clarity," the last requiring a condition of general agreement about proper behavior. The more clearly a role is defined the better it is likely to be performed, and the greater its impact is likely to be on the personality of the performer. Thus, it may be that to some degree one's personality consists of the roles one plays.

Applying these ideas to the southern plantation slave, the Elkins hypothesis runs something like this: In a closed system from which there was virtually no escape, the master, whose authority was absolute, who dispensed rewards and punishments, was the only significant other in the slave's life. The master defined the slave's role, provided him with a clear and simple script, judged his performance, and rewarded him according to its quality. The result was Sambo, the perpetually dependent, irresponsible child. Elkins does not claim that Sambo was the universal slave personality, for he recognizes that there were "a great profusion of individual types." A "significant number," including house servants, skilled craftsmen, slaves who hired their own time, slave foremen, and those who lived in single families on small farms managed "to escape the full impact of the system and its coercions upon personality." For these slaves "there was a margin of space denied to the majority . . . ," and few of them took on the character of Sambo. But of the mass of field hands on large and small plantations, though Elkins recognizes that some did not fit the classic Sambo type, it is clearly his intention to suggest that Sambo embraced the majority.[15]

Finally, to illuminate certain aspects of southern slavery, Elkins resorts to the analogy of the Nazi concentration camp. He warns that an analogy must not be taken literally, for things that are analogous are not identical. His purpose is to examine two situations which, in spite of their "vast dissimilarities," contain "mechanisms that are metaphorically comparable and analytically interchangeable." In this analogy the mechanism was "the infantilizing tendencies of absolute power."[16] Elkins sees a rough similarity between the Sambo produced by slavery on the southern plantation and the human product of the concentration camp, whose experiences often led to personality disintegration, infantilization, and even a tendency to look on SS guards in a child-like way as father figures.

Both the master of the plantation and the commander of the concentration camp were the sole significant others in the lives of the people under their control. Both could mete out punishment or grant protection, while the slaves and inmates were reduced to complete dependence. "A working adjustment to either system," Elkins concludes, "required a childlike conformity . . ."; the crucial factor

> was the simple "closedness" of the system, in which all lines of authority descended from the master. . . . The individual, consequently, for his very psychic security, had to picture his master in some way as the "good father," even when, as in the concentration camp, it made no sense at all. But why should it not have made sense for many a simple plantation Negro whose master did exhibit, in all the ways that could be expected, the features of the good father who was really "good"? If the concentration camp could produce in two or three years the result that it did, one wonders how much more pervasive must have been those attitudes, expectations, and values which had, certainly, their benevolent side and which were accepted and transmitted over generations.[17]

It is no small tribute to Elkins's achievement that his essay should have provided the focus for virtually all scholarly discussion of slave personality for the past decade and that a volume of commentary, with a response from Elkins, has recently been published.[18] I doubt that any future historian of slavery will fail to recognize Sambo as an authentic personality type among the slaves on southern plantations. More generally, Elkins has contributed much to arousing interest in the problem of slave personality and to making historians aware of the possibility of dealing with the problem through an interdisciplinary approach. On the other hand, I believe that the discussion has been rather too much preoccupied with his hypothesis; that, in consequence, we have made little additional progress during the past decade; and that the time has come for renewed investigation. Elkins, after all, intended his essay to be the start of a new approach, suggestive rather than definitive; and, accordingly, he left plenty of work for others to do. Moreover, his essay contains a number of flaws, which give the remaining work a special urgency.

Because of their fascination with the essay's methodology and conceptualization, many scholars seem to have overlooked its lack of empirical evidence—its bland assumption that the prevalence of Sambo on the plantations can be taken for granted. The concentration-camp analogy, of course, proves nothing; at most, Elkins can argue that *if* the typical plantation slave was a Sambo, the literature on the camps might suggest an explanation of *why* he was a Sambo.[19] Elkins, as I have noted, takes Sambo for granted because Sambo appears so prominently in antebellum plantation literature. But most of this literature was written by white men, and much of it is in defense of slavery. To accept it at face value would be only slightly more justifiable than to accept at face value a body of literature on the concentration camps written not by former inmates and competent scholars, such as Bruno Bettelheim, but by the SS guards. Moreover, the public testimony of white witnesses does not by any means invariably support the Elkins hypothesis, for contemporary writers often speak of the resourcefulness and guile of Negroes, and numerous essays on the governing of slaves warn masters never to trust them.[20] Elkins is certainly mistaken when he asserts that the prevalence of Sambo was part of the Negro's own lore. Neither the slave narratives nor the Negro's oral tradition give validity to Sambo as the typical plantation slave; rather, their emphasis is on the slave dissemblers and the ways in which they deceived their masters.

In an essay on sources, Elkins explains why he did not use manuscript plantation records, which constitute the private testimony of the white slaveholders. Manuscripts, he writes, "are useful principally on questions of health and maintenance, and they have already been worked over with great care and thoroughness by eminent scholars."[21] But the plantation manuscripts are in fact quite valuable for the study of slave personality, and even information on maintenance and health (including mental health) is decidedly relevant. If the manuscripts have been worked over by other scholars, that is really of little help to Elkins, because no one has used them for precisely his purpose and with his hypothesis in mind. He offers no explanation for his failure to examine other sources, especially newspapers, with their extremely revealing fugitive-slave advertisements, and contemporary periodicals, with their countless essays on the management of slaves and their descriptions of slave behavior. As a result, Elkins is obliged in the end to offer corroborating testimony from sources such as John Pendleton Kennedy's *Swallow Barn* (1832), where we learn that the slave had "the helplessness of a child—without foresight, without faculty of contrivance, without thrift of any kind; and from Edward Pollard's *Black Diamonds Gathered in the Darkey Homes of the South* (1859), which assures us that "The Negro . . . in his true nature, is always a boy, let him be ever so old. . . ." "Few Southern writers," Elkins concludes, "failed to describe with obvious fondness . . . the perpetual good humor that seemed to mark the Negro character, the good humor of an everlasting childhood."[22]

David C. McClelland, one of Elkins's authorities on personality, devotes two chapters of his book to the problems of collecting and interpreting data. In one of them, McClelland observes that an individual's personality may change "as he changes or as the scientist's insights improve."[23] This is an important point, for the accumulation of an ample supply of data is often the beginning of improved insight. Eugene D. Genovese, after paying tribute to Elkins's achievement, reminds us "that all psychological models may only be used suggestively for flashes of insight or as aids in forming hypotheses and that they cannot substitute for empirical investigation."[24]

The remaining shortcomings of the Elkins essay concern its conceptual and methodological strategies and its apparent misunderstanding of the life of plantation slaves. Several critics have already questioned Elkins's comparative approach, particularly his exaggerated notion of the success of church and state in Latin America in protecting the slave's humanity. They have also demonstrated that Sambo was not a unique product of North American slavery, for he appeared in Brazil, in the French colonies, and in Spanish America as well. "On close inspection," writes Genovese, "the Sambo personality turns out to be neither more nor less than the slavish personality; wherever slavery has existed, Sambo has also."[25] Since the antebellum South did not actually produce a distinct slave personality, the explanation for Sambo may be sought not there alone but everywhere in the Western World.

Elkins's concentration-camp analogy, as I will try to demonstrate, may help to illuminate the condition of one small group of plantation slaves, but it is of little value as an aid to understanding Sambo. He would be quite justified in using his analogy for limited purposes, provided, first, that he could establish a controlling mechanism that is in truth "analytically interchangeable," and, second, that the obvious and admitted elements of dissimilarity between slavery and the concentration camps did not themselves have an important bearing on the formation of personality. To Elkins, the "shock and detachment" experience of adult camp inmates—an experience that slaves born into the system did not endure—was less crucial to personality than adjusting to "the requirements of a 'closed system' of absolute authority."[26]

However, Elkins dismisses far too easily certain vital elements of dissimilarity that did have a profound impact on adult personality, and first among them is the systematic policy of terror and brutality in the concentration camps. Slaves were rarely treated as cruelly as camp inmates. The realities of slavery dawned on them gradually over a period of years, while the realities of the concentration camp hit the inmates with one stunning and often disintegrating blow. Moreover, plantation slavery was a rational institution; it had a logic and purpose that was utterly missing in the camps, where life, with its total unpredictability, had about it a nightmarish quality. The extermination policy eventually adopted in the camps destroyed all belief in the value of human life. Everybody in the camps, as Bettelheim observed, "was convinced that his chances for survival were very slim; therefore to preserve himself as an individual seemed pointless."[27] It was this hopelessness, rather than the absolute authority of one significant other, that explains the phenomenon of inmates walking with resistance to the gas chambers. Slavery, though its influence on personality was severe, still afforded its victims something a good deal closer to normal life, and therefore it did not ordinarily have anything like as shattering an impact on personality as did the concentration camps.

The most momentous difference between the two institutions is evident in the fact that only about 700,000 out of nearly eight million inmates survived the camps. Elkins declares that he is necessarily concerned only with the survivors, but among those he thus eliminates from consideration are nearly all who in some manner resisted the system and whose personalities were not crushed by it.[28] To establish a comparable situation in slavery, one would have to imagine that the system had become vastly more brutal in the 1850s and that, in consequence, only 400,000 rather than four million slaves were alive in 1860, the rest having been murdered by their masters for resistance or rules infractions, or in medical experiments, or as victims of a Negro extermination policy. One could hardly argue seriously that such a profound change in the nature of slavery—in terms of the slave's expectations of survival—would have had no significant impact on personality. Nor would one then want to limit a study of slave personality to the cringing 400,000 survivors. It would appear, therefore, that absolute power was not the controlling mechanism as much as the manner in which the power was used.

Turning finally to the theoretical foundation of the Elkins essay, the important question is whether personality theory, when applied to the available data, points unmistakably to Sambo as the typical plantation slave. This does not seem to be the case, for there are important aspects of the theories that Elkins uses, together with much data, that suggest other plausible hypotheses.[29] In addition, personality theory contains more than a few ambiguities. For example, role psychology does not provide a clear answer to the question of whether the Sambo role played by many plantation slaves was internalized and became part of their personalities, or whether it was a form of conscious hypocrisy, a mere accommodation to the system. David Mc-Clelland asserts that the roles an individual plays are part of his knowledge "and therefore part of his personality."[30] But Ralph Linton thinks that playing a role proves nothing about an individual's personality, "except that he has normal learning ability." The psychologist must be able "to penetrate behind the façade of social conformity and cultural uniformity to reach the authentic individual."[31] Two recent writers on role theory, Theodore R. Sarbin and Vernon L. Allen, illustrating a new trend, hardly touch on the matter of role and personality. They are far more interested in the interaction between role and social identity, and they state explicitly that they "are not using 'social identity' and 'self' as synonyms. Selfhood . . . embodies more residuals of behavior than those generated through role enactment."[32]

At times Elkins approaches this problem warily, suggesting only that the roles an individual plays are internalized to "an extent," or that "deliberate" role-playing and "natural" role-playing grade into each other "with considerable subtlety." Returning to the problem in an appendix, Elkins again refuses to generalize: "The main thing I would settle for would be the existence of a broad belt of indeterminacy between 'mere acting' and the 'true self' "; to the extent that they "grade into one another" it seems "permissible to speak of Sambo as a personality 'type.' "[33]

These cautious statements are hardly disputable, but they do not represent the tone of the essay as a whole. The clear inference to be drawn from Elkins's comparison of North American and Latin American slavery, from his introduction of the concentration-camp analogy, and from his use of personality theory is that Sambo was not a dissembler but a distinct personality type and the typical plantation slave. Indeed, in one footnote, Elkins explicitly rejects the possibility that the Sambo role was only a form of conscious accommodation. Not until after emancipation, he insists, did the Negro's "moral and psychological orientation" permit the development of "the essentially intermediate technique of accommodation . . . as a protective device beneath which a more independent personality might develop."[34]

Yet the theory of role psychology, when applied to the information we have concerning the life and behavior of plantation slaves, provides plenty of room for personalities other than Sambo. This theory, which stresses the importance of "role clarity," holds that adequate role performance will be unlikely if there is uncertainty concerning the nature of an appropriate role. In addition, role conflict occurs when a person finds himself occupying more than one status at a given time, each requiring different behavior, or when there is more than one source of advice about how a role is properly played. Conflicting obligations or conflicting expectations may lead to a personal crisis and to difficulty in playing any role successfully.[35] These were problems that troubled plantation slaves in their daily lives—problems whose psychic strains they resolved in ways that varied with their individual natures and experiences.

Harry Stack Sullivan's model of interpersonal relationships, when fully utilized, also provides theoretical support for a variety of plantation slave personalities. Sullivan describes a highly complex and subtle interplay between an individual and the significant others in his life. One side of it—the side that Elkins explores—is the anxiety that helps to mold an individual's personality as he behaves in certain ways to meet the expectations of authority figures. But there is another side, which involves the conscious manipulation of significant others to the individual's own advantage. By the time a child is ready for school, Sullivan observes, he has "evolved techniques" for handling his parents "with only a modicum of pain"; he now encounters other adults "who have to be managed."[36] In addition to manipulation, there is still another and less fortunate way that a person deals with tendencies in his personality that are strongly disapproved by his significant others. These tendencies are neither lost nor resolved but simply "dissociated from personal awareness." In the process of dissociation they are "excluded from the self" and become part of the "extra-self." But the tendencies still remain an integral part of the personality, manifesting "themselves in actions, activities, of which the person himself remains quite unaware."[37]

Sullivan's concept of dissociation describes a condition which, at a certain point, may lead to serious psychic problems. Generally speaking, he believes that the "healthy development of personality is inversely proportionate to the amount, to the number, of tendencies which have come to exist in dissociation."[38] In Elkins's conceptualization we encounter the significant other of Sullivan's interpersonal theory but not the phenomena of manipulation and dissociation; yet all three concepts are relevant to the problem of slave personality.

I believe that a historian utilizing the available evidence on slave behavior and master-slave relationships and taking account of all aspects of the personality theories used by Elkins will be forced to abandon his hypothesis that Sambo was the typical plantation slave. Several historians have already briefly suggested other possibilities,[39] and at present several have more ambitious projects under way. The following is my own sketch of an alternative to the Elkins hypothesis.

I would begin by accepting Elkins's description of southern slavery as a closed system from which few escaped and in which the slaves had only limited contacts with free society; his emphasis on the de-humanizing tendencies of slavery (though not in North America alone); his belief that the system had built into it powerful pressures toward dependent, infantilized, emasculated personalities;[40] and his conception of the master as a formidable significant other in the life of nearly every slave—partly an object of fear, partly a Freudian father figure. But I would reject his assertions that the master's power was absolute; that he was the only significant other in the lives of his slaves; that he was the sole author of the role, or roles, they played; and that southern slaves were almost totally dehumanized. Finally, I would suggest that plantation slaves encountered significant others in their own families and communities; that dissembling, manipulation, dissociation, role conflict, and lack of role clarity were important ingredients of slave behavior; and that plantation life enabled most slaves to develop independent personalities—indeed, provided room for the development of a considerable range of personality types.

In his concentration-camp analogy Elkins observes that a small minority of the inmates, who held minor administrative jobs, was able to escape the full impact of the system on personality. This minority could engage in petty underground activities, such as stealing blankets, getting medicine from the camp hospital, and negotiating black-market arrangements with the guards. These activities turned out to be crucial for the fortunate prisoner's psychological balance. For him the SS was not the only significant other, and the role of the child was not the only one open to him—he was able to do things that had meaning in adult terms.[41]

If these trivial activities could preserve the psychic balance of camp inmates, then the plantations afforded the great mass of field hands infinitely greater opportunities to preserve theirs. Though plantation slaves were exposed to influences that encouraged childlike dependency and produced emasculated personalities, the system nevertheless permitted them a degree of semiautonomous community life and the opportunity to do many things that had meaning in adult terms. They lived in their own separate quarters where they could escape the constant scrutiny of their masters. Unlike the slaves on the sugar and coffee plantations of Brazil and Cuba, where men outnumbered women by as much as three to one, those on the plantations of the Old South could experience something like a normal sex life, because the sexes were usually evenly divided. Though slave marriages had no legal support and families were ever in danger of being broken up by sales, southern slaves nevertheless lived in family groups more often than those on the commercialized plantations of Latin America. In fact, it was customary for them to live in family groups.[42]

Slave families, because of their relative lack of economic significance, their instability, and the father's severely restricted role, may well have been less important in the lives of slaves than the broader plantation slave communities. The latter provided opportunities for self-expression in their celebrations of holidays, in their music and folklore, and in other aspects of community life. Historians have perhaps viewed religion among plantation slaves too much in terms of the nonreligious uses to which it was put. We know that masters used religious indoctrination as a means of control and that slaves found in their religious services subtle ways of protesting their condition. But there were other and deeper ways in which religion served them. It provided a system of beliefs that comforted and sustained them in their bondage, and it afforded additional means of self-expression that helped them retain their psychic balance. I do not believe that a truly autonomous Afro-American subculture developed in slavery days, but some of the ingredients for one were certainly there.

Both the family and the community provided plantation slaves with roles other than that defined by the master, and with significant others besides the master. For the very young child the mother, not the master, was the significant other in the sense that Sullivan uses this concept. Though the near impossibility of fathers acting as true authority figures was of great psychic importance, meaningful relationships did sometimes exist between fathers and sons. As the child grew, the master's role as a significant other became increasingly vital, but he was always in competition with significant others in the slave community: with husbands, wives, fathers, and mothers; with religious leaders; with strong male models, some of whom may even on occasion have served as substitute father figures;[43] with slaves believed to possess mystical powers; and with those whose wisdom was respected. Few planters had any illusions about being the only authority figures on their estates; as one of them noted, there were always slaves who held "a kind of magical sway over the minds and opinions of the rest."[44]

In his community, in the presence of these significant others, the slave could play a role decidedly different from the one prescribed by his master. This situation often led to the psychologically important problem of role conflict. An obvious illustration is the dilemma of a slave being questioned by his master concerning the whereabouts of a fugitive. Here the rules of proper conduct that the master tried to instill in him came in conflict with the values of his community. If we can trust the testimony of the masters themselves, community values usually triumphed, even though punishment might be the consequence.

Was there any sense in which the master's power was really absolute? Only in the sense that if a master killed a slave by overwork, or by cruel punishment, or in a fit of rage, it was nearly impossible to convict him in a court of law. But southern state laws did not themselves give the master absolute power over his slaves, for the laws recognized their humanity and attempted to control the degree of punishment that might be inflicted, the amount of labor that could be required, and the care that was to be provided. Where the laws failed, the master might be restrained by his own moral standards or by those of the white community. If law and custom were not enough, he was still confronted by the fact that, unlike the inmates of a concentration camp, his slaves had monetary value and a clear purpose —to toil in his fields—and therefore had bargaining power. The master got work out of his slaves by coercion, by threats, by promises of rewards, by flattery, and by a dozen other devices he knew of. But if he were prudent, he knew that it was not wise to push slaves too far—to work them too long, punish them too severely or too often, or make too many threats. Slaves had their own standards of fair play and their own ways of enforcing them.[45] The relationship between master and slave was not one in which absolute power rested on one side and total helplessness on the other; rather, the relationship was one of everlasting tensions, punctuated by occasional conflicts between combatants using different weapons.

If the master had the *de facto* power of life and death over his slaves, the slaves knew that he was most unlikely to use it. They knew that rules infractions and certain forms of resistance did not ordinarily lead to death but to milder and often quite bearable forms of punishment, or to sale to another master, or, on occasion, to no penalty at all. In the conflicts between masters and slaves, the masters or their overseers sometimes suffered defeat, and the resulting collapse of discipline led inflexibly to economic disaster. To read the essays "On the Management of Negroes" that frequently appeared in southern periodicals is to appreciate the practical limits of the master's power. Clearly, for the slave, as he responded to the problems of his existence, the choices open to him were a good deal more complex than a simple one between life and death.

Role psychology, as those who have written on the subject observe, tempts one to view the whole problem metaphorically as drama.[46] But in slavery the theatrical situation was seldom one in which the master wrote the script and the slaves played their roles and read their lines precisely as their master had written them. The instructions masters gave to their overseers, which describe the qualities they hoped to develop in their slaves, suggest something quite different. Significantly, the model slave described in these instructions is not Sambo but a personality far more complicated. Masters wanted their slaves, like Sambo, to be docile, humble, and dependent; but they also wanted them to be diligent, responsible, and resourceful—in short, as Earle E. Thorpe has noted, "to give a very efficient and adult-like performance."[47] The slaves in turn had to find ways to resolve the obviously incongruent role expectations of their masters, and many of them responded as persons troubled with this or other forms of role conflict often do. They resorted to lying and deceit.

Eugene Genovese, in an otherwise valuable essay on slave personality, is not very perceptive when he argues that slaves who tricked their masters, rather than coping with problems of role conflict and role definition, were merely playing a game which the masters enjoyed and had themselves written into the script.[48] True, a master might occasionally be amused when a house servant outwitted him, but there is scant evidence that he enjoyed this "game" when played by field hands. This was certainly not in the script, and masters frequently expressed their anger or perplexity at the "untrustworthiness" of Negroes. Their appreciation of the slave trickster was confined mostly to their public defenses of slavery and to sentimental plantation literature. In private they were seldom amused.

Plantation field hands, finding no escape from slavery but plenty of elbow room within it, usually managed to preserve their individuality and therefore revealed a considerable variety of personality types. Among the types, there were, to be sure, genuine Sambos who seemed to have internalized much of the role, for some slaves simply lacked the psychic strength to withstand the infantilizing pressures of the system. They looked on the master as a father figure, accepted his values, identified with him, and perhaps even viewed themselves through his eyes.

We may assume that the slave who internalized the Sambo role did accept his master as his only significant other and that he was relatively untroubled by the problem of role conflict. But he must have been sorely disturbed by the psychic process of dissociation—that is, exclusion from the self of disapproved personality tendencies, which then become part of what Sullivan calls the "extra-self." Such dissociated tendencies, we must remember, still remain part of the personality; and, therefore, Sambo was Sambo only up to a point—in Genovese's words, "up to the moment that the psychological balance was jarred from within or without. . . ."[49] Plantation records often reveal the astonishment of masters when slaves, who had long given evidence of Sambo personalities, suddenly behaved in disturbingly un-Sambo ways.

Another personality type was evident on certain large plantations, especially on those of absentee owners in new areas of the Southwest, where labor was sometimes exploited ruthlessly and punishments were brutal. This type displayed none of the silliness of Sambo, none of his childlike attachment to master or overseer; rather, he was profoundly apathetic, full of depression and gloom, and seemingly less hostile than indifferent toward the white man who controlled him. One slaveholder observed that slaves subjected to overwork and cruel punishments were likely to fall "into a state of impassivity" and to become "insensible and indifferent to punishment, or even to life. . . ."[50] These brutalized slaves had their counterparts on Latin American plantations, where extreme cruelty produced in some a state of psychic·shock manifested in apathy and depression. In colonial Brazil this condition was sufficiently common to be given a special name: banzo.[51] It is this condition that seems to be analogous to the concentration camps, where life had lost its meaning, and to prisons and asylums, where "situational withdrawal" is a form of institutional adaptation.[52]

More numerous among plantation personalities were the men and women with sufficient strength of character to escape the emasculating tendencies of the system, a group whose size Elkins seriously underestimates. These slaves were not only not Sambos, but they did not *act* like Sambos—their behavior was in no respect infantile. Though observing all the niceties of interracial etiquette, they maintained considerable dignity even in their relations with their masters. Judging from plantation diaries, masters often treated slaves of this kind with genuine respect and seldom made the mistake of regarding them as children. Slaves such as these were not troublemakers; they were rarely intransigent as long as what was asked of them and provided for them was reasonable by their standards. They worked well and efficiently and showed considerable initiative and self-reliance. They tended to be fatalistic about their lot, expected little of life, and found their satisfaction in the religious and social activities of the slave communities. No doubt their psychic balance and their relative tranquillity was sometimes disturbed by a certain amount of role conflict; and they could hardly have escaped the phenomenon of dissociation described by Sullivan.

Herbert Aptheker's rebels must also be included among those whose personalities were far removed from the traditional Sambo. I would not limit these to the organizers of or participants in rebellions, for their number was very small.[53] Rather, I would include all who were never reconciled to the system and engaged in various acts of resistance: running away, arson, the damaging of crops and tools, and sometimes even assaults on masters, overseers, or other whites. Needless to say, it is often impossible to distinguish conscious resistance from the unconscious carelessness and indifference of slaves, but the evidence of genuine resistance is clear enough in some cases.[54] Genovese argues that the slaves did not develop a genuine revolutionary tradition, that their acts of resistance were usually nihilistic, and that at best they came out of slavery with a tradition of recalcitrance—"of undirected, misdirected or naively directed violence." George M. Frederickson and Christopher Lasch object even to calling the acts of slave rebels "resistance" and insist that it was only "intransigence." They define the former as organized, purposeful political action, the latter as mere "personal strategy of survival" which can easily lead to "futile and even self-destructive acts of defiance."[55] Surely, little that was done by the rebels could form the basis for a revolutionary tradition or satisfy so narrow a definition of resistance; but these were rebels, nonetheless, who never internalized the masters' standards of good conduct and never dissociated from their conscious selves all the disapproved tendencies of their personalities.

All of these slave types, with myriad individual variations, were recognizable on the plantations. But I believe that the personalities of most slaves are less easily classified, because their behavior when observed by whites was usually that of conscious accommodators. They played the role of Sambo with varying degrees of skill and consistency,[56] but, in contrast to the authentic Sambos, most characteristics of the role did not become part of their true personalities. For them the Sambo routine was a form of "ritual acting"—that is, they went through the motions of the role, but with a rather low degree of personal involvement.[57]

Several aspects of role theory support this hypothesis. One assumption of this theory is that the average normal person plays not one but several roles, and often two or more simultaneously. To think of the slave as playing but one role—that of Sambo—is to assume that he responded to a single social situation, which was clearly not the case. Moreover, when a role performance is demanded primarily in terms of the pains and penalties for non-performance, as it was on the typical plantation supervised by an overseer and run as a business enterprise, the role is likely to be enacted with little conviction and minimal personal involvement. The Sambo role doubtless was performed more convincingly and with more feeling in a paternalistic situation. Finally, the extent to which a given role makes an impact on the self depends on its "preemptiveness"—on how much of a person's time is spent playing the role.[58] Therefore, one must ask how preemptive the Sambo role actually was. During the week the plantation field hand spent most of his waking hours as an agricultural worker, planting, cultivating, or harvesting, and the demand on him was for a responsible adult performance. He spent evenings and holidays in the slave community playing a variety of roles, only occasionally being observed by master and overseer. The one occasion that called for the Sambo role was that of a direct contact with a member of the white race, when the Negro was forced to acknowledge in some way not only that he was a slave but that he belonged to a degraded caste. However, for the average field hand such contacts were brief and relatively infrequent; therefore the pressures on him most of the time were to play roles other than Sambo.

In short, most plantation slaves avoided the internalization of

Sambo, first, because they were able to play different roles in their communities; second, because the Sambo role was not unduly pre-emptive; third, because masters were not the only significant others in the lives of slaves; fourth, because slaves found abundant opportunities to behave in ways that had meaning in adult terms; and, last, because conditions on the average plantation were not so brutal that they were destroyed as human beings. In consequence, slaves could use the essentially external Sambo role, in Elkin's words, "as a protective device beneath which a more independent personality might develop."[59] Those who consciously and purposefully acted the part of Sambo, thereby reducing sources of friction and putting limits on what would normally be expected of them, were in no sense being childish or infantile; rather, their behavior was rational, meaningful, and mature.

In an essay based on studies of other total institutions, George Fredrickson and Christopher Lasch suggest that conditions in prisons and asylums are more analogous to slavery than conditions in concentration camps. They note that the inmates of such institutions do not usually internalize a sense of obligation to obey their rules and accept their values. In the case of slavery, they conclude, "a system that rigorously defined the Negro slave not merely as an inferior but as an alien, a separate order of being," could hardly have instilled in him "the sense of belonging on which internalized obedience necessarily has to rest."[60]

However, I think there is a better approach to understanding the personalities of plantation slaves than that provided by either of these analogies. Much more can be learned from a study of ex-slaves and their descendants in the rural South in the decades after Reconstruction, when, for all practical purposes, the system was still a closed one from which few escaped, and when powerful forces again generated tendencies toward emasculated personalities. Now their humanity was assaulted and their race denigrated by the most extreme forms of prejudice, segregation, and discrimination; and they felt strong pressures, both subtle and crude, to internalize the white man's opinion of them. After emancipation there was still a white landlord to serve as a counterpart to the slaveowner as a significant other. More important, the whole white community now became, collectively, a significant other, imposing a subservient and dependent role on the Negro and enforcing an etiquette of race relations with sanctions equal to those available to masters in slavery days. Yet, most Negroes, as in slavery days, found ways of maintaining a degree of psychic balance. Through their churches, their music, and a great variety of organized social activities, they gradually developed a semiautonomous Afro-American subculture; in their communities and families they responded to their own significant others; and in their mature years they had a variety of adult roles to play, even though whites persisted in calling black men boys and black women girls.

In circumstances whose psychic impact had many parallels to slavery, Negroes once more resorted to conscious accommodation. The investigations of twentieth-century social scientists provide much evidence that most post-Reconstruction Negroes did not internalize the Sambo role they played before the white community. For example, in the 1930s, John Dollard observed that the southern Negro played two roles:

> one that he is forced to play with white people and one the "real Negro" as he appears in his dealings with his own people. What the white southern people see who "know their Negroes" is the role that they have forced the Negro to accept, his caste role. . . . It is perhaps this fact which often makes Negroes seem so deceptive to white people; apparently our white caste wishes the Negro to have only one social personality, his caste role, and to *be* this with utter completeness.[61]

The testimony of post-Reconstruction Negroes themselves, especially in their music and folklore, also suggests a prevalent pattern of conscious accommodation.[62]

Similarly, the slaves, in their scattered records, and the masters, in their private papers and published essays on the management of Negroes, indicate that conscious accommodation was a widespread behavior pattern on the antebellum plantations. Whatever the masters may have said about the loyal, childlike "darky" in their public defenses of slavery, the dissembling pseudo-Sambo was the most common reality that confronted them in their daily lives. As one planter wrote: "The most general defect in the character of the Negro, is hypocrisy; and this hypocrisy frequently makes him pretend to more ignorance than he possesses; and if the master treats him as a fool, he will be sure to act the fool's part. This is a very convenient trait, as it frequently serves as an apology for awkwardness and neglect of duty."[63]

However, the fact that some masters saw through the Sambo act, as this one did, suggests that slave accommodators may often have missed their lines. Playing this intricate role could never have been easy, and it may have caused even the most skilled of them serious psychic problems, especially if there was a basic incongruence between the self and this role.[64] I suspect that many had profound difficulties with role conflict, as the weaker characters who internalized the Sambo role suffered from dissociation. Those who study slave personality would be well advised to watch for signs of character disorders in these seemingly gay dissemblers. I want to point again, as I did in *The Peculiar Institution*, to the astonishing frequency of speech problems among slaves. Time after time, owners advertising for runaways reported that a slave "stutters very much," "stammers very much," "speaks quickly and with an anxious expression of countenance," or is "easily confused when spoken to."[65] Such data are open to several interpretations, but one respectable theory suggests that speech impediments are symptoms of buried hostility. Dr. Murry Snyder of the Speech Rehabilitation Institute of New York City believes that "Underneath the cloak of inhibition and mild manner, the stutterer often seethes with anger."[66] In the case of slaves, speech problems may also have been a manifestation of role conflict or of incompatibility between self and role.

The art of conscious accommodation, along with all its psychic consequences, is one of the skills that Negroes carried with them from slavery to freedom. Accommodation continued to be a part of life for many of them, especially in the rural South, for another century. Being obliged to wear the mask of Sambo, whatever they may have been inside, doubtless they were, as in slavery days, troubled to an extraordinary degree by the problem of role conflict. To escape this problem seems to be one of the aims of the present black revolution, for the search for black identity is in part a search for role clarity. To end the dissembling, to be all of a piece, to force the white community to accept them as they really are, not as it so long wanted to see them, is quite obviously one determined goal of the new generation of blacks.

NOTES

1. Drew, *The Refugee: or the Narratives of Fugitive Slaves in Canada* (Boston, 1856).

2. John B. Cade, "Out of the Mouths of Ex-Slaves," *Journal of Negro History*, XX (July 1935), 294-337; Fisk University Social Science Institute, *Unwritten History of Slavery* (Nashville, 1945); Benjamin A. Botkin, ed., *Lay My Burden Down* (Chicago, 1945). See also Norman R. Yetman, "The Background of the Slave Narrative Collection," *American Quarterly*, XIX (Fall

1967), 534-53. My evaluation of these collections of slave narratives is based on the above published extracts. A careful study of the more than two thousand narratives collected by the Federal Writer's Project in the 1930s may lead to a more favorable assessment of their historical value.

3. A good case for the value of this material is presented in Lawrence W. Levine, "Slave Songs and Slave Consciousness: An Exploration in Neglected Sources," in Tamara Hareven, ed., *Anonymous Americans* (New York, 1971), 99-130. See also Sterling Stuckey, "Through the Prism of Folklore: Black Ethos in Slavery," *Massachusetts Review*, IX (Summer 1968), 417-37.

4. Aptheker, *American Negro Slave Revolts* (New York, 1943).

5. Elkins, *Slavery: A Problem in American Institutional and Intellectual Life* (2d ed., Chicago and London, 1968).

6. Aptheker, *Slave Revolts*, 374.

7. Elkins, *Slavery*, 82.

8. Aptheker, *Slave Revolts*, 162.

9. *Ibid.*, 325-36.

10. Elkins, *Slavery*, 84-86, 88-89.

11. *Ibid.*, 81-82, 84, 134-37.

12. *Ibid.*, 130, 242.

13. Sullivan defines personality as "the relatively enduring pattern of recurrent interpersonal situations which characterize a human life." *The Interpersonal Theory of Psychiatry* (New York, 1953), 111.

14. "A role is a cluster of traits (or pattern of behavior) which serves as the culturally normal or modal solution to recurrent, usually social problems peculiar to a particular status or position in society." David C. McClelland, *Personality* (New York, 1951), 293. See also Eugene L. and Ruth E. Hartley, *Fundamentals of Social Psychology* (New York, 1952), 485-86.

15. Elkins, *Slavery*, 86-87, 137-38.

16. *Ibid.*, 104, 225.

17. *Ibid.*, 128-30.

18. Ann Lane, ed., *The Debate over Slavery: Stanley Elkins and His Critics* (Urbana, Ill., 1971). In his response, except for one important point mentioned in note 34 below, Elkins concedes very little to his critics. Therefore, since he has neither changed his position significantly nor added any supporting empirical evidence, my comments on his use of analogy, his use of personality theory, and his view of the life of plantation slaves are as relevant to the new essay as to the old.

19. It is unlikely that Elkins thought of his analogy as more than an explanation. Yet he creates a small ambiguity by labeling one of the sections of Appendix A (p. 225) "*Analogy as evidence.*"

20. Winthrop D. Jordan has called my attention to an important question about when Sambo first began to appear prominently in southern plantation literature. He was not the typical slave depicted in the seventeenth and eighteenth centuries. In those earlier years the slave was more often thought of as a dangerous element in the population—a threat to the peace and safety of the English colonies. Of course, it is possible that the Negro's personality had changed by the nineteenth century, when Sambo first became important in southern literature; but there may have been a connection between the appearance of Sambo and the growing moral attack on slavery. Sambo was always

one of the proslavery writers' major arguments for keeping the Negro in bondage.

21. Elkins, *Slavery*, 224.

22. *Ibid.*, 131-32. It hardly needs to be said that Elkins does not endorse the racist implications of these statements. He uses them merely to illustrate the Sambo character that slavery allegedly forced on the Negro in the South. Still, it is worth noting that, except for the racist overtones, his description of the plantation slave is almost identical with that found in the writings of Ulrich B. Phillips.

23. McClelland, *Personality*, 70.

24. Genovese, "Rebelliousness and Docility in the Negro Slave: A Critique of the Elkins Thesis," *Civil War History*, XIII (December 1967), 314.

25. *Ibid.*, especially 295-98; quote on page 297. See also David B. Davis, *The Problem of Slavery in Western Culture* (Ithaca, 1966), especially Chap. VIII. Carl N. Degler, "Slavery in Brazil and the United States: An Essay in Comparative History," *American Historical Review*, LXXV (April 1970), 1004-28; Marvin Harris, *Patterns of Race in the Americas* (New York, 1964), 65-78.

26. Elkins, *Slavery*, 229.

27. Bettelheim, *The Informed Heart* (Glencoe, Ill., 1960), 138. For statements of the crucial differences between slavery and the concentration camps see Genovese, "Rebelliousness and Docility in the Negro Slave," 308-9; and Earle E. Thorpe, "Chattel Slavery and Concentration Camps," *Negro History Bulletin*, XXV (May 1962), 173.

28. The literature on the camps indicates that there was resistance, but such behavior is not taken into account in Elkins's essay. See especially Eugen Kogon, *The Theory and Practice of Hell* (New York, 1950). See also Genovese, "Rebelliousness and Docility in the Negro Slave," 312-13; Thorpe, "Chattel Slavery and Concentration Camps," 175.

29. Since psychologists cannot agree on a definition of personality, the literature gives the historian plenty of latitude. One psychologist compiled a list of almost fifty definitions of personality. Calvin S. Hall and Gardner Lindzey, *Theories of Personality* (New York, 1957), 7-10. Though I am not here considering the personality theories that Elkins does not use, I do question whether he was justified in making so little use of Freud, especially Freud's emphasis on the molding of the child's superego through experiences with the parents. Elkins explains why he thinks that Freud is not very useful in understanding the impact of the concentration camps on personality, but he never explains adequately why he thinks that Freudian concepts would not help us to understand the personality of the slave. While on the subject of what Elkins has neglected, I must note his failure to use the decidedly relevant writings of Erik H. Erikson on the problem of identity.

30. McClelland, *Personality*, 296. See also Hartley and Hartley, *Fundamentals of Social Psychology*, 509-11. However, it is important to note that those who relate roles to personality are usually writing about children and the role the parents prescribe. In the case of the slave child, it was the mother or the father or a slave nurse, not the master, who taught the child a role in his early years. The master's direct involvement in child training did not usually begin until the child was old enough to perform some chores—say, at the age of seven

or eight. By that time a large part of the child's personality had been formed. In the early formative years the master was not so much the one who prescribed a role as he was an object whom the child was taught to cope with in one way or another.

31. Ralph Linton, *The Cultural Background of Personality* (New York, 1945), 26.

32. Sarbin and Allen, "Role Theory," in Gardner Lindzey and Elliot Aronson, eds., *The Handbook of Social Psychology* (2d ed., 5 vols., Reading, Mass., 1968–1969), I, especially 550-57; quote on page 554.

33. Elkins, *Slavery*, 86n, 125, 227-28.

34. *Ibid.*, 132n-33n. In his recent essay Elkins claims that his statement about "a broad belt of indeterminacy between 'mere acting' and the 'true self' " expresses the position he had taken in the original essay. Lane, ed., *The Debate over Slavery*, 359. However, in my opinion, this claim represents a shift in his basic position rather than an accurate statement of his original point of view.

35. McClelland, *Personality*, 316-18; Hartley and Hartley, *Fundamentals of Social Psychology*, 521-32; Sarbin and Allen, "Role Theory," 540-44.

36. Sullivan, *Conceptions of Modern Psychiatry* (Washington, 1947), 18. Speaking of the child and his relations with his parents, Sullivan notes the child's "realistic appreciation of a necessity and a human development of devices to meet the necessity. . . . that marvelous human thing, great adaptive possibilities applied successfully to a situation." *Ibid.*, 19-20.

37. *Ibid.*, 13, 21-22.

38. *Ibid.*, 22.

39. Genovese, "Rebelliousness and Docility in the Negro Slave," 293-314; Genovese, "American Slaves and Their History," *New York Review of Books*, December 5, 1970, pp. 34-43; George M. Fredrickson and Christopher Lasch, "Resistance to Slavery," *Civil War History*, XIII (December 1967), 315-29; Levine, "Slave Songs and Slave Consciousness," 99-130; Willie Lee Rose, "Childhood in Bondage," unpublished paper read at the annual meeting of the Organization of American Historians, Los Angeles, April 1970. I have suggested other possibilities in Chapters III and VIII of *The Peculiar Institution: Slavery in the Ante-Bellum South* (New York, 1956).

40. My study of slavery also called attention to these pressures: "Ideally [slavery] was the relationship of parent and child. . . . The system was in its essence a process of infantilization. . . ." Stampp, *Peculiar Institution*, 327.

41. Elkins, *Slavery*, 134-35. I suspect that the ability of these petty administrators to escape the full impact of the terror and brutality of the camps was even more crucial to their psychological balance.

42. In her unpublished paper, "Childhood in Bondage," Willie Lee Rose argues that historians have underestimated the importance of the slave family, especially the role of the father in raising children. See also Genovese, "American Slaves and Their History," 37-38.

43. In discussing the problem that boys without fathers have in learning the male role, Eugene and Ruth Hartley note that the situation changes quickly when such boys find other opportunities to observe the male role: "They learn from their playmates and from any adult males with whom they come into repeated contact." *Fundamentals of Social Psychology*, 504.

44. *Southern Cultivator*, IX (1851), 85.

45. Fredrickson and Lasch, in "Resistance to Slavery," 322-25, suggest that slaves developed their own standards of fair play through their varying experiences with different masters and overseers.

46. "*Role*, a term borrowed directly from the theater, is a metaphor intended to denote that conduct adheres to certain 'parts' (or positions) rather than to the players who read or recite them." Sarbin and Allen, "Role Theory," 489, 547-50.

47. Thorpe, "Chattel Slavery and Concentration Camps," 174-75. This is an excellent example of one kind of role conflict—the kind that results when an authority figure holds "simultaneous contradictory expectations for one role." Sarbin and Allen, "Role Theory," 540.

48. Genovese, "Rebelliousness and Docility in the Negro Slave," 310-11.

49. *Ibid.*, 312.

50. *De Bow's Review*, XXV (July 1858), 51.

51. Davis, *Problem of Slavery*, 238.

52. See Fredrickson and Lasch, "Resistance to Slavery," 325-27, and their sources for behavior in total institutions, especially Erving Goffman, *Asylums: Essays on the Social Situation of Mental Patients and Other Inmates* (Garden City, N. Y., 1961).

53. For persuasive explanations of why there were relatively few insurrections in the antebellum South see Degler, "Slavery in Brazil and the United States," 1013-16; Eugene D. Genovese, "The Legacy of Slavery and the Roots of Black Nationalism," *Studies on the Left*, VI (November–December 1966), 4-6. I believe that a major factor contributing to the larger number of insurrections in Brazil was the imbalance of the sexes on the plantations, whereas most southern slaves lived in family groups. The presence of a large number of young men without women and the absence of the stabilizing influence of the family on Brazilian plantations were bound to create a condition highly conducive to rebellions.

54. See Raymond A. and Alice H. Bauer, "Day to Day Resistance to Slavery," *Journal of Negro History*, XXVII (October 1942), 388-419; Stampp, *Peculiar Institution*, Chap. III; Vincent Harding, "Religion and Resistance Among Ante-bellum Negroes, 1800–1860," in August Meier and Elliott Rudwick, eds., *The Making of Black America* (2 vols., New York, 1969), I, 179-97.

55. Genovese, "The Legacy of Slavery," 7-11 (quote on page 9); Fredrickson and Lasch, "Resistance to Slavery," 317, 326.

56. Sarbin and Allen note the great qualitative differences in role performance among individuals: "One person may enact a role convincingly and skillfully, while another may be inept." "Role Theory," 514.

57. *Ibid.*, 492-96; Hartley and Hartley, "*Fundamentals of Social Psychology*," 493.

58. Sarbin and Allen, "Role Theory," 491, 496-97, 535; Hartley and Hartley, *Fundamentals of Social Psychology*, 498.

59. Elkins, *Slavery*, 133n.

60. Fredrickson and Lasch, "Resistance to Slavery," 320-23.

61. Dollard, *Caste and Class in a Southern Town* (3d ed., Garden City, N. Y., 1957), 257-59.

62. See, for example, Lawrence W. Levine, "The Concept of the New Negro and the Realities of Black Culture," in Nathan I. Huggins, Martin Kilson, and Daniel M. Fox, eds., *Key Issues in the Afro-American Experience* (2 vols., New York and other cities, 1971), II, 125-47.

63. *Farmer's Register*, V (May 1837), 32. For an excellent analysis of "Quashee," the Jamaican counterpart of Sambo, and of the degree to which he was a conscious role-player, see Orlando Patterson, *The Sociology of Slavery: An Analysis of the Origins, Development and Structure of Negro Slave Society in Jamaica* (London, 1967), 174-81.

64. Sarbin and Allen, "Role Theory," 524.

65. One must, of course, ask whether runaways were not exceptional slaves with special psychic problems. I do not think that this was the case, because many kinds of slaves ran away for a variety of reasons. But this is a matter that requires further investigation.

66. *Time*, XCVI (August 24, 1970), 42. See also Sarbin and Allen, "Role Theory," 527.

V: ASSESSMENTS

On Eugene D. Genovese's "Roll, Jordan, Roll:
The World the Slaves Made," and Other Works

RICHARD H. KING

> *The Political Economy of Slavery.* By Eugene Genovese. New York: Pantheon, 1966.
>
> *The World the Slaveholders Made.* By Eugene Genovese. New York: Pantheon, 1969.
>
> *In Red and Black: Marxian Explorations in Southern and Afro-American History.* By Eugene Genovese. New York: Vintage, 1972.
>
> *Roll, Jordan, Roll.* By Eugene Genovese. New York: Pantheon, 1974.

Eugene Genovese's work has made plain what most American historians have been loath to admit: "no theory, no history." And if Genovese's commitment to theoretical clarity is not enough, his Marxist vision is neither congenial nor comprehensible to most historians, even those who are Marxists in much the same way that Jefferson was a Federalist or Nixon a Keynesian.

Most of Genovese's critics are reluctant to attend to his Marxism in a thoroughgoing way or to investigate the differences it makes in his work. I would like to examine some of the crucial theoretical notions which inform Genovese's writings and elaborate upon the way they shape his writings on slavery and the antebellum South. My critique will thus be internal, taking Genovese on his own terms; but at certain junctures I will compare Genovese's version of the antebellum South with other accounts and offer suggestions as to how his account might be extended or enriched.

Genovese's brand of Marxism is unusual, at least in this country where the diversity of twentieth century Marxist thought has yet to be appreciated. As Genovese himself has asserted, what passes for Marx-

From "Marxism and the Slave South" by Richard H. King, *American Quarterly* 29 (Spring, 1977): 117-31. Copyright © 1977 by the Trustees of the University of Pennsylvania. Reprinted by permission of the publisher and the author.

ist historiography in America has consisted of an admirable but sentimental commitment to the oppressed, Popular Front cheerleading for
"progressive" forces, or flat-footed economic determinism.[1] Allowing
for the polemical context in which he made these remarks, his judgment is not far off the mark.

Genovese's theoretical mentors are those European Marxists who, in
response to Bolshevism, the collapse of revolutionary hopes in Central
Europe, and the emergence of Fascism in Italy and Germany, redrew
the contours of Marxist social theory. What linked such diverse thinkers as Georg Lukács, the Frankfurt School in Germany, the Freudian-
trained Erich Fromm and Wilhelm Reich, and Antonio Gramsci was
a rejection of the economic determinism, the political passivity, and
the psychological and epistemological naiveté of orthodox Marxism.
They rejected the notion that consciousness and its collective expression—culture—were epiphenomena, the methodological and causal
stepchildren of economic forces. Class interests, an idea which included but was not exhausted by economic interests, became their
central focus. In Lukács' terms they made central the "concrete totality," the social-historical *Gestalt* in which material and ideal forces
were *aufgehoben*.

Specifically, the Italian Marxist Gramsci (1891–1937) has been the
major theoretical influence on Genovese, who has lauded him as "the
greatest Western Marxist theorist of our century."[2] For Gramsci
the ruling class maintained its position not by violence alone, but by
imposing a world view upon the underclasses as well. This "hegemony"
linked the classes by a common set of assumptions, values, and attitudes which masked class contradictions. Hegemony was not necessarily
planned; rather cultural domination was in the nature of class rule.
Gramsci implied that the social revolution had also been cultural and
guided by a new world view which would incorporate as well as transcend the older hegemonic culture. In Italy, Marxism was to serve that
purpose as had Protestantism in northern Europe and the ideals of the
Revolution in France.

It is not hard to see the importance of Gramsci's notion of hegemony for Genovese's analysis of the antebellum South. Genovese's early
work consisted in a delineation of the hegemonic role of a "precapitalist" slave-holding class in the backward, rural South. In his latest work,
Roll, Jordan, Roll, he has detected the stirrings of a "national" consciousness among the slave class, an idea which parallels Gramsci's concern with the "national" question and the role of the southern Italian
peasantry in the proletarian revolution.

Genovese's Marxism has scarcely cost him professional standing. One suspects that American historians are relieved to have a "good" Marxist in their ranks, particularly one who is as kind to the reputation of U. B. Phillips as he is to the work of liberals such as C. Vann Woodward and David Potter. If that were not enough, Genovese has cultivated what Freud called the "narcissism of small differences" and has directed his major criticisms against a fellow Marxist, Herbert Aptheker, and a fellow radical, Staughton Lynd.[3]

Cloaked as he is in Marxism, Genovese has also deflected suspicions of reactionary and racist sympathies which his attention to Southern slaveholders has elicited. Marxism is not, however, without its own moral ambiguities which arise from the uneasy coexistence of two impulses: to describe "objectively" historical development *and* to pass judgment. The uneasy (and unsatisfactory) resolution has been to equate the "moral" with that which is historically "progressive." In 1968, for instance, Genovese attacked Lynd's natural rights ideology as one "which could justify anything." "Marxism," countered Genovese, "sees freedom as an historical process, not an absolute."[4]

Following upon such pronouncements, historians such as Irwin Unger have wondered whether Genovese, as a Marxist, could morally condemn slavery at all. Genovese responded by granting that a Marxist must acknowledge the "positive role of class exploitation" and conceded that slavery was historically necessary for the emergence of society from primitive conditions.[5] The problem was that Genovese failed to explain why modern slavery could not be justified along similar lines. "Modern slavery," he wrote in 1967, was "far from indispensable" for capitalism.[6] To match Lynd's justification of "anything," Genovese responded to Unger with an invocation of the wisdom of "Comrade Stalin, who remains dear to some of us for the genuine accomplishments that accompany his crimes."[7] If this was not a justification of the unjustifiable, it came close to it. Finally, in *Roll, Jordan, Roll,* Genovese asserts that slavery was "one of history's greatest crimes" and "an evil social system."[8] Few would disagree, but it is not clear how Genovese can make this assertion.

Genovese's Marxism also influences the "shape" of his work. By historical analysis Marxists refer not so much to analyzing the historical development of a society or a class as to analyzing that society or class in all its aspects at a given historical moment. Genovese thus tends to posit and then dissect a "synchronic" whole, within which change is all but ignored.

His focus established, Genovese proceeds according to the dialectical "principle of interrelatedness."[9] All aspects of a historical totality are dependent, and transformations in one realm lead necessarily to transformations in the others. But this approach involves more than a methodological imperative. Genovese also assumes that the social world contains the seeds of its own destruction and supersession. The task of the Marxist historian is to reveal the social contradictions at work, the driving force of historical change.

The static quality of the world which Genovese sets forth contrasts with E. P. Thompson's *The Making of the English Working Class* where class in the "making" remains uppermost. (Thompson's book also attends to politics in a way that Genovese's books do not.) Genovese is less a historian of the slaveholders and slaves than he is an analyst of their world(s). He does not so much tell a story as paint a mural in which time is stopped. We are called upon to witness the clash of classes and "nations," but rarely of individuals. It is a fascinating panorama, rich in detail and insight, but frozen, bereft of the differences of time and place.[10]

A defender might reply that Genovese's account captures the static quality of antebellum Southern society. Still I wonder if Marxism is the most fruitful analytic framework for that society. At best it sheds light on what was *not* present in the antebellum South. To be sure Lukács has claimed that Marxism must be considered as a way of thinking rather than as dogma. The principle of interrelatedness and the notion of hegemony can be applied with much insight. But Genovese's efforts recall the medieval Christian theologians and historians who interpreted the classical world with categories derived from Christian theology. This lack of "fit" between his subject and his interpretive framework may explain the air of perversity lingering over his work.

Taking his cue from Hegel, Genovese places the master-slave relationship at the center of his interpretation of the slave South. In their organic relationship, the master was dependent, psychologically and economically, upon the slave, who thus had a certain "mastery" over him and was his "truth." Within each slave resided both Sambo and Nat Turner.[11] The slave was chattel; the slave was human. This contradiction lay at the heart of the planter's world view; from it can be constructed the economic, social, and cultural realities of the world which slave and slaveholder made.

According to Genovese the planter did not exercise his dominance for reasons of survival alone or primarily to turn a profit. Had subsistence been at issue, the peculiar institution would scarcely have been necessary. Had maximizing profits come first, the planters would have acted more "rationally" by capitalist standards. Rather mastery was a way of being before and among other men; it was a way of life. This follows Hegel's contention that to be human is precisely *not* to act for reasons of survival alone. Man desires recognition as autonomous and he will enslave others to win that recognition. For this recognition to be satisfactory, however, it must issue from another autonomous being. In short, the master desires the impossible—free recognition from a slave—and mastery in any final sense is foreclosed.

This makes psychological and even historical sense, but it does not account for the central reality of antebellum slavery—its racial nature. The history of slavery is a history of ideological attempts to define the slave as naturally inferior, not fully human.[12] That such an ideological reflex is so pervasive testifies to a primordial uneasiness, guilt if you will, of the master for enslaving another human being. The Southern planters hoisted themselves on their own petard. In transforming the social fact of black weakness into theological or biological inferiority, the Southern master defeated his own purpose—if we follow Genovese's Hegelian paradigm. Of such shortcomings in the paradigm Genovese speaks not at all.

Another aspect of the master-slave relationship needs clarification. Genovese generally equates the master-slave relationship with "paternalism." In discussing George Fitzhugh he notes that such an elision of meaning was disingenuous, since paternalistic relationships are founded upon provisional domination.[13] And this was precisely not the case in the relationship of master and slave. Yet Genovese continues to equate the two. On this matter, as well as in discussing race in the master-slave relationship, Genovese has not clarified his guiding theoretical concept or identified the problems involved in applying it to history. The failure to think through the master-slave relationship sufficiently (which in Hegel is not intended as a piece of historical analysis) explains Genovese's obtuseness on race and leads him to Fitzhugh's writings as the "logical outcome" of the proslavery apologies. Indeed Genovese admits that Fitzhugh was "neither typical nor representative."[14]

This raises the question of how firmly Southerners were committed to slavery as *the* essential social institution. In *Slaves Without Masters* Ira Berlin has indicated that most Southerners, even in the Deep

South, found such a commitment foreign. Not only did Southern state legislatures refuse to extend slavery to the common whites, they rejected legislation which would have enslaved free blacks.[15] Berlin's findings cast doubt on the strength of the commitment to slavery as a "positive good," even in hardcore slavery areas, and show the relatively shallow roots of the planters' world view on this point.

What then of Southern "guilt" over the enslavement of Africans? Even in the ancient world manumission was an act of virtue or atonement, and freedom has always been seen as good. This was true of the slave South as well and points to a certain universal discomfort with the enslavement of other human beings. (The defenses of animal domestication would scarcely fill a page.) *The World the Slaveholders Made* takes W. J. Cash and others to task for encouraging what Genovese breezily names "guiltomania."[16] His dismissal of white guilt is understandable: to grant otherwise would admit that the planters' world view was neither so monolithic nor so historically "exceptional" as he argues. Genovese can grant that a planter felt guilt over the treatment of a slave—but only within the framework of the institution. Guilt over the institution itself, he contends, was hardly a factor.

When Genovese confronts the "guilt" problem head-on, he flounders and belies his claim to be a Freudian.[17] First, he dismisses stirrings of guilt by speculating that they "probably concerned unconscious wishes about mother or sister or something equivalent. . . ."[18] So much for Genovese the Freudian. A few pages later he tries to have it both ways by arguing that if evidence of ethical conflict did emerge, it "was manifesting itself in the form of feelings that had entirely different roots and his [the slaveowner's] sense of guilt, which probably arose from deeply personal and early experiences having little to do with the social order, was being given a public face."[19] Private and public are linked mechanically, a strange position for a sophisticated Marxist. He confuses matters further when he suggests, following H. Hoetink, that genuine feelings of guilt are often buried in the psyche, an argument which refutes his own position.[20] We never learn whether misgivings about slavery decreased over time and, if so, why this couldn't be attributed to defensiveness against abolitionist attacks rather than any commitment to the institution per se. Genovese ends by pronouncing the argument over guilt "irrelevant." It may be unresolvable, but the only thing irrelevant is Genovese's attempt to refute the notion of guilt.

Indeed, it is undialectical to deny a strong component of guilt in the world view of the slaveholders. Surely if their world was riven with contradictions on the political and economic plane, such contradictions would be present in the intellectual and emotional life of the class. And in *Roll, Jordan, Roll* he has grudgingly admitted that the planters were guilty about everything and thus guilty over slavery too, at least in contrast with the slave's "shame" culture.[21] To admit guilt is not to deny the hegemonic role of the planters; but it is to complicate a simple depiction of the planter class.

There are also problems with Genovese's use of hegemony. His concentration has fallen on the relationship of master and slave, but the problem of the antebellum South is less how master dominated slave than how planter controlled yeoman farmer, poor white, and the commercial bourgeoisie. On this matter Cash remains superior to Genovese. In positing a unitary "mind," Cash too asserted the hegemonic world view, the instrument of Southern unity which stunted class consciousness and generated a "democracy of feeling." Cash also noted the growing importance of the paternalistic ideal. He too saw an aristocracy, but an undeveloped one, while Genovese reads back into this fledgling aristocracy a fully developed ideal and reality. Genovese chides Cash for failing to realize that aristocracies have always been rude and vulgar and asserts that ideology, not origins or length of existence, defines an aristocracy. Yet a few pages earlier Genovese states that time is of the essence in the emergence of an authentic aristocracy.[22] Surely there are more "objective" criteria for assessing the planter class than its ideology.

In his essay, "Yeoman Farmers in a Slaveholders' Democracy," published since *Roll, Jordan, Roll,* Genovese tries to explain, rather than to assume, the dominance of planter over common white.[23] He explores the various components of the planter hegemony and skillfully sketches the relationship within one Southern family of a rich planter and a not-so-prosperous relative; how the latter resents yet is proud of his successful kinsman, and how the planter condescends to his yeoman relatives who "aspired to become slaveholders themselves."[24] It convincingly renders the hegemonic relationship. Yet aside from a few references to the organic relationship of master and slave, Genovese talks little of the planters' premodern mentality. Implicitly, he separates the hegemony question from the question of the nature of the planters' world view. His analysis reveals that, though white Southern society and politics were hierarchically structured, the South remained committed to the equalitarian ideal, for whites, by which every man could become or at least entertain the notion of becoming a planter. Genovese meets Cash.

In this essay Genovese also cautions against the judgment that the nonslaveholding whites violated their class interests in supporting slavery and following the leadership of the planters. This cautionary note raises another aspect of his work for consideration: how does the historian judge individuals or classes? As a Marxist Genovese holds that world views are class-determined. An important point in *The Political Economy of Slavery* was that the historian should evaluate the Southern planter class according to how its values and actions advanced its class interests. Of it no more nor less could be demanded. Thus Genovese has scorned those who hold that the planters were bent on making a profit, rather than strengthening their position as a class. And conversely he has scored the Southern industrialists for irrationally betraying their class interests, thereby indicating their "ultimate ideological commitment" to the slaveholders.[25]

There is something valuable in Genovese's strictures against easy moralizing; yet there are problems as well. What are given class' interests and who is to decide? As Carl Degler has observed, many Whig slaveholders opposed secession because they felt it would endanger slavery more than remaining in the Union would.[26] And they were correct. Nor is it clear that, because the Southern bourgeoisie and the Whig planters fought with their section, this indicated a commitment to the "slave-holding civilization." Surely, as with the yeoman and the poor whites, motives transcending class interests can plausibly be suggested.

Genovese now seems less confident of a glib answer on such matters. In the essay on Southern yeomanry, he asserts that "if a social class acts against its own apparent collective interests," we must assume a "rational basis for its action."[27] Thus Genovese separates rationality from class interest, hiding behind the equivocal "apparent." Here he needs to distinguish between relatively conscious interests and the underlying motivational structure, formed under earlier conditions. As both Wilhelm Reich and Erich Fromm (in their Marxist incarnations) noted, conscious and unconscious interests may diverge. The notion of hegemony is a step toward explaining such a divergence, but it does not penetrate the unconscious of individuals or classes.

What of the achievements of the planter class in "high" culture? Genovese has devoted little or no attention to such matters, nor has he dealt that much with the daily life of the planter class. Only very sketchily in *Roll, Jordan, Roll* do we sense the daily round, the social fabric, and the cultural activities of the slaveholders. The Southern "gift" for politics and rhetoric are scarcely touched upon. The reason, I suspect, for these lacunae is that the prebourgeois style was undeveloped and that attempts to live up to their "ideal" appeared as ridiculous to the planters as they do to us, a point which Genovese inadvertently supports in *Roll, Jordan, Roll*.[28] They rode to the coon hounds and not the fox hounds. Nowhere do we learn anything which would contradict Cash's indictment of the planters' culture as evanescent, bereft of lasting value.

Indeed from the master-slave model we should expect as much, since Hegel noted that the master was a parasitic consumer of what the slave wrests from nature. Genovese grants this in the economic realm, but fails to explore the cultural implications. In fact to encompass the lifestyle of the planters, neither Marx nor Gramsci are as informative as, for instance, Thorstein Veblen's *The Theory of the Leisure Class* would have been.

An authentic aristocracy had dominated premodern Europe with considerable cultural achievement to its name. Its demise was no unambiguous good—therein lay the tragedy. But the Southern planter class exemplifies one of Marx's historical farces.

In the late 1960s and early 1970s Genovese published several essays laying the groundwork for *Roll, Jordan, Roll*. In them, he contended that a slave culture had existed in the prewar South, something which went against the grain of most major studies of slavery.[29] His "Treatment of Slaves in Different Countries" (1969) clarified the debate over the "merits" of slavery in its various hemispheric settings and suggested three meanings of the term "treatment." Genovese argued that if the term referred to day-to-day living conditions, slaves in North America probably had things better. But if treatment referred to viable social and cultural structures, then the Caribbean and Latin American settings were more advantageous, though evidence pointed to a U.S. slave culture which was no mere reflection of the dominant European culture. Finally, if treatment meant access to freedom, slavery outside of the United States was superior.[30] Subsequently in *Roll, Jordan, Roll* Genovese emphasized the second meaning of treatment and, to a lesser degree, the first.

Astonishingly, except for David Brion Davis, most reviewers of Genovese's latest book have missed or chosen to soften Genovese's central claim, one which resembles Stanley Elkins' "Sambo" thesis, though Genovese's account is more nuanced and locates the American slave culture among the cultures of oppressed classes generally.[31] His thesis is that, though the slaves had no commitment to slavery, they incorporated its paternalistic ethos into their culture. The result was a psycho-cultural dependence upon the master class and, to a lesser degree, whites, lasting to the present. Thus David Donald's claim that Genovese has become a "House Honky" is absurd, and Stanley Elkins' more measured assertion that *Roll, Jordan, Roll* belongs with the historiography of slavery stressing "cultural autonomy" as opposed to "damage" is a half-truth.[32]

In the section "On Paternalism" Genovese analyzes the way in which slaves won an implicit recognition of their humanity and a precarious space of freedom by playing off overseer against master. Later he notes in "The Hegemonic Function of Law" that, despite the positive law which considered the slave as chattel, the slaves forced the masters to follow an informal plantation code by which slaves were married, had some privacy of worship, and received days of rest and holidays. The dialectic of the situation was, however, that a personal dependence upon the master was established, since the claims of the slaves could not be recognized legally and hence impersonally. In the short run small triumphs allowed the slaves a certain breathing room; in the long run the master was kind only to be cruel.

This analysis traces back to the logic of Hegel's master-slave relationship as developed by such critics of colonialism as Fanon and Memmi: autonomy can be won only by the slave's risking his life against the master. Genovese would add that this risk of life must be a collective one. Because, Genovese claims, the slaves did not win their freedom but were freed, they never developed the requisite independence from the masters. This is not to deny that individual slaves wrested autonomy (Frederick Douglass provides the prototypical example). Genovese cites cases where slaves refused to be whipped or protected their wives and families, thereby facing down the master in a literal risk of life. Nor is it to deny the acts of violence against the master and his property. Rather, resistance remained apolitical or prepolitical; only rarely was it collective. As Genovese stressed in discussing Fanon's notion of the therapeutics of violence, it is not violence but joint action, whether violent or not, which undercuts the master's claim to superiority and the slaves' feelings of inferiority. "It was not that the slaves did not act like men. Rather it was that they could not grasp their collective strength as people and act like political men."[33]

By itself this is too much an "idealist" reading of the situation. As *Roll, Jordan, Roll* stresses, the objective conditions made collective revolt suicidal. Thus culture and context shaped one another. The slaves knew this. If they were not heroic in a superficial sense, it was because they realized what the outcome would be. The compromise was an accommodation to slavery which Genovese refuses to call "Uncle Tomism," and which stopped short of collective rebellion. In short, the slave culture was one of passive aggression, gaining for the slaves a respite from domination. Coping with the sociopathology of everyday slave life was as much as could be managed.

At the heart of Genovese's analysis is the religion of the slaves, shaped by and shaping the "concrete totality." Though some reviewers have been puzzled that a Marxist would pay serious attention to religion, Marxism originated as a critique of religion and forms of idealism. They forget the words which accompany Marx's famous "opium of the people" dictum: religion is "the heart of the heartless world." This is also Genovese's view.

Slave religion was a form of Christianity, leavened with African carry-overs and exhibiting many of the traits of preindustrial spiritual life. In no sense was it a reflection of the masters' religion, which ironically Genovese must nudge toward the puritanism of Northern Protestantism when he compares it with slave spirituality. (Similarly Genovese must push the planters in the direction of sexual puritanism when discussing the sexual morality of the slaves.) Slave religion was life- and world-affirming and never took seriously the doctrines of original sin and guilt. But it contained a flaw which reenforced or accommodated the paternalistic ethos and collective inaction. Lacking the spur of guilt, the ascetic predisposition, or an activating sense of chosenness, slave religion thereby lacked a revolutionary dynamism. With the exception of a Nat Turner, whom Genovese considers an isolated and aberrant case, the prophetic tradition and millennial vision never took hold. In shorthand terms, the religion of the slave lacked a collective and political component; culture never became politics. It gave the slaves a "profound spiritual strength . . . but also imparted political weakness."[34] Though authentic and coherent rather than fragmented and derivative, the slave culture was essentially defensive. While it protected and even nurtured the will to individual resistance, it blunted the revolutionary impulse.

Roll, Jordan, Roll offers myriad other local insights. Yet the second half lacks the coherence and energy of the first half and all too often is marked by equivocation. One of Genovese's concerns is to rehabilitate the slave family and to demonstrate its strength. His strongest claim is that the *ideal* of the family and a coherent sexual morality were established in the slave culture, contrary to the standard view of demoralized families, emasculated husbands, and promiscuous wives. Yet he often generalizes from anecdotal examples. He writes that "many black women fiercely resisted such aggression and many black men proved willing to die in defense of their women."[35] What does "many" mean in such a context? Nor does Genovese distinguish between the disruption of slave marriages and the disruption of slave families; and he slights the effects which the threat of disruption had on overall morale of the family.[36] He does remind us here that our view of such matters must be complex. Many planters knew that male slaves were less rebellious or inclined to run away if they were responsible for their wives and children. The perniciousness of slavery as a "total institution" was that both family stability and fragility could be used to bolster the slave regime.

Despite Genovese's theoretical bent, the material on the slave family is under-interpreted and demands connection with the paternalism thesis and his analysis of slave religion. Genovese's Marxism lacks, however, a psychology to illuminate the relationships within the slave family and community, specifically the internalizations of and identifications with the actual and symbolic parental figures. As it stands, the notion of hegemony remains abstract.

In this connection it is important to call attention to a certain sentimentality which has grown up around the slave family and slave culture. Such sentimentality urges that the slave family was adaptive and healthy, despite its divergences from the European model. Adaptive it may have been and strengths it may have possessed, but in no sense can it be called strong or healthy. A family structure cannot be called such when it exists under the constant threat of disruption, when fathers possess little power over their fate or that of their families, and when mothers bear the burden of child care and nurturing. It is irrelevant whether slave fathers were courageous and slave wives faithful. The fact remains that the white planter disposed over the instrumentalities of violence, as well as the symbolic and material accoutrements of life. For Genovese to say that the slaves developed a coherent sexual and familial ethic is to point up the tremendous gap between that ideal and the possibility of its realization.

From Genovese's account we can glean that the nursing of children was exigent and irregular, though long lasting; that the young slave child roamed relatively freely and was sometimes spoiled by the white owners; and that as puberty approached, the child was impressed into the labor force, separated from former white playmates and the white world generally. Slave parents also severely punished their children as protections against the greater brutality from the "free" world. If such a pattern was relatively common, surely we need some suggestion from Genovese concerning "typical" slave personalities or the range of possibilities open to the slave psyche.

Genovese's emphasis on paternalism and the family also calls attention to the "split father." Though the slaveholder was the source of power, neither his values nor his role could be internalized by the slave. In Oedipal terms, he could neither be done away with nor identified with. Too far removed, yet too all-pervasive, as "Father" he was the source of no inheritance or succession which marks the normal relationship of parents and children. On the other hand the actual slave father, even when "present," was "absent." Parental roles and values could be internalized but this provided nothing to pass on to the children, except the defensive wisdom of a community under duress. It was not a matter of the child's despising his father for his weakness, but more a matter of intuiting over the years from whence power came and the lack of inner authority with which the slave fathers were plagued.

Finally there is slave religion. Here Genovese fails to follow Marx's cue that to understand the heavenly family we must first understand the earthly family. Though Genovese adverts several times to spirituals referring "to God ('de Big Massa . . .') as living in a 'mansion in de sky,'" and notes how such reflected the paternalistic hegemony,[37] the source of transcendent aid was a combination Moses-Jesus figure, the emblem of deliverance and suffering, nearer a brother than a father.[38] In seeing God as brother the slaves seem to have rejected in part the patriarchal impulse. Perhaps the planter as symbolic father was not quite so central as Genovese would have it; or perhaps this is an example of an ideological reaction-formation. Whatever the case Genovese does not enlighten us on why the patriarchal ideology did not receive straightforward expression in slave religion. And finally it seems that Genovese has forgotten what he once criticized Stanley Elkins for: neglecting the dialectic within slave personality and culture. It is not that his paternalism thesis is wrong; it is one-sided. The slave was split between two worlds, possessed by and possessing a "doubleness" which could not be superseded.

Undoubtedly the paternalism thesis will and should be hotly argued in the future. Whatever the plausibility of the thesis, Genovese has opened himself to charges of having illicitly extended it to contemporary black culture with little or no evidence. Genovese has also sidestepped an important area of speculation—whether the paternalistic relationship was stronger in some parts of the South than in others—by minimizing the disparities between life on the large plantations and slave life on small farms.

Roll, Jordan, Roll marks a shift from Genovese's earlier "class" focus and his reluctance to make "race" a major factor in the operation or understanding of slavery. In a review of Harold Cruse's *The Crisis of the Negro Intellectual* (1968) Genovese acknowledged the importance of ethnicity and the "national struggle" in the history of black Americans: "American blacks constitute not so much a class as a nation." Two years later he noted that one effect of black nationalism had been to show "a common body of interest, strong elements of a discrete culture, and a general sense of being a distinct people. . . ."[39]

Such statements anticipate Genovese's argument in his latest book that "slaves as an objective social class laid the foundation for a separate black national culture. . . ."[40] His not-so-hidden agenda stresses the commonality of the slave experience, while minimizing the "class" distinctions within the slave community and the distinctions between free blacks and slaves. With the unifying power of religion and language we have the elements for an emerging nation. Thus race may shape class, a corrective to his earlier position in which class outweighed race.

This is the weakest part of Genovese's analysis. It is not clear in what sense we are to understand the claim for national status. Is it from the viewpoint of the slaves or that of the modern historian, acquainted with the various national liberation movements of recent years? "Nation" is a slippery term (why not ethnic group?). On his account slaves were a proto-nation within a Southern nation which was moving toward a conflict with the American (Northern?) nation. Thus the term loses meaning and usefulness.

The value of Genovese's work has been to correct the conventional understanding of slavery and the antebellum South. For this task his Marxist vision has served him and historians well. As with most Marxists of this century, particularly those who have caught the spirit of thinkers such as Gramsci, Genovese's work displays a mixture of pessimism and optimism, detachment and engagement. Things appear bleak and analysis leads to revolutionary dead ends; yet contradictions are at work and a better future is possible. This stance can best be summed up in the famous phrase of Romain Rolland which Gramsci was fond of quoting: "pessimism of the intelligence, optimism of the will." There is no better way to describe the overall thrust of Genovese's efforts.

NOTES

1. Genovese, "Marxian Interpretations of the Slave South," in Barton Bernstein (ed.), *Towards A New Past* (New York: Pantheon, 1968), 90-125.

2. Genovese, "On Antonio Gramsci," *In Red and Black*, 391-422. See also John Cammett, *Antonio Gramsci and the Origins of Italian Communism* (Palo Alto: Stanford Univ. Press, 1967) and Guiseppi Fiori, *Antonio Gramsci: Life of a Revolutionary* (New York: Dutton, 1971).

3. Genovese, "Potter and Woodward on the South," "U. B. Phillips: Two Studies," and "Staughton Lynd as Historian and Ideologue" in *In Red and Black.*

4. "Staughton Lynd . . . ." 354-67.

5. "A Question of Morals," *In Red and Black*, 374.

6. "Marxian Interpretations . . . ." 114.

7. "A Question of Morals," 371.

8. *Roll, Jordan, Roll,* xvi.

9. "Materialism and Idealism in the History of Slavery," *In Red and Black*, 43.

10. This is not the case when Genovese analyzes the differences among North American, Caribbean, and Latin American slave systems. Thus his work in the area of comparative slavery is so valuable.

11. "Rebelliousness and Docility in the Negro Slave: A Critique of the Elkins Thesis," *In Red and Black*, 73-101.

12. David Brion Davis, *The Problem of Slavery in the Western World* (Ithaca: Cornell Univ. Press, 1966).

13. *The World the Slaveholders Made*, 196.

14. Ibid., 129.

15. Ira Berlin, *Slaves Without Masters* (New York: Pantheon, 1974), chap. 11.

16. *World*, 137-50.

17. Genovese offered this bit of intellectual biography at a session devoted to *Roll, Jordan, Roll* at the meeting of the Southern Historical Association in Washington, D.C., on November 14, 1975.

18. *World*, 146.

19. Ibid., 149.

20. Ibid.

21. *Roll, Jordan, Roll,* 120.
23. *World,* 121.
23. Genovese, "Yeoman Farmers in a Slaveholders' Democracy," *Agricultural History,* 49 (April 1975), 331-42.
24. Ibid., 338.
25. *The Political Economy of Slavery,* 206-8.
26. Carl Degler, *The Other South* (New York: Harper Torchbooks, 1974).
27. "Yeoman Farmers . . . ," 332.
28. *Roll, Jordan, Roll,* 116.
29. "American Slaves and Their History," *In Red and Black,* 102-08.
30. "The Treatment of Slaves in Different Countries," ibid., 158-72.
31. David Brion Davis, "Slavery and the Post-World War II Historians," *Daedalus,* 103 (Spring 1974), 1-16.
32. David H. Donald, "Writing About Slavery," *Commentary,* 59 (January 1975), 86-90; Stanley Elkins, "The Slavery Debate," *Commentary,* 60 (December 1975), 40-54.
33. *Roll, Jordan, Roll,* 149.
34. Ibid., 284.
35. Ibid., 422-3.
36. See Herbert Gutman, *Slavery and the Numbers Game* (Urbana: Univ. of Illinois, 1975) for an extensive discussion of this matter in reference to *Time on the Cross.*
37. *Roll, Jordan, Roll,* 533.
38. Ibid., 252-3.
39. "Class and Nationality in Black America," *In Red and Black,* 57.
40. *Roll, Jordan, Roll,* xv.

On Herbert G. Gutman's "The Black Family in Slavery and Freedom, 1750–1925"

GEORGE M. FREDRICKSON

Whatever else the civil rights movement of the 1960s may have accomplished or failed to accomplish, it at least liberated Afro-Americans from historical invisibility. As recently as 1965, the dean of American historians produced a best-selling history of the United States in which black leaders and cultural achievements received scarcely more attention than horses and horse-raising.[1] It is hard to imagine such a thing happening again. Not only has black history gained academic respectability, but it has even become a preoccupation of the press and television.

Most of this burgeoning interest has focused on the slave experience. Everyone now seems to agree that the struggle of Afro-Americans to survive under servitude was not only an important episode in American history but somehow even a glorious one. But the exact nature of this struggle and the question of how the white masters influenced its outcome remain matters of great controversy among historians. Every year or so the discussion seems to take a new turn. In 1974, Robert Fogel and Stanley Engerman offered a radical reinterpretation of these issues by using elaborate quantitative methods.[2] Later that year Eugene Genovese published his sophisticated Marxian analysis with its emphasis on "paternalism" as the setting within which slaves made a world for themselves.[3] In 1976 the work of Herbert Gutman, ostensibly more modest and specialized than that of his immediate predecessors, promises to force still another rethinking of the meaning of the Afro-American slave experience.

To understand the significance of what Gutman has done, it may be useful to review the modern debate on the impact of enslavement on black culture and personality. The debate really began in earnest in the early to mid Sixties when there was a delayed reaction to a book published without fanfare in 1959—Stanley Elkins's *Slavery: A Prob-*

lem in American Institutional and Intellectual Life.[4] Since Elkins
stressed the harshness of servitude and its allegedly devastating effect
on the black personality, he had little reason to anticipate the ideological storm that his work would eventually provoke. For in the late
Fifties there was general agreement among liberal historians and sociologists—both white and black—that an emphasis on victimization
was the best reply to the racist argument of innate inferiority and
might also serve to counter the view, still enshrined in most textbooks,
that slavery was a beneficent institution—a kind of school for the
civilization of primitive Africans, where kindly masters presided over
the Americanization of contented slaves. But Elkins planted the seeds
of controversy by likening the slave plantation to a Nazi concentration camp and arguing that such a totalitarian institution tended to
reduce its victims to childlike dependency. He thus gave a new envi-
ronmentalist sanction to an old and unflattering black stereotype—the
grinning, shuffling "Sambo" of pro-slavery lore.

Initial criticisms of Elkins's work came mainly from orthodox historians who objected to his freewheeling use of hypotheses derived
from the behavioral sciences more than to his conclusions. But the
book was welcomed by sociologists and "interdisciplinary" historians
who admired it precisely because of this bold use of social science
"models." The book had a powerful influence for a time not only
within academic circles but outside as well. In his famous report on
the Negro family, prepared for the Johnson administration in 1965,
Daniel Patrick Moynihan quoted a summary of the Elkins thesis
which asserted that slavery "stripped [blacks] of their African heritage," placed them in "a completely dependent role," and "most important of all . . . vitiated family life."[5] Such a background, Moynihan argued, helped to account for "pathological" weaknesses in the
contemporary black family. William Styron's prize-winning novel,
The Confessions of Nat Turner, published in 1967, was also influenced by Elkins's work, both in some of its characterizations of slaves
and in its general portrayal of the cultural chaos out of which Nat
Turner emerged. But the hostile reaction, particularly from blacks,
which greeted both the Moynihan Report and Styron's novel was
symptomatic of a growing attack on the Elkins thesis itself.[6]

Elkins's view of what slavery had done to its black victims became
increasingly unacceptable in the Sixties, not simply, or even mainly,
because of its inherent flaws. Flaws there were, but much of the bitter
antagonism generated by the book was due to its direct collision with

emerging ideologies. Its argument, first of all, was anathema to proponents of black nationalism, whose search for historical sources of pride and community led them to reject the idea that their grandfathers were dehumanized "Sambos." Furthermore Elkins's thesis seemed to provide support for a new "racism," based on the concept of "cultural deprivation," which was replacing crude notions of biological inferiority as a rationale for denying equal justice to Afro-Americans. Elkins's premise of black docility and passivity was also incompatible with a New Left historiography that took it for granted that oppressed classes always resist their oppressors.

There were, however, some historians (this reviewer among them) who acknowledged that Elkins had given a fruitful new direction to the study of slavery by attempting to use analogies or models drawn from contemporary experience in coercive or "total" institutions. Instead of rejecting his approach *in toto*, they sought to build upon it and refine it, by using analogies that seemed to do greater justice to the variety of plantation experience and the wide range of personal adjustments that slaves could make to their predicament. They sought illumination from apparently comparable situations, such as prisons, mental hospitals, and boot camps, in which the great differences in power between those in charge of such institutions and those incarcerated in them did not inevitably result in the successful "internalization" of the authority of the superintending class but left the subordinates or inmates with enough leeway or "breathing space" to erect a variety of defenses against "dehumanization."[7] If some slaves were reduced to passivity, others "played it cool" by opportunistically masking their true feelings, and a few resisted the regime every step of the way. When their own standards of justice were flagrantly affronted, slaves who had hitherto seemed perfectly docile could suddenly turn into rebels or runaways.

Later scholarship, culminating in Gutman's study, showed that the view of the plantation as a total institution had one significant shortcoming: it failed to take into account the fact that slaves, unlike inmates, lived in family groups. Hence it tended to overlook the more collective aspects of slave response in favor of an overemphasis on individualistic "strategies for survival."

John Blassingame's *The Slave Community*, published in 1972, was the first substantial effort to do justice to this collective or communal side of the slave experience.[8] Furthermore it seemed to bury Elkins's thesis once and for all because of the effective way it summed up and synthesized almost all the lines of attack that had developed over a decade. Blassingame described a plantation community in which slaves, far from being utterly dependent on their masters, used substantial cultural resources of their own to resist oppression and maintain a sense of their dignity and worthiness as human beings.

Among these resources were surviving African traditions in the form of folklore, music, and beliefs about the supernatural; "significant others" like black preachers and conjurors who could blunt the psychological impact of the masters; and strong family ties that persisted despite the frequent break-ups resulting from the slave trade. Almost point by point, therefore, Elkins's thesis was refuted, and on the whole convincingly. Yet major questions remained about how precisely this slave community developed, maintained itself over time, and adjusted to the realities of white power and dominance. Not conclusively resolved was the crucial issue of whether it was slave initiative or planter patronage that was mainly responsible for family life and other sources of communal health and vitality.

The next major work on slavery, Fogel and Engerman's *Time on the Cross,* was mostly concerned with somewhat different issues from those we have been considering. Yet it did have important implications for the question of how and to what extent slaveholders were able to shape the personalities and belief systems of their slaves. Arguing from a conviction that the plantation was not merely a profitable enterprise but a model of capitalistic efficiency, Fogel and Engerman made their controversial claim that the slave was a willing collaborator in this economic miracle, as well as a beneficiary of it. He was thus neither a degraded and infantilized instrument of his master's will, as Elkins contended, nor a deliberately non-cooperative and inefficient worker, asserting his manhood by sabotaging his master's interests, as many of Elkins's critics argued. According to Fogel and Engerman, slaves were induced to work efficiently because of real incentives—which included material rewards equivalent to wages, opportunities for upward mobility within a plantation hierarchy, and positive protection for a stable pattern of family life.

The slaves thus accepted the capitalistic work ethic of their masters because it was in their own interest to do so. It would seem to follow, therefore, that many of the signs of health, or at least absence of "pathology," that Blassingame had discovered in the quarters, were due to the deliberate policies of enlightened capitalistic owners who understood that the encouragement of worker morale and *esprit de corps* was the essence of good management.

In *Roll, Jordan, Roll,* Eugene Genovese vigorously rejected any notion that the master-slave nexus was influenced by a capitalistic ethos. In his view, the opportunity for blacks to develop a community and culture of their own resulted from a "paternalistic" compromise or bargain between masters and slaves. Using as his model the kind of reciprocity between lords and dependents characteristic of precapitalist "seigneurial" societies, he portrayed the slave as fulfilling his obligations to his master in return for a recognition of certain "customary rights" and privileges. Although there was constant tension within the system, as slaves struggled for greater autonomy and masters sought to perfect their mechanisms of control, the result was a kind of dynamic equilibrium in which both sides made the necessary concessions. Despite his relish for dialectical paradox and his basic disagreement with Fogel and Engerman on the processes involved, Genovese also concluded in effect that the master-slave relationship was a collaborative or accommodationist arrangement. To put it simply, blacks avoided being degraded and dehumanized by accepting what their masters offered and making it their own.

Hence, according to both of the most recent major interpretations of slavery, blacks could indeed assert their manhood and enjoy a limited sense of autonomy under slavery, but *only* within a larger scheme of beliefs and values imposed by the master class. Although they differed from Elkins by stressing consensus rather than coercion, these historians of the Seventies agreed with him in seeing planter power and ideology as decisive influences on slave consciousness. Unlike Fogel and Engerman, Genovese paid considerable attention to the growth of a distinctive black culture and even an incipient black nationalism. But these developments occurred as the result of the paternalistic compromise, not in spite of it; for it was within the "breathing space" conceded by paternalistic masters that slaves forged an Afro-American world view that was culturally sustaining and psychologically satisfying, but incapable of providing revolutionary consciousness because it incorporated the slaves' own acceptance of a paternalistic order.

II

Herbert Gutman's *The Black Family in Slavery and Freedom* should serve as a valuable counterweight to this new tendency to domesticate the Afro-American slave experience as part of some larger pattern of interracial cooperation or adjustment. Like other post-Elkins historians of slavery, Gutman stresses the creativity and achievement of blacks rather than the crippling effects of oppression. But unlike Fogel and Engerman or Genovese, he gives the white planters very little credit for what happened. According to him, one does not need to assume an atmosphere of capitalistic opportunity or paternalistic mutuality to explain the rise of the slave communities. Slaves made a life for themselves not so much by reacting to particular modes of white domination as by adapting to highly diverse conditions of servitude in certain uniform ways that were truly their own. Using cultural forms that whites did not even perceive—much less impose, promote, or concede to them as part of a paternalistic compromise or out of a rational concern for industrial morale—they built up a complex and distinctive Afro-American heritage that shielded them not only from the kind of psychological damage and dependency posited by Elkins but also from the cultural dominance or hegemony of the planter class.

For Gutman there is nothing unique or miraculous in such a process of autonomous cultural adaptation on the part of a lower class or dependent group. In his notable essays on the American working class, also published in book form this year, he describes similar phenomena among immigrants and others reacting for the first time to industrial society.[9] Rather than being hollow receptacles for the new concepts of work discipline and laissez-faire capitalism pressed upon them by the ruling class, they clung tenaciously to older, pre-industrial values. As recently as 1902 there was a classic type of "food riot" in New York City, as Jewish immigrants protested a rise in the price of Kosher meat and called on rabbis to fix prices in accordance with traditional standards of fairness. In all his work, Gutman seeks to demonstrate that the poor and underprivileged, whether black or white, are not simply acted upon by the rich and powerful, but behave in ways that can only be understood with reference to the persistence and resiliency of traditional cultures, which are sometimes richer and more complex than those of their overlords. Ruling classes of course must attribute such "deviant" behavior to congenital inferiority or "cultural deprivation," because to do otherwise would undermine their rationalizations for dominance and exploitation. But conservative cultural adaptation serves the relatively weak and powerless as a defense against psychic exploitation and may, under some circumstances, provide a platform for collective action against the world their masters are trying to make.

The Black Family does not attempt to exhaust the subject of how the cultural experience of blacks helped them to adapt to slavery and to what followed. Rather Gutman examines in detail the one institution that he finds was central to the growth of communal consciousness and was the vehicle for transmitting the folk heritage from generation to generation. His initial research was aimed at questioning the Moynihan Report's generalization about a legacy of black family disorganization going back to the slave era. Looking first at census data for a number of cities in the period between 1880 and 1925, Gutman discovered that two-parent households were the norm in poor black communities and that families headed by females were scarcely, if at all, more common than among comparable whites. Some of these findings are presented in the concluding section of the book. But most of his current study is devoted to explaining how this stable family pattern among freedmen and their immediate descendants could have arisen in the first place, given the prevailing view among historians and sociologists that slavery and emancipation had wrecked the black family.

Gutman finds the answer not in some rush to imitate white norms in the Reconstruction era (which has been the view of some recent historians) but rather in family and kinship patterns that had arisen under slavery. He recreates this family and kinship structure mainly through an ingenious use of quantifiable data, derived mostly from plantation birth registers and to a lesser extent from marriage applications that freedmen submitted to Union officers after emancipation. He also makes considerable use of the direct testimony of ex-slaves as he seeks to probe the human reality behind his charts and statistical tables.

He establishes, first of all, that the two-parent household predominated in the slave quarters just as it did among freedmen after emancipation. This is perhaps the least unexpected of his findings; in less conclusive fashion Blassingame, Fogel and Engerman, and Genovese had asserted much the same thing. But Gutman provides a fuller sense than his predecessors of what these unions meant. They tended to be remarkably long-lasting, except when broken prematurely by sale. Indeed if one were to try to calculate a voluntary divorce rate among slaves it would probably be considerably lower than what exists in the United States today. Yet forced separation by sale was frequent enough to make it misleading to describe slave marriages as "stable" or to ascribe their normative character to the patronage of planters (as Fogel and Engerman had done).

Nearly one-sixth of all the slaves over twenty who registered to be married by Union Army chaplains in Mississippi in 1864 and 1865 reported that an earlier marriage, often of long duration, had been broken by force. But to the extent that slaves had their own way, as reflected most clearly on plantations where sale was infrequent, they showed a strong preference for stable monogamy. Since these unions resulted in children who constituted capital gains for the masters, one might suppose that the owners encouraged them. Not so, argues Gutman; for masters were fully aware of the biological fact that women can have children without living with one man in a stable relationship, and most of them in fact professed indifference to the specific kinds of sexual arrangements existing in the quarters so long as offspring resulted.

The slaves' propensity to live in settled monogamous unions was not, however, accompanied by the same high regard for female virginity that characterized the culture of the planters. It was relatively common for a young slave woman to have a child by one man before settling down to a permanent relationship with another. Marital fidelity, Gutman finds, was highly regarded and zealously defended, but prenuptial sex was regarded with tolerance and no stigma was attached to illegitimacy.

The long-lasting conjugal unions could have represented an imitation of white norms, and the tolerance for illegitimacy and premarital experimentation might have resulted from defective social controls or from the fact that for slaves there were none of the problems involving the inheritance of property or lineage rights that have discouraged premarital sex and especially birth out of wedlock among most free populations. But Gutman uncovers other facets of kinship that cannot be explained in this way. Most importantly his birth registers reveal that cousins almost never married. This "exogamous" tendency contrasts sharply with the "endogamy" practiced by the masters, who showed so little fear of inbreeding that according to one contemporary observer "the marriage of cousins" was "almost the rule rather than the exception."

The distinctive slave preference for exogamy, Gutman cautiously suggests, may have been adapted from African kinship patterns. Although the rules governing the choice of marriage partners in West Africa were extremely variable, differing markedly from one cultural or tribal group to another, all involved some kind of prohibition on unions with close kin, and it seems probable that slaves preserved from the diverse practices of their ancestors a general sense that it was wrong to marry blood relations.

To practice exogamy one has to have a good sense of exactly how people are related to each other, and the apparent taboo against cousin marriages is only one of the many indications Gutman finds of a strong awareness of an extended kinship network. The frequency with which children were named after parents or grandparents suggests to him a regard for lineage or family continuity extending over at least three generations. He even disputes the common view that slaves had no family names and simply took on those of their masters when they were emancipated. Although last names did not appear in the records kept by the owners, the recollections of ex-slaves reveal that they frequently used such names among themselves and that they were usually derived from a former master or even the master of an ancestor rather than from the current owner. Gutman cites, among others, the example of Daniel Payne, a slave of George Washington, who ran off during the Revolution and was evacuated by the British. The function of these family names was not so much to memorialize an earlier, and perhaps kindlier, master, as to keep alive some sense of identification with a slave family of origin.

The consciousness of being part of an extended family—including spouses, siblings, grandparents, aunts, uncles, and cousins—provided Afro-Americans with the foundations for a sense of community that could extend over time and across space. When original families were broken up and individual members carried to new plantation areas in the nineteenth century the effect was of course traumatic; yet the kinship ideal was not lost. When congenial relationships were lacking, as on newly stocked plantations in the Southwest, "fictive" kinship arrangements tended to take their place until a new pattern of consanguinity had time to develop. Out of such situations, Gutman believes, arose such habits as addressing all elderly slaves as "uncle" or "aunty." Thus blood ties could become the model for a broader conception of the slave community, in which individuals, whether actually related or not, came to view their social obligations and allegiances as kin-like in character.

The kinship structure and sense of slave interdependence associated with it developed quite early in the Afro-American experience, Gutman believes—probably by the middle to late eighteenth century.

Since Africans were arriving in great numbers during that period, it may well have been the principal mechanism by which African traditions were adapted to slave circumstances. The resulting cultural forms—which were neither African nor American but Afro-American— were passed down to future generations of slaves. Their resiliency was such that they could survive disruptive economic and geographical changes, such as the transplantation of slavery from relatively small economic units in one region to vast plantations in another. Since the slave family was the principal agency for the socialization of slave children, it served as the means for transmitting other aspects of the Afro-American cultural tradition from one generation to the next. Without it the rich and distinctive legacy of folklore, music, and religious expression that slaves were continually fashioning out of African and American materials could not have survived.

Gutman's discoveries enable him to challenge explicitly some of the central assumptions of previous scholarship on Afro-American slavery. He scores his predecessors for assuming that slave socialization and culture were predetermined by the kind of "treatment" they received from the masters. This approach, he argues, underestimates the cultural resources that enabled the slaves to make certain kinds of adaptations regardless of how they were treated.

A related shortcoming of the historiography of slavery has been its tendency to exaggerate the extent to which black consciousness was influenced by white cultural models. One of Gutman's most striking revelations is that slaveholders were generally not only indifferent to the complex kinship arrangements prevailing in the quarters but not even aware of their existence. He explains this myopia quite convincingly as the result of an unwillingness to attribute "adult" behavior to folk who had to be seen as "child-like" in order to justify their enslavement. This strikes me as another way of saying that racism so clouded the vision of the whites that they could not deal with blacks as responsible human beings. Even when whites tried to influence black behavior and beliefs out of some sense of paternalistic duty, their efforts were seriously inhibited by their lack of understanding of the people they were dealing with. Blacks of course did learn from whites what they needed to know to get along, but this was not necessarily what the whites wanted to teach them.

The question still remains how it was possible for the planters to maintain effective control over people who were so profoundly alien to them. Gutman's work seems to me to rule out the possibility that the planters could do so because they were able to persuade or brainwash the slaves into accepting or "internalizing" the idea that whites had some legitimate right to rule over them. Although he does not concern himself directly with the sources of white power and authority, Gutman does suggest a new explanation when he points out in passing that "kin and quasi-kin obligations often militate against the development of 'class consciousness.' " It seems likely that slavery was a satisfactory labor system for the master class, as well as an effective means of social control, partly because the satisfactions of kinship and quasi-kinship took the edge off black discontent and gave the owners a kind of leverage that could work against the growth of revolutionary attitudes and actions.

A culture in which social obligations are defined by kinship is likely under most circumstances to be a conservative culture where the main concern is holding on to what one already has rather than seeking radical changes. As Gutman makes clear, many slaves were reluctant to run away because this meant the breaking of strong ties to family and friends. Similarly, defiance and rebellion could lead to reprisals not only against oneself but against kinfolk as well. The threat of sales that could break up families may have been the most powerful device that the masters possessed to ensure discipline and economic performance.

In short, the masters may have been the entirely undeserving beneficiaries of the kinship system that Gutman describes. The verdict of comparative historians that slave rebellions were less frequent and smaller in scale in the American South than in other New World slaveholding societies may be supported not only by the factor most often mentioned—the relatively high proportion of whites to blacks—but also by the growth of a more highly developed and comprehensive kinship structure. In areas such as Brazil and Cuba where the African slave trade lasted longer than in the United States, there was a constant influx of unattached Africans who had relatively little to lose by rebelling. Afro-Americans, once the network of kin and quasi-kin had matured and stabilized, would have had a great deal to lose by overt acts of resistance.

If kinship does not promote militancy, proponents of revolution searching for a "usable past" may in the end be as disappointed by Gutman's interpretation as they are with the work of Fogel and

Engerman and Genovese. Yet surely there was great nobility in the cultural achievement of Afro-American slaves. If they were not consciously making a revolution to overthrow white power, they were doing a great deal more than simply "surviving" under slavery. They were creatively fashioning a life for themselves by making what choices they could and putting to use whatever resources they had. As Herbert Gutman's magnificent study shows, the chance to live, even precariously, in family groups provided the means to create a distinctive Afro-American culture.

Since Gutman formally ends his study in 1925, he makes no attempt to describe in detail how the black family has fared in more recent times. But in a brief postscript he endorses the view of some critics of the Moynihan Report that "massive structural unemployment" among urban blacks, and not some deeply rooted legacy of family instability, accounts for the increase since the 1940s in the proportion of female-headed families. He also cites studies showing that much of the statistical gap between the races (93 percent of all white families in 1960 had a male present as compared to 79 percent of all black families) disappears when one compares blacks and whites of the same economic level. Blacks with incomes above the poverty line differ very little from similarly situated whites in the percentage of families that are headed by women. A catastrophic lack of steady jobs for young black males, which has become a chronic feature of ghetto life, is clearly a main factor in preventing many of them from becoming effective husbands and fathers.

This does not mean, however, that the adaptive capacities of the black lower class have failed them under modern urban conditions. Carol Stack's recent anthropological study, *All Our Kin: Strategies for Survival in the Black Community*, describes vividly how extended networks of kin and quasi-kin meet some of the needs of poor urban blacks.[10] These "domestic networks" function by sharing limited resources and services—a pattern of exchanges reflecting the principle that those who for the moment have something are obliged to share with those who do not, with the expectation that the roles may be reversed in the future. This system conceivably suggests a new adaptation of the extended kinship structure that originated under slavery. But Stack also describes how a combination of widespread unemployment and a welfare system that rewards fatherless families has given the kin group a vested interest in discouraging the development of stable conjugal unions. For a poor black woman to enter into conventional marriage might well mean her withdrawal from full participation in the network. Her ADC payments, if any, would no longer be available to the kin group, and her own energies and earnings would now tend to be devoted exclusively to her smaller nuclear family rather than to her larger extended one.

Such middle-class behavior would normally make little sense even from the woman's point of view, since a potential husband would be unlikely to be a successful breadwinner. Greater security can usually be found by remaining in the network and avoiding marital commitments. Thus the contemporary situation has apparently created a new kind of tension or conflict between the two sides of the black family tradition that Gutman describes as coexisting in the past—conjugal affection and loyalty to an extended kin group. Two aspects of family life that even under slavery could reinforce each other may now turn out to be harsh alternatives for the poorest and most deprived blacks. Stack's work suggests that many will continue to choose the kinship network over the conjugal union so long as severe unemployment and the current welfare system persist.

But reformers should not be too quick to set as their goal the isolated nuclear family that is the norm among middle-class whites. These islands of self-contained tension and neurosis hardly represent familial perfection. A better objective would be to try to restore the complementary relationship between the ties of marriage and the obligations of extended kinship that, according to Gutman, is the essence of the black folk tradition.

NOTES

1. Samuel Eliot Morison, *The Oxford History of the American People* (Oxford University Press).
2. *Time on the Cross: The Economics of American Negro Slavery* (Little, Brown & Co.).
3. *Roll, Jordan, Roll: The World the Slaves Made* (Pantheon).
4. University of Chicago Press. A new edition (the third) is being published this year and contains Elkins's latest response to his critics.
5. See Lee Rainwater and William L. Yancey, *The Moynihan Report and the Politics of Controversy* (MIT Press, 1967), p. 62.
6. Published by Random House. See also John Henrik Clarke, ed., *William Styron's Nat Turner: Ten Black Writers Respond* (Beacon Press, 1968).
7. See George M. Fredrickson and Christopher Lasch, "Resistance to Slavery," and Roy Bryce-Laporte, "Slaves as Inmates, Slaves as Men: A

Sociological Discussion of the Elkins Thesis," in Ann J. Lane, ed., *The Debate over Slavery: Stanley Elkins and His Critics* (University of Illinois Press, 1971), pp. 223-44, 269-92.

8. Oxford University Press.

9. *Work, Culture and Society in Industrializing America: Essays in Working-Class and Social History* (Alfred A. Knopf).

10. Harper and Row, 1974.

A Selected Modern Bibliography

General Works

State and Local Studies of Slavery
      The North
      The South

The Antebellum Negro and the Problem of Race
      General studies and slave narratives
      Patterns of slave resistance
      Race relations
      Special studies
      Slavery
      Free Negroes: North and South

The Old South
      General studies
      The slave trade
      Special studies
      Chronological
      The Southern economy
      Slavery and ideology
      Miscellaneous
      Collections and edited volumes

Guides to Further Reading
      Historiography
      Bibliographic aids

American Slavery in World Perspective
      Greece and Rome
      Latin America and the West Indies
      Other cultures

General Works

John W. Blassingame, *The Slave Community: Plantation Life in the Ante-Bellum South* (New York, 1972).

Paul A. David, et al., *Reckoning with Slavery: A Critical Study in the Quantitative History of American Negro Slavery* (New York, 1976).

David Brion Davis, *The Problem of Slavery in Western Culture* (Ithaca, 1966).

———, *The Problem of Slavery in the Age of Revolution, 1770–1823* (Ithaca, 1975).

Stanley M. Elkins, *Slavery, A Problem in American Institutional and Intellectual Life* (Chicago, 1959).

Philip S. Foner, *History of Black Americans: From Africa to the Emergence of the Cotton Kingdom* (Westport, 1975).

Eugene D. Genovese, *In Red and Black: Marxian Explorations in Southern and Afro-American History* (New York, 1971).

———, *The Political Economy of Slavery: Studies in the Economy and Society of the Slave South* (New York, 1965).

———, *Roll, Jordan, Roll: The World the Slaves Made* (New York, 1974).

———, *The World the Slaveholders Made: Two Essays in Interpretation* (New York, 1969).

Herbert G. Gutman, *The Black Family in Slavery and Freedom, 1750–1925* (New York, 1976).

Barnett Hollander, *Slavery in America: Its Legal History* (New York, 1963).

Herbert S. Klein, *Slavery in The Americas: A Comparative Study of Cuba and Virginia* (Chicago, 1967).

Lawrence W. Levine, *Black Culture and Black Consciousness: Afro-American Folk Thought from Slavery to Freedom* (New York, 1977).

Leslie Howard Owens, *This Species of Property: Slave Life and Culture in the Old South* (New York, 1976).

Ulrich B. Phillips, *American Negro Slavery* (New York, 1918).

———, *Life and Labor in the Old South* (Boston, 1929).

Donald L. Robinson, *Slavery in the Structure of American Politics, 1765–1820* (New York, 1971).

Abbot Emerson Smith, *Colonists in Bondage: White Servitude and Convict Labor in America, 1607–1776* (Chapel Hill, 1947).

Kenneth M. Stampp, *The Peculiar Institution: Slavery in the Ante-Bellum South* (New York, 1956).

Frank Tannenbaum, *Slave and Citizen: The Negro in the Americas* (New York, 1946).

Eric Williams, *Capitalism and Slavery* (Chapel Hill, 1944).

C. Vann Woodward, *American Counterpoint: Slavery and Racism in the North-South Dialogue* (New York, 1971).

Arthur Zilversmit, *The First Emancipation: The Abolition of Negro Slavery in the North* (Chicago, 1967).

State and Local Studies of Slavery

THE NORTH

Noel P. Conlon, "Rhode Island Negroes in the Revolution: A Bibliography," *Rhode Island History* (Winter-Spring 1970).

Lorenzo J. Greene, *The Negro in Colonial New England, 1620–1776* (New York, 1942).
Norman Dwight Harris, *The History of Negro Servitude in Illinois* . . . (Chicago, 1909).
David M. Katzman, "Black Slavery in Michigan," *Midcontinent American Studies Journal*, XI (Fall 1970).
Gwendolyn Evans Logan, "The Slave in Connecticut During the Revolution," *Connecticut Historical Society Bulletin*, XXX (July 1965).
Elaine MacEacheren, "Emancipation of Slavery in Massachusetts: A Reexamination, 1770–1790," *Journal of Negro History*, LV (October 1970).
Edgar J. McManus, *Black Bondage in the North* (Syracuse, 1973).
———, *A History of Negro Slavery in New York* (Syracuse, 1966).
Richard C. Twombly and Robert H. Moore, "Black Puritan: The Negro in Seventeenth-Century Massachusetts," *William and Mary Quarterly*, 3rd series, XXIV (April 1967).
Donald D. Wax, "The Demand for Slave Labor in Colonial Pennsylvania," *Pennsylvania History*, XXXIV (October 1967).
Arthur Zilversmit, *The First Emancipation: The Abolition of Slavery in the North* (Chicago, 1967).
———, "Liberty and Property: New Jersey and the Abolition of Slavery," *New Jersey History*, LXXXVIII (Winter 1970).
———, "Quok Walker, Mumbet, and the Abolition of Slavery in Massachusetts," *William and Mary Quarterly*, XXV (October 1968).

THE SOUTH

Richard C. Wade, *Slavery in the Cities, The South, 1820–1860* (New York, 1964).
Claudia Dale Goldin, *Urban Slavery in the American South, 1820–1860: A Quantitative History* (Chicago, 1976).
Charles S. Davis, *The Cotton Kingdom in Alabama* (Montgomery, 1939).
Weymouth T. Jordan, *Ante-Bellum Alabama, Town and Country* (Tallahassee, 1957).
James B. Sellers, *Slavery in Alabama* (Tuscaloosa, 1950).
Orville W. Taylor, *Negro Slavery in Arkansas* (Durham, 1958).
John A. Munroe, "The Negro in Delaware," *South Atlantic Quarterly*, LVI (1957).
Julia Floyd Smith, *Slavery and Plantation Growth In Antebellum Florida, 1821–1860* (Gainesville, 1973).
Norman J. Cobb and Don McWalters, "Historical Report on Evelyn Plantation," *Georgia Historical Quarterly*, LV (Fall 1971).
William G. Proctor, Jr., "Slavery in Southwest Georgia," *Georgia Historical Quarterly*, XLIX (March 1965).
Donald D. Wax, "Georgia and the Negro Before the American Revolution," *Georgia Historical Quarterly*, LI (March 1967).
J. Winston Coleman, Jr., *Slavery Times in Kentucky* (Chapel Hill, 1940).
John S. Kendall, "New Orleans' 'Peculiar Institution,'" *Louisiana Historical Quarterly*, XXIII (July 1940).
Joseph Karl Menn, *The Large Slaveholders of Louisiana, 1860* (New Orleans, 1964).

V. A. Moody, "Slavery on Louisiana Sugar Plantations," *Louisiana Historical Quarterly*, VII (1924).

John Milton Price, "Slavery in Winn Parish," *Louisiana History*, VIII (Spring 1967).

Robert C. Reinders, "Slavery in New Orleans in the Decade Before the Civil War," *Mid-America*, XLIV (October 1962).

William L. Richter, "Slavery in Baton Rouge, 1820–1860," *Louisiana History*, X (Spring 1969).

Roger Shugg, *Origins of Class Struggle in Louisiana . . . 1840–1875* (Baton Rouge, 1939).

Joe Gray Taylor, *Negro Slavery in Louisiana* (Baton Rouge, 1963).

———, "Slavery in Louisiana During the Civil War," *Louisiana History*, VIII (Winter 1967).

Jonathan L. Alpert, "The Origin of Slavery in the United States—The Maryland Precedent," *American Journal of Legal History*, XIV (July 1970).

Charles S. Sydnor, *Slavery in Mississippi* (New York, 1933).

Lester B. Baltimore, "The Fight for Slavery on the Missouri Border," *Missouri Historical Review*, LXII (October 1967).

Lyle W. Dorsett, "Slaveholding in Jackson County, Missouri," *Bulletin of the Missouri Historical Society*, XX (October 1963).

George R. Lee, "Slavery and Emancipation in Lewis County, Missouri," *Missouri Historical Review*, LXV (April 1971).

Philip V. Scarpino, "Slavery in Callaway County, Missouri: 1845–1855," *Missouri Historical Review*, LXXI (October, 1976).

Arvarh E. Strickland, "Aspects of Slavery in Missouri," *Missouri Historical Review*, LXV (July 1971).

Guion G. Johnson, *Ante-Bellum North Carolina: A Social History* (Chapel Hill, 1937).

Edward W. Phifer, "Slavery in Microcosm: Burke County, North Carolina," *Journal of Southern History*, XXVII (May 1962).

Rosser H. Taylor, *Slaveholding in North Carolina: An Economic View* (Chapel Hill, 1926).

Frank Klingberg, *The Negro in Colonial South Carolina: A Study in Americanization* (Washington, 1941).

Peter Wood, *Black Majority: Negroes in South Carolina from 1670 Through the Stono Rebellion* (New York, 1974).

Robert E. Corlew, "Some Aspects of Slavery in Dickson County," *Tennessee Historical Quarterly*, X (September–December 1951).

Chase C. Mooney, *Slavery in Tennessee* (Bloomington, 1957).

Earl W. Fornell, "The Abduction of Free Negroes and Slaves in Texas," *Southwestern Historical Quarterly* (January 1957).

George R. Woolfolk, "Cotton Capitalism and Slave Labor in Texas," *Southern Social Science Quarterly* (June 1956).

———, "Sources of the History of the Negro in Texas, With Special Reference to Their Implications for Research in Slavery," *Journal of Negro History*, XLII (January 1957).

Dennis L. Lythgoe, "Negro Slavery in Utah," *Utah Historical Quarterly*, 39 (Winter 1971).

Susie M. Ames, *Studies of the Virginia Eastern Shore in the Seventeenth Century* (Richmond, 1940).

Richard R. Beeman, "Labor Forces and Race Relations: A Comparative View of the Colonization of Brazil and Virginia," *Political Science Quarterly*, LXXXVI (December 1971).

Wesley Frank Craven, *White, Red and Black: The Seventeenth-Century Virginian* (Charlottesville, 1971).

Robert McColley, *Slavery and Jeffersonian Virginia* (Urbana, Ill., 1964).

Edmund S. Morgan, *American Slavery, American Freedom: The Ordeal of Colonial Virginia* (New York, 1975).

Joseph Clarke Robert, *The Road from Monticello: A Study of the Virginia Slavery Debate of 1832* (Durham, 1941).

Thad W. Tate, *The Negro in Eighteenth-Century Williamsburg* (Charlottesville, 1965).

Alden T. Vaughan, "Blacks in Virginia: A Note on the First Decade," *William and Mary Quarterly*, 3rd series, XXIX (July 1972).

Constance McLaughlin Green, *Washington, Village and Capitol, 1800–1878* (Princeton, 1962).

A number of older studies, many originally published as part of the Johns Hopkins University series of historical studies, are still useful to modern historians of the question. Among them are the following:

Bernard C. Steiner, *History of Slavery in Connecticut* (Baltimore, 1893).

Edward Ingle, *The Negro in the District of Columbia* (Baltimore, 1893).

N. Dwight Harris, *The History of Negro Servitude in Illinois, 1719–1864* (Chicago, 1904).

Ivan E. McDougle, *Slavery in Kentucky, 1792–1865* (Lancaster, Pa., 1918).

John H. T. McPherson, *History of Liberia* (Baltimore, 1891).

Jeffrey R. Brackett, *The Negro in Maryland: A Study of The Institution of Slavery* (Baltimore, 1904).

Eugene I. McCormac, *White Servitude in Maryland* (Baltimore, 1904).

Harrison A. Trexler, *Slavery in Missouri, 1804–1865* (Baltimore, 1914).

Henry S. Cooley, *Slavery in New Jersey* (Baltimore, 1896).

Edward Raymond Turner, *The Negro in Pennsylvania, 1639–1861* (American Historical Association, 1911).

John S. Bassett, *History of Slavery in North Carolina* (Baltimore, 1899).

R. H. Taylor, *Slaveholding in North Carolina: An Economic View* (Chapel Hill, 1926).

H. M. Henry, *Police Control of the Slave in South Carolina* (Emory, Va., 1914; Ph.D. thesis, Vanderbilt University).

Edson L. Whitney, *Government in the Colony of South Carolina* (Baltimore, 1895).

Caleb P. Patterson, *The Negro in Tennessee, 1790–1865* (Austin, Texas, 1922).

The Antebellum Negro and the Problem of Race

GENERAL STUDIES AND SLAVE NARRATIVES

Herbert Aptheker, *A Documentary History of the Negro People in the United States*, 2 vols. (New York, 1951).

———, *Essays in the History of the American Negro* (New York, 1964).

Richard Bardolph, *The Negro Vanguard* (New York, 1959).

John F. Bayliss (ed.), *Black Slave Narratives* (New York, 1970).

Arna Bontemps, *Five Slave Narratives: A Compendium* (New York, 1968).
———— (ed.), *Great Slave Narratives* (Boston, 1969).
Benjamin F. Botkin (ed.), *Lay My Burden Down: A Folk History of Slavery* (Chicago, 1945).
Helen T. Catterall (ed.), *Judicial Cases Concerning American Slavery and the Negro*, 5 vols. (Washington, 1926–37).
Daedalus, The Negro in America, 2 vols. (1966).
Basil Davidson, *The Lost Cities of Africa* (Boston, 1959).
Frederick Douglass, *A Narrative of the Life of Frederick Douglass, an American Slave, Written by Himself* (Boston, 1845). (Ten years later expanded into *My Bondage and My Freedom* [New York, 1855].)
Stanley Feldstein (ed.), *Once a Slave: The Slaves' View of Slavery* (New York, 1971).
Leslie Fishel and Benjamin Quarles (eds.), *The Negro American: A Documentary History* (Chicago, 1967).
Miles Mark Fisher, *Negro Slave Songs in the United States* (Ithaca, N. Y., 1953).
Fisk University, *God Struck Me Dead, Religious Conversion Experiences and Autobiographies of Negro Ex-Slaves* (Nashville, 1945). (Reprinted in paperback, Clifton Johnson [ed.], Philadelphia, 1969.)
Fisk University, *Unwritten History of Slavery: Autobiographical Accounts of Negro Ex-Slaves* (Nashville, 1945). (Reprinted Washington, D. C., 1968.)
John Hope Franklin, *From Slavery to Freedom: A History of Negro Americans*, 3rd ed. (New York, 1967).
E. Franklin Frazier, *The Negro in the United States*, 2nd ed. (New York, 1957).
George M. Fredrickson, *The Black Image in the White Mind: The Debate on Afro-American Character and Destiny, 1817–1914* (New York, 1971).
J. C. Furnas, *Goodbye to Uncle Tom* (New York, 1956).
Oscar Handlin, *Race and Nationality in American Life* (Boston, 1957).
Marvin Harris, *Patterns of Race in the Americas* (New York, 1964).
Robert V. Haynes (ed.), *Blacks in White America Before 1865* (New York, 1972).
Melville J. Herskovits, *The Myth of the Negro Past* (New York, 1941).
Nathan I. Huggins, Martin Kilson, and Daniel M. Fox (eds.), *Key Issues in the Afro-American Experience*, 2 vols. (New York, 1971).
James Weldon Johnson and J. Rosamund Johnson (eds.), *The Book of American Negro Spirituals* (New York, 1925).
J. W. Johnson and J. R. Johnson (eds.), *The Second Book of Negro Spirituals* (New York, 1926). (Both first and second books reprinted in one vol., *The Books of American Negro Spirituals* [New York, 1956].)
J. Ralph Jones, "Portraits of Georgia Slaves" (interviews with ex-slaves), Tom Landess (ed.), *Georgia Review* (Spring, Summer, Fall, and Winter 1967, Spring and Summer 1968).
Winthrop D. Jordan, *White Over Black: The Development of American Attitudes Toward the Negro, 1550–1812* (Chapel Hill, 1968).
Abraham Kardiner and Lionel Ovesey, *The Mark of Oppression: A Psycho-Social Study of the American Negro* (New York, 1951).

Bernard Katz (ed.), *The Social Implications of Early Negro Music in the United States* (New York, 1969).

William Loren Katz (gen. ed.), *The American Negro: His History and Literature* (New York, 1969). (141 vols. reprinted.)

Julius Lester (ed.), *To Be a Slave* (New York, 1968).

Leon Litwack, *North of Slavery: The Negro in the Free States, 1790–1860* (Chicago, 1961).

Joseph Logsdon, "Diary of a Slave: Recollection and Prophecy," in William G. Shade and Roy C. Herrenkohl (eds.), *Seven on Black: Reflections on the Negro Experience in America: Selected Essays* (Austin, Tex., 1970).

August Meier (ed.), *Studies in American Negro Life Series* (New York, 1968–   ).

August Meier and Elliott Rudwick (eds.), *The Making of Black America:* Vol. 1, *The Origins of Black Americans* (New York, 1969).

———, *From Plantation to Ghetto*, rev. ed. (New York, 1970).

Gunnar Myrdal *et al.*, *An American Dilemma: The Negro Problem and Modern Democracy*, 2 vols. (New York, London, 1944).

Charles H. Nichols, *Many Thousand Gone: The Ex-Slaves' Account of Their Bondage and Freedom* (Leiden, 1963).

Gilbert Osofsky (ed.), *Puttin' on Ole Massa* (three slave narratives) (New York, 1969).

Talcott Parsons and Kenneth B. Clark (eds.), *The Negro American* (New York, 1967).

Jane H. and William H. Pease (eds.), *Austin Steward: Twenty-Two Years a Slave and Forty Years a Freeman* (Reading, Mass., 1969).

Newton M. Puckett, *Folk Beliefs of the Southern Negro* (Chapel Hill, 1926).

A Report of the Ninth Newberry Library Conference on American Studies, "The Question of 'Sambo,'" *The Newberry Library Bulletin*, V (December 1958).

George P. Rawick (ed.), *The American Slave: A Composite Autobiography* (Westport, Conn., 1972). (18 vols. of reprinted W. P. S. Federal Writers' Project slave narratives and interviews with ex-slaves.)

———, *From Sundown to Sunup: The Making of the Black Community* (Westport, Conn., 1972).

Peter I. Rose (ed.), *Americans from Africa: Slavery and its Aftermath* (New York, 1970).

Marion L. Starkey, *Striving to Make it My Home: The Story of Americans from Africa* (New York, 1964).

Maxwell Whiteman (ed.), *Afro-American History Series*, 10 vols. (Wilmington, Del., 1970).

Robin W. Winks, *The Blacks in Canada: A History* (New Haven, 1971).

Robin W. Winks (gen. ed.), *Four Fugitive Slave Narratives* (Reading, Mass., 1969).

Carter Woodson, *The Mind of the Negro as Reflected in Letters Written during the Crisis, 1800–1860* (Washington, D. C., 1926).

Carter F. Woodson and Charles H. Wesley, *The Negro in Our History*, 10th ed. (Washington, 1962).

Norman R. Yetman, "The Background of the Slave Narrative Collection" (of the Federal Writers' Project), *American Quarterly*, XIX (Fall 1967).

Norman R. Yetman (ed.), *Life Under the "Peculiar Institution": Selections from the Slave Narrative Collection* (New York, 1970).

PATTERNS OF SLAVE RESISTANCE

Wendell G. Addington, "Slave Insurrections in Texas," *Journal of Negro History*, XXXV (October 1950).

Jervis Anderson, "Styron and His Black Critics," *Dissent*, XVI (March-April 1969).

Herbert Aptheker, *American Negro Slave Revolts* (New York, 1943).

——, *Nat Turner's Slave Rebellion* . . . (New York, 1966).

——, "Slave Guerilla Warfare," in *To Be Free: Studies in American Negro History* (New York, 1948).

Herbert Aptheker and William Styron, "Truth and Nat Turner: An Exchange," *Nation*, CCVI (April 22, 1968).

Raymond A. Bauer and Alice H. Bauer, "Day to Day Resistance to Slavery," *Journal of Negro History*, XXVII (October 1942).

Elwood L. Bridner, Jr., "The Fugitive Slaves of Maryland," *Maryland Historical Magazine*, 66 (Spring 1971).

Joseph C. Carroll, *Slave Insurrections in the United States, 1800–1865* (Boston, 1938).

William F. Cheek (ed.), *Black Resistance Before the Civil War* (Beverly Hills, Calif., 1970).

John Hendrik Clarke (ed.), *William Styron's Nat Turner: Ten Black Writers Respond* (Boston, 1968).

T. Wood Clarke, "Negro Plot, 1741," *New York History*, XXV (April 1944).

Thomas J. Davis, "The New York Slave Conspiracy of 1741 as Black Protest," *Journal of Negro History*, LVI (January 1971).

John W. Dobbs, "Crispus Attucks, one of America's First and Noblest Heroes," *Negro History Bulletin*, 34 (February 1971).

William S. Drewry, *Slave Insurrections in the United States* (Washington, 1900).

John B. Duff and Peter M. Mitchell (eds.), *The Nat Turner Rebellion: The Historical Event and the Modern Controversy* (New York, 1971).

Robert F. Durden, "William Styron and His Black Critics," *South Atlantic Quarterly*, LXVIII (Spring 1969).

George M. Frederickson and Christopher Lasch, "Resistance to Slavery," *Civil War History*, XIII (December 1967).

Larry Gara, *The Liberty Line: The Legend of the Underground Railroad* (Lexington, Ky., 1961).

Eugene Genovese, "The Nat Turner Case," *New York Review of Books*, XI (September 12, 1968).

Eugene D. Genovese, "Rebelliousness and Docility in the Negro Slave: A Critique of the Elkins Thesis," *Civil War History*, XIII (December 1967).

Richard Gilman, "Nat Turner Revisited," *New Republic*, CLVIII (April 27, 1968).

Lorenzo J. Greene, "Mutiny on the Slave Ships," *Phylon*, V (4th quarter 1944).

Seymour L. Gross and Eileen Bender, "History, Politics and Literature: The Myth of Nat Turner," *American Quarterly*, XXIII (October 1971).

Nicholas Halasz, *The Rattling Chains: Slave Unrest and Revolt in the Ante-Bellum South* (New York, 1966).

Thomas Wentworth Higginson, *Black Rebellion*, James M. McPherson (ed.) (New York, 1969).

Donald M. Jacobs, "David Walker: Boston Race Leader, 1825–1830," *Essex Institute Collections*, CVII (January 1971).

——, "William Lloyd Garrison's *Liberator* and Boston's Blacks, 1830–1865," *New England Quarterly*, XLIV (June 1971).

F. Roy Johnson, *The Nat Turner Slave Insurrection* (Murfreesboro, N. C., 1966).

Howard Jones, "The Peculiar Institution and National Honor: The Case of the *Creole* Slave Revolt," *Civil War History* (March 1975).

Sidney Kaplan, "Black Mutiny on the Amistad (1840)," *Massachusetts Review*, (Summer 1969).

John Oliver Killens (ed.), *The Trial Record of Denmark Vesey* (Boston, 1970).

Marion D. deB. Kilson, "Towards Freedom: An Analysis of Slave Revolts in the United States,' *Phylon*, XXV, No. 2 (1964).

Ann J. Lane (ed.), *The Debate Over Slavery: Stanley Elkins and His Critics* (Urbana, 1971).

Mary Agnes Lewis, "Slavery and Personality: A Further Comment," *American Quarterly* (Spring 1967).

John Lofton, *Insurrection in South Carolina: The Turbulent World of Denmark Vesey* (Yellow Spring, Ohio, 1964).

Katherin Lumpkin, " 'The General Plan was Freedom': A Negro Secret Order on the Underground Railway," *Phylon* (Spring 1967).

David B. McKibber, "Negro Slave Insurrections in Mississippi, 1800–1865," *Journal of Negro History*, XXXIV (January 1949).

Christopher Martin, *The Amistad Affair* (New York, 1970).

Edwin A. Miles, "The Mississippi Slave Insurrection Scare of 1835," *Journal of Negro History*, XLII (January 1957).

Clarence L. Mohr, "Samboization: A Case Study," *Research Studies* (June 1970).

Gerald W. Mullin, *Flight and Rebellion: Slave Resistance in Eighteenth-Century Virginia* (New York, 1972).

——, "Gabriel's Insurrection," in Peter I. Rose (ed.), *Americans from Africa*, Vol. II: *Old Memories, New Moods* (New York, 1970).

William A. Owens, *Slave Mutiny: The Revolt on the Schooner Amistad* (New York, 1953). (Retitled in paperback *Black Mutiny*.)

Orlando Patterson, "Slavery and Slave Revolts," *Social and Economic Studies*, Vol. 19, No. 3 (1970).

George Rawick, "The Historical Roots of Black Liberation," *Radical America*, II (July–August 1968).

Marion J. Russell, "American Slave Discontent in Records of the High Courts," *Journal of Negro History*, XXXI (October 1946).

Kenneth Scott, "The Slave Insurrection in New York in 1712," *New York Historical Society Quarterly*, XLV (January 1961).

Kenneth M. Stampp, "Rebels and Sambos: The Search for the Negro's Personality in Slavery," *Journal of Southern History*, XXXVII (August 1971).

Robert S. Starobin (ed.), *Denmark Vesey: The Slave Conspiracy of 1822* (Englewood Cliffs, N. J., 1970).

Sterling Stuckey, "Remembering Denmark Vesey," *Negro Digest*, XV (February 1966)

William Styron, *The Confessions of Nat Turner* (New York, 1966).

William Styron, C. Vann Woodward, R. W. B. Lewis interviewed in *The Yale Alumni Magazine* (November 1967).

Ferenc M. Szasz, "The New York Slave Revolt of 1741: A Re-Examination," *New York History*, XLVIII (July 1967).

R. H. Taylor, "Slave Conspiracies in North Carolina," *North Carolina Historical Review* (January 1928).

Earle E. Thorpe, "Chattel Slavery and Concentration Camps," *Negro History Bulletin*, XXV (May 1962).

Henry Irving Tragle (ed.), *The Southampton Slave Revolt of 1831* (Amherst, Mass., 1971).

Richard C. Wade, "The Vesey Plot: A Reconsideration," *Journal of Southern History*, XXX (May 1964).

William W. White, "The Texas Slave Insurrection of 1860," *Southwestern Historical Quarterly*, LII (January 1949).

Harvey Wish, "American Slave Insurrections before 1861," *Journal of Negro History*, XXII (July 1937).

J. Leitch Wright, Jr., "A Note on the First Seminole War as Seen by the Indians, Negroes, and Their British Advisers," *Journal of Southern History*, XXXIV (November 1968).

RACE RELATIONS

Jonathan L. Alpert, "The Origin of Slavery in the United States—the Maryland Precedent," *American Journal of Legal History*, XIV (July 1970).

Michael Banton, *Race Relations* (New York, 1967).

Richard R. Beeman, "Labor Forces and Race Relations: A Comparative View of the Colonization of Brazil and Virginia," *Political Science Quarterly*, LXXXVI (December 1971).

Eugene H. Berwanger, *The Frontier Against Slavery: Western Anti-Negro Prejudice and the Slavery Extension Controversy* (Urbana, 1967).

Lee Calligaro, "The Negro's Legal Status in Pre-Civil War New Jersey," *New Jersey History*, LXXXV.

Alfred A. Cave, "The Case of Calvin Colton: White Racism in Northern Antislavery Thought," *New York Historical Society Quarterly*, LIII (July 1969).

Daedalus, Color and Race (A Symposium) (Spring 1967).

Carl Degler, *Neither Black Nor White: Slavery and Race Relations in Brazil and the United States* (New York, 1971).

Carl N. Degler, "Slavery and the Genesis of American Race Prejudice," *Comparative Studies in Society and History*, II (October 1959).

Robert C. Dick, *Black Protest: Issues and Tactics* [1827–1861] (Westport, 1974).

Roger A. Fischer, "Racial Segregation in Ante-Bellum New Orleans," *American Historical Review*, LXXIV (February 1969).

James A. Fisher, "The Struggle for Negro Testimony in California, 1851–1863," *Southern California Quarterly*, LI (December 1969).

Eric Foner, *Free Soil, Free Labor, Free Men: The Ideology of the Republican Party Before the Civil War* (New York, 1970).

George M. Fredrickson, *Toward a Social Interpretation of the Development of American Racism* in Huggins, Kilson, Fox, Vol. 1 (New York, 1971).

Thomas F. Gossett, *Race, the History of an Idea in America* (Dallas, 1963).

Constance McLaughlin Green, *The Secret City; A History of Race Relations in the Nation's Capitol* (Princeton, N. J., 1967).

John S. Haller, Jr., "Concepts of Race Inferiority in Nineteenth-Century Anthropology," *Journal of the History of Medicine and Allied Sciences*, XXV (January 1970).

John S. Haller, "Civil War Anthropometry: The Making of a Racial Ideology," *Civil War History* (December 1970).

Oscar and Mary Handlin, "Origins of the Southern Labor System," *William and Mary Quarterly*, 3rd series, XIX (April 1962).

James Hugo Johnston, *Race Relations in Virginia and Miscegenation in the South, 1776–1860* (Amherst, Mass., 1970).

Winthrop D. Jordan, "American Chiaroscuro: The Status and Definition of Mulattoes in the British Colonies," *William and Mary Quarterly*, 3rd series, XIX (April 1962).

Winthrop D. Jordan, "Modern Tensions and the Origins of American Slavery," *Journal of Southern History*, XXVIII (February 1962).

Linda K. Kerber, "Abolitionists and Amalgamation: The New York City Race Riots of 1834," *New York History*, XLVIII (January 1967).

Eileen S. Kraditor, *Means and Ends in American Abolitionism . . . 1834–1850* (New York, 1950).

Donald G. Mathews, "The Abolitionists on Slavery: The Critique Behind the Social Movement," *Journal of Southern History*, XXXIII (May 1967).

James M. McPherson, "A Brief for Equality: The Abolitionist Reply to the Racist Myth, 1860–1865," in Martin Duberman (ed.), *The Anti-Slavery Vanguard* (Princeton, 1965).

Richard B. Morris, "The Measure of Bondage in the Slave States," *Mississippi Valley Historical Review* (September 1954).

Phillips Moulton, "John Woolman's Approach to Social Action—As Exemplified in Relation to Slavery," *Church History*, XXXV (December 1966).

Gary B. Nash, "Red, White and Black: The Origins of Racism in Colonial America," in Gary B. Nash and Richard Weiss (eds.), *The Great Fear: Race in the Mind of America* (New York, 1970).

Gilbert Osofsky (ed.), *The Burden of Race: A Documentary History of Negro-White Relations* (New York, 1967).

298 A Selected Modern Bibliography

Rembert W. Patrick, *Race Relations in the South* (Tallahasse, Fla., 1958).

Jane H. Pease and William H. Pease, *They Who Would Be Free: Blacks' Search for Freedom, 1830–1861* (New York, 1974).

Lorman Ratner, *Powder Keg: Northern Opposition to the Anti-Slavery Movement, 1831–1840* (New York, 1968).

Leonard L. Richards, *"Gentlemen of Property and Standing": Anti-Abolition Mobs in Jacksonian America* (New York, 1970).

Louis Ruchames, "The Sources of Racial Thought in Colonial America," *Journal of Negro History*, LII (October 1967).

William R. Stanton, *The Leopard's Spots: Scientific Attitudes Toward Race in America, 1815–1859* (Chicago, 1960).

Ronald Takaki, "The Black Child-Savage in Ante-Bellum America," in Gary B. Nash and Richard Weiss (eds.), *The Great Fear: Race in the Mind of America* (New York, 1970).

V. J. Voegeli, *Free but not Equal: The Midwest and the Negro During the Civil War* (Chicago, 1967).

Donald D. Wax, "The Image of the Negro in the *Maryland Gazette*, 1745–75," *Journalism Quarterly*, 46 (Spring 1969).

Mary W. Williams, "The Treatment of Negro Slaves in the Brazilian Empire: A Comparison with the United States," *Journal of Negro History*, XV (1930).

Forrest G. Wood, *Black Scare: The Racist Response to Emancipation and Reconstruction* (Berkeley, 1968).

SPECIAL STUDIES

Slavery

S. Sydney Bradford, "The Negro Ironworker in Ante-Bellum Virginia," *Journal Southern History*, XXV (May 1959).

Kathleen Bruce, "Slave Labor in the Virginia Iron Industry," *William and Mary Quarterly*, series 2, VII (January 1927).

Mina Davis Caulfield, "Slavery and the Origins of Black Culture," in Peter I. Rose (ed.), *Americans from Africa*, Vol. I (New York, 1970).

M. Ray Della, Jr., "The Problems of Negro Labor in the 1850's," *Maryland Historical Magazine*, 66 (Spring 1971).

Charles B. Dew, "Disciplining Slave Ironworkers in the Antebellum South . . . ," *American Historical Review*, 79 (April 1974).

Thomas E. Drake, *Quakers and Slavery in America* (New Haven, 1950).

Clement Eaton, "Slave-Hiring in the Upper South: A Step Toward Freedom," *Mississippi Valley Historical Review*, XLVI (March 1960).

Walter Fisher, "Physicians and Slavery in the Antebellum Southern Medical Journal," *Journal of History of Medicine* (January 1968).

Edward A. Freeman, "Negro Baptist History," *Baptist History and Heritage*, 4 (July 1969).

Romeo B. Garrett, "African Survivals in American Culture," *Journal of Negro History*, LI (October 1966).

Eugene D. Genovese, "American Slaves and Their History," *New York Review of Books* (December 3, 1970).

———, "The Legacy of Slavery and the Roots of Black Nationalism," Commentary by Aptheker and C. Vann Woodward, *Studies on the Left*, 6 (November-December 1966).

———, "Materialism and Idealism in the History of Negro Slavery in the Americas," *Journal of Social History*, 1 (Summer 1968).

Lyle Glazier, "The Uncle Remus Stories: Two Portraits of American Negroes," *Hacettepe Bulletin of Social Sciences and Humanities*, 1 (June 1969).

Lorenzo J. Greene, *The Negro in Colonial New England, 1620–1776* (New York, 1942).

Harold B. Hancock (ed.), "William Yates's Letter of 1837: Slavery and Colored People in Delaware," *Delaware History*, XIV (April 1971).

Chadmich Hansen, "Jenny's Tow: Negro Shaking Dances in America," *American Quarterly*, XIX (Fall 1967).

Vincent Harding, "Religion and Resistance Among Antebellum Negroes, 1800–1860," in August Meier and Elliott Rudwick (eds.), *The Making of Black America*, 2 vols. (New York, 1969), Vol. I.

G. B. Johnson, *Folk Culture on St. Helena Island, South Carolina* (Chapel Hill, 1930).

———, *A Social History of the Sea Islands* (Chapel Hill, 1930).

Leonard Kriegel, "Uncle Tom and Tiny Tim: Some Reflections on the Cripple as Negro," *American Scholar*, 38 (Summer 1969).

Lawrence W. Levine, "Slave Songs and Slave Consciousness: An Exploration in Neglected Sources," in Tamara Hareven (ed.), *Anonymous Americans* (Englewood Cliffs, N. J., 1971).

Donald G. Mathews, *Slavery and Methodism: A Chapter in American Morality, 1780–1845* (Princeton, 1965).

Jack M. Moore, "Images of the Negro in Early American Short Fiction," *Mississippi Quarterly*, XXII (Winter 1968–69).

John H. Moore, "Simon Gray, Riverman: A Slave Who was Almost Free," *Mississippi Valley Historical Review*, XLIX (December 1962).

LeRoy Moore, Jr., "The Spiritual: Soul of Black Religion," *American Quarterly*, XXIII (December 1971), also *Church History*, 40 (March 1971).

William Dostite Postell, *The Health of Slaves on Southern Plantations* (Baton Rouge, La., 1951).

Walter Rodney, "Upper Guinea and the Significance of the Origins of Africans Enslaved in the New World," *Journal of Negro History*, LIV (October 1969).

Milton C. Sernett, *Black Religion and American Evangelicalism . . . 1787–1865* (Metuchen, N.J., 1975).

Lewight Sikes, "Medical Care for Slaves. A Review of the Welfare State," *Georgia Historical Quarterly*, LII (December 1968).

M. Eugene Simans, "The Legal Status of the Slave in South Carolina, 1670–1740," *Journal of Southern History*, XXVIII (November 1962).

Kenneth Stampp, "The Daily Life of the Southern Slave," in Nathan I. Huggins, Martin Kilson, and Daniel M. Fox (eds.), *Key Issues in the Afro-American Experience*, 2 vols. (New York, 1971), Vol. I.

Robert Starobin, "Disciplining Industrial Slaves in the Old South," *Journal of Negro History*, LIII (April 1968).

————, *Industrial Slavery in the Old South* (New York, 1970).

Sterling Stuckey, "Through the Prism of Folklore: The Black Ethos in Slavery," *Massachusetts Review*, IX (Summer 1968).

William C. Suttles, Jr., "African Religious Survivals as Factors in American Slave Revolts," *Journal of Negro History*, LVI (April 1971).

Robert Farris Thompson, "African Influence on the Art of the United States," in Armstead L. Robinson *et al.* (ed.), *Black Studies in the University* (New Haven, 1969).

Howard Thurman, *Deep River: Reflections on the Religious Insight of Certain of the Negro Spirituals*, rev. ed. (New York, 1955).

William Toll, "The Crisis of Freedom: Toward an Interpretation of Negro Life," *Journal of American Studies*, 3 (December 1969).

Lorenzo D. Turner, "African Survivals in the New World with Special Emphasis on the Arts," in John A. Davis, *Africa Seen by American Negro Scholars* (New York, 1963).

Mary A. Twining, "An Anthropological Look at Afro-American Folk Narrative," *CLA Journal* (September 1970).

David O. Whitten, "Slave Buying in 1835: Virginia as Revealed by Letters of a Louisiana Negro Sugar Planter," *Louisiana History*, XI (Summer 1970).

Bell I. Wiley, *Southern Negroes, 1861–1865* (New Haven, 1938).

Free Negroes, North and South

Richard H. Abbott, "Massachusetts and the Recruitment of Southern Negroes, 1863–1865," *Civil War History*, IV (September 1963).

Warren B. Armstrong, "Union Chaplains and the Education of the Freedmen," *Journal of Negro History*, LII (April 1967).

George R. Bentley, *A History of the Freedmen's Bureau* (Philadelphia, 1955).

Ira Berlin, *Slaves Without Masters: The Free Negro in the Antebellum South* (New York, 1974).

Mary F. Berry, "Negro Troops in Blue and Gray: The Louisiana Native Guards, 1861–1863," *Louisiana History*, VIII (Spring 1967).

John W. Blassingame, "The Recruitment of Colored Troops in Kentucky, Maryland, and Missouri, 1863–1865," *Historian*, XXIX (August 1967).

Letitia Woods Brown, *Free Negroes in the District of Columbia, 1790–1846* (New York, 1972).

J. W. Cook, "Freedom in the Thoughts of Frederick Douglass, 1845–1860," *Negro History Bulletin*, 32 (February 1969).

Dudley T. Cornish, *The Sable Arm: Negro Troops in the Union Army, 1861–1865* (New York, 1956).

Alfred E. Cowdrey, "Slave into Soldier," *History Today* (October 1970).

Edwin A. Davis, "William Johnson: Free Negro Citizen of Ante-Bellum Mississippi," *Journal of Mississippi History*, XV (1953).

Edwin A. Davis and William R. Hogan, *The Barber of Natchez* (Baton Rouge, La., 1954).

C. Ashley Ellefson, "Free Jupiter and the Rest of the World: The Problems of a Free Negro in Colonial Maryland," *Maryland Historical Magazine*, 66 (Spring 1971).

J. Merton England, "The Free Negro in Ante-Bellum Tennessee," *Journal of Southern History*, IX (February 1943).

Horace Fitchett, "The Origin and Growth of the Free Negro Population of Charleston, South Carolina," *Journal of Negro History*, XXVI (October 1941).

Ralph B. Flanders, "The Free Negro in Ante-Bellum Georgia," *North Carolina Historical Review*, IX (July 1932).

Philip S. Foner, "The First Negro Meeting in Maryland," *Maryland Historical Magazine*, 66 (Spring 1971).

———, *Frederick Douglass* (New York, 1964).

Jack D. Forbes, "Black Pioneers: The Spanish-Speaking Afro-Americans of the Southwest," *Phylon* (Fall 1966).

John Hope Franklin, *The Free Negro in North Carolina, 1790–1860* (Chapel Hill, 1943).

———, "James Boon, Free Negro Artisan," *Journal of Negro History*, XXX (April 1945).

E. Franklin Frazier, *The Free Negro Family* (Nashville, 1932).

Russell Garvin, "The Free Negro in Florida Before the Civil War," *Florida Historical Quarterly*, XLVI (July 1967).

Carl E. Hatch, "Negro Migration and New Jersey—1863," *New Jersey History*, LXXXVII (Winter 1969).

William R. Hogan and Edwin A. Davis (eds.), *William Johnson's Natchez* (Baton Rouge, La., 1951).

James Oliver Horton, "Generations of Protest: Black Families and Social Reform in Ante-Bellum Boston," *New England Quarterly*, XLIX (June, 1976).

James C. Jackson, "The Religious Education of the Negro in South Carolina Prior to 1850," *Historical Magazine of the Protestant Episcopal Church* (March 1967).

Luther Porter Jackson, *Free Negro Labor and Property Holding in Virginia, 1830–1860* (New York, 1942).

Partrena L. James, "Reconstruction in the Chickasaw Nation: The Freedmen Problem," *Chronicles of Oklahoma*, LXV (Spring 1967).

Harold D. Langley, "The Negro in the Navy and Merchant Service 1789–1860," *Journal of Negro History*, LII (October 1967).

Hollis R. Lynch, "Pan-Negro Nationalism in the New World Before 1862," *Boston University Papers on Africa*, Vol. II, *African History*, Jeffrey Butler (ed.) (Boston, 1966).

William McFeely, *Yankee Stepfather: General O. O. Howard and the Freedmen's Bureau* (New Haven, 1968).

Tom McLaughlin, "Sectional Responses of Free Negroes to the Idea of

Colonization," *Washington State University Research Studies* (September 1966).

Richard K. MacMaster, "Henry Highland Garnet and the African Civilization Society," *Journal of Presbyterian History*, 48 (Summer 1970).

James M. McPherson, *The Negro's Civil War; How American Negroes Felt and Acted During the War for the Union* (New York, 1965).

————, *The Struggle for Equality; Abolitionists and the Negro in the Civil War and Reconstruction* (Princeton, 1964).

August Meier, "Negroes in the First and Second Reconstructions of the South," *Civil War History*, XIII (June 1967).

John L. Meyers, "American Antislavery Society Agents and the Free Negro, 1833–1838," *Journal of Negro History*, LII (July 1967).

Floyd J. Miller, *The Search for a Black Nationality: Black Emigration and Colonization, 1787–1863* (Urbana, 1975).

Alice D. Nelson, "People of Color in Louisiana," *Journal of Negro History*, I (October 1916); and II (January 1917).

Daniel Perlman, "Organizations of the Free Negro in New York City, 1800–1860," *Journal of Negro History*, LVI (July 1971).

Richard W. Pih, "Negro Self-Improvement Efforts in Ante-Bellum Cincinnati, 1836–1850," *Ohio History*, 78 (Summer 1969).

William A. Poe, "Lott Cary [of American Colonization Society]: Man of Purchased Freedom," *Church History*, 39 (March 1970).

Kenneth W. Porter, "Florida Slaves and Free Negroes in the Seminole War, 1835–1842," *Journal of Negro History*, XXVIII (October 1943).

————, "Negroes and the Seminole War, 1835–1842," *Journal of Southern History*, XXX (November 1964).

C. Daniel Potts and Annette Potts, "The Negro and the Australian Gold Rushes, 1852–1857," *Pacific Historical Review*, XXXVII (November 1968).

Benjamin Quarles, *Black Abolitionists* (New York, 1969).

————, *Frederick Douglass* (Washington, D. C., 1948).

————, *Lincoln and the Negro* (New York, 1962).

————, *The Negro in the American Revolution* (Williamsburg, Va., 1961).

————, *The Negro in the Civil War* (Boston, 1953).

Joe M. Richardson, "Christian Abolitionism: The American Missionary Association and the Florida Negro," *Journal of Negro Education*, XXXX (Winter 1971).

Henry S. Robinson, "Some Aspects of the Free Negro Population of Washington, D. C., 1800–1862," *Maryland Historical Magazine*, 64 (Spring 1969).

Willie Lee Rose, *Rehearsal for Reconstruction: The Port Royal Experiment* (Indianapolis, 1964).

Judith P. Ruchkin, "The Abolition of 'Colored Schools' in Rochester, New York, 1832–1856," *New York History*, LI (July 1970).

John H. Russell, *The Free Negro in Virginia 1617–1865* (Baltimore, 1913).

Harold Schoen, "The Free Negro in the Republic of Texas," *Southwestern Historical Quarterly*, XXXIX (April 1936); XL (July 1936); (October 1936); (January 1937); (April 1937); XLI (July 1937).

Loren Schweninger, "The Free-Slave Phenomenon . . . in Ante-Bellum Nashville," *Civil War History,* XXII (December, 1976).

Terry L. Seip, "Slaves and Free Negroes in Alexandria, 1850–1860," *Louisiana
History,* X (Spring 1969).

James B. Sellers, "Free Negroes of Tuscaloosa County Before the Thirteenth
Amendment," *Alabama Review,* XXIII (April 1970).

Donald J. Senese, "The Free Negro and the South Carolina Courts, 1790–
1860," *South Carolina Historical Magazine,* 68 (July 1967).

Roger W. Shugg, "Negro Voting in the Ante-Bellum South," *Journal of Negro
History,* XXI (October 1936).

Robert M. Spector, "The Quack Walker Cases (1781–83): The Abolition of
Slavery and Negro Citizenship in Early Massachusetts," *Journal of
Negro History* (January 1968).

Annie L. W. Stahl, "The Free Negro in Ante-Bellum Louisiana," *Louisiana
Historical Quarterly,* XXV (April 1942).

John L. Stanley, "Majority Tyranny in Tocqueville: America: The Failure of
Negro Suffrage in 1846," *Political Science Quarterly,* LXXXIV (September 1969).

Philip J. Staudenraus, *The African Colonization Movement* (New York,
1961).

Aaron Stopak, "The Maryland State Colonization Society: Independent State
Action in the Colonization Movement," *Maryland Historical Magazine,* 63 (September 1968).

Charles S. Sydnor, "The Free Negro in Mississippi before the Civil War,"
American Historical Review, XXXII (July 1927).

David Y. Thomas, "The Free Negro in Florida before 1965," *South Atlantic
Quarterly,* X (October 1911).

Emma L. Thornbrough, *The Negro in Indiana: A Study of a Minority* (Indianapolis, 1957).

Miriam L. Ustey, "Charles Lenox Remond, Garrison's Ebony Echo: World
Anti-Slavery Convention, 1840," *Essex Institute History Colloquium*
(April 1970).

Arthur O. White, "The Black Movement Against Jim Crow Education in
Lockport, New York, 1835–1876," *New York History,* L (July 1969).

James E. Winston, "The Free Negro in New Orleans, 1803–1861," *Louisiana
Historical Quarterly,* XXI (October 1938).

Carter G. Woodson, *Free Negro Heads of Families in the United States in
1830* (Washington, D. C., 1925).

———, *Free Negro Owners of Slaves in the United States in 1830* (Washington, D. C., 1925; reprinted, 1968).

James M. Wright, *The Free Negro in Maryland, 1634–1860* (New York,
1921; reprinted New York, 1969).

Wilbur Zelinsky, "The Population Geography of the Free Negro in Ante-
Bellum America," *Population Studies,* III (March 1950).

THE OLD SOUTH

GENERAL STUDIES

David Bertelson, *The Lazy South* (New York, 1967).

Carl Bridenbaugh, *Myths and Realities: Societies of the Colonial South* (Baton Rouge, La., 1952).

Jesse T. Carpenter, *The South as a Conscious Minority, 1789–1861; A Study in Political Thought* (New York, 1930).

Wilbur J. Cash, *The Mind of the South* (New York, 1941).

William E. Dodd, *The Cotton Kingdom* (New Haven, 1919).

Clement Eaton, *The Growth of Southern Civilization, 1790–1860* (New York, 1961).

——, *A History of the Old South*, 2nd ed. rev. (New York, 1966).

John Hope Franklin, *The Militant South, 1800–1861* (Cambridge, Mass., 1956).

Lewis C. Gray, *History of Agriculture in the Southern United States in 1860*, 2 vols. (Washington, D. C., 1933).

William Sumner Jenkins, *Pro-Slavery Thought in the Old South* (Chapel Hill, 1935). (Reprinted Gloucester, Mass., 1960.)

Fabian Linden, "Economic Democracy in the Slave South: An Appraisal of Some Recent Views," *The Journal of Negro History*, XXXI (April 1946).

Arthur Young Lloyd, *The Slavery Controversy, 1831–1860* (Chapel Hill, 1939).

Frank L. Owsley, *Plain Folk of the Old South* (Baton Rouge, La., 1949).

David M. Potter, *The South and the Sectional Conflict* (Baton Rouge, La., 1968).

Francis B. Simkins, *A History of the South*, 2nd ed. rev. (New York, 1953).

Wendell H. Stephenson, *A Basic History of the Old South* (Princeton, 1959).

——, *The South Lives in History* (Baton Rouge, La., 1955).

C. Vann Woodward, *The Burden of Southern History* (Baton Rouge, La., 1960).

THE SLAVE TRADE

Frederic Bancroft, *Slave-Trading in the Old South* (Baltimore, 1931).

Thomas D. Clark, "The Slave Trade between Kentucky and the Cotton Kingdom," *Mississippi Valley Historical Review*, XXI (December 1934).

Reginald Coupland, *The British Anti-Slavery Movement* (London, England, 1933).

——, *East Africa and its Invaders* . . . (Oxford, England, 1956).

Phillip D. Curtin, "Epidemiology and the Slave Trade," *Political Science Quarterly*, LXXXIII (June 1968).

Basil Davidson, *Black Mother: The Years of the African Slave Trade* (Boston, 1961).

Kenneth G. Davies, *The Royal African Company* (London, England, 1957).

Robert R. Davis, Jr. (ed.), "Buchanian Espionage: A Report on Illegal Slave Trading in the South in 1859," *Journal of Southern History* XXXVII (May 1971).

Elizabeth Donnan (ed.), *Documents Illustrative of the History of the Slave Trade to America*, 4 vols. (Washington, D. C., 1930–35).

W. E. B. DuBois, *The Suppression of the African Slave Trade to the United States of America, 1638–1870* (New York, 1896).

Peter Duignan and C. Clendenen, *The United States and the African Slave Trade, 1619–1862* (Stanford, 1963).

J. D. Fage, "Slavery and the Slave Trade in the Context of West African History," *Journal of African History*, 10 (1969).

James Paisley Hendrix, Jr., "The Effort to Reopen the African Slave Trade in Louisiana," *Louisiana History*, X (Spring 1969).

Melville J. Herskovitz, *Dahomey: An Ancient West African Kingdom* (New York, 1938).

James High, "The African Gentleman: A Chapter in the Slave Trade," *Journal of Negro History*, XLIV (October 1959).

Warren S. Howard, *American Slavers and the Federal Law, 1837–1862* (Berkeley, 1963).

James F. King, "The Evolution of the Free Slave Trade Principle in Spanish Colonial Administration," *Hispanic American Historical Review* (February 1942).

Kenneth F. Kipte, "The Case Against a Nineteenth-Century Cuba-Florida Slave Trade," *Florida Historical Quarterly*, XLIX (April 1971).

Herbert S. Klein, "North American Competition and the Characteristics of the African Slave Trade to Cuba, 1790 to 1794," *William and Mary Quarterly*, 3rd series, XXVIII (January 1971).

———, "Slaves and Shipping in Eighteenth-Century Virginia," *Journal of Interdisciplinary History*, V (Winter, 1975).

William T. Laprade, "The Domestic Slave Trade in the District of Columbia," *Journal of Negro History*, XI (January 1926).

Averil Mackenzie-Grieve, *The Last Years of the English Slave Trade: Liverpool, 1750–1807* (London, England, 1941).

Daniel Mannix, *Black Cargoes: A History of the Atlantic Slave Trade, 1619–1862* (Stanford, 1963).

William L. Miller, "A Note on the Importance of the Interstate Slave Trade of the Ante-Bellum South," *Journal of Political Economy*, LXXIII (April 1965).

Karl Polanyi, *Dahomey and the Slave Trade* . . . (Seattle, 1966).

James Pope-Hennessey, *Sins of the Fathers: A Study of the Atlantic Slave Traders, 1441–1807* (New York, 1968).

Simon Rottenberg, "The Business of Slave Trading," *South Atlantic Quarterly*, LXVI (Summer 1967).

R. B. Sheriden, "Commercial and Financial Organization of the British Slave Trade, 1750–1807," *Economic History Revue*, 2nd series, XV (December 1958).

Francis T. Stafford, "Illegal Importations Enforcement of the Slave Trade Laws Along the Florida Coast, 1810–1828," *Florida Historical Quarterly* (October 1967).

Wendell H. Stephenson, *Isaac Franklin, Slave Trader and Planter of the Old South* (Baton Rouge, La., 1938).

Ronald T. Takaki, *A Pro-Slavery Crusade: The Agitation to Reopen the African Slave Trade* (New York, 1971).

W. E. F. Ward, *The Royal Navy and the Slavers: The Suppression of the Atlantic Slave Trade* (New York, 1969).

E. Richmond Ware, "Health Hazards of the West African Trader 1840–1870," *American Neptune*, XXVII (April 1967).

Howard S. Warren, *American Slavers and the Federal Law, 1837–1862* (Berkeley, 1963).

Darold D. Wax, "A Philadelphia Surgeon on a Slaving Voyage to Africa [1749–51]," *Pennsylvania Magazine of History and Biography* (October 1968).

———, "Quaker Merchants and the Slave Trade in Colonial Pennsylvania," *Pennsylvania Magazine of History*, LXXXVI (April 1962).

Charles H. Westey, "Manifests of Slave Shipments Along the Waterways, 1808–1864," *Journal of Negro History*, XXVII (April 1942).

H. A. Wyndham, *The Atlantic and Slavery* (London, England, 1935).

SPECIAL STUDIES

Chronological

Wesley Frank Craven, *The Southern Colonies in the Seventeenth Century, 1607–1689* (Baton Rouge, La., 1949).

John R. Alden, *The South in the Revolution, 1763–1789* (Baton Rouge, La., 1957).

Thomas P. Abernethy, *The South in the New Nation, 1789–1819* (Baton Rouge, La., 1961).

Glover B. Moore, *The Missouri Controversy, 1819–1821* (Lexington, Ky., 1953).

William W. Freehling, *Prelude to Civil War: The Nullification Controversy in South Carolina, 1816–1836* (New York, 1966).

Charles S. Sydnor, *The Development of Southern Sectionalism, 1819–1848* (Baton Rouge, La., 1948).

Avery D. Craven, *The Growth of Southern Nationalism, 1848–1861* (Baton Rouge, La., 1953).

Steven A. Channing, *Crisis of Fear: Secession in South Carolina* (New York, 1970).

Emory M. Thomas, *The Confederacy as a Revolutionary Experience* (Englewood Cliffs, N. J., 1971).

The Southern Economy

Agricultural History, XLIV (January 1970) issue devoted to Ante-Bellum Cotton Economy and Slavery.

Hugh G. J. Aitken (ed.), *Did Slavery Pay? Readings in the Economies of Black Slavery in the United States* (Boston, 1971).

Ralph V. Anderson and Robert E. Gallman, "Slaves as Fixed Capital: Slave Labor and Southern Economic Development," *Journal of American History*, LXIV (June, 1977).

R. Keith Aufhauser, "Profitability of Slavery in the British Caribbean," *Journal of Interdisciplinary History*, V (Summer, 1974).

Kathleen Bruce, *Virginia Iron Manufacturer in the Slave Era* (New York, 1931).

Stuart Bruchey (ed.), *Cotton and the Growth of the American Economy, 1790–1860* (New York, 1967).

Alfred H. Conrad, "Econometrics and Southern History," *Explorations in Entrepreneurial History*, 2nd series, VI (Fall 1968). (Comments by Fogel, Bruchey, and Chandler.)

A. Conrad, D. Dowd, S. Engerman, E. Ginzberg, C. Icelso, John R. Meyer, H. N. Scheiber and R. Sutch, "Slavery as an Obstacle to Economic Growth in the United States. A Panel Discussion," *Journal of Economic History*, XXVII (December 1967).

Alfred H. Conrad and John R. Meyer, *The Economics of Slavery* (Chicago, 1964).

Charles B. Dew, *Ironmaker to the Confederacy: Joseph R. Anderson and the Tredegar Iron Works* (New Haven, 1966).

Douglas F. Dowd, "A Comparative Analysis of Economic Development in the American South and West," *Journal of Economic History*, XVII (December 1956).

Stanley L. Engerman, "The Effects of Slavery upon the Southern Economy. A Review of the Recent Debate," *Explorations in Entrepreneurial History*, 2nd series, 4 (Winter 1967).

Marvin Fischbaum and Julius Rubin, "Slavery and the Economic Development of the American South," *Explorations in Entrepreneurial History*, 6 (Fall 1968).

Heywood Fleisig, "Slavery, the Supply of Agricultural Labor, and the Industrialization of the South," *Journal of Economic History*, XXXVI (September 1976).

Robert W. Fogel and Stanley L. Engerman (eds.), *The Reinterpretation of American Economic History* (New York, 1968). Part VII, "The Economics of Slavery."

Robert W. Fogel and Stanley L. Engerman, "The Relative Efficiency of Slavery. A Comparison of Northern and Southern Agriculture in 1860," *Explorations in Economic History*, 8 (Spring 1971).

———, *Time on the Cross: The Economics of American Negro Slavery*, 2 vols. (Boston, 1974).

James D. Foust and Dale E. Swan, "Productivity and Profitability of Antebellum Slave Labor: A Micro-Approach," *Agricultural History*, XLIV (January 1970).

Herbert G. Gutman, *Slavery and the Numbers Game: A Critique of Time on the Cross* (Urbana, 1975).

Ernest M. Lander, Jr., "Slave Labor in South Carolina Cotton Mills," *Journal of Negro History*, XXXVIII (April 1953).

Richard Lowe and Randolph Campbell, "Slave Property and the Distribution of Wealth in Texas, 1860," *Journal of American History*, LXIII (September 1976).

Arthur Pierce Middleton, *Tobacco Coast: A Maritime History of Chesapeake Bay in the Colonial Era* (Newport News, Va., 1953).

Warren L. Miller, "Slavery and the Population of the South," *Southern Economic Journal*, XXVIII (July 1961).

John H. Moore, *Agriculture in Ante-Bellum Mississippi* (New York, 1958).

Louis Morton, *Robert Carter of Nomini Hall: A Virginia Planter of the Eighteenth Century* (Williamsburg, Va., 1941).

William N. Parker, "Slavery and Southern Economic Development: An Hypothesis and some Evidence," *Agricultural History*, XLIV (January 1970).

William N. Parker (ed.), *The Structure of the Cotton Economy of the Antebellum South* (Washington, D. C., 1970).

U. B. Phillips, *The Slave Economy of the Old South: Selected Essays in Economic and Social History*, Eugene Genovese (ed.) (Baton Rouge, La., 1968).

Norris W. Preyer, "The Historian, the Slave, and the Ante-Bellum Textile Industry," *Journal of Negro History*, XLVI (April 1961).

Joseph Clarke Robert, *The Tobacco Kingdom: Plantation, Market, and Factory in Virginia and North Carolina, 1800–1860* (Durham, N. C., 1938).

Morton Rothstein, "The Antebellum South as a Dual Economy: A Tentative Hypothesis," *Agricultural History*, XLI (October 1967).

William K. Scarborough, *The Overseer: Plantation Management in the Old South* (Baton Rouge, La., 1966).

Joseph C. Sitterson, *Sugar Country: The Cane Sugar Industry in the South, 1753–1950* (Lexington, Ky., 1953).

Robert S. Starobin, "The Economics of Industrial Slavery in the Old South," *Business History Review*, XLIV (Summer 1970).

———, *Industrial Slavery in the Old South* (New York, 1970).

Richard Stutch, "The Profitability of Ante-Bellum Slavery—Revisited," *Southern Economic Journal* (April, 1965).

Edgar T. Thompson, "The Natural History of Agricultural Labor in the South," in David K. Jackson (ed.), *American Studies in Honor of William Kenneth Boyd* (Durham, N. C., 1940).

David O. Whitten, "Sugar Slavery: A Profitability Model for . . . Antebellum Louisiana," *Louisiana Studies*, XII (Summer 1973).

Harold D. Woodman, "The Profitability of Slavery: A Historical Perennial," *Journal of Southern History*, XXIX (August 1963).

Harold D. Woodman, *Slavery and the Southern Economy* (New York, 1966).

Yasukichi Yasuba, "The Profitability and Viability of Plantation Slavery in the United States," *The Economic Studies Quarterly*, 12 (September 1961).

Slavery and Ideology

Kenneth M. Bailor, "John Taylor of Caroline: Continuity, Change, and Discontinuity in Virginia's Sentiments toward Slavery," *Virginia Magazine of History and Biography* (July 1967).

Leland J. Bellot, "Evangelicals and the Defense of Slavery in Britain's Old Colonial Empire," *Journal of Southern History*, XXXVII (February 1971).

Paul F. Boller, Jr., "Washington, The Quakers and Slavery," *Journal of Negro History*, 46 (January 1961).

Jack J. Cardoso, "Southern Reaction to *The Impending Crisis*," *Civil War History*, XVI (March 1970).

Guy A. Cardwell, "Jefferson Renounced: Natural Rights in the South," *Yale Review*, LVIII (March 1969).

William Cohen, "Thomas Jefferson and the Problem of Slavery," *Journal of American History*, LVI (December 1969).

W. Harrison Daniel, "Virginia Baptists and the Negro in the Antebellum Era," *Journal of Negro History*, LVI (January 1971).

David Brion Davis, *The Slave Power Conspiracy and the Paranoid Style* (Baton Rouge, La., 1969).

——, *Was Thomas Jefferson an Authentic Enemy of Slavery?* (Oxford, England, 1970).

Donald J. D'Ella, "Dr. Benjamin Rush and the Negro," *Journal of the History of Ideas* (July–September 1969).

John P. Diggins, "Slavery, Race, and Equality: Jefferson and the Pathos of the Enlightenment," *American Quarterly*, XXVIII (Summer, 1976).

David Donald, "The Proslavery Argument Reconsidered," *Journal of Southern History*, XXXVII (February 1971).

John L. Eighmy, "The Baptists and Slavery. An Examination of the Origins and Benefits of Segregation," *Social Science Quarterly* (December 1968).

Gordon E. Finnie, "The Antislavery Movement in the Upper South Before 1840," *Journal of Southern History*, XXXV (August 1969).

William W. Freehling, "The Founding Fathers and Slavery," *American Review*, 77 (February 1972).

Eugene D. Genovese, "The Logical Outcome of the Slaveholders' Philosophy . . . The Social Thought of George Fitzhugh," in Genovese, *The World the Slaveholders' Made* (New York, 1969).

John C. Greene, "The American Debate on the Negro's Place in Nature, 1780–1815," *Journal of the History of Ideas*, XV (June 1954).

Kenneth S. Greenberg, "Revolutionary Ideology and the Proslavery Argument . . . in Antebellum South Carolina," *Journal of Southern History*, XLII (August, 1976).

James D. Guillory, "The Pro-Slavery Arguments of Dr. Samuel A. Cartwright," *Louisiana History*, IX (Summer 1968).

David C. Harell, Jr., "Sin and Sectionalism: A Study of Morality in the Nineteenth-Century South," *Mississippi Quarterly*, XIX (Fall 1966).

William E. Juhnke, "Benjamin Franklin's View of the Negro and Slavery," *Pennsylvania History*, XLI (October, 1974).

Don B. Kates, Jr., "Abolition, Deportation, Integration: Attitudes Toward Slavery in the Early Republic," *Journal of Negro History*, LIII (January 1968).

David S. Lovejoy, "Samuel Hopkins, Religion, Slavery, and the Revolution," *New England Quarterly*, XL (June 1967).

Dennis L. Lythgoe, "Negro Slavery and Mormon Doctrine," *Western Humanities Review*, XXI (Autumn 1967).

Duncan J. MacLeod, *Slavery, Race and the American Revolution* (London, 1974).

Edmund S. Morgan, "Slavery and Freedom: The American Paradox," *Journal of American History*, LIX (June 1972).

Howard A. Ohline, "Republicanism and Slavery: Origins of the Three-Fifths

Clause in the United States Constitution," *William and Mary Quarterly*, 28 (October 1971).

Ulrich B. Philips, "The Central Theme of Southern History," *American Historical Review*, XXXIV (October 1928).

Valerie Quinney, "Decisions on Slavery . . . in the Early French Revolution," *Journal of Negro History*, LV (April 1970).

Tommy W. Rogers, "Dr. Frederick A. Ross and the Presbyterian Defense of Slavery," *Journal of Presbyterian History*, 45 (June 1967).

Charles Grier Sellers, Jr., "The Travail of Slavery," from Sellers (ed.), *The Southerner as American* (Chapel Hill, 1960).

Lynda Worley Skelton, "The States Rights Movement in Georgia, 1825–1850," *Georgia Historical Quarterly*, 6 (December 1966).

Douglas C. Stange, " 'A Compassionate Mother to Her Poor Negro Slaves': The Lutheran Church and Negro Slavery in Early America," *Phylon* (Fall 1968).

———, "Our Duty to Preach the Gospel to Negroes: Southern Lutherans and American Slavery," *Concordia Historical Institute Quarterly* XLII (November 1969).

Gaston H. Wamble, "Negroes and Missouri Protestant Churches Before and After the Civil War," *Missouri Historical Review*, LXI (April 1967).

Henry Warnoch, "Southern Methodists, the Negro, and Unification: The First Phase," *Journal of Negro History*, LII (October 1967).

Harvey Wish, *George Fitzhugh: Propagandist of the Old South* (Baton Rouge, La., 1943).

C. Vann Woodward, "George Fitzhugh, Sui Generis," introduction to Woodward (ed.), Fitzhugh's *Cannibals All!*

Miscellaneous

Florence R. Beatty-Brown, "Legal Status of Arkansas Negroes Before Emancipation," *Arkansas Historical Quarterly*, XXVIII (Spring 1969).

Joseph C. Burke, "The Proslavery Argument and the First Congress," *Duquesne Review*, XIV (1969).

Penelope Campbell, "Some Notes on Frederick County's Participation in the Maryland Colonization Scheme," *Maryland Historical Magazine*, 66 (Spring 1971).

Stanley W. Campbell, *The Slave Catchers: Enforcement of the Fugitive Slave Law, 1850–1860* (Chapel Hill, 1970).

Evsy D. Domar, "The Causes of Slavery or Serfdom: A Hypothesis," *Journal of Economic History*, XXX (March 1970).

Walter Ehrlich, "Was the Dred Scott Case Valid?" *Journal of American History*, LV, No. 2 (September 1968).

Larry Gara, "Slavery and the Slave Power: A Crucial Distinction," *Civil War History*, XV (March 1969).

E. D. Genovese, "A Georgia Slaveholder [1859] Looks at Africa," *Georgia Historical Quarterly* (June 1967).

Adele Hast, "The Legal Status of the Negro in Virginia, 1705–1765," *Journal of Negro History*, LIV (July 1969).

Michael S. Hindus, "Black Justice Under White Law: Criminal Prosecutions of Blacks in Antebellum South Carolina," *Journal of American History*, LXIII (December 1976).

Vincent C. Hopkins, *Dred Scott's Case* (New York, 1951).

Bertram W. Korn, "Jews and Negro Slavery in the Old South, 1789–1865," *Publication of the Jewish Historical Society*, L (March 1961).

Harold D. Moser, "Reaction in North Carolina to the Emancipation Proclamation," *North Carolina Historical Review*, XLIV (January 1967).

A. E. Keir Nash, "A More Equitable Past? Southern Supreme Courts and the Protection of the Antebellum Negro," *North Carolina Law Review*, XLVIII (February 1970).

———, "Fairness and Formalism in the Trials of Blacks in the State Supreme Courts of the Old South," *Virginia Law Review*, LVI (February 1970.)

———, "The Texas Supreme Court and Trial Rights of Blacks, 1845–1860," *Journal of American History*, LVIII (December 1971).

Jane H. Pease, "A Note on Patterns of Conspicuous Consumption Among Seaboard Planters, 1820–1860," *Journal of Southern History*, XXXV (August 1969).

Walter F. Peterson, "Slavery in the 1850's: The Recollections of an Alabama Unionist [Wade Hampton Richardson]," *Alabama Historical Quarterly* (Fall–Winter 1968).

Arthur G. Pettit, "Mark Twain, Unreconstructed Southerner, and His View of the Negro, 1835–1860," *Rocky Mountain Social Science Journal*, VII (April 1970).

Tommy W. Rogers, "D. R. Hundley: A Multi-Class Thesis of Social Stratification in the Ante-Bellum South," *Mississippi Quarterly*, XXIII (Spring 1970).

Donald M. Roper, "In Quest of Judicial Objectivity: the Marshall Court and the Legitimation of Slavery," *Stanford Law Review*, XXI (February 1969).

Sudie Duncan Sides, "Southern Women and Slavery," *History Today*, XX (January and February 1970).

Albert F. Simpson, "The Political Significance of Slave Representation, 1787–1821," *Journal of Southern History*, VII (August 1941).

Patrick Sowle, "The Abolition of Slavery [in Georgia]," *Georgia Historical Quarterly*, LII (September 1968).

John C. Staley III, "The Responsibilities and Liabilities of the Barter of Slave Labor in Virginia," *American Journal of Legal History*, 12 (October 1968).

Carl Brent Swisher, "Dred Scott One Hundred Years After," *Journal of Politics*, XIX (May 1957).

Martin Torodash, "Constitutional Aspects of Slavery," *Georgia Historical Quarterly*, LV (Summer 1971).

Richard D. Brown (ed.), *Slavery in American Society* (Lexington, Mass., 1969).

Thomas D. Clark, *Travels in the Old South: A Bibliography*, 3 vols. (Norman, Okla., 1956–59).

Katherine M. Jones (ed.), *The Plantation South* (Indianapolis, 1951).

Eric McKitrick (ed.), *Slavery Defended: The Views of the Old South* (Englewood Cliffs, N. J., 1963).

Frederick Law Olmsted, *The Cotton Kingdom*, Arthur M. Schlesinger (ed.) (New York, 1953).

Willard Thorp (ed.), *A Southern Reader* (New York, 1955).

Irwin Unger and David Reimars (eds.), *The Slavery Experience in the United States* (New York, 1970).

Ian W. Van Noppen, *The South, A Documentary History* (Princeton, 1958).

Harvey Wish (ed.), *Slavery in the South: A Collection of Contemporary Accounts . . .* (New York, 1964).

Harold D. Woodman (ed.), *Slavery and the Southern Economy* (New York, 1966).

C. Vann Woodward (ed.), George Fitzhugh, *Cannibals All!* or *Slaves Without Masters* (Cambridge, Mass., 1960).

GUIDES TO FURTHER READING

HISTORIOGRAPHY

James C. Bonner, "Plantation and Farm: The Agricultural South," in Arthur S. Link and Rembert W. Patrick (eds.), *Writing Southern History: Essays in Historiography in Honor of Fletcher M. Green* (Baton Rouge, La., 1965).

Eugene D. Genovese, "Marxian Interpretations of the Slave South," in Barton J. Bernstein (ed.), *Towards a New Past: Dissenting Essays in American History* (New York, 1968).

———, Race and Class in Southern History: An Appraisal of the Work of Ulrich Bonnel Phillips," *Agricultural History*, XLI (October 1967).

———, "Recent Contributions to the Economic Historiography of the Slave South," *Science and Society*, XXIV (Winter 1960).

Louis R. Harlan, "The Negro in American History," *Service Center for Teachers of History*, Publication No. 61 (Washington, D. C., 1965).

Richard Hofstadter, "U. B. Phillips and the Plantation Legend," *Journal of Negro History*, XXIX (April 1944).

William Issel, "History, Social Science, and Ideology: Elkins and Blassingame on Ante-Bellum American Slavery," *History Teacher*, IX (November, 1975).

Ruben F. Kugler, "U. B. Phillips' Use of Sources," *Journal of Negro History*, XLVII (July 1962).

Staughton Lynd, "On Turner, Beard and Slavery," *Journal of Negro History*, XLVIII (October 1963).

Chase C. Mooney, "The Literature of Slavery: A Re-evaluation," *Indiana Magazine of History*, VII (April 1965).

Orlando Patterson, "Rethinking Black History," *Harvard Educational Review*, Vol. 41 (August 1971).

David M. Potter, "The Work of Ulrich B. Phillips: A Comment," *Agricultural History* (October 1967).

Daniel Joseph Singal, "Ulrich B. Phillips: The Old South as the New," *Journal of American History*, LXIII (March, 1977).

Arnold A. Sio, "Interpretations of Slavery," *Comparative Studies in Society and History*, VII (April 1965).

Kenneth M. Stampp, "The Historian and Southern Negro Slavery," *American Historical Review*, LVII (April 1952).

Robert Starobin, "The Negro: A Central Theme in American History," *Journal of Contemporary History*, 111 (April 1968).

Robert S. Starobin and Dale Tomich, "Black Liberation Historiography," *Radical America*, II (September–October 1968).

Raymond Starr, "Historians and the Origins of British North American Slavery, *Historian* XXXVI (November, 1973).

Bennett H. Wall, "African Slavery" in Arthur S. Link and Rembert W. Patrick (eds.), *Writing Southern History: Essays in Historiography in Honor of Fletcher M. Green* (Baton Rouge, 1965).

C. S. Wesley, *Neglected History: Essays in Negro-American History by a College President* (Wilberforce, Ohio, 1965).

Harold D. Woodman, "The Profitability of Slavery: A Historical Perennial," *Journal of Southern History*, XXIX (August 1963).

C. Vann Woodward, "Clio With Soul," *Journal of American History*, LVI (June 1969).

BIBLIOGRAPHIC AIDS

John W. Blassingame, "Using the Testimony of Ex-Slaves: Approaches and Problems," *Journal of Southern History*, XLI (November, 1975).

Rita M. Cassidy, "Black History: Some Basic Reading," *History Teacher*, 2 (May 1964).

W. E. B. DuBois *et al.*, *Encyclopedia of the Negro: Preparatory Volume with Reference Lists and Reports* (New York, 1946).

The Journal of Negro History (1916–present).

James McPherson *et al.*, *Blacks in America: Bibliographic Essays* (New York, 1971). This book is the best one-volume annotated bibliography in the general field of black studies and is highly recommended.

Elizabeth W. Miller (compiler), *The Negro in America: A Bibliography* (Cambridge, Mass., 1966).

Monroe N. Work, *A Bibliography of the Negro in Africa and America* (New York, 1928).

Excellent bibliographies of American slavery can be found in the footnotes of two previously cited works; Stanley M. Elkins, *Slavery* . . . , and David Brion Davis, *The Problem of Slavery in Western Culture*. All of the historiographic articles listed also contain good bibliographies.

AMERICAN SLAVERY IN WORLD PERSPECTIVE

GREECE AND ROME

Victoria Cuffel, "The Classical Greek Concept of Slavery," *Journal of Historical Ideas* (July–September 1966).

David Brion Davis, *The Problem of Slavery in Western Culture* (Ithaca, 1966).

A. M. Duff, *Freedmen in the Early Roman Empire*, 2nd ed. (Cambridge, England, 1958).

Moses I. Finley (ed.), *Slavery in Classical Antiquity: Views and Controversies* (Cambridge, England, 1960).

Moses I. Finley, *The World of Odysseus* (Meridian Paperback edition, New York, 1959).

C. A. Forbes, "The Education and Training of Slaves in Antiquity," *Transactions of the American Philological Association*, 86 (1955).
F. M. Snowden, *Blacks in Antiquity* (Cambridge, Mass., 1970).
William Linn Westerman, *The Slave Systems of Greek and Roman Antiquity* (Philadelphia, 1955).

LATIN AMERICA AND THE WEST INDIES

Richard R. Beeman, "Labor Forces and Race Relations: A Comparative View of the Colonization of Brazil and Virginia," *Political Science Quarterly*, LXXXVI (December 1971).
Gonzalo Aguirre Beltran, "The Slave Trade in Mexico," *Hispanic American Historical Review*, XXIV (1944).
J. Harry Bennett, Jr., *Bondsmen and Bishops: Slavery and Apprenticeship . . . Barbados, 1710–1838* (Berkeley, 1958).
Leslie Bethell, *The Abolition of the Brazilian Slave Trade: Britain, Brazil and the Slave Trade Question 1807–1869* (New York, 1970).
C. R. Boxer, *The Golden Age of Brazil, 1690–1750: Growing Pains of a Colonial Society* (Berkeley, 1962).
———, *Race Relations in the Portuguese Empire, 1415–1825* (Oxford, England, 1963).
Peter Boyd-Bowman, "Negro Slaves in Early Colonial Mexico," *The Americas*, XXVI (October 1969).
George Breathitt, "Religious Protection and Haitian Slaves," *Catholic Historical Review*, LV (April 1969).
W. L. Burn, *Emancipation and Apprenticeship in the British West Indies* (London, England, 1937).
David W. Cohen and Jack P. Greene (eds.), *Neither Slave Nor Free: The Freedman of African Descent in the Slave Societies of the New World* (Baltimore, 1972).
Robert Conrad, "The Contraband Slavery Trade to Brazil, 1831–1845," *Hispanic American Historical Review*, XLIX (November 1969).
Arthur F. Corwin, *Spain and the Abolition of Slavery in Cuba* (Austin, Texas, 1967).
David M. Davidson, "Negro Slave Control and Resistance in Colonial Mexico," *Hispanic American Historical Review*, XLVI (1966).
David Brion Davis, "Slavery" in C. Vann Woodward (ed.), *The Comparative Approach to American History* (New York, 1968).
Carl N. Degler, *Neither Black nor White: Slavery and Race Relations in Brazil and the United States* (New York, 1971).
———, "Slavery in Brazil and the United States: An Essay in Comparative History," *American Historical Review* (April 1970).
Donald Gray Eder, "Time Under the Southern Cross: The Tannenbaum Thesis Reappraised," *Agricultural History*, L (October, 1976).
Stanley L. Engerman, "Some Economic and Demographic Comparisons of Slavery in the United States and the British West Indies," *Economic History Review*, XXIX (May, 1976).
Stanley L. Engerman and Eugene D. Genovese (eds.), *Race and Slavery in the Western Hemisphere: Quantitative Studies* (Princeton, 1975).

Laura Foner and Eugene D. Genovese (eds.), *Slavery in the New World: A Reader in Comparative History* (Englewood Cliffs, N. J., 1969).

Gilberto Freyre, *The Masters and the Slaves: A Study in the Development of Brazilian Civilization* (New York, 1946).

Eugene D. Genovese, *The World the Slaveholders Made: Two Essays in Interpretation* (New York, 1969).

Elsa V. Goveia, *Slave Society in the British Leeward Islands . . .* (New Haven, 1965).

Richard Graham, "Brazilian Slavery Re-Examined: A Review Article," *Journal of Social History*, 3 (Summer 1970).

———, "Causes for the Abolition of Negro Slavery in Brazil," *Hispanic American Historical Review*, XLIV (May 1966).

Ramiro Guerra y Sánchez, *Sugar and Society in the Caribbean* (New Haven, 1964).

Gwendolyn Midlo Hall, *Social Control in Slave Plantation Societies: A Comparison of St. Domingue and Cuba* (Baltimore, 1972).

Jerome S. Handler, *The Unappropriated People: Freedmen in the Slave Society of Barbados* (Baltimore, 1974).

Lewis Hanke, *Aristotle and the American Indians* (Chicago, 1959).

Marvin Harris, *Patterns of Race in the Americas* (New York, 1964).

Harry Hoetink, *The Two Variants in Caribbean Race Relations* (London, England, 1967).

Harry Hoetink, *Slavery and Race Relations in the Americas . . .* (New York, 1973).

Norman Holub, "The Brazilian Sabinada (1837–38) Revolt of the Negro Masses [Bahia]," *Journal of Negro History* (July 1969).

C. L. R. James, *The Black Jacobins' Toussaint L'Ouverture and the San Domingo Revolution*, rev. ed. (New York, 1968).

Winthrop D. Jordan, *White Over Black: American Attitudes Toward the Negro, 1550–1812* (Chapel Hill, 1968).

———, "The Influence of the West Indies on the Origins of New England Slavery," *William and Mary Quarterly*, XVIII (April 1961).

James F. King, "The Negro in Continental Spanish America: A Select Bibliography," *Hispanic American Historical Review*, XXIV (August 1944).

James Ferguson King, "Negro Slavery in New Granada," in *Greater America: Essays in Honor of Herbert Eugene Colton* (Berkeley, 1945).

Herbert S. Klein, *Slavery in the Americas: A Comparative Study of Cuba and Virginia* (Chicago, 1967).

Franklin W. Knight, *Slave Society in Cuba During the Nineteenth Century* (Madison, 1970).

Claude Levy, "Slavery and the Emancipation Movement in Barbados, 1650–1833," *Journal of Negro History*, LV (January 1970).

John V. Lombardi, *The Decline and Abolition of Negro Slavery in Venezuela, 1820–1854* (Westport, Conn., 1970).

Edgar F. Love, "Legal Restrictions on Afro-Indian Relations in Colonial Mexico," *Journal of Negro History*, LV (April 1970).

Alexander Marchant, *From Barter to Slavery: The Economic Relations of Portuguese and Indians in the Settlement of Brazil, 1500–1580* (Baltimore, 1942).

Sidney W. Mintz, "Slavery and the Afro-American World," in John F. Szwed (ed.), *Black America* (New York, 1970).

Vienna Moog, *Bandeirantes and Pioneers* (New York, 1964).

Magnus Morner, "The History of Race Relations in Latin America," *Latin American Research Review*, I (1966).

———, *Race Mixture in the History of Latin America* (Boston, 1967).

Richard Pares, *Merchants and Planters*, (Cambridge, England, 1960).

Orlando Patterson, *The Sociology of Slavery: An Analysis of the Origins, Development and Structure of Negro Slave Society in Jamaica* (London, England, 1967).

Oriol Pi-Sunyer, "Historical Background to the Negro in Mexico," *Journal of Negro History*, XLII (October 1957).

Caio Prado, Jr., *The Colonial Background of Modern Brazil* (Berkeley, 1967).

Mary Reckord, "The Jamaica Slave Rebellion of 1831," *Past and Present*, No. 40 (July 1968).

J. H. Rodrigues, *Brazil and Africa* (Berkeley, 1965).

Monica Schuler, "Ethnic Slave Rebellions in the Caribbean and the Guianas," *Journal of Social History*, 3 (Summer 1970).

Richard B. Sheridan, "The Crisis of Slave Subsistence in the British West Indies during and after the American Revolution," *William and Mary Quarterly*, XXXIII (October, 1976).

———, *Sugar and Slavery: An Economic History of the British West Indies, 1623–1775* (Baltimore, 1974).

Stanley J. Stein, *Vassouras: A Brazilian Coffee County, 1850–1900* (Cambridge, Mass., 1957).

Frank Tannenbaum, *Slave and Citizen: The Negro in the Americas* (New York, 1946).

D. W. Thoms, "Slavery in the Leeward Islands in the Mid-Eighteenth Century: A Reappraisal," *Bulletin Institute Historical Research* (May 1969).

Ralph H. Vigil, "Negro Slaves and Rebels in the Spanish Possessions, 1503–1558," *Historian*, XXXIII (August 1971).

Eric Williams, *Capitalism and Slavery* (Chapel Hill, 1944).

C. Vann Woodward, "Protestant Slavery in a Catholic World," in C. Vann Woodward, *American Counterpoint: Slavery and Race in the North-South Dialogue* (Boston, 1971).

OTHER CULTURES

Abdel-Moshen Bakir, *Slavery in Pharaonic Egypt* (Cairo, 1952).

Dev Raj Chanana, *Slavery in Ancient India, As Depicted in Pali and Sanskrit Texts* (New Delhi, 1960).

Hannah S. Goldman, "American Slavery and Russian Serfdom: A Study in Fictional Parallels" (unpublished Ph.D. thesis, Columbia University, 1955, University Microfilms No. 11, 453).

Melville Herskovits, *Dahomey: An Ancient West African Kingdom* (New York, 1938).

Isaac Mendelsohn, *Slavery in the Ancient Near East: A Comparative Study of Slavery in Babylonia, Assyria, Syria, and Palestine, from the Middle of the Third Millennium to the End of the First Millennium* (New York, 1949).

Virginia S. Platt, "The East India Company and the Madagascar Slave Trade," *William and Mary Quarterly*, XXVI (October 1969).

E. G. Pulleyblank, "The Origins and Nature of Chattel Slavery in China," *Journal of the Economic and Social History of the Orient*, I, pt. 2 (1958).

Lowell J. Ragatz, *The Fall of the Planter Class in the British Caribbean, 1763–1833* (New York, 1928).

C. Martin Wilbur, *Slavery in China During the Former Han Dynasty, 206 B.C.–A.D. 25* (Chicago, 1945).